Contents

Understanding
the human body

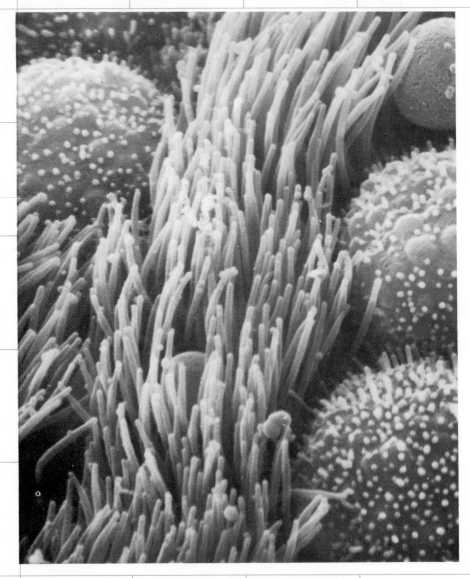

Scanning electron micrograph of the surface of the trachea (windpipe)

Understanding the human body

E R Tudor MSc Dip Ed

E McI Tudor BVSc (Hons)

Illustrations by
Kate Crowle

Pitman

Pitman Books Limited
128 Long Acre, London WC2E 9AN

Associated Companies
Pitman Publishing Pty Ltd, Melbourne
Pitman Publishing New Zealand Ltd, Wellington

© E R Tudor, E Mcl Tudor 1981

First published in Australia by Pitman Publishing Pty Ltd 1981
ISBN 0 85896 819 3

First published in Great Britain 1983

Text set in English Times by Richard Clay (SE Asia) Pte Limited
Printed and bound by Koon Wah Printing Pte Ltd
Singapore

ISBN 0 273 01952 X

Acknowledgments

The stimulus for this book came from a course in human and social biology introduced at Melbourne Church of England Grammar School by Mr Alan Patterson. To both the school and Mr Patterson we are indebted. Writing was begun during the latter part of a teaching exchange at King's School, Bruton, Somerset, in the United Kingdom. For the contribution that this teaching exchange made to the book we are most grateful.

A number of people read parts of the manuscript, and we thank them for their valuable suggestions: in particular Dr J N Santamaria, Mr J Cheetham, Mrs E Clements, Dr C R Hunter and Mr B Jones. For the preparation of scanning electron micrographs we are most grateful to Mr C Mayberry. Mr T Martin and Mr G Perkins assisted with the preparation of photographic material. Finally we thank particularly Mrs Barbara Gray for typing each draft of the manuscript with such interest and care.

We are grateful to the following for permission to reproduce copyright material: Blackwell Scientific Publications for Fig 7.14, redrawn from Fig 7.9 in I M Roitt, *Essential Immunology* (1971); The English Universities Press for Figs 6.6 and 6.11, redrawn from pp 65 and 66 of C H Barnett et al, *The Human Body* (1975); Miss Shirley Jennings for the extract in Chapter 19 from *Challenging Years*, a publication of the Australian Council on the Ageing; Macmillan Publishing for Fig 6.15, redrawn from Fig 15.2 in M Griffiths, *Introduction to Human Physiology* (1974); the Royal College of Physicians and Pitman Medical for Figs 9.1, 9.2 and 9.3, adapted from pp 44, 54 and 66 of *Smoking or Health*, 3rd edn (1977); Prentice Hall Inc for Fig 6.16, adapted from Fig 5.8, and Fig 13.14, redrawn from Fig 10.2, in R Macey, *Human Physiology*, 2nd edn (1975); the Road Safety and Traffic Authority of Victoria for Fig 16.8 (unpublished data, 1976); and W B Saunders Co for Figs 19.2, 19.3 and 19.4, adapted from D W Smith and E L Bierman (ed), *The Biologic Ages of Man* (1975).

ERT, E McI T

Chapter 1

The living world and how we view it

- Characteristics of living things
- Classifying the living world
- Humans and their place in the animal kingdom
- Human control of the environment

We don't need a great deal of imagination to appreciate that the earth is composed of an extremely large number and variety of things. A casual glance at our surroundings will reveal rocks, trees, buildings, mountains, flowers, animals, roads and so on. Each object has its own form, colour, texture and composition—the features by which we recognise it and give it a name.

Young children learn step by step to recognise objects and features of their environment and in turn to give them names. As this process of recognition develops, children learn subconsciously to place different objects in different groups. That is, the child learns to classify the objects in the world around him. Perhaps the first difference a child becomes aware of is that between 'mother' and 'not mother'. A little later, as the child becomes aware of more objects around him, he realises that some objects move, others are soft, warm or furry and some make characteristic noises. Other objects may be hard, immobile, shiny or cold. In this mental process the child is grappling with one of the most basic classifications of the world he lives in—he is making the distinction between living and non-living things.

Living or dead: how do we know?

Characteristics of living things

Biology is the study of living things. The word biology comes from two Greek words—*bios*, meaning life, and *logos*, meaning a study. What, then, are the characteristics of living things?

It is almost impossible to define life itself. It is not so difficult, however, to describe what living things are. This is because all living things have certain common characteristics. Some of these may also be found in some non-living things. For example, cars can move, and crystals may grow. However, only living organisms share all these characteristics.

We can demonstrate all of these characteristics in some of the very simplest forms of living things—tiny plants and animals, some made of a single cell and visible only under a microscope. The same living processes are basic to all forms of life, however. Although they may not be as easy to demonstrate, life depends on these same processes in trees, seaweed, mice and human beings.

Feeding

Feeding is probably one of the most obvious characteristics of living things. We are well aware that all living organisms feed—so many of the animals we can see around us appear to spend much of their time in search of food. Under a microscope we can observe tiny one-celled animals feeding on particles from their environment. Plants, too, 'feed' on molecules in the soil and air around them.

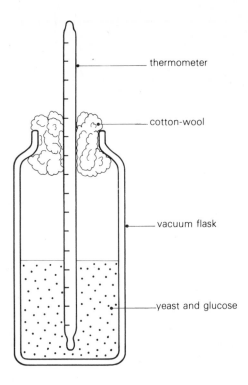

Fig 1.1 *Apparatus used to demonstrate respiration*

Living organisms use these 'food' molecules which they obtain from their environment to repair themselves and grow. They may also use them as a fuel, which they burn in chemical reactions, to release the energy they need for other life processes.

Respiration

Experiment Yeast cells, tiny one-celled plants, are placed in a vacuum flask, in a solution of 0.1 per cent glucose. A thermometer is placed in the yeast–glucose suspension, and the top of the flask is closed with cotton wool (Fig 1.1). The temperature of the suspension is recorded. A second temperature recording is made after 24 hours. The concentration of glucose after 24 hours is found to be zero. The temperature of the suspension has risen considerably.

Respiration—the release of energy

Explanation Yeast cells have used the glucose in a process called **respiration**. This is a chemical process which goes on inside all living organisms. It involves the chemical breakdown of glucose (sugar) to release energy. This chemical reaction can be summarised:

Glucose $\xrightarrow{\text{yeast}}$ energy + ethyl alcohol + carbon dioxide

The energy is the most important part of this reaction. It is the energy that enables the yeast to carry on all its living functions:

- cell division (splitting) or reproduction
- building up its cellular structures (growth)
- breaking down unwanted structures and materials
- moving molecules into and out of the cell.

But why does the temperature increase in the vacuum flask? As the glucose is broken down, much of the energy in the glucose is trapped and used for the yeast's life processes. However, some of the energy escapes and is wasted. This waste energy becomes heat—hence the temperature increase.

During the breakdown of glucose in yeast cells, to release energy, two waste products are formed: ethyl alcohol (commonly referred to as alcohol) and a gas, carbon dioxide. Yeast cells break down sugar without using oxygen—this kind of respiration is called **anaerobic respiration**.

Most living organisms assist the breakdown of glucose by using oxygen. When oxygen is used, much more energy can be released. The process of breaking down glucose with oxygen is called **aerobic respiration**. Aerobic respiration is similar to anaerobic respiration in that glucose is broken down in order to release energy. However, instead of carbon dioxide and ethyl alcohol, the waste products of aerobic respiration are carbon dioxide and water. This reaction can be summarised as follows:

$$\text{Glucose} + \text{oxygen} \rightarrow \text{energy} + \text{carbon dioxide} + \text{water}$$

As in yeast cells, some of the energy resulting from this process is wasted as heat.

The human body is like a very complex machine. Huge amounts of energy must be provided all the time for the highly specialised life processes. Aerobic respiration provides most of the energy which the body cells need. However, sometimes oxygen cannot be supplied quickly enough to allow aerobic respiration to proceed. At these times, the cells must release energy from glucose without oxygen, that is by anaerobic respiration. This process is similar to anaerobic respiration in yeast cells. However, in all animals, the waste product of anaerobic respiration is lactic acid. The equation for anaerobic respiration in animal cells can be written:

$$\text{Glucose} \rightarrow \text{energy} + \text{lactic acid}$$

Excretion

Experiment   Some milk is placed in a test tube and an indicator used to test its acidity. The milk is slightly acidic. The milk is left for 5 days at room temperature, and its acidity is tested again. The acidity of the milk has increased considerably.

At the same time, another sample of milk is placed in the refrigerator. The acidity of this milk also is tested at the beginning and the end of the 5-day period. The acidity of this milk has not increased.

Explanation Bacteria in the milk sample kept at room temperature have used up sugars in the milk to release energy. The waste product of this process is lactic acid.

As explained in the previous section, this process is known as anaerobic respiration. The bacteria have no use for the lactic acid. In fact, if it collects inside the cells in high concentrations it becomes poisonous or toxic. To overcome this, lactic acid is eliminated or excreted by the bacteria. Lactic acid is thus called an excretory product.

(In the milk kept in the refrigerator, very little lactic acid is produced. This is because bacteria are unable to continue energy-releasing reactions when the temperature is low.)

All living organisms excrete some kind of waste material. In humans, the waste product resulting from the breakdown of proteins is very toxic. It is converted into urea (Chapters 4 and 12), which is excreted through the kidneys. Carbon dioxide, the waste product of aerobic respiration, is excreted through the lungs (see Chapter 8).

Movement

Watch a number of small aquatic organisms moving under a microscope, for example paramecium, amoeba and euglena (Fig 1.2). Each of these organisms moves by a different method. Although our bodies, as a whole, are moved by more complex systems (discussed in Chapter 18), each of these simple types of movements is important in particular cells in our bodies.

Paramecium moves by means of rows of small hairs which are attached to its surface. These are called **cilia**. As the cilia beat, they propel the microscopic animal forwards or backwards. Cilia are also found in the gullet of the paramecium. Here, their beating action wafts tiny food particles into this small hollow, ready for 'swallowing' by the animal. (We shall see later that cilia have an important job moving different particles on several of our body surfaces, too.)

Amoebae move by quite a different process. You can think of an amoeba as being like a loose jelly (cytoplasm) inside a thin plastic bag (cell membrane). The jelly flows around inside the plastic bag, and occasionally pushes slightly harder in a particular direction. When it does this it forms a projection or **pseudopod** (false foot). The rest of the cytoplasm (jelly) may flow in the same direction, so that the whole amoeba is brought to a new position (Fig 1.2b). Because it was first described in the amoeba, this type of movement is known as **amoeboid movement**. In our bodies, certain types of white blood cells move through the tissues by this means (see Chapter 7).

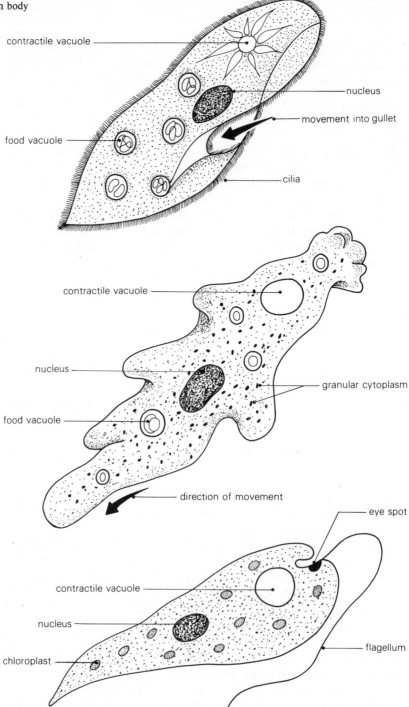

Fig 1.2 *Three small water organisms, each using a different method of locomotion*
(a) Paramecium (movement using cilia)
(b) Amoeba (movement using pseudopodia)
(c) Euglena (movement using a flagellum)

Many organisms move by means of a single, whip-like tail called a **flagellum**. As the tail lashes, the organism is propelled through the water. Euglena is an example of an organism that moves in this way (Fig 1.2c). Sperm cells (see Chapter 17) also move by means of a flagellum.

Reproduction

Experiment   A yeast cell is placed on a cavity slide in a 0.1 per cent glucose solution at room temperature. (These cells can be handled using a very small pipette and a binocular dissecting microscope.) When the slide is examined under the dissecting microscope 24 hours later, a number of cells can be seen. The cell has multiplied. In biological terms we say that the yeast cell has reproduced.

Explanation   How has this reproduction occurred? If you could observe the cells for some time under the microscope, you would see them form small side buds (Fig 1.3a). The small buds grow and then finally break off to form new individual cells. This very simple type of reproduction is known as **budding**.

Reproduction, the ability of an organism to create new organisms like itself, is a basic feature of all living things. It is not an essential part of the survival of an individual, but the survival of that species depends on at least some of the individuals of the species reproducing themselves. Reproduction by budding, which occurs in yeast cells, is one of the simplest forms   of reproduction. There are several other types of reproduction.

Very simple organisms like bacteria (see Chapter 7) divide by a method known as **binary fission**. In this method, the bacterial cell grows longer, until it reaches a size at which it can divide into two portions. The nuclear (genetic) material separates into two parts, and then a new cell wall grows down the centre of the cell. Finally, the divided cell splits to form two new bacteria (Fig 1.3b).

Other one-celled animals, like the amoeba, can also reproduce by simple fission. However, the division is more complex. The process of cell division is called **mitosis**. The important feature of mitosis is that it ensures equal division of both nucleus and cytoplasm between the two 'daughter' cells (Fig 1.3c). Mitosis involves a complex sequence of events which are discussed in Chapter 5 and illustrated in Fig 5.1.

Mitosis occurs in all multicelled animals and plants. It is the process by which their cells divide. However, cell division of this type, in complex organisms, does not normally result in reproduction of a new daughter individual. Instead, cell division results in an increase in cell number and tissue volume, that is, in growth.

Reproduction by binary fission, budding and mitosis are all examples of reproduction in which the daughter organisms are identical to the parent organisms. This type of reproduction is called **asexual reproduction**. Reproduction of larger organisms such as humans involves a far more

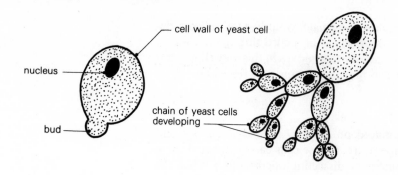

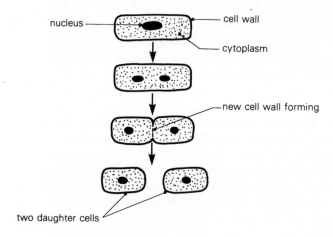

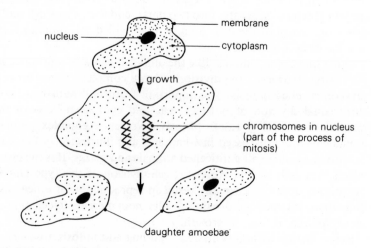

Fig 1.3   *Three methods of reproduction*
(a) Budding (yeast)
(b) Binary fission (bacteria)
(c) Division involving mitosis (amoeba)

complex process called **sexual reproduction**. Sexual reproduction differs from asexual reproduction in several important ways:

● The formation of the new individual begins with the union (fusion) of two cells. This union is called **fertilisation**.

● The two cells which fuse to form the new individual are called **gametes**.

● In animals, the gametes are always of two kinds—male and female.

The process of reproduction of the human species is discussed in detail in Chapter 17.

Irritability

Experiment   A number of euglena (single-celled animals) are placed in a drop of water on a microscope slide. Part of the slide is illuminated, the other part remains in darkness. Very soon, most of the organisms are found on the illuminated part of the slide.

Explanation   The organisms have responded to a change in their environment. In biological terms this change is called a **stimulus**. Because the euglena are able to detect the stimulus and respond to it, they are said to be **irritable**.

All living things, plants included, are irritable in some way. Different organisms are sensitive (or can respond) to different types of stimuli. You may have observed how a plant bends slowly towards *light* from a window in a dark room, or how a tendril of a climbing plant curls in response to *touch*. Woodlice move away from light, and moths fly towards it. People, of course, can detect and respond to a huge variety of stimuli—they have special communication systems which enable them to do this. These are discussed in detail in Chapters 13 and 15.

Classifying the living world

The biologist classifies living organisms by grouping them according to their permanent and useful characteristics. For example, the kingdom of animals can be broken up into smaller, but still very large, groups called phyla (singular phylum), into which are placed animals with similar characteristics. The animals which make up a phylum can be split into a number of smaller groups called classes. Classes can in turn be subdivided into: orders, families, genera (singular genus) and finally into the smallest category, the species.

Every organism is given a name according to the genus and species groups it belongs to. Because organisms belonging to the same genus and species groups possess particular characteristics, knowing the genus and species name of an organism tells us a great deal about the organism.

Figure 1.4 illustrates this process of classification by showing the place of humans amongst living things.

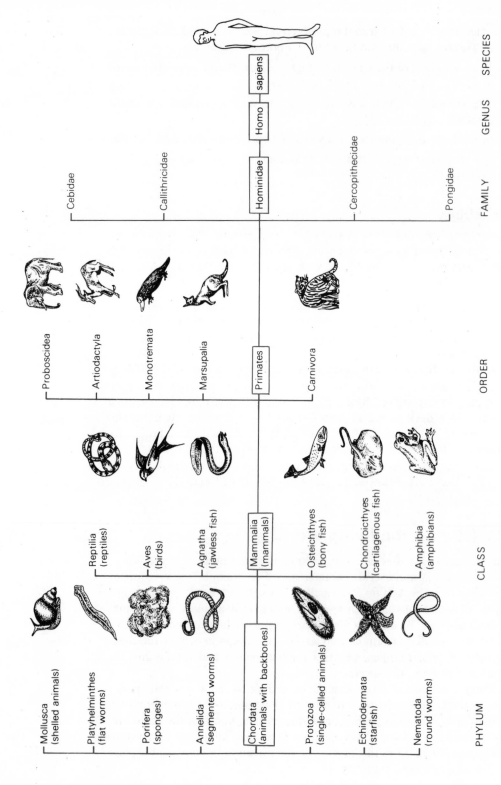

Fig 1.4 *The place of humans in the animal kingdom*

Humans and their place in the animal kingdom

Let us now examine some of the characteristics of the groups which the human being or *Homo sapiens* belongs to. First, humans belong to the phylum Chordata. Members of the phylum Chordata possess a hollow nerve cord in the back or dorsal region. Some of the Chordates possess a chain of bones, running down their backs, which protects this nerve cord. Each of the individual units in this backbone is called a **vertebra**. These animals with backbones are therefore known as the vertebrates.

Although many vertebrate classes are successful, the **mammals** are perhaps the most advanced and efficient class. There seems to be a number of reasons for this; they are worth considering in more detail if we are to get a true picture of humans as members of the class of mammals.

Vertebrates

Mammals can be distinguished from other vertebrates by a number of characteristics:

Mammals

- Most mammals (although humans appear to be the exception) are covered with thick hair or fur. This hair helps to insulate the animal from the cold, and helps to maintain a high, constant body temperature.

- Mammals have large brains and complex behaviour. Unlike most creatures they are able to learn from past experience and to act with what we might call intelligence. The ability to reason is a feature particularly well developed in the human species, and is a major reason for its success.

- All mammals feed their young on milk, a fluid secreted from special glands called mammary glands.

- The offspring of mammals develop to a large or small degree within the uterus of the mother. This contrasts with other animals such as fish, in which the young develop outside the mother from the point of fertilisation. In placental mammals the developing animal comes into intimate contact with the wall of the female uterus and is fed through the placenta and the mother's circulatory system.

- The heart of mammals consists of four chambers: two atria and two ventricles. This contrasts with reptiles (such as snakes) and amphibians (such as frogs), which have hearts with only three chambers, whilst fish have only two.

- The teeth of mammals are usually of four distinct types: incisors, canines, premolars and molars.

These, then, are the characteristics which enable us to place a number of animals, including humans, in the class Mammalia. A quick glance at Fig 1.4 will show that humans belong to a further subdivision of the mammals, the order of primates. The animals belonging to this group (monkeys, apes etc) share a number of characteristics including a well-developed ability to see and judge distance, giving birth to fewer young, taking part in a relatively long period of parental care, and the development of nails rather than claws.

Primates

Further characteristics make humans members of the family Hominidae. The most striking of these characteristics are forelimbs that are shorter than the hind limbs, an upright stance, and the presence of a thumb for grasping.

Family Hominidae

Of the family Hominidae, 'Modern Man' (*Homo sapiens*) is the only living representative. What characteristics are unique to Modern Man? There are a number of these, but perhaps the most significant is the extremely large brain size relative to the size of the body. For example, the braincase of Modern Man (1000–1800 cm³) is almost three times as large as that of the gorilla (390–650 cm³), and almost four times that of the chimpanzee (230–480 cm³), man's closest living relative.

Human control of the environment

A large brain has enabled Modern Man to achieve the status of the most successful organism on earth today. The human ability to communicate and to store information, and to pass knowledge and experience on to the next generation, has led to rapid advances in technology over the past 20 000 years. A growing understanding of the surrounding world has enabled humans to improve their own environment, and in particular to cut down the wastage of life from disease and malnutrition, and to understand the conditions necessary for maintaining good health.

But as well as using their increased understanding of themselves and their environment to their advantage, this increased understanding has enabled people to abuse these developments also. For example, although the medical use of drugs such as penicillin has made possible the control of a large number of serious diseases, the development and abuse of other drugs have taken their toll on human health and, in some cases, life. Alcoholic drinks have become very much a part of our society and our way of life—acceptable within limits—but abuse of alcohol causes physical and social damage to large proportions of our communities. Tobacco-smoking may cause cancer, heart disease and other respiratory diseases. Processed foods may cause rapid and irreversible dental decay (Fig 1.5).

On a more positive note, improved medicine has allowed more people to reach old age than ever before. This, in turn, means that there is an increased need for greater understanding, by society, of old people and their needs, and of the biological processes involved in ageing. Medical knowledge has also enabled us to control the birth rate and to detect some serious deficiencies in the young child well before birth. It is again essential that people learn how to live with and use such knowledge, particularly when it encroaches on the areas of human feeling and respect, or even upon decisions involving human life.

The purpose of this book is to describe in detail how our bodies function, and to relate this information to ourselves as members of society. We shall come to see that understanding how our bodies work can help us not only to make decisions about our own health and lifestyle, but also to understand others better.

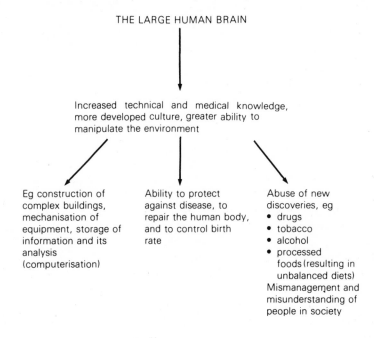

THE LARGE HUMAN BRAIN

Increased technical and medical knowledge, more developed culture, greater ability to manipulate the environment

Eg construction of complex buildings, mechanisation of equipment, storage of information and its analysis (computerisation)

Ability to protect against disease, to repair the human body, and to control birth rate

Abuse of new discoveries, eg
• drugs
• tobacco
• alcohol
• processed foods (resulting in unbalanced diets)
Mismanagement and misunderstanding of people in society

Fig 1.5 *Man's impact on the environment*

Chapter 2

Cells, tissues and organs

- Importance of cells
- Cells and their parts
- How plant cells differ from animal cells
- How molecules enter and leave cells
- Structure and function of specialised cells
- Levels of organisation

Importance of cells

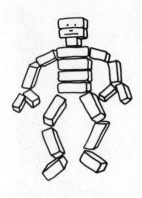

By the seventeenth century scientists had made many observations about the structure and function of living organisms. However, their observations were limited by the power of their eyesight. With the invention of the microscope, smaller and smaller objects could be studied. One early scientist to use the microscope was an Englishman named Robert Hooke, who observed a variety of familiar objects. In 1665, when examining a thin section of cork, he discovered that it was made up of many little 'boxes' for which he coined the term 'cell'. Robert Hooke was therefore credited with the discovery of the cell.

The significance of these cells to all forms of life was not appreciated for many years. For some time scientists assumed that the basic units of an organism were the visible structures, such as legs, heart, lungs and stomach in animals, and roots, stems and flowers in plants. Then, in 1839, a German physiologist named Schwann, with the assistance of a botanist, Schleiden, wrote a book setting forward the 'cell theory'. Although others before him had suggested the basic importance of cells in living organisms, Schwann was the first to convince the scientific world of the cellular basis of life. His cell theory set forward the following ideas:

Cell theory—all living organisms are composed of cells

- All living organisms are composed of cells.
- The life of a new organism begins with a single cell.
- Organisms develop by creating new cells.

Cells and their parts

Today, cells are recognised as the basic unit of any living organism (Fig 2.1). The size, shape, chemical composition and arrangement of cells in any organism are specifically related to the functions the cells perform. It is therefore difficult to talk about a typical cell. For example, cells involved with movement (muscle cells) are quite different from cells involved with communication (nerve cells), which are in turn different from cells involved in supporting (such as bone cells). However, there are certain features which all cells have in common.

Cell membrane

All cells are surrounded by a membrane

All cells are surrounded by a very thin flexible layer of fat and protein known as a membrane. This membrane holds the jelly-like contents of the cell together. However, the cell membrane does allow certain substances to pass backwards and forwards between the external environment and the living material of the cell. Because only certain substances

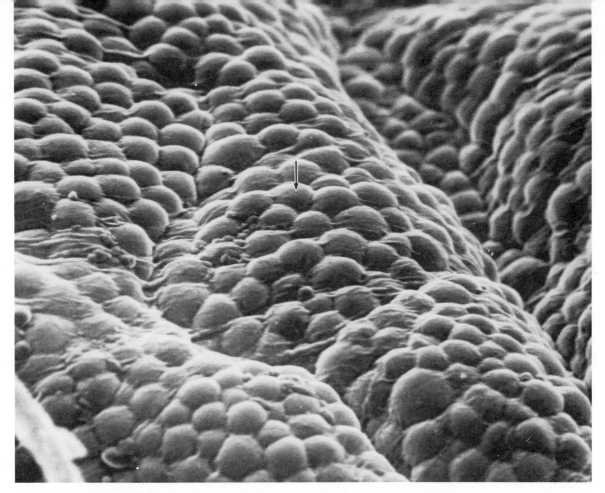

Fig 2.1 *All living organisms are composed of cells (scanning electron micrograph of fat cells). The arrow points to the surface of one fat cell in a mass of fatty tissues*

can penetrate the membrane, it is said to be **semipermeable**. Substances which can penetrate cell membranes are usually in the form of small molecules. Figure 2.2 shows the cell membrane of a cheek cell in relation to the other cell structures.

Cell membranes are semipermeable

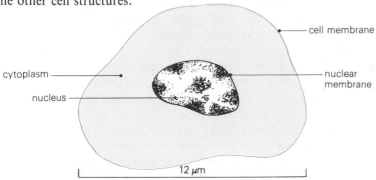

Fig 2.2 *A cheek cell (diagrammatic)*

Nucleus

The nucleus contains DNA

The nucleus is a small, often circular structure clearly visible inside the cell. It can often be distinguished from the rest of the cell because it stains more strongly with certain dyes. It contains a chemical called de-oxyribonucleic acid, or DNA, which is responsible for controlling all the activities of the cell. Because of this the nucleus is said to be the 'control centre' of the cell. It plays a part in determining the shape, size and function of the cell, and controls most of the chemical processes within it. Without the nucleus, a cell is unable to continue its normal life-giving processes.

The nucleus controls
• shape
• size
• function
• chemical processes of the cell

Within the nucleus is the nucleolus, which contains RNA

Within the nucleus another body can often be seen. This is the **nucleolus**, which contains another kind of chemical, ribonucleic acid, or RNA. The nucleolus is thought to manufacture RNA for the rest of the cell.

During the process of cell division the nucleus divides in two. After division is complete, the two daughter cells must be left with sufficient nucleic acid to continue their normal functions. To ensure this, the amount of DNA in the nucleus must *double* between divisions. As a result of this doubling, both daughter nuclei formed from a dividing cell receive a full amount of nuclear material. The role of the nucleus in the life of the cell will be discussed further in Chapter 5.

Cytoplasm

The nucleus controls processes occurring in the cytoplasm

Cytoplasm looks like a transparent jelly-like soup

Cytoplasm could be termed the 'soup' of the cell. It is here that the chemical processes essential to life are carried on. There is a strong link between this jelly-like, transparent fluid and the nucleus, as it is the nucleus that controls the processes occurring in the cytoplasm. When observed through a light microscope, the cytoplasm is seen as a pale-staining unstructured material. However, it may contain particles which appear as distinct units within the uniform background.

Cytoplasm can be examined more closely using an electron microscope

A great deal more can be discovered about the cytoplasm with the help of a different type of microscope. Electron microscopes make use of electrons rather than light to 'view' tissue. The thinly sectioned specimen is stained with a heavy metal stain and placed on a fine-meshed copper grid. It is then positioned inside the electron microscope. The electron microscope has a large evacuated tube with an electron gun at the top end, and a screen at the bottom which fluoresces when struck by electrons. Electrons pass through the specimen and then strike the fluorescent screen, producing an 'image' of the specimen. Different structures inside the cells of the specimen take up the heavy metal stain in different concentrations. Those which stain strongly with the metal stain stop the electrons from passing through and hitting the screen, and so cause less fluorescence to appear on corresponding areas of the screen. Because of their different staining reactions, many different structures inside cells can be viewed in this way. Objects can be magnified up to 200 000 times with this type of microscope (Fig 2.3).

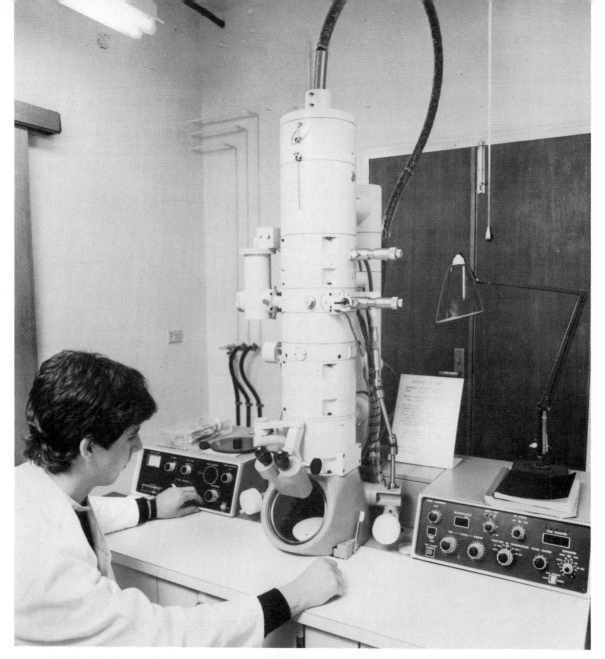

Fig 2.3 *An electron microscope*

A number of previously unseen cell structures called **organelles** were discovered with the electron microscope. Several of these are illustrated in Figs 2.4 to 2.7.

Cytoplasm contains organelles

- The **mitochondrion** is the structure in which most of the energy of the cell is produced.

Energy is produced in the mitochondrion

- The **endoplasmic reticulum** (ER) is a network of flattened sacs extending throughout the cytoplasm, and has small granules of RNA attached to its surface. These granules are called ribosomes.

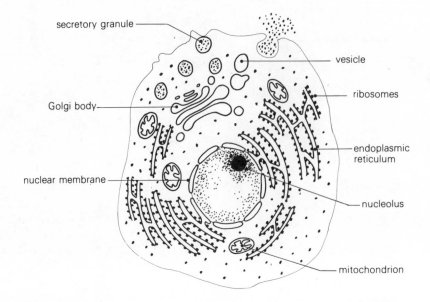

secretory granule

vesicle

Golgi body

ribosomes

endoplasmic reticulum

nuclear membrane

nucleolus

mitochondrion

Fig 2.4 *Structures inside a cell (as seen with an electron microscope)*

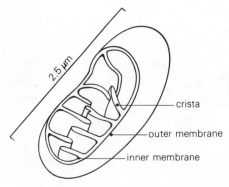

2.5 μm

crista

outer membrane

inner membrane

Fig 2.5 *A mitochondrion*

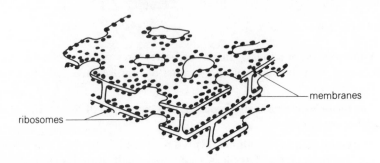

membranes

ribosomes

Fig 2.6 *Endoplasmic reticulum (ER) and ribosomes*

secretory vesicles

secretory vesicles
leaving Golgi body

membrane sacs

Fig 2.7 *A Golgi body*

- **Ribosomes** are responsible for the construction of important cellular chemicals called proteins. These proteins are then concentrated in the sacs of the endoplasmic reticulum and transported to different sites in the cell.

- The **Golgi body** packages the protein from the ER and mixes it with carbohydrates. This material is then carried in small membrane sacs called **vesicles** to the cell membrane, where it is released from the cell.

Using a microscope, the most detailed analysis we can make of any cell is a study of the different cell organelles. If we are to learn more about the cell and how it operates we have to resort to chemical techniques, which bring us into the field of biochemistry.

Ribosomes are responsible for protein construction

Endoplasmic reticulum receives newly formed protein

Golgi bodies package protein and carbohydrate for release from the cell

How plant cells differ from animal cells

There are several differences in the structures of animal and plant cells. Some of the most important of these are discussed below. Figure 2.8 illustrates the structure of a typical plant cell viewed with a light microscope. In later chapters we shall see how these differences in structure are related to the roles of animals and plants in the living world.

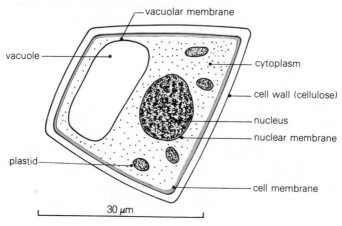

vacuolar membrane

vacuole

cytoplasm

cell wall (cellulose)

nucleus

nuclear membrane

plastid

cell membrane

30 μm

Fig 2.8 *A plant cell*

Cell wall

Plant cell walls consist of cellulose

Unlike animal cells, plant cells possess a wall of cellulose outside the cell membrane. The cellulose takes the form of extremely thin interlocking fibres (or fibrils), which form a structure something like that of a closely woven basket. Most substances can travel through the gaps between the cellulose fibrils, and so the cell wall can be regarded as fully permeable to most substances. Sometimes the gaps in the wall are filled with chemicals, as in the cells of corky tree bark. In such cases, not much water and not even much gas is able to pass through the wall.

Cell walls are fully permeable

The function of the cell wall is to give the cell some sort of shape and rigidity. While a plant cell is growing, the cell wall can be stretched, but once the cell has reached its adult size, its wall becomes harder and resistant to stretching.

The cell wall gives the cell shape and rigidity

Vacuole

Vacuoles are surrounded by a membrane

The vacuole is a permanent area of a mature plant cell, bounded by a membrane known as the vacuolar membrane. The vacuole contains fluid. The fluid may contain substances such as mineral salts, sugar or even dissolved pigments. A full vacuole exerts a pressure outwards on the cell wall, making the cell firm and adding to the definite shape already given by the cell wall. Many young plant cells do not have vacuoles, which appear as the cell matures.

Vacuoles hold fluid containing mineral salts, sugars or dissolved pigments

Animal cells rarely possess large single vacuoles. They may contain small droplets of fluid substances surrounded by membranes; these resemble small vacuoles.

Shape

Plant cells have a more distinctive shape than animal cells

Because plant cells are surrounded by a cellulose wall they tend to have a more definite shape than animal cells, which are encased only by a membrane. That is not to say that all plant cells are always more regular in shape than animal cells, but plant cells tend to have more distinctive outlines. This is probably due to the presence of the cell wall material.

Plastids

Plant cells possess, in their cytoplasm, a number of structures that are not found in animal cells. These structures are known as **plastids**. Some plastids are green and contain a green pigment called chlorophyll. These are called **chloroplasts**. There are two other types of plastids that are not green. One of these is filled with starch grains, and its function is to store food. The other type contains different pigments which give colour to the structures of many plants, such as fruit (eg tomatoes or oranges) or petals.

Plastids containing chlorophyll are called chloroplasts

Plastids may store starch

How molecules enter and leave cells

As we said earlier, the membrane which surrounds a cell is a semi-permeable membrane. In other words, it provides a barrier to the movement of some molecules but allows other chemical substances to enter or leave the cell. Just which chemicals can enter and leave the cell is very important. The life of the cell depends on a network of chemical reactions. All cells are constantly exchanging molecules between their cytoplasm and the fluid which surrounds them in the body. The cell membrane therefore has a vital role, both as a passive barrier, preventing some molecules from leaving the cell and others from entering, and as an active envelope, regulating the movement of needed and unwanted substances into and out of the cell.

Understanding how substances move into and out of cells is basic to understanding almost all of the body's functions. How are food molecules absorbed from the intestine? How does oxygen in the lungs enter the bloodstream? And how is blood filtered to form urine? The answers to all these questions involve understanding how chemical substances enter and leave cells. Let us now see how this movement takes place.

Movement of substances in or out of cells occurs in one of four basic ways. Three of these are discussed below. A fourth process, by which larger particles may be taken into some special cells, is discussed in Chapter 7. This process is known as phagocytosis.

Diffusion

If a drop of red dye is placed in a beaker of water, the drop remains visible for only a few seconds. After this the red dye spreads itself throughout the water until finally the whole volume of water has a uniform pale pink colour. The dye particles have spread themselves from an area in which they are in high concentration to areas in which they are in low concentration. (The water surrounding the drop of red dye originally had zero dye concentration.) This natural spreading of small particles is called diffusion and is shown diagrammatically in Fig 2.9.

Diffusion—movement of particles (or molecules) from areas of high concentration to areas of low concentration

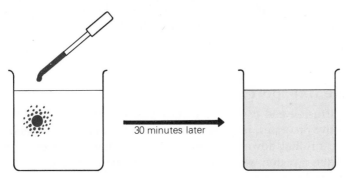

30 minutes later

Fig 2.9 *An example of diffusion*

Cells obtain food and rid themselves of waste by diffusion

Diffusion is one method by which cells both take in food material and get rid of waste products. For example, both oxygen and glucose enter cells by diffusion; that is, they move from an area of high concentration outside the cell to an area of low concentration inside the cell. Carbon dioxide diffuses out of cells for the same reason.

Osmosis

Osmosis can be regarded as a special type of diffusion—the diffusion of water molecules from a weaker solution to a stronger solution. Now you will probably realise that in a weaker solution there will be less dissolved substance and more water. In a strong solution there is more dissolved substance and less water.

Osmosis—movement of water molecules from a more dilute solution to a more concentrated solution through a semipermeable membrane

There is, therefore, another way of defining osmosis. That is, as the movement of water molecules from an area in which water molecules are in high concentration to an area in which water molecules are in low concentration. One further point must be added to this definition—that the two solutions must be separated by a semipermeable membrane. This membrane allows movement of water, but not of dissolved substances.

Osmosis can be demonstrated in an experiment using distilled water and a concentrated starch solution. A length of dialysis tubing (which is like cellophane and is semipermeable) is filled with a strong solution of starch. It is then fitted over the end of a capillary tube and held in place by an elastic band. The dialysis tube is lowered into a beaker of distilled water. After 30 minutes, the level of liquid in the capillary tube will have risen many centimetres, and fluid may even overflow from the top of the tube. A diagram of the apparatus is shown in Fig 2.10a.

Figure 2.10b illustrates the movement of water molecules in the process of osmosis.

Red blood cells placed in distilled water absorb water by osmosis. They finally burst

Both plant and animal cells will take in water by osmosis. This occurs whenever the concentration of water inside the cell is *less* than the concentration of water outside the cell. For example, when a red blood cell (whose cytoplasm has a very high concentration of protein) is placed in distilled water, it will absorb water and finally burst. (Some special animal cells (particularly tiny, aquatic animals) possess apparatus to remove excess water absorbed by osmosis.)

Active transport

Both diffusion and osmosis are automatic processes. We say that they are passive processes, because they occur without any energy being spent. Like a car rolling down a hill, molecules move down a concentration gradient from a region where they are in high concentration to one where they are in lower concentration.

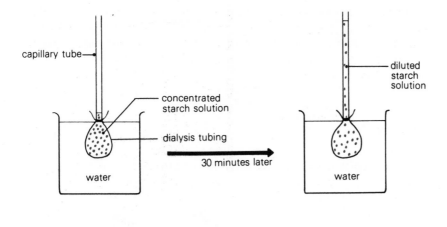

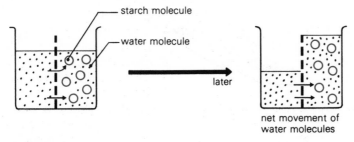

Fig 2.10 *Osmosis*
(a) Apparatus to demonstrate osmosis
(b) Movement of water molecules during osmosis

Sometimes, however, cells require particular substances, even though their concentration inside the cell is already greater than their concentration outside the cell. The natural tendency is for the substance to travel in the opposite direction (out of the cell), as would occur by diffusion. In these situations, energy must be spent to pump the molecules up the concentration gradient, from areas of low concentration to areas of high concentration. When energy is used to move molecules across membranes, the process is known as active transport. (Think again of the car on the slope. The force of diffusion is like gravity tending to pull the car down the hill. Only when the engine is switched on and energy is used can the car make any progress up the slope.) The principles of active transport are illustrated simply in Fig 2.11.

Exactly how chemicals are pumped across membranes in this way is unclear. There are examples of active transport in many parts of the body. In the intestine, glucose is absorbed into epithelial cells at ten times the concentration found in the digested food.

Active transport—substances moved from areas of low concentration to areas of high concentration through a cell membrane. The process requires energy

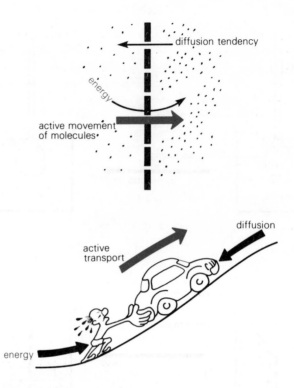

Fig 2.11   *The principles of active transport*

Structure and function of specialised cells

Each operation in the body is carried out by cells

It is not hard to appreciate the vast number of different operations that go on in the human body. Each operation is made possible by many types of cells. For example, limbs are moved by muscle cells. The message to make a muscle cell contract (or shorten in length) is conveyed by a nerve cell. Some cells secrete chemicals, such as those in the stomach wall. Some cells, like sperm, have to move long distances in comparison with their size. The task of many cells is to cover and protect the body surfaces.

The structure of a cell is related to its function

In all these examples the cells mentioned have a particular job or task. In biological terms this job or task is called the function. That is, different cells have different functions. (Refer to Figs 2.16 and 2.17, which show two cells with quite different functions. One, the nerve cell, relays electrical messages to a muscle cell. The other, the muscle cell, contracts and relaxes, to produce movement of parts of the body.) In order to carry out these different tasks or functions, the cells have different shapes and arrangements of organelles. This is called the structure of the cells. In any part of the body, cells with the same function have similar structures. Cells with different functions have different structures. In general, the structure of cells is related to their function. Cells that are

Specialised cells have a particular structure which helps them to carry out a particular function

constructed in order to carry out a certain function are said to be *specialised*.

Probably the best method of looking at the structure of cells and relating this to their function is to use the electron microscope. In this way we can observe not only the shape of the cell, but also the particular cellular organelles it contains. Figure 2.12 shows line drawings of electron micrographs of a cell involved with absorption of chemicals in the kidney tubule (Fig 2.12a) and one involved with secretion of protein chemicals in the pancreas (Fig 2.12b).

The shape of the absorptive cell is such that it has a large surface area, over which it can absorb molecules from the kidney tubule. This absorption is a living process which requires energy. You may remember that the cellular organelle concerned with supplying energy is the mitochondrion. It is no surprise, therefore, to observe that the kidney tubule cell has many mitochondria, particularly in areas of the cytoplasm close to the cell membrane.

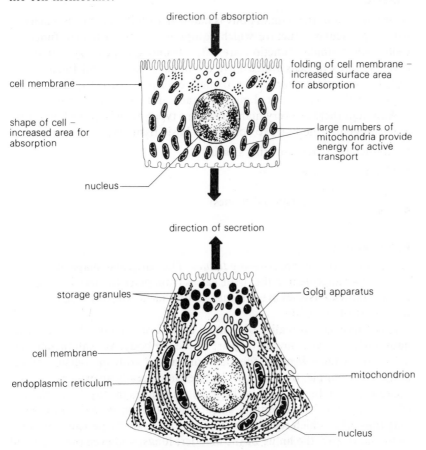

Fig 2.12 *Two cells with different functions (line drawings of electron micrographs)*
(a) Kidney tubule cell, involved with absorption
(b) Pancreas cell, involved with secretion of protein (enzyme)

The cell from the pancreas is one whose function is to form and secrete some of the proteins necessary for digestion. With the help of the electron microscope, we can see cellular organelles inside the pancreatic cell, which equip it for this particular function. The pancreatic cell has vast quantities of endoplasmic reticulum (ER) and ribosomes, which together help to manufacture proteins. The top portion of the cell is filled with Golgi bodies, which 'package' the proteins in vesicles ready for release from the cell (secretion), and vesicles of protein awaiting secretion.

Levels of organisation

The human body is an organised structure with several levels of organisation: cells, tissues, organs, systems and the whole organism.

Tissues

As we have said, the human body is made up of billions of cells, each one with a particular structure which equips it for its particular function. Cells with a similar function are often found grouped together in the body. Groups of cells which have a similar structure and function are called tissues. It is from these tissues, or groups of cells, that all the organs of the body (heart, lungs, stomach and so on) are built.

Tissues—groups of cells with similar structure and function

Although there are very many different types of cells in the body, they are arranged in the body to form four basic tissue types. These are:

- Epithelial tissues (covering tissues)
- Connective tissues
- Muscle tissues ⎫
- Nerve tissues   ⎬ (special tissues)

Epithelial tissues

All epithelial tissues are *covering tissues*. The particular shape of the cells and their arrangement in the tissue varies from place to place in the body, but all epithelial tissues are designed to provide a covering or a lining for some part of the body.

It is important to realise that many organs of the body have external body surfaces, even though they are inside the body. We call them external body surfaces because they are continuous with the outside of the body. For example, the lining of the intestine is really an external surface because it can be reached without cutting through any body tissues. (Photographs of the intestinal surface are sometimes taken through a long thin tube, which reaches the intestine through the patient's mouth.) In the same way, the lining of the bladder, lungs, and even the ducts and glands which pour secretions into the mouth, stomach and intestines are external surfaces. All these surfaces are covered with epithelial tissues.

Epithelial tissues cover all the external surfaces of the body, eg
- *skin*
- *lung*
- *bladder*
- *stomach*
- *ducts of breasts*

Because of this special job (or function) of covering body surfaces, all epithelial tissues have some common structural features. In epithelial tissues the cells are packed tightly together in sheets, with no spaces between adjacent cells. The sheet of cells may be only one cell thick, as is the case in the lungs, or it may be many cells thick, as is the case in the skin, where it provides protection from dehydration, 'wear and tear', and infection. Some examples of the different shapes and arrangements of epithelial cells and tissues are shown in Figs 2.13 and 2.14.

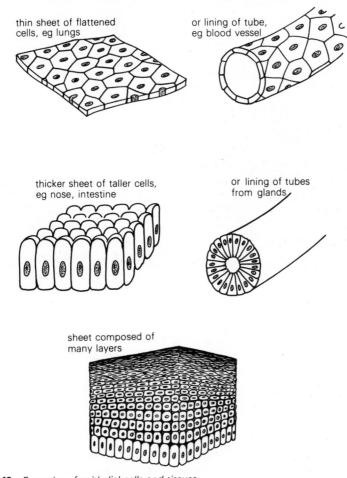

thin sheet of flattened cells, eg lungs

or lining of tube, eg blood vessel

thicker sheet of taller cells, eg nose, intestine

or lining of tubes from glands

sheet composed of many layers

Fig 2.13 *Examples of epithelial cells and tissues*

Connective tissues

As its name suggests, connective tissue has the special function of holding the body together and supporting other tissues. Different organs and parts of the body often require very different types of support. For example, bone is one type of connective tissue, designed to provide the strength and resilience needed to support the body's weight and allow

Connective tissues:
• supporting tissues
• cells widely spaced
• spaces between cells filled with non-living material—matrix

Fig 2.14 *'Pavement' epithelium lining the bladder—note the absence of spaces between cells (scanning electron micrograph). The arrows mark the junctions between cells*

movement. Cartilage and tendons are other types of connective tissue. All the organs of the body are held together by connective tissue. The covering (epithelial) surface of the skin sits on a layer of connective tissue which provides blood vessels and nerves for the surface layer.

The characteristic feature of the many varied forms of connective tissue is that they are all made up of cells which are widely spaced. The spaces between the cells are filled with a non-living material (usually produced by the cells) called the **matrix**. The matrix can be very different in different connective tissues. For example, the matrix of bone contains fibres and a cementing substance which is hardened with chemicals similar to limestone. The loose, fibrous connective tissue which is found around and within organs has a soft matrix of collagen and elastic fibres. Fat tissue is a special type of connective tissue in which the cells become filled with fat. The fat cells are held together by fibres called collagen fibres. (Blood is sometimes called a connective tissue. The blood cells are surrounded by a fluid matrix called plasma.) Figure 2.15 shows some examples of types of connective tissue.

bone—a hard connective tissue

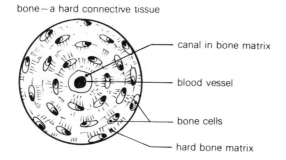

- canal in bone matrix
- blood vessel
- bone cells
- hard bone matrix

cartilage—a flexible connective tissue

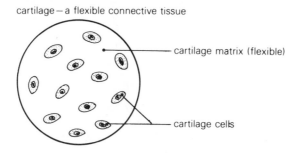

- cartilage matrix (flexible)
- cartilage cells

fibrous tissue

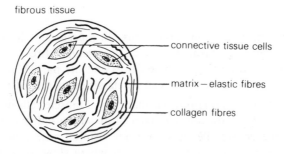

- connective tissue cells
- matrix—elastic fibres
- collagen fibres

Fig 2.15 *Examples of connective tissues*

Nerve tissue

Nerve tissue consists of nerve cells, whose function is to transmit signals (as electrical impulses) from one part of the body to another. (Nerve tissue also includes some special cells which support and nourish nerve cells, for example Schwann cells—see Chapter 13.) A nerve cell is shown in Fig 2.16.

Nerve tissue is a special tissue designed to transmit electrical impulses

Long extensions of cytoplasm are a feature of nerve cells

Muscle tissue

Muscle tissue is the fourth type of tissue. All muscle tissues have the very special function of *contraction*, that is shortening in length and the

Muscle tissues are tissues capable of contracting

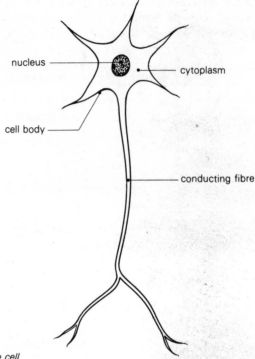

nucleus

cytoplasm

cell body

conducting fibre

Fig 2.16 *A nerve cell*

Muscle cells contain
contractile fibres in their
cytoplasm

Smooth muscle:
• involuntary
• slow movements
• found in viscera, eg
  stomach, uterus,
  bladder, blood vessels

Striated (skeletal) muscle:
• voluntary (conscious)
  control
• rapid contraction

development of tension. To do this, all muscle cells have special structures in their cytoplasm, known as contractile fibres. According to the
appearance (structure) of these fibres and the particular ways in which
they contract, muscle tissue can be classified as one of three types:

- **Smooth** or **visceral muscle** is made up of muscle cells in which the contractile fibres are not arranged in an organised pattern. Because of
  this, the contractile fibres are not visible under a light microscope.
  Smooth muscle is found in places where slow, involuntary (unconscious) movements take place, such as the stomach, uterus, bladder
  and blood vessels. Another feature of smooth muscle is that a contraction which begins in one cell of a muscle may spread as a wave of
  contraction over a large area.

- **Striated** or **skeletal muscle** is so specialised that some cell membranes
  have disappeared altogether. Each muscle cell is very long and has
  numerous nuclei. The contractile fibres are arranged in a highly
  organised pattern which results in very efficient contraction. They can
  be seen under the microscope as stripes or striations inside the muscle
  cells. Most of the muscles of the limbs and trunk are of this type. The
  contraction of striated muscle is under the control of the brain—that
  is to say, conscious control.

- **Cardiac muscle** is the special muscle of the heart. It is striated like skeletal muscle, but cells branch and link together so that it is impossible for one cell to contract on its own. Another special feature of cardiac muscle is that a contraction may begin even in the absence of nerve stimulation. (If the nerves supplying a skeletal muscle are cut, the muscle will no longer contract. If the nerves to the heart are cut, the heart muscle will continue to contract automatically.)

Cardiac (heart) muscle:
- cells branch and link
- impossible for one cell to contract alone
- contraction occurs even without signals from nerves

The different types of muscle tissue are illustrated in Fig 2.17.

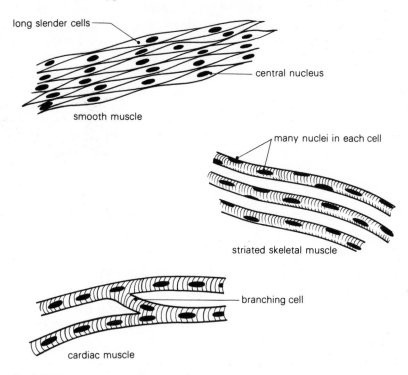

long slender cells

central nucleus

smooth muscle

many nuclei in each cell

striated skeletal muscle

branching cell

cardiac muscle

Fig 2.17   *The three types of muscle tissue*

Organs

The different types of tissues are joined together in the body to form organs. Organs are thus the third level of organisation that can be identified within the body. Organs are structures that perform one or more special functions. For example, the stomach is an organ with the particular function of breaking down food particles. It is an organ built from all four tissue types: an epithelial or lining layer, a connective tissue or holding-together layer, and a muscle layer, as well as nerve fibres which supply all these layers. The heart, bladder, lungs and eyes are other examples of organs.

Organs—structures built from different tissues that perform one or more special functions

Systems

In the body, organs very rarely work alone. Usually organs work together, in a coordinated way, as members of a system. Each system in the body has one general function. For example the heart, blood vessels and blood make up the circulatory system whose function is transport. Similarly, the digestive system is responsible for providing food for the cells of the body. During digestion, food passes from the mouth through a number of organs: the oesophagus, stomach and small and large intestines. In addition, a number of other organs of the digestive system provide chemical secretions to break down food: the salivary glands, pancreas and liver. Table 2.1 summarises the systems of the body, their organs and functions.

Table 2.1   *Body systems – their organs and functions*

System	Process carried out	Organs or structures
Skeletal	Support, protection	All bones of the body
Muscular	Movement	Muscles of limbs and trunk
Circulatory	Transport	Heart, blood vessels, blood, lymph vessels, lymph
Nervous	Response to stimuli; coordination, intelligence and emotions	Brain, nerves, sense organs
Endocrine	Growth, development and coordination	Ductless glands
Respiratory	Breathing	Lungs, air passages (nose, trachea (windpipe) etc)
Digestive	Food processing	Alimentary (food) canal, salivary glands, liver, pancreas
Urinary	Excretion	Kidneys, ureters, bladder, urethra
Reproductive	Reproduction	Different sex organs in the male and female

The organism

The final level of organisation in the body is the coordination of all the systems to make an organism (Fig 2.18). In the following chapters we shall be discussing how each of the organ systems works, and how they all interact in the course of the body's daily activity. Each system is of equal and vital importance to the body. The failure of any one will cause damage to all the other systems and so to the body as a whole.

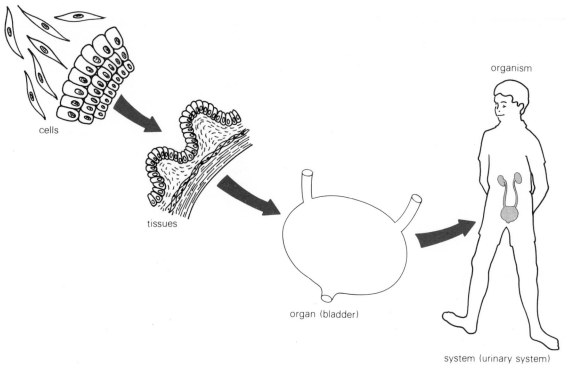

Fig 2.18   *Levels of organisation in the body*

Chapter 3

The chemicals of life

- Organisms contain chemicals
- Role of carbohydrates, fats and proteins
- Enzymes
- Vitamins and minerals

Organisms contain chemicals

Just as a prospector can investigate a piece of rock and analyse it to find the types of metals present, so the biologist is able to determine the types of chemicals which make up living cells. From the eighteenth century onwards, many compounds were extracted from both plant and animal material. These compounds were found to contain many of the known elements. Many of the compounds were identical to those found in non-living matter; others were found to be unique to living organisms.

We now know that chemical compounds can be divided into two main groups. Those that are complex in structure, and contain carbon, are called **organic compounds.** All others are termed **inorganic.** A large number of organic compounds are formed in living organisms. Many, however, can be formed by chemical operations in the laboratory.

All cells of living organisms contain a mixture of organic and inorganic compounds. On analysis, 20 per cent of the average cell is found to be organic in nature. The main organic compounds in cells are carbohydrates, fats, proteins and nucleic acids. A special group called vitamins is also organic in nature. Inorganic compounds found in cells include minerals and water.

Organic compounds contain carbon and are complex in structure

Organic compounds of the cell:
• carbohydrates
• fats
• proteins
• nucleic acids

Four organic compounds found in cells

Most cells contain compounds that are composed only of the elements carbon, hydrogen and oxygen. These compounds can be divided into two groups: carbohydrates and lipids.

Carbohydrates and lipids contain only carbon, hydrogen and oxygen

Carbohydrates

In carbohydrates there are always twice as many hydrogen atoms as oxygen atoms. A common carbohydrate is glucose, in which there are 6 carbon atoms, 12 hydrogen atoms and 6 oxygen atoms arranged in a ring structure:

For simplicity we can draw this without showing all the carbon, hydrogen and oxygen atoms:

It is also possible to express glucose as a chemical formula:

$$C_6H_{12}O_6$$

Carbohydrates made of a single ring structure like the one above are called **monosaccharides** (*mono* = one; *saccharide*, meaning a compound consisting of carbohydrate ring structure). Different monosaccharides can be formed by changing the arrangement of the hydrogen and oxygen atoms around the basic ring. Fructose is a monosaccharide which differs in another way—its basic structure contains only five carbon atoms. Galactose is yet another example of a monosaccharide.

Monosaccharides have a single ring of carbon atoms, eg glucose, ribose and galactose

Sometimes single ring carbohydrates are joined together in pairs to form **disaccharides** (*di* = two). This can be represented diagrammatically by showing two simple rings joined by an oxygen:

Disaccharides are made from two rings of carbon atoms, eg maltose, sucrose and lactose

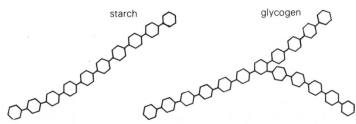

An example of a disaccharide is maltose, in which two glucose rings are joined. Other examples are sucrose, which consists of fructose + glucose, and lactose, which is made from a combination of glucose and galactose.

Often, monosaccharide rings are joined into long chains to form **polysaccharides** (*poly* = many), which, unlike monosaccharides and disaccharides, are insoluble in water. For example, starch (found only in plants) consists of long chains of glucose molecules and is the form in which plants store carbohydrate. The same kind of storage compound in animals is called glycogen, which is different from starch only in the fact that it consists of branched chains of glucose molecules. A simple diagram comparing these two polysaccharides is shown below:

Polysaccharides—many monosaccharide rings joined together, eg glycogen, starch and cellulose

Another important polysaccharide is present in the walls of plant cells. This compound is cellulose and consists of long chains of glucose molecules which are linked sideways to each other:

This forms a three-dimensional lattice which enables cellulose to act as a supporting structure around the contents of the plant cell.

Lipids

Lipids are composed of glycerol and fatty acids

The second group of compounds containing carbon, hydrogen and oxygen are lipids. These include both fats and oils, the difference between these being that at room temperature fats are solid whereas oils are liquids. All lipid molecules are composed of two parts: **glycerol** and **fatty acids.** The formula of glycerol is $C_3H_8O_3$ and it has the structure shown below. A simplified diagram of the glycerol molecule is shown on the right:

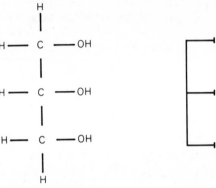

Fatty acids are composed of chains of carbon atoms of varying lengths

The other component of lipids, fatty acids, are chains of carbon atoms of varying lengths, surrounded mainly by hydrogen atoms. The structure of a fatty acid containing three carbon atoms is shown below:

A simple way of drawing this might be:

The number of carbon atoms in the fatty acid chain can vary from 2 to 18. Two types of fatty acids are found in fats. Fatty acids with two bonds between each pair of carbon atoms are called **unsaturated fatty acids.** These are normally found in plants. Fatty acids with one bond between each pair of carbon atoms are called **saturated fatty acids.** Most of these are found in animal tissues.

One lipid = 3 fatty acids + 1 glycerol

A lipid is a combination of three fatty acids and one glycerol molecule. Each fatty acid joins to the glycerol where there is an –OH attached to the carbon atoms of the glycerol molecule. The three fatty acids could be of any chain length, ranging from 3 to 18 carbon atoms. The structure of a lipid is shown in simplified form as follows:

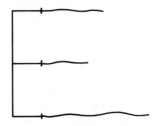

Lipids in which long fatty acid chains are attached to the glycerol tend to be solids at room temperature. Lipids with short-chained fatty acids tend to move more freely in relation to each other and are liquids at room temperature. Thus, long-chained fatty acids are a feature of fats, whereas short-chain molecules belong to oils. In addition, saturated fatty acids are more usually present in fats, whereas unsaturated fatty acids are common in oils.

Proteins

The third important organic compound found in cells is protein. All proteins possess one more element than carbohydrates and lipids—they possess nitrogen. Proteins are composed of chains of subunits called **amino acids.** The structure of an amino acid is shown below, with a simplified diagram on the right:

Proteins contain the element nitrogen, in addition to carbon, hydrogen and oxygen

Proteins consist of chains of amino acids

The part of the molecule labelled R can be one of twenty different shapes. The smallest R group is $-CH_3$, whereas the largest one is a ring structure:

There are 20 amino acids

There are 20 naturally occurring amino acids, each one having a different R side group.

A dipeptide is composed of 2 amino acids

When two amino acids join together, the molecule is called a **dipeptide** (*di* = two). Similarly, three amino acids linked to each other would be termed a **tripeptide.** An example of a tripeptide is shown below in simple diagrammatic form:

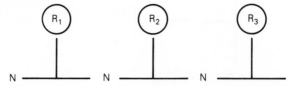

A polypeptide is composed of many amino acids

Often, large numbers of amino acids are joined together. These molecules are then known as **polypeptides** (*poly* = many). A particular polypeptide may be composed of as many as 100 amino acids.

Proteins contain one or more coiled or folded polypeptide chains

Very often, long polypeptide chains become coiled and knotted, or folded in a particular manner. Such a coiled polypeptide is called a protein. Sometimes a number of polypeptide chains become joined together, each polypeptide chain itself being coiled in a special way. Figure 3.1 shows, in simplified form, a protein molecule formed in this way, from three polypeptides.

Different proteins contain different numbers of each amino acid, arranged in a particular order

It is important to realise that the number of proteins which can be constructed from 20 amino acids is very large. Proteins consist of long chains of the 20 amino acids, in any number of different orders. Some amino acids may occur more than once. Each protein has a particular number and order of amino acids. For example, the protein insulin contains a total of 51 amino acid components; 17 of the 20 known amino acids are found in this molecule. Another protein called lysozyme has 129 amino acid components in its long chain.

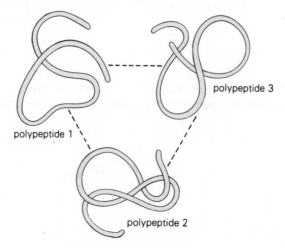

Fig 3.1   *A protein molecule, made up of three polypeptide chains*

Nucleic acids

The fourth important organic compound found in cells is nucleic acids. These are formed from the elements carbon, hydrogen, oxygen, nitrogen and phosphorus. They exist in two forms: RNA and DNA. Both of these chemicals control the types of proteins made in a cell; they will be considered more fully in Chapter 5.

Nucleic acids (RNA and DNA) contain
- carbon
- hydrogen
- oxygen
- nitrogen
- phosphorus

Role of carbohydrates, fats and proteins

To understand the part that carbohydrates, fats and proteins play in the day by day, minute by minute, second by second operation of the cell, we must first consider what basic activities are carried out by the cell. First, the cell must enlarge or grow. Second, cells must divide. (As we saw in Chapter 2, no cell will live for ever.) Third, cells must repair themselves constantly—adding new membrane, cytoplasm (including ·organelles) and nuclear material. Fourth, it is essential that the concentration of the different chemicals in the cytoplasm remains fairly constant. All cells must work to ensure this. Finally, the most important activity carried out by any cell is to provide energy for the building, repair and maintenance processes of the cell.

Main activities of the cell:
- enlargement
- division
- repair
- maintenance of constant concentrations of chemicals in cytoplasm
- release of energy

A very useful way of thinking about the cytoplasm of a cell is to regard it as a storehouse of molecules for the enlargement and repair of structures inside the cell. Chemicals are constantly being removed from the cytoplasm to construct cell organelles such as the cell membrane, nuclear membrane, endoplasmic reticulum, Golgi apparatus and so on, or perhaps to build large molecules such as DNA or RNA. At the same time, certain chemicals are resupplied to the cytoplasm to maintain their correct concentrations. This is shown schematically in Fig 3.2.

Cytoplasm is the cell's chemical reservoir

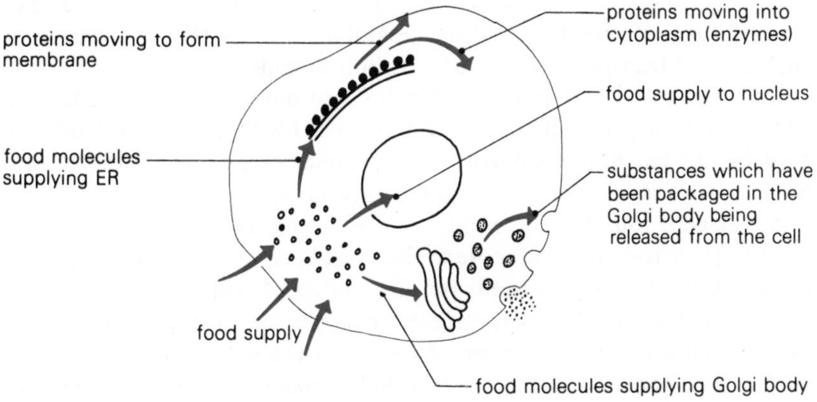

proteins moving to form membrane

proteins moving into cytoplasm (enzymes)

food supply to nucleus

food molecules supplying ER

substances which have been packaged in the Golgi body being released from the cell

food supply

food molecules supplying Golgi body

Fig 3.2 *Chemical supply in a cell*

Chemicals of cytoplasm:
- small molecules, eg glucose
- large molecules, eg RNA and globular proteins

The chemicals of the cytoplasm fall into two groups. In one group are small molecules such as glucose, glycerol, fatty acids or amino acids. In the other are large molecules such as RNA or proteins. (Some proteins are insoluble and are not found in the 'soupy' cytoplasm. They make up the structure of the cell and are called **structural proteins**.) Others are **soluble globular** proteins, which form a large part of the 'soupy' cytoplasm of the cell. The large globular proteins function mainly as organic catalysts called enzymes. The small chemicals are used to build up these large molecules and structures in the cell.

Globular proteins in cytoplasm function as enzymes

Structural proteins play an important part in cells. All cellular membranes, both inside the cell and on the cell surface, have a basic framework of protein and lipid. The arrangement of the protein and lipid is rather like that of a sandwich—lipid in the centre and protein on the outsides. This is shown in Fig 3.3. Sometimes carbohydrate is joined to the protein of membranes. Amino acids from the cytoplasm link up to form the protein of these membranes, while glycerol and fatty acids join to form the lipid portion. Although these reactions occur to a large extent just before a cell divides, they in fact continue throughout the cell's life, as part of the repair and growth processes.

Structural proteins are found in membranes

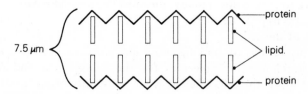

7.5 μm

protein

lipid.

protein

Fig 3.3   *Structure of a cell membrane*

Proteins are found in
- 'soup' of cytoplasm
- ribosomes
- nucleus
- membrane

Proteins are also found in other parts of the cell, serving a variety of functions. The ribosomes attached to the endoplasmic reticulum are composed of protein and RNA. There is a small amount of protein present in the nucleus, with the DNA. The red blood cells contain a specialised form of protein called haemoglobin, the function of which is to pick up and transport oxygen and carbon dioxide.

Both structural and globular proteins have roles outside the cell

Both structural and globular proteins also have functions outside the cell (though they are, of course, still produced within the cell). Globular proteins are an important part of the fluid component of the blood. Structural proteins include keratin, found in hair and nails, and elastin and collagen, found in different types of connective tissues.

The major role of the glucose in the cytoplasm of the cell is to provide the cell with the energy it needs for all its other activities: growth, repair, division and so on. Energy is released from glucose through a large number of chemical reactions in which oxygen is usually involved. These reactions are known collectively as **cellular respiration**. Fatty acids and glycerol can also provide cellular energy through a similar set of reactions. Energy is temporarily stored in the cell in a molecule called ATP (adenosine triphosphate) (see Chapter 4).

In a well-fed animal the rate at which glucose is supplied to the cells is often faster than the rate at which glucose is used in the cell. As a result, glucose is stored in the form of glycogen, which appears in the cytoplasm as distinct granules. (Starch is a similar storage material formed in plant cells. It does not occur in animal cells.) When the supply of glucose to the cell falls below a certain level, insoluble glycogen splits into single, soluble glucose rings which become free in the cytoplasm for use in cellular respiration. This mechanism is illustrated in the diagram below.

Glycogen and starch are storage forms of glucose

Enzymes

If you were to place large quantities of glucose molecules in a test tube at 37°C (body temperature), after waiting for a day you would find no evidence that the glucose molecules had joined to form glycogen or even maltose molecules. And yet glucose molecules are very readily linked together in liver cells to produce disaccharides and glycogen. Furthermore, in the liver cells, this process occurs extremely rapidly.

The reason why these reactions occur so much more readily inside cells is that liver cells contain globular proteins called enzymes. Enzymes are usually made from very long polypeptide chains curled up in a very special way in three dimensions. The way in which the polypeptide chains curl up depends on the types and order of the amino acids present. Within this curled-up polypeptide chain is a space into which other molecules can fit. This space is called an **active site**. The arrangement of an enzyme and its active site is shown in Fig 3.4.

Enzymes are polypeptide chains curled into a 3-D pattern

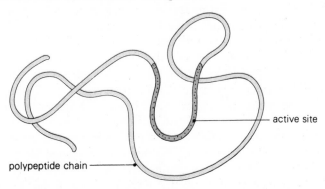

active site

polypeptide chain

Fig 3.4 *The active site of an enzyme*

Understanding the human body

46 Understanding the human body

Each enzyme has a space called an active site, which has a shape unique to that enzyme

The active site of a particular enzyme has a shape which is unique to that particular enzyme. Other enzymes, formed from different polypeptide chains, possess differently shaped active sites. If an enzyme's active site has the correct shape to fit two glucose molecules, then it is likely that two glucose molecules can be held closely side by side in the active site. Under these conditions they will become joined. Figure 3.5 shows how this happens. Thus, with a supply of glucose molecules in the cytoplasm, and the presence of the enzyme shown above, a large number of disaccharides (maltose molecules) form in the cell. However, these molecules are of no use in the cell unless they are released from the 'clutches' of the enzyme which assisted in their formation. The final stage of the linking reaction is therefore the release of the newly formed molecule back into the cytoplasm.

Fig 3.5 *Example of an enzyme acting as a 'builder'*

If another enzyme were present that could add another glucose molecule to the disaccharide in the same way, a trisaccharide would form. This process could continue until a complete glycogen chain had been built up. It is important to realise that in such a joining process only the glucose units being joined fit into the enzyme's active site. The remainder of the glycogen chain floats outside the enzyme.

Not only do enzymes join small molecules together, they also assist in breaking large molecules into small subunits. For example, in the process of breaking starch into maltose, a different enzyme, whose active site can fit maltose molecules, participates. Figure 3.6 shows how this enzyme might operate. At the active site, the bond between the end maltose and the remainder of the starch chain is twisted in order to break off this end maltose. When this happens, the maltose is released from the enzyme, and the next maltose in the chain moves along into the active site. This process occurs extremely rapidly in the presence of the correct enzyme. Without the enzyme the process would virtually stop.

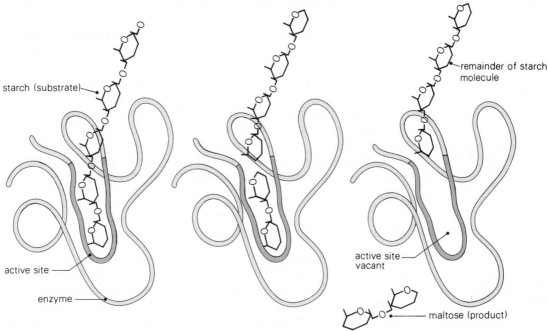

starch (substrate)

remainder of starch molecule

active site

enzyme

active site vacant

maltose (product)

Fig 3.6   *Example of an enzyme acting as a molecule 'splitter'*

A number of other important points should be noted about enzymes. You have seen that enzymes can help to break up molecules into smaller subunits or build up large molecules from small ones. After these reactions the enzyme is unchanged. But for these processes to occur as rapidly as possible the active site *must* have a very special shape. Anything that distorts the shape even slightly will prevent the enzyme operating at maximum efficiency. For example, there is a temperature at which an enzyme operates best. If the temperature of a cell rises slightly above this temperature, the coiled structure of the enzyme will begin to uncoil, and the shape of the active site will be changed. At very high temperatures, enzymes uncoil completely and show no activity at all. At a slightly lower temperature than this, the active site will shrink slightly, and although the substrate may fit, it will not fit well enough for the reaction to occur rapidly. Acids or alkalis can also help to unwind the polypeptide chain of the enzyme and thus destroy the active site. The unwinding of a polypeptide chain as a result of high temperatures, acid or alkali is known as **denaturation**.

The removal of water from a cell can also result in the destruction of an enzyme's active site. The shape of an active site depends on how the polypeptide chain of the enzyme is coiled up in three dimensions. Water is the medium in which the coiled structure floats, and if it is removed, the coiled structure collapses. Thus a constant supply of water to cells is essential if enzymes are to remain operational.

Enzymes speed up
• the breaking down of large molecules
• the building up of small molecules into large molecules

Enzymes are unchanged after a reaction

Enzymes operate most efficiently at a particular temperature

High temperatures destroy an enzyme's active site

Low temperatures shrink the active site, causing an enzyme to act more slowly

Acids or alkalis can destroy the active site

Water is essential for enzyme action

Finally, one other important point needs to be made about enzymes. Although each cell has many thousands of enzymes, and thousands of chemicals, each type of enzyme can act only on one **substrate**. (A substrate is the compound the enzyme acts upon; in other words, the compound which fits into the active site.) An enzyme's active site has a particular shape into which only the molecule with the corresponding shape can fit. Enzymes are thus said to be *specific* for their substrates.

One enzyme acts on one substrate, ie enzymes are specific

Sometimes enzymes are freed from the cells in which they are produced and are used to carry out reactions outside the cell. Examples of this are digestive enzymes released from the salivary glands, pancreas, stomach and intestine to break down food in the alimentary canal. These types of enzymes are called **extracellular enzymes**.

Extracellular enzymes are those that are released from the cell

Vitamins and minerals

Two further chemicals which occur in the cytoplasm of the cell in small quantities are vitamins and minerals. Vitamins are organic compounds whose function is to assist enzymes in their role of breaking down or building up. Minerals also perform this role, in addition to a number of other functions in the body. Humans rely almost entirely on plants and other animals for their source of vitamins, as only two vitamins (vitamins K and D) can be formed in the human body. All minerals come to us from plants, or via other animals from plants.

Vitamins are organic compounds which assist enzymes

Mineral salts may assist enzymes

As we have said, vitamins assist enzymes in speeding up chemical reactions in cells. They often do this by joining on to part of the enzyme, where they are able to add or subtract small chemical groups to or from the substrate molecule. Minerals also function with enzymes by helping to make the active site a better fit for the substrate. Many enzymes do not act effectively in the absence of a particular mineral ion. Magnesium is one example of a mineral which is required in a number of different enzyme reactions.

We take many vitamins into our bodies daily through food. Although vitamins are needed in only very small quantities, the lack of different vitamins causes particular diseases. For example, a deficiency of vitamin A causes night-blindness; lack of vitamin D results in the malformation of bones, a condition known as rickets; lack of vitamin C causes scurvy, a condition in which the gums bleed and swell and the teeth become loose; deficiency of vitamin B_1 results in fatigue, muscular wasting and nervous disorders. Table 10.4 (Chapter 10) outlines the important vitamins, their sources in the human diet and their roles in the working of the body.

Lack of vitamins causes disease

Minerals are involved in a variety of cellular functions other than those connected with enzyme action. For example, cells of the thyroid gland require iodine in the making of the chemical thyroxine. Thyroxine circulates throughout the body in the bloodstream and affects the rate of chemical activity in all body cells (see Chapter 13).

Iodine is necessary for the production of thyroxine

Another mineral, iron, is necessary to form haemoglobin, which is present in red blood cells. The function of haemoglobin is to carry oxygen around the body. When combined with oxygen, the iron gives haemoglobin its red colour. People deficient in iron have less haemoglobin in their red blood cells. This lack of haemoglobin causes them to look pale, and the lack of oxygen (resulting from the lack of haemoglobin) causes them to lack energy and tire easily. Iron deficiency is a common cause of the condition known as anaemia.

Other minerals, too, play an important part in the body. The hard material of bones and teeth which is produced by living cells contains calcium, magnesium and phosphorus. Sodium and potassium are vital parts of the blood fluid, and play an important role in the transmission of nerve impulses along nerve cells. Throughout our discussions of the different systems of the human body, we shall come across many more examples of the important part played by minerals.

Iron is necessary to form haemoglobin, which carries oxygen in red blood cells

Calcium, magnesium and phosphorus are a major part of bones

Sodium and potassium are important to body fluids and nerve cells

Chapter 4

The chemical network
in living organisms

Energy and action

All forms of transport require fuel. Motor vehicles, aeroplanes and diesel locomotives all need a constant supply of organic chemicals. In some way this fuel releases energy which enables the vehicle to move. The energy present in the fuel as **chemical energy** is converted into the movement energy of the car, locomotive or aeroplane. This movement energy is often called **kinetic energy**.

A running athlete also has kinetic energy. Like the motor vehicle, the athlete obtains his kinetic energy from a fuel. Between races the athlete eats food which contains the fuel he needs for racing. This fuel, like that used by transport vehicles, is organic in nature and possesses chemical energy. Within the cells of the athlete's body, the chemical energy of the food is changed into the movement or kinetic energy of his muscles.

All people move and so must have a supply of chemical energy in the form of food. As well as chemical energy for movement, energy must be available for many other processes in the body. For example, chemical energy is required to build up large molecules from small molecules (eg proteins from amino acids, or polysaccharides from monosaccharides), or to build organelles from large molecules. Chemical energy is needed for active transport, cell division and growth, and to enable nerves to transmit nerve impulses.

Energy release

If we take a fully grown mouse and feed it solely on glucose and water, we find that the mouse can continue to live and move normally for some weeks. Other compounds, if fed to the mouse in place of glucose, are not as efficient in allowing the animal to continue normally, and the mouse soon begins to show signs of weakness, fatigue and general slowing down. Apparently glucose is the compound which most readily provides the mouse with chemical energy. (However, even glucose, by itself, cannot maintain the mouse in normal health indefinitely. Other compounds are needed as well.)

Two further experiments tell us something more about the way in which glucose is used up to release energy for the animal's living processes. If a mouse is placed in a large bell jar for a day, we find that as the day progresses the amount of oxygen in the bell jar decreases dramatically. Apparently the mouse has used oxygen (Fig 4.1a). In a second experiment, the air entering the bell jar is first passed through soda lime, which absorbs all the carbon dioxide present. It is then bubbled through limewater to check that no carbon dioxide remains, and is then directed into the bell jar. The bell jar contains a mouse, which is fed on glucose and water. As the gas leaves the bell jar it is again pumped through limewater. This time, the limewater becomes milky, indicating that carbon dioxide has been added to the air in the bell jar (Fig 4.1b). Similar results would be obtained if the same experiments were carried out on human beings.

A further clue to the way in which energy is provided for living processes can be gained by breathing on to a cold glass pane. The glass soon becomes misty, owing to the buildup of water droplets, which have condensed from the exhaled air on to the cold surface. (The deposit on the glass can be positively identified as water by testing with cobalt chloride paper and seeing whether it turns from blue to pink.)

If we put these pieces of evidence together, we come up with an equation for the release of energy from glucose:

Glucose + oxygen → carbon dioxide + water + energy

In symbols this equation can be written:

$$C_6H_{12}O_6 + 6\,O_2 \rightarrow 6\,CO_2 + 6\,H_2O + energy$$

Cellular respiration:
Glucose + oxygen
↓
carbon dioxide
+
water
+
energy

This process is called cellular respiration, and occurs in most living organisms. Chemical research has shown that this single reaction is made up of approximately 25 chemical reactions arranged in a complicated chain. Further studies using the electron microscope have shown that a large number of these reactions occur in the mitochondria of the cell.

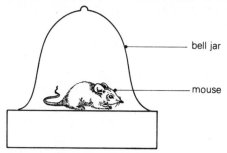

bell jar

mouse

after a short time the air in the bell jar barely supports a burning splint, indicating that oxygen has been used up

(a) Showing that oxygen is used up

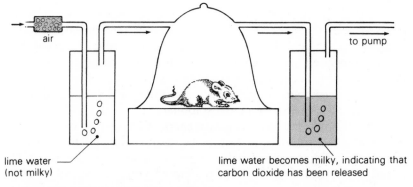

air

to pump

lime water
(not milky)

lime water becomes milky, indicating that carbon dioxide has been released

(b) Showing that carbon dioxide is produced

Fig 4.1 Experiments to demonstrate cellular respiration

How energy is transferred

If you think a little further about cellular respiration and its role in the cell, several other questions may come to mind. What is meant by *energy release*? How is the energy which is obtained from glucose *transferred* to the different processes of the cell? How can the energy be *stored* temporarily before it is used by the cell? The answers to these questions involve concepts which may seem rather difficult.

To help answer these questions, we shall compare the energy transfer process to a physical system of springs. In the cell, energy from glucose is passed to another molecule called ATP (adenosine triphosphate). The ATP can then provide the energy necessary for any one of a number of cell processes. Think of the glucose molecule as a spring whose two ends have been joined. The ATP molecule is another spring structure, which forms part of a spring system with the glucose spring. Let us see how energy may be transferred through this system of springs. (The sequence of events is illustrated in Figs 4.2a and 4.2b.)

Consider a strong, tightly wound spring, about 20 cm long, with a coil diameter of approximately 3 cm. You now take the two ends of the spring and join them. This is not easy, requiring considerable physical effort on your part. Having done this, you put the spring on a smooth table surface next to a small plastic sphere (P) of about 3 cm diameter. The small sphere is close to a shorter, thinner, spring. This weaker spring is attached to a wooden block which is firmly held to the table surface so that it cannot move. A thin metal rod is also attached to the wooden block. The small sphere can attach itself to the rod by means of a catch if it is pushed towards the wooden block. At the same time, this movement of the sphere would cause compression of the small spring.

You are now ready for operation. Holding the end of the strong spring marked A, cut the joined ends of the large spring. The B end of the spring whips to the right (see dotted arrow, Fig 4.2a) and pushes the small sphere. This movement of the sphere compresses the small spring and at the same time the small sphere then becomes attached to the thin rod.

Now that the sphere P is securely held on the wooden block, you can release the wooden block and slide it across the table towards another small plastic sphere S. The two spheres are lined up next to one another. A slight pressure exerted on the catch of the metal rod causes the sphere P to be released. The small spring rapidly expands, throwing the sphere P towards its neighbour. On contact, the second sphere S is pushed firmly across the table, P now becoming stationary.

In this example you have witnessed energy being passed from one object to another, in different forms. As the two ends of the spring are joined, a certain amount of potential energy is stored in the spring. On releasing one end of the spring, the stored potential energy becomes movement or kinetic energy. As the small spring is compressed it gains potential energy. Finally, when the small spring is released, this stored

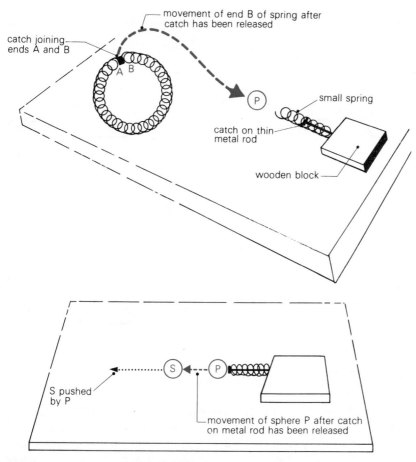

Fig 4.2 *A model for energy release in cells*
(a) Energy release from the large spring (glucose)
(b) Energy release from the smaller spring (ATP)

potential energy is transferred to the sphere P as kinetic energy, which is further transferred to the sphere S as kinetic energy. The main energy changes in these events are shown below:

Joined spring (potential energy)	Compressed small spring (potential energy)	Sphere P (kinetic energy)	Sphere S (kinetic energy)
→	→	→	

This model provides an example which can help us understand how energy is released in the cell. The joined spring represents the glucose molecule in its ring form. The wooden block and small spring represent a molecule called ADP (adenosine diphosphate), the sphere P represents another phosphate group, and the sphere S represents a muscle cell. The ADP molecule consists of a complex ring structure with two phosphate groups attached. This is shown in Fig 4.3a.

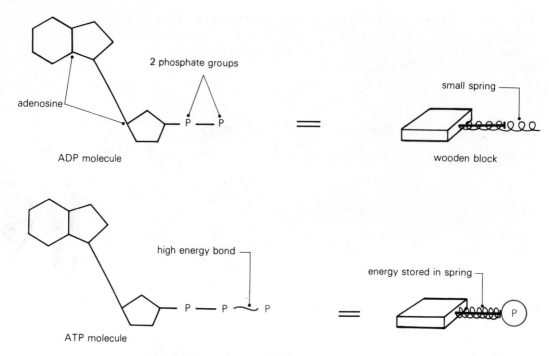

Fig 4.3   *The energy-storing molecule of the cell*
(a) Adenosine diphosphate (ADP) — the molecule and model
(b) Adenosine triphosphate (ATP) — the molecule and model

ADP + P + energy
↓
ATP

ATP
↓
ADP + P + energy

The addition of a third floating phosphate group to ADP (like the sphere P being added to the small spring) results in the formation of ATP (adenosine triphosphate) (Fig 4.3b). Just as potential energy was stored in the small spring when the sphere P became attached, chemical energy is stored in the bond formed between ADP and the third P. When the third phosphate is removed, this chemical energy is freed to supply one of a number of cellular processes.

The events described above are outlined and compared in the following summary:

Large spring with A, B joined—potential energy is stored in the spring.

Glucose molecule—chemical energy is stored in the molecule.

A, B are separated by cutting the spring—the potential energy of the spring is released.

Glucose breaks down to form CO_2 + H_2O—the chemical energy of the molecule is released.

The potential energy of the large spring is transferred to the small spring, which becomes compressed.

The chemical energy of the glucose molecule is transferred to ADP—a third P is joined to the ADP, which is then known as ATP.

As the catch holding the small spring is released, the spring releases its potential energy. (Some of this potential energy is passed to the sphere P, which gains kinetic energy.)

When the third P is removed from ATP, chemical energy is released from ATP.

Sphere P transfers its kinetic energy to sphere S.

Chemical energy from ATP is transferred to different cellular processes.

Thus glucose molecules contain chemical energy which can be transferred to ADP to form ATP. The chemical energy from the ATP can then be passed on to other processes, perhaps in a different form. For example, muscle cells can be made to contract and move (kinetic energy). The chemical energy of ATP can also be used to construct other compounds which also contain chemical energy, such as proteins. Often, in the processes of energy transfer from ATP to other processes, a certain amount of energy is wasted. This shows itself as heat energy, and has the function of helping to maintain body temperature:

Glucose molecules contain chemical energy

Chemical energy from glucose is transferred to ATP

Energy from ATP is used for cellular processes

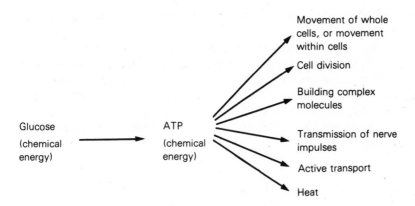

Glucose—the centre of the network

In order to find out where glucose comes from in the first place, we need to look at the leaves of a green plant. A cross-section of a leaf is shown in Fig 4.4. Glucose is produced in the mesophyll and palisade cells of leaves by a process called **photosynthesis**. Scientific research has shown that this process, like cellular respiration, consists of a whole chain of complex reactions, whose effect can be summarised in one reaction:

Glucose is produced in green leaves by photosynthesis

$$\text{Carbon dioxide} + \text{water} \xrightarrow{\text{sunlight energy}} \text{glucose} + \text{oxygen}$$

In symbols:

$$6\,CO_2 + 6\,H_2O \xrightarrow{\text{sunlight energy}} C_6H_{12}O_6 + 6\,O_2$$

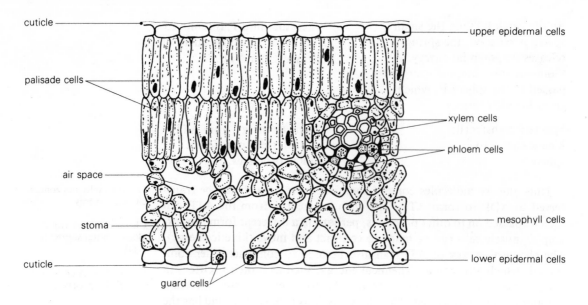

cuticle — upper epidermal cells
palisade cells —
— xylem cells
— phloem cells
air space —
— mesophyll cells
stoma —
cuticle — — lower epidermal cells
guard cells —

Fig 4.4 *Cross-section of a leaf*

The sun is the source of energy

This equation, you will recognise, is the reverse of that for cellular respiration.

The single equation for photosynthesis can be broken into two parts. In the first part, light is trapped, and its energy is changed into chemical energy in the form of ATP. At the same time water is split to form oxygen and hydrogen ions (H^+) and electrons (e). In the second part, the ATP is used, in the absence of light, to produce glucose from carbon dioxide, hydrogen ions (H^+) and electrons (e). This can be summarised as follows:

(1) $H_2O \rightarrow O_2 + H^+ + e$ }
(2) $CO_2 + H^+ + e \rightarrow C_6H_{12}O_6$ }   unbalanced equations

Chlorophyll traps sunlight energy and converts it to chemical energy

The leaf has a number of features which allow it to carry out photosynthesis. Palisade and mesophyll cells possess small organelles known as chloroplasts, which contain a chemical called chlorophyll. Chlorophyll can trap sunlight energy and convert it to chemical energy. In this respect chlorophyll acts rather like a modern solar cell, which converts light energy into electrical energy. Small pores in the surfaces of the leaf allow gases like carbon dioxide and oxygen to enter and leave the body of the leaf. These pores are known as stomata. There are also numerous spaces between the cells into which carbon dioxide can diffuse after passing through the stomata, or into which oxygen can diffuse after being released from the photosynthesising mesophyll or palisade cells. Water is supplied to the leaf via the roots and stem in specialised water-conducting cells called xylem cells. Water moves from the xylem cells in the leaf to those involved in photosynthesis by diffusion. Glucose formed in the process of photosynthesis is stored in leaf cells as insoluble starch granules. The activities of a photosynthesising cell are summarised in Fig 4.5.

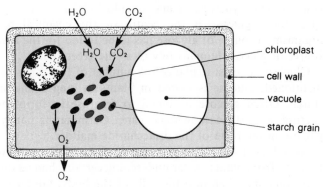

Fig 4.5 *Activities of a photosynthesising cell*

Once glucose has been formed by photosynthesis in a plant cell, it is able to be changed into a number of other different compounds. For example, glucose can be converted to fructose which can then be joined to another glucose to form the disaccharide sucrose. Glucose can be made into cell wall material in the form of cellulose. Glucose is also capable of forming fatty acids and glycerol, which together make up fats.

In order to form amino acids, a plant must have access to a source of nitrogen. This element is present in the soil as nitrates. Nitrogen-fixing bacteria in the soil are capable of combining nitrogen gas (N_2) with oxygen to form nitrites (NO_2^-) and finally nitrates (NO_3^-). The plant cell then uses this nitrate to construct amino acids, by combining the nitrate with a by-product of glucose. This again involves a number of complex reactions. Amino acids so formed can then be joined in long chains to produce proteins.

The chemical reactions involving glucose formation and use in plants are summarised in Fig 4.6.

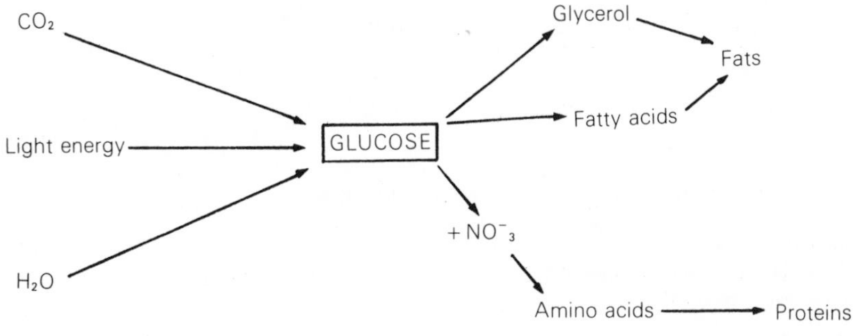

Glucose can be converted into
• other monosaccharides (eg fructose)
• disaccharides (eg sucrose)
• polysaccharides (eg cellulose)
• fatty acids and glycerol—fats

Plants obtain nitrogen from nitrates in the soil

Glucose by-product
+
nitrate
↓
amino acid

Many amino acids = protein

CO₂

Light energy

H₂O

GLUCOSE

Glycerol

Fats

Fatty acids

+ NO⁻₃

Amino acids ⟶ Proteins

Fig 4.6 *Glucose formation and uses in plants*

The chemical network in humans

Humans are not able to produce their own glucose

Like other animals, humans have no means of producing their own glucose. None of their cells possess chlorophyll which can trap the light energy required for the photosynthetic process. And none of their cells contain the enzymes necessary to build CO_2 into a six-carbon-ring structure. Since glucose is the centre of the chemical network of any organism, a source of glucose has to be found for the human body. The source of glucose humans rely on is the green plant.

Humans obtain glucose from green plants

Glucose can be found in plants as
• starch
• sucrose
• maltose

Glucose can exist in plants in a number of forms. As has already been mentioned, glucose is stored in plants in long chains in the form of starch. Often glucose is joined to fructose to form the disaccharide sucrose, as is the case in sugar cane. Germinating barley seeds contain glucose in the form of the disaccharide maltose.

Plants can also provide
• fats
• fatty acids
• glycerol

As well as using plants as a direct source of glucose, humans also obtain fats from plants. After undergoing certain changes during digestion, these fats are taken into the cells of the body. Glycerol and fatty acid molecules may also be part of the cell's food directly obtained from plants.

In humans:
• glucose can form glycerol and fatty acids
• glycerol + fatty acids form fats

• glycerol and fatty acids produce carbon dioxide + water + energy

• glucose can be stored as glycogen

Once carbohydrates and fats have been taken into a cell in the human body, a number of chemical changes can occur to them. For example, glucose can form glycerol and some fatty acids. Fatty acids of different chain length can join with glycerol to form fats. Glycerol and fatty acids can both be broken down, by a process similar to cellular respiration, to form carbon dioxide and water and release energy. Fats may be stored in fat cells. Glucose can be stored as glycogen. These chemical changes which occur in the cells of humans are referred to as carbohydrate and fat metabolism. (The word **metabolism** refers to both the breakdown and buildup reactions considered together as a 'network'.)The network of reactions is summarised in Fig 4.7.

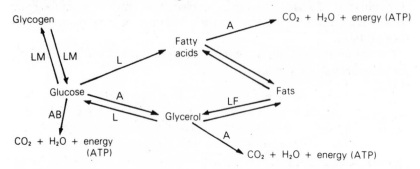

Note: Although this is a general scheme for carbohydrate and fat metabolism, some of these reactions occur only in particular types of cells. This is indicated by letters:
A = all cells (except those of the brain) B = brain cells
L = liver cells M = muscle cells F = fat cells

Fig 4.7 *Carbohydrate and fat metabolism in animals*

Plants are also a source of amino acids and proteins for the human body. Of the 20 amino acids needed to build cellular proteins, 8 can be obtained from plants only. These are given the name **essential amino acids**. From these, the human body can produce the other 12 **non-essential amino acids** in its cells. This may be achieved by an amino group ($-NH_2$) being removed from one of the essential amino acids and transferred to one of the breakdown products of glucose. We shall call these breakdown products carbohydrate-like compounds. This combination of an amino group and a carbohydrate-like compound results in the formation of a non-essential amino acid (Fig 4.8). It is important to realise that the cell is *not* able to manufacture *any* of the essential amino acids in this way. This is why it is necessary to have these provided by the plant in their complete form.

Essential amino acids are obtainable only from plants

12 non-essential amino acids are produced in human cells

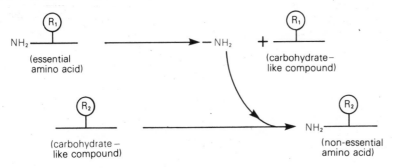

Fig 4.8 *Formation of a non-essential amino acid from an essential amino acid*

For humans, plants are not the only source of carbohydrates, fats and proteins. If they feed on the tissue of other animals, glucose, amino acids, proteins, glycerol and fatty acids will all be part of their diet. *However, it is important to realise that these chemicals which make up the cells of an animal such as a cow all began as plant glucose, glycerol, fatty acids or amino acids in grass or leaves.* Plants are also the ultimate source of mineral ions and vitamins (except vitamins D and K), and any of these that are passed from the animal to man have been formed, originally, in plants.

Humans can obtain
• glucose
• fats
• fatty acids
• glycerol
• proteins
• amino acids
from other animals

Plants provide mineral salts and vitamins

Like carbohydrates and fats, proteins can also be used as a source of energy. In the liver an amino acid can lose its amino group ($-NH_2$), leaving a carbohydrate-like compound. This compound can be fed into the sequence of cellular respiration reactions. Carbon dioxide and water are released when such a compound is broken down, and energy is then released for use in the cell. ATP again forms the temporary store for the released energy. The carbohydrate-like compound can also be used to reform glucose. If excess glucose is present in the cell, this can be converted to and stored as glycogen.

Amino acids can be used as an energy source, after they have lost the amino group ($-NH_2$)

The removal of an amino group from an amino acid is known as **deamination**. The amino group is converted to ammonia, which is highly

The removal of an ($-NH_2$) group from an amino acid is known as deamination

-NH₂ groups are
converted to urea

toxic, or poisonous, to the cell. It is therefore rapidly converted to a compound of low toxicity called **urea**. This chemical change is achieved in the liver, and urea is constantly removed from the bloodstream in the kidneys.

These reactions involving the formation and breakdown of amino acids and proteins are known collectively as protein metabolism. The major reactions of protein metabolism are summarised in Fig 4.9.

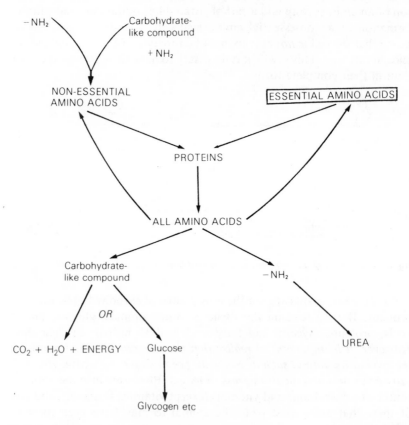

Fig 4.9   *A summary of protein metabolism*

Cellular respiration without oxygen

On some occasions insufficient oxygen is able to reach rapidly respiring cells, and as a result they are unable to break down glucose completely to carbon dioxide and water. Although the bloodstream carries oxygen to the muscle cells as fast as possible, oxygen may not be arriving at the cells in large enough quantities. The oxygen is needed to assist in the breakdown of glucose and release of the energy needed for continued muscle contraction. When this happens your muscles start to tire.

When oxygen is in short
supply, anaerobic
respiration occurs

Under these circumstances, when oxygen cannot be obtained quickly enough to break down all the glucose to carbon dioxide and water, another method is also used—anaerobic respiration. In anaerobic respiration, glucose is broken down to lactic acid. The overall process may be summarised:

Lactic acid is the waste product of anaerobic respiration

$$\text{Glucose} \rightarrow \text{lactic acid} + \text{energy}$$

The energy released from this reaction is approximately one-sixteenth of the energy released from the complete breakdown of glucose to carbon dioxide and water, in the presence of oxygen. Thus anaerobic respiration is a far less efficient process than aerobic respiration. Moreover, lactic acid must be rapidly removed from the cells. If lactic acid accumulates in cells, it interferes with their normal working. In addition, it may cause pain and often severe cramp.

Aerobic respiration is 16 times as efficient as anaerobic respiration

What happens to this lactic acid which accumulates in the muscle cells? The lactic acid is really a waste product of the muscle cells and must be removed from the tissues in the bloodstream. It is carried in the bloodstream to the liver. The liver cells are able (because they possess the required enzymes) to convert the lactic acid back to glucose and then to glycogen (the storage form of glucose). To do this, however, they require oxygen and energy (ATP). This process can be summarised:

In liver cells, lactic acid is converted to glucose. This process requires oxygen and energy

$$\text{Lactic acid} + \text{oxygen} + \text{energy (ATP)} \rightarrow \text{glucose} \rightarrow \text{glycogen}$$

Understanding this process of energy release also helps us to understand another feature of our response to severe physical exercise. Consider, again, your body's reaction to a running race. For some time after you stop running, you continue to pant heavily. You do this because your body needs oxygen to replenish its energy reserves. Physiologists say that your body has an 'oxygen debt' to repay. We now know why this is so. In times of anaerobic respiration, glycogen reserves are broken down to glucose and then to lactic acid, in the absence of oxygen. To convert the lactic acid back to glycogen, oxygen and energy (ATP) are needed. You continue to breathe deeply until all the lactic acid has been reconverted to glucose and the stores of ATP and glycogen are replenished.

Sources of energy

All three of the major food materials, carbohydrates, fats and proteins, are capable of releasing energy. The exact amount released can be found by measuring the amount of heat produced when a measured quantity of each food type is burned. The apparatus used for this is a strong steel chamber filled with oxygen and then tightly sealed. It is known as a bomb calorimeter. After a known quantity of the food has been placed inside, it is ignited by a small electric heating coil. The amount of heat

The amount of energy able to be released from fat, protein or carbohydrate is measured in a bomb calorimeter

produced is estimated by measuring the rise in temperature of a known volume of water contained in a water jacket around the steel chamber. Figures for the heat released from, or the *energy value* of, one gram of carbohydrate, fat and protein are shown in Table 4.1. (The metric unit of energy release is the kilojoule. In the past another unit was used to measure the energy value of food. This unit is the calorie. A calorie is the amount of heat required to raise the temperature of one litre of water by one degree centigrade. 1 calorie = 4.2 kilojoules.)

Table 4.1 *Energy value of the three types of food*

Food type	Energy value per gram	
	Kilojoules	Calories
Carbohydrate	17.2	4
Fat	38.5	9
Protein	17.2	4

One gram of fat releases almost twice as much energy as one gram of carbohydrate or protein

As you can see from Table 4.1, one gram of fat releases approximately twice as much energy as one gram of carbohydrate or protein. In addition, alcohol can be a source of energy for the body, releasing as much as 29 kJ per gram.

Order of use of food materials as energy sources in the body:
• glucose
• glycogen/fat
• proteins

When energy is required by the body, not all three energy sources are used at once. Carbohydrates and fats are the body's primary sources of energy. Glucose contains energy in its most available form, and some tissues, for example the brain, under normal conditions can use *only* glucose to obtain their energy supplies. Glycogen is a storage form of glucose, present in liver and muscle cells. When glucose supplies are depleted, glycogen is broken down to replenish glucose levels. If the body's demands for energy are great, fats also are broken down to release energy. This process requires oxygen, and the fats are converted into carbon dioxide and water. Proteins are needed for growth and repair processes in cells, and excess protein in the diet may be used to provide energy. The large-scale use of tissue proteins for energy release usually occurs only in periods of extreme starvation, after body fats have been used up. This situation can be thought of as the body using its own material for its preservation and maintenance.

Energy requirements of the human body

We are all aware of the fact that we need energy to carry out physical tasks such as chopping wood or throwing a ball. We are probably equally aware that the source of energy is the food we eat. Just how much energy do we need for different activities?

The energy needed for basic body processes is called the basal energy requirement

The human body needs a certain amount of energy to maintain basic body processes such as heart beat, breathing and tissue repair. We call this energy requirement the **basal energy requirement**. The amount of basal energy depends upon the size of the individual. For an average-sized adult man this energy requirement is about 7500 kJ per day. For a larger person it will be more than this, and for a smaller person it will be less.

Energy required for running, walking, lifting and even thinking is energy which must be available in addition to the basal energy. This extra energy plus the basal energy requirement makes up the **total energy** needed by a person. This too is measured on a daily basis and depends on the mass of the person. Using average figures, these total energy requirements are about 13 000 kJ per day for a man and 9500 kJ per day for a woman. Vigorous daily exercise such as farm work or labouring can take the total energy requirement to as high as 20 000 kJ.

These figures can be related to the energy available from ATP. One mole of ATP, when split into ADP plus phosphate, releases 34 kJ of energy. Some of this is lost as heat, but some can be channelled into the operation of body activities.

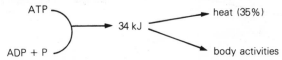

You could probably work out the number of moles of ATP you might need to convert to ADP + P during a normal day's work. In doing this, it is important to remember that during the day some of the ATPs which are converted to ADP + P can be converted back to ATP and then re-used. The energy for this reconstruction comes from the breakdown of carbohydrates, fats and proteins through respiration.

In most individuals there is normally a balance between the amount of energy required for all the activities of daily living (total energy requirement) and the energy intake in food. An energy imbalance occurs, however, if the energy intake (food) exceeds the body's energy requirements, or if the energy intake is not sufficient to meet the body's energy needs.

Extra energy is required for activities such as walking, thinking, lifting

Total energy requirement = basal energy + extra energy requirements

$$ATP \\ \downarrow \\ ADP + energy$$

The energy released from ATP is used for body activities or wasted as heat

Energy input greater than energy use   *Energy use greater than energy input*

We have already discussed what happens when energy needs are greater than the energy intake in food. The body uses its own energy reserves: glycogen, fat and finally proteins. Obviously, if these reserves are broken down to provide energy, body weight will decrease. On the other hand, if energy intake exceeds the body's total energy requirement, the excess energy will be stored in the body's energy reserves, particularly in the form of fat. As a result of these increased stores of energy, body weight increases. These principles of energy balance in the fully grown person are summarised in Fig 4.10. How would this chart differ for a growing child?

In Chapter 10 we shall look in more detail at the food substances we eat—what their ingredients are, how they are used in the body, and how their energy value contributes to the body's energy requirements.

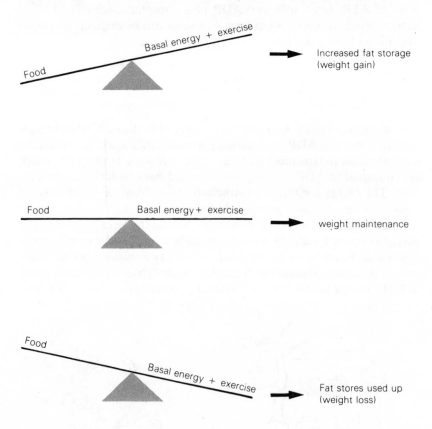

Fig 4.10   *Energy balance in the fully grown person*

Chapter 5

DNA—the key to life

- Growth and development of the young organism
- Cell division
- Importance of the nucleus
- The chemical mystery of the nucleus
- How DNA codes for cellular proteins
- DNA, proteins and people
- DNA switches

Growth and development of the young organism

Each human individual is unique

In Chapter 2 we saw how organisms are built from millions of different types of cells. Where does the story of the organism begin? Before your birth, no one quite like you had ever existed on this earth. Both your physical make-up and inbuilt personality traits are unique—you are a unique individual of the species *Homo sapiens*. Where did your thousands of cells come from, how have they formed, and how do they come to make up the individual you?

Sperm from father
+
egg from mother
↓
zygote
↓
embryo
↓
foetus

Your beginning can be traced back to the joining of two cells—a sperm cell from your father and an egg cell from your mother. After joining or fusing, these two cells formed a single cell called a **zygote**. This was the first cell that could be identified as 'you'. As time progressed, hundreds of other cells formed from that one zygote. By the twelfth day you could be described as an **embryo**, and by the eighth week as a **foetus**—a mass of many thousands of cells. At birth your cell count had reached millions. Your size had increased dramatically, too. A human zygote is about the same size as the tip of a needle (or 1.2×10^{-4} metres in diameter). At birth you were an individual of about 50 cm in length and weighing perhaps 3 kg.

As the zygote grows, it
• increases in size, ie increases in number of cells
• develops different tissues, organs and systems
• develops individual external characteristics

As well as having grown, you were different from the original zygote in another way. The zygote from which you developed was simply a cell with a nucleus, cytoplasm, cell membrane, another outer membrane and a surrounding jelly coat. How unlike the individual born about nine months later, with all its facial and bodily structures, with perhaps a little hair and features distinctive enough to encourage such comments as 'how like his mother he is'. By birth you were finally recognisable as 'you'. As well as all your external characteristics, the different tissues, organs and systems of your body developed. From that original simple zygote cell, nerve cells, muscle cells, blood cells, bone cells and many more had formed.

Two basic processes occur during growth of a new individual:
• cell division
• cell differentiation

During the nine months of development within the mother's uterus, two basic processes have been occurring to produce, finally, the new individual ready for birth. One of these processes is **cell division**—one cell has divided to form a mass of many cells. The other process is **cell differentiation**—during growth one zygote has formed many different *types* of cells, each with particular jobs to perform in the body.

Cell division

Cells divide in order to
• add more cells (growth)
• replace damaged tissue

In any animal, cells are constantly dividing to form more cells. Division takes place for either of two reasons: to *replace* tissue which has been damaged or to *add* new tissue to the existing organism (growth). Even in the adult, there are particular areas of any animal in which cell division occurs very frequently. For example, the epithelial cells lining the intestine have a life-span of only two to three days. This means that intestinal cells must divide to replace these lost cells at a similar rate. Surface layers of the skin also divide rapidly, to replace the cells that are constantly being rubbed off.

How do cells divide? If you examine a stained preparation of intestinal epithelium or skin under the microscope, it is possible to see cells dividing. These cells can be recognised because their nuclei look different from those of all other cells.

The majority of cells have roughly spherical nuclei finely dotted with dark-staining material. As we said in Chapter 2, this is the genetic material of the cell. The nuclei of dividing cells, however, look conspicuously different. In these cells the dark-staining material forms heavy clumps or thin threads, sometimes clearly separated at either end of the cell, at other times bunched and intertwined with one another. What is the significance of these changes in the nucleus of the dividing cell?

Almost a hundred years ago, a German scientist named Flemming described these changes in the nuclei of cells, and established that this division of the nucleus is the first stage of cell division. He was the first to describe the appearance of thread-like structures within the nucleus. He showed that these threads split along their length and that half of each thread then moved into each daughter cell. He called the process mitosis (from the Greek *mitos*, meaning a thread) and called the dark-staining material inside the nucleus **chromatin**. Later, the threadlike bodies were named **chromosomes**.

Most of the details of cell division or mitosis were worked out in the years that followed. Scientists discovered that *every cell of an organism* (except sperm and egg cells) *contains the same number of chromosomes*. During mitosis, each of these chromosomes splits in half, so that *each daughter cell has the same set of chromosomes as the parent*. The sequence of events in mitosis is summarised in Fig 5.1.

Importance of the nucleus

We have now seen that equal division of the chromosomes of the nucleus is the most important aspect of cell division. But why are these chromosomes so important for the newly formed cells? Experiments with the single-celled amoeba show clearly that a cell is incapable of surviving and reproducing without its nucleus. In one such experiment (see Fig 5.2), an amoeba is divided into two parts, one part including the nucleus and the other part without the nucleus. The portion with the nucleus continues to grow and produce daughter amoebae, whereas the portion without the nucleus dies. Other experiments show that the nucleus determines the

Rapid cell division is always seen in certain tissues of the body

Division of the nucleus is the first stage of cell division

During normal cell division (mitosis) the nucleus breaks up into a series of threads called chromosomes

Each chromosome then splits lengthwise

Half of each chromosome moves to each daughter nucleus

In mitosis, each daughter cell receives a set of chromosomes identical to that of the parent cell

Cells without nuclei die

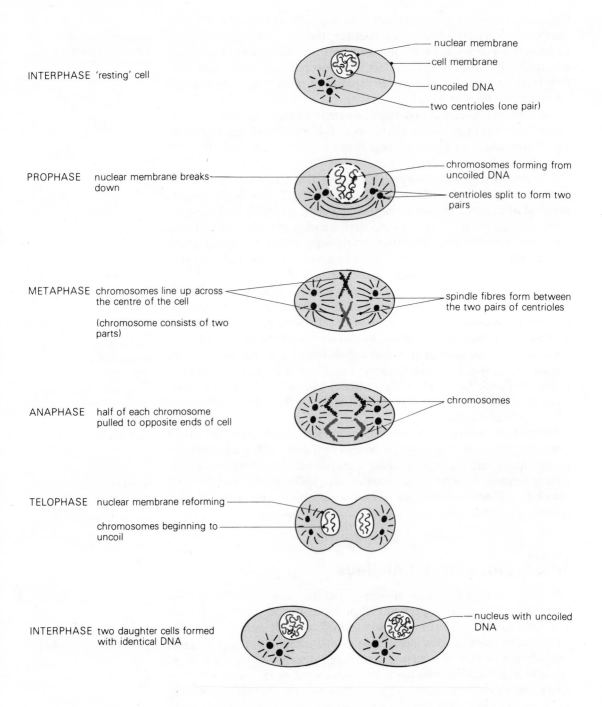

Fig 5.1 *Animal cell undergoing mitosis (only two chromosomes are shown)*

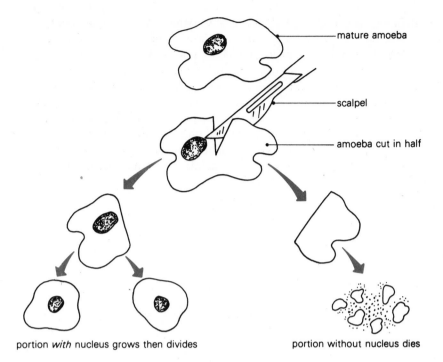

mature amoeba

scalpel

amoeba cut in half

portion *with* nucleus grows then divides

portion without nucleus dies

Fig 5.2   *Vital role of the nucleus (an experiment with an amoeba)*

shape and type of a cell. For example, the nucleus controls the growth of the long fibres of a nerve cell along which nerve impulses are relayed. The nucleus of a pancreatic cell is responsible for the development of a very large amount of endoplasmic reticulum (ER). This is the 'factory' where digestive enzymes are produced inside the pancreatic cell. Similarly, the nucleus of a muscle cell controls the growth of protein fibres which can contract, and of a specially large number of mitochondria, to provide energy during contraction.

As explained in Chapter 2, the structure of a cell determines the job that cell performs. Therefore, *since the nucleus of a cell controls its structure it must also control its function.*

The nucleus of a cell controls its structure and function

Each individual person is in fact a collection of different cell types arranged into tissues, organs and systems. We can say, then, that the nuclei of the cells in a human body control what the body looks like. It is the nuclei of millions of cells which control characteristics such as height, hair colour, eye colour, facial features and muscle build. It may even be true to say that the nuclei of body cells govern some personality traits such as patience, intelligence or temper. But how does the nucleus carry out its controlling function?

Nuclei in the cells of an individual control
• appearance
• personality traits

It has been shown that all the chemical processes occurring in the cytoplasm are controlled by biological catalysts called enzymes. In Chapter 3 we explained that enzymes cause cellular reactions to occur more rapidly

All chemical reactions occurring in the cytoplasm of cells are catalysed by enzymes

Enzymes are proteins

than they otherwise would. Without enzymes, many reactions in the cell would almost stop. Furthermore, it was emphasised that all enzymes belong to the important group of organic compounds called proteins. Research has shown that the nucleus of the cell controls the production of proteins in the cell. Some of these proteins are structural proteins, others are enzymes. As explained in Chapter 3, particular enzymes are responsible for particular cellular reactions. Thus the types of enzymes present in a cell determine which reactions occur in that cell. These reactions determine which type of cellular machinery is built, and which jobs that cell will perform. This principle is summarised in Fig 5.3.

Enzymes determine
• cell structure
• cell function

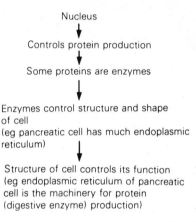

Nucleus

↓

Controls protein production

↓

Some proteins are enzymes

↓

Enzymes control structure and shape
of cell
(eg pancreatic cell has much endoplasmic
reticulum)

↓

Structure of cell controls its function
(eg endoplasmic reticulum of pancreatic
cell is the machinery for protein
(digestive enzyme) production)

The nucleus is like the
computer of the cell

Fig 5.3   *Role of the nucleus in determining the structure and function of the cell*

The chemical mystery of the nucleus

Nuclei (and chromosomes)
contain a special chemical
called DNA

All experiments had shown that the key to the structure and working of all the cells in our bodies lay in the nuclei. Analysis of chromosomes had shown that they contained two types of chemicals: a nucleic acid, known as DNA, and proteins. For a long time people wondered which of these two substances controlled the operations of the cell. Then a number of experiments were conducted which proved that it was the **nucleic acid**—DNA—which governed protein production in the cell, and so held the key to life. The structure or shape of this key to life proved difficult to establish, however.

DNA (a nucleic acid)
controls protein
production in a cell and
thus controls
• cell type
• structures within a cell
• cell function

DNA is a remarkable molecule with quite a complex shape. Many research workers had pondered over the arrangement of the atoms within the molecule, until in 1953 Watson and Crick, working at the Cavendish Laboratories in Cambridge, put forward a possible structure for the DNA molecule. This was a landmark in biology and to this day there has been no change to the model of 1953.

The structure of the DNA molecule can be likened to a ladder. Whereas the sides of a ladder consist of long wooden members, the sides of the DNA molecule consist of long chains of sugar and phosphate molecules, joined alternately: sugar–phosphate–sugar–phosphate——. Just as sides of a ladder are joined by struts, the two long chains of DNA are joined by four types of 'strut' molecules, given the labels A (adenine), T (thymine), C (cytosine) and G (guanine). Each strut molecule is attached on one side to the sugar–phosphate chain and on the other side to a strut molecule from the other chain. Figure 5.4 shows this basic structure. The four strut molecules are arranged in *pairs* which fit together between the two chains in a very particular way—A joins only with T, and C pairs only with G. Finally, the two long chains are twisted in the form of a double helix.

DNA consists of
• two chains of sugar–phosphate molecules
• four different strut molecules which join the chains

Strut molecules:
• A always pairs with T
• C always pairs with G

What importance do the different parts of this DNA molecule have for the cell? The two chains are important only in that they support the struts. The vital parts of the molecule are the struts themselves. If we were to tear apart the two long chains with the struts still attached to their respective chains, we would end up with two rows of struts arranged in a particular order. Watson and others discovered that it is the order of these struts along the chain which determines the shape, structure and function of a cell. The nucleus of the cell contains many DNA molecules, and each of these contains many millions of struts. In fact, the DNA strand can be likened to a long computer tape, with information punched into the tape all along its length.

The order of the strut molecules in DNA determines the shape, structure and function of a cell

A DNA molecule can be compared to a piece of computer tape

How DNA codes for cellular proteins

How does the DNA molecule control the types of cell proteins that are made? The DNA molecule itself can be likened to the plan for making a piece of machinery such as a motor car. This plan tells us everything we need to know to enable us to build a motor car, including:

The DNA molecule is like the plan for the manufacture of a piece of machinery

• the moulds to be used as a framework
• the order in which the moulds must be assembled to fit the parts of the car together correctly
• the pieces of machinery (cranes, winches etc) needed to lower sections of the car into the moulds
• the equipment needed to join the sections of the car together (rivets, screws, welders etc).

This is illustrated in Fig 5.5a.

The construction of cellular protein is, in principle, similar to the construction of the motor car described above. You will remember from Chapter 3 that proteins are made up of long chains of units called amino acids. Twenty different amino acids are found in the proteins of animals.

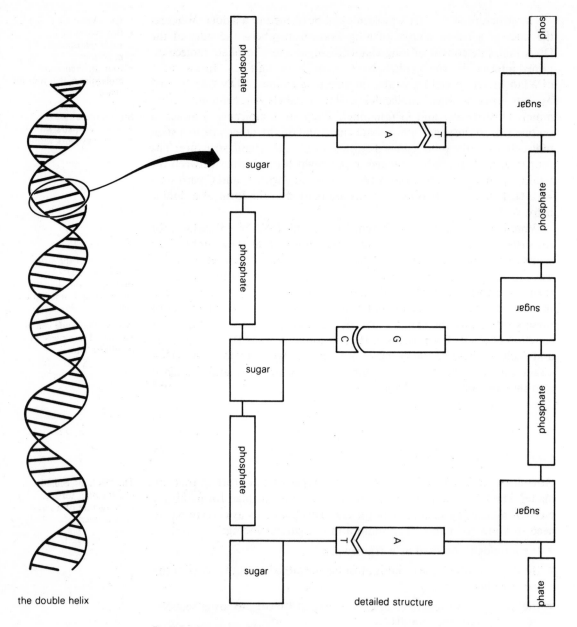

the double helix

detailed structure

Fig 5.4 *Structure of DNA*

Just as the master plan for the motor car told us all we needed to know to construct the motor car, so the DNA in the nucleus tells the cell everything it needs to know to build a huge variety of proteins. How does it store this information?

The order of the DNA struts is the code for the protein construction programme

We have already said that the DNA molecule can be likened to a piece of computer tape. In fact, *it is the order of the struts in the DNA which forms the code* (like the computer tape) for the protein construction programme.

First of all, the code instructs the cell to make the machinery needed for the protein 'production line'. This consists of special molecules which are built from a plan held in the DNA code (Fig 5.5b).

What are these molecules? The protein production molecules are all another type of nucleic acid, known as RNA. The important feature of RNA molecules is that they all have struts which can form pairs, in the same way as the struts of DNA molecules. In other words, a G strut will pair only with a C strut, and an A strut only with a T strut on the DNA molecule. (One difference of the RNA molecules is that they have no T struts themselves. Instead, A struts of the DNA molecules pair with another strut molecule found only in RNA molecules—U or uracil. Another difference of RNA molecules from DNA molecules is that they only ever consist of one strand—in other words, only one 'member' of a ladder.)

The formation of the RNA or protein production molecules is directed by the DNA 'plan' molecule by pairing of appropriate RNA strut molecules with the struts of one half of a DNA molecule. These struts are joined together by a sugar–phosphate backbone, similar to that of the DNA molecule. This process is shown in Fig 5.6.

There are three different RNA molecules, and each one has a different task in the production of proteins. They form the machinery of the production line in much the same way as moulds, carriers and welders form the machinery of a motor car production line. Each different RNA molecule is given a particular name:

- Messenger RNA acts as the mould. It is attached to the surfaces of the endoplasmic reticulum in the cytoplasm. The amino acids line up on the messenger RNA mould before they are joined to form a polypeptide (protein).

  Messenger RNA acts as the mould for lining up the amino acids

- The carrier which brings the amino acids to the mould is called **transfer RNA**. Transfer RNA floats freely in the cell cytoplasm and picks up individual amino acid molecules.

  Transfer RNA is the amino acid carrier

- The molecule which joins the amino acids together, once they are lined up on the mould, is called **ribosomal RNA**. As the name implies, ribosomal RNA is found in structures in the cytoplasm called ribosomes. We referred to these structures in Chapter 2. You may remember that they are frequently attached to endoplasmic reticulum, where they play a part in protein synthesis.

  Ribosomal RNA assists in joining amino acids together

DNA codes for the formation of all three types of RNA molecules in the nucleus. The formation of RNA from the DNA plan is shown in Fig 5.6. Once formed, the RNA molecules move from the nucleus into the cytoplasm to begin their different tasks. Figure 5.7 summarises these events.

DNA codes for RNA in the nucleus. RNA then moves out into the cytoplasm

There is a little more to be said about these RNA molecules before showing how they operate. Messenger RNA is often long, with up to 600 struts in its chain. Transfer RNA molecules have shorter chains, which

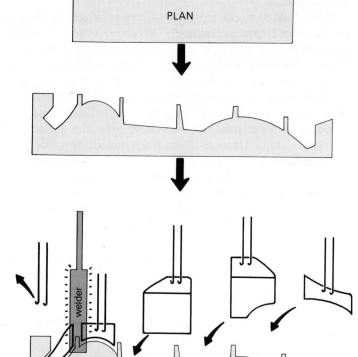

mould for car

beginning of car construction

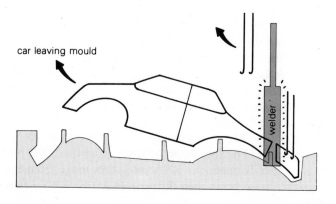

car leaving mould

car construction almost complete

Fig 5.5 *Construction of protein is similar in principle to the building of a motor car*

(a) Construction of a car, using car parts, carrier hooks, welder and a mould
(b) Construction of a section of protein, using amino acids, transfer RNA and messenger RNA

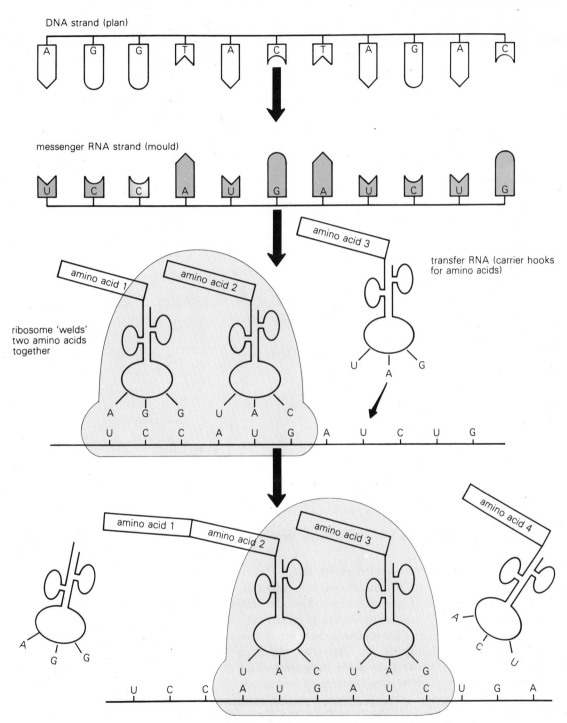

DNA strand (plan)

messenger RNA strand (mould)

transfer RNA (carrier hooks for amino acids)

ribosome 'welds' two amino acids together

ribosome moves along messenger RNA and 'welds' next amino acid to chain

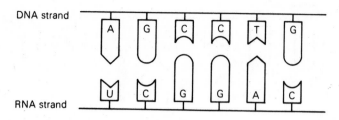

Fig 5.6 *Method by which a DNA strand instructs the formation of an RNA strand*

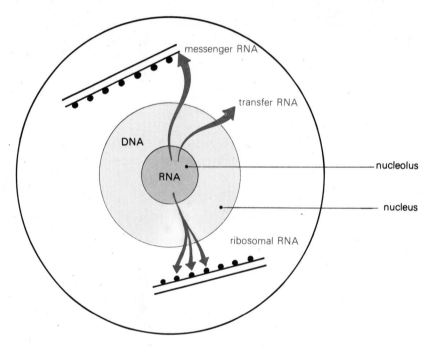

Fig 5.7 *Summary of the paths taken by three RNA molecules after being coded by DNA*

are folded rather like a clover leaf. There are many different transfer RNA molecules, but each one carries only one particular amino acid. Figure 5.8 shows how the amino acid is carried. The amino acid is attached to the 'stalk' end of the transfer RNA. At the opposite ('leaf') end of the molecule there are three struts, which stick out prominently. These struts can pair with matching struts on messenger RNA molecules. *Transfer RNA molecules which carry different amino acids have different combinations of end struts.*

The process of protein production involves all three types of RNA (refer back to Fig 5.5b). Each transfer RNA molecule in the cytoplasm picks up its own amino acid. It then carries the amino acid to a messenger RNA mould or 'work bench', where the three special end struts of the transfer RNA pair up with three struts of the messenger RNA molecule.

Different transfer RNA molecules with different end struts carry different amino acids

Three struts of a transfer RNA molecule pair with three struts of a messenger RNA molecule

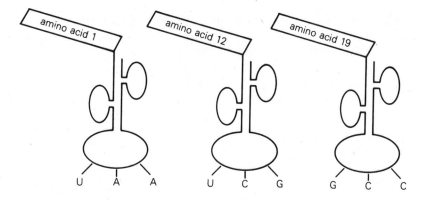

Fig 5.8 *Transfer RNAs with different end struts pick up different amino acids*

(Again, when these struts form pairs, U pairs with A, C pairs with G, and so on.) Another transfer RNA molecule may pair with the next three struts on the messenger RNA molecule. The two amino acids carried by these two transfer RNA molecules are thus brought to lie side by side. At this stage, a ribosome containing ribosomal RNA moves along the messenger RNA and joins the two amino acids. Once the amino acids are joined by a peptide bond, the carrier transfer RNA molecules are released and return to the cytoplasm to collect more amino acids. This same process is repeated many times, so that a large number of amino acids become joined together by peptide bonds. This amino acid chain is called a polypeptide, and several polypeptides join together to form a protein. After a polypeptide chain has been completed, it is released from the messenger RNA and the ribosomes.

(One DNA strand can code for all three types of RNA. Remember, in addition, that a cell contains many DNA strands and is thus equipped to produce many different messenger and transfer RNA molecules.)

It is important that we do not forget the significance of this apparently rather complex process. Remember that it is the DNA of the nucleus that controls cell shape, structure and function. The polypeptide just described would perhaps form part of an enzyme which may control cell shape and structure (see Fig 5.3). This polypeptide is related indirectly to the order of DNA struts in the nucleus. Three DNA struts code for three messenger RNA struts, which in turn code for one amino acid. *The order of the amino acids in a polypeptide chain is determined by the order of DNA struts (sometimes called bases).*

DNA, proteins and people

At this stage, think back to the young organism or embryo, growing by cell division and differentiation in the mother's uterus. Already, cells in different parts of the embryo are developing into special cell types with special jobs to perform: nerve cells, muscle cells, 'covering' cells and so

A ribosome joins two amino acids

A chain of amino acids = a polypeptide chain

Several polypeptide chains = a protein

One DNA strand can code for
• messenger RNA strands
• transfer RNA strands
• ribosomal RNA strands

Three DNA struts:
|
code for
↓
three messenger RNA struts
|
code for
↓
one amino acid

Differentiation—the development of special cells with particular functions from simple cells

Cells in the embryo differentiate to form nerve, epithelial, muscle cells etc

Cells group together to form the bodily features of the new individual

DNA controls cell shape, structure and function

Meiosis is a special type of cell division in which the amount of DNA in the daughter cells is half that of a normal body cell

Gametes are cells with half the quantity of DNA found in normal body cells

Meiosis results in the formation of gametes with slightly different DNA molecules in their nuclei

on. This process is called differentiation. These special cell types become organised to form tissues, organs and systems in the foetus. Even before birth it may be possible to distinguish certain features which are special to that developing individual. These bodily features which become the person are being formed by the arrangements of different groups of cells. More and more cells of different types are added, so that, by the time of birth, division and differentiation of cells have resulted in a body that is distinctly you and no one else. Both processes continue after birth to build a unique adult body. Each cell in the body relies on its DNA for the development of its type, shape and structure.

The differences between individuals are not due only to the process of differentiation, however. People differ from one another because no two people (with the exception of identical twins) have identical chromosomes. That is, no two people have DNA molecules with exactly the same orders of DNA struts. Let us see why this is so.

As we have already said, life of a new individual begins when a sperm cell from the father joins with an ovum (egg cell) from the mother to form a zygote. The zygote therefore receives some chromosomes (DNA) from each parent. If both the sperm and ovum contained the normal quantity of DNA found in body cells, the zygote would contain twice the normal quantity of DNA. To overcome this problem, when sperm and ova form from normal body cells a process of reduction and division occurs—the amount of DNA is halved, and at the same time cell division occurs. The process is called **meiosis**. The resulting cells, with half the amount of DNA found in body cells, are called gametes. Following this halving of the amount of DNA, a sperm and ovum can then join to form a zygote with the correct amount of the body cell DNA. However, this reduction and division does more than just halve the amount of DNA in the daughter cells. If all daughter cells resulting from meiosis contained the same DNA molecules, all children of the same parents would have the same DNA in their nuclei and would be identical. Clearly, however, brothers and sisters are often markedly different from one another. This is because when the body cell divides to form two gametes, different DNA molecules pass to each gamete nucleus. *No two gamete molecules will have identical DNA molecules.* As a result, each zygote (and individual) which forms, even from the same two parents, will be distinctly different from any other zygote.

As we have already mentioned, there is one important exception to this general rule—that of identical twins. Identical twins develop from a single zygote, formed by the fusion of one sperm and ovum. Very early in the development of the embryo it splits in half, and each half of the embryo then develops to form a complete individual. Two individuals who develop from one zygote are called identical twins. Non identical (or fraternal) twins, however, may be as dissimilar as any brothers and sisters. They develop when two eggs are released from the ovary at the one time and are fertilised by two different sperm.

Another question may occur to you at this point. How does each cell of your body happen to contain the same quantity of DNA? To answer this we should go back and look at cell division, focusing again on the nucleus. The life of a cell can be broken into two main phases: a *resting* phase (which scientists call interphase) and a *dividing* phase—mitosis, which we described earlier. If cells divided a number of times without any increase in the chromosomal material of the nucleus, the daughter cells would very soon contain almost no DNA. In order to maintain the same quantity of DNA in the nucleus, the DNA amount doubles in a cell during the resting phase of the cell cycle; that is, before each cell division. This is shown in Fig 5.9.

Two phases in the life of a cell:
• resting phase
• dividing phase

DNA doubles during the resting phase

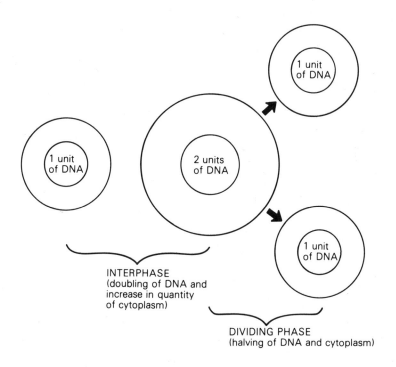

INTERPHASE
(doubling of DNA and increase in quantity of cytoplasm)

DIVIDING PHASE
(halving of DNA and cytoplasm)

Fig 5.9   *The quantity of DNA in a cell doubles before cell division*

How is this doubling of DNA carried out? The structure of the DNA molecule was shown in Fig 5.4. During doubling, the molecule splits down the middle between the struts, rather like undoing a zip. Once this has happened, new struts, with their pieces of sugar–phosphate chain attached, pair up with the old DNA struts—A pairs with T, and C pairs with G. The result is that two DNA molecules are formed that are identical to the one original molecule (Fig 5.10). One of each of these identical DNA molecules passes to each of the daughter nuclei.

DNA doubling occurs by
• unzipping of the DNA molecule
• new struts pairing with old struts

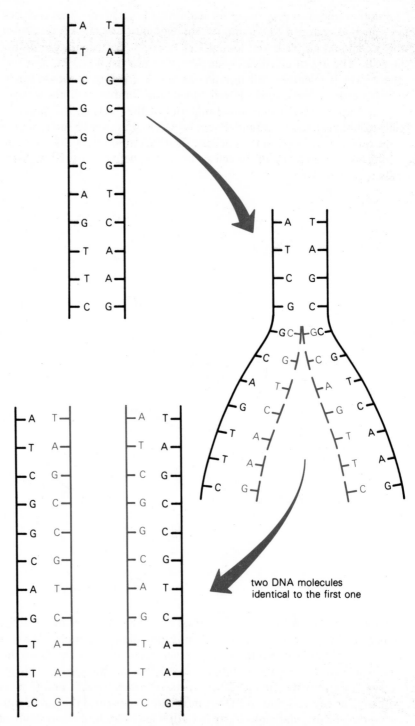

Fig 5.10   *The doubling of DNA during interphase, to produce two new DNA molecules*

DNA switches

One more question now remains to be answered. If each cell in the body contains the same quantity and type of DNA with the same arrangement of struts, how does the body come to develop different cell types? We have already discussed how the DNA controls cell shape and structure. Why then are all the cells in the body not a mixture of characteristics from eye cells, nerve cells, pancreatic cells and so on?

The process by which a general cell type forms a particular cell type such as a nerve cell is known as differentiation. The key to differentiation is DNA 'switching'. As the body develops, certain portions of DNA in the nucleus of different cells are prevented from operating, or are 'switched off'. This switching is done by particular chemicals within the cell. For example, those cells developing into stomach epithelium have DNA coding for nerve cells, muscle cells, bone cells and many others switched off. That is, these sections of DNA are inactive. Similarly, nerve cells contain inactive DNA coding for muscle, connective and epithelial cells.

Differentiation of cells is controlled by gene switching

DNA not required to form a particular tissue is switched off by a chemical in the cell

There are still many questions to be answered about the causes of differentiation: what triggers it in the first place; what chemicals are responsible for switching the DNA off; and indeed what other chemicals are responsible for switching DNA back on again? These are questions to which scientists continue to seek answers. In asking questions about differentiation we are asking the deepest questions about why we are as we are.

Chapter 6

The circulatory system— lifeline of the cells

The need for a circulatory system

All cells
- require food and oxygen to provide themselves with energy
- need to rid themselves of wastes

We have already seen in Chapter 4 that all cells require food molecules to provide the energy they need in order to live. They need oxygen too, to burn these foods or fuels. In this process poisonous waste products are produced, and these must be removed from the cell before they cause damage.

Movement of food and wastes into and out of single-celled animals occurs by diffusion

For simple, one-cell animals such as the amoeba, this presents few problems. No part of the animal's cytoplasm is very far from the external environment at any time. Molecules move in and out of the cell mainly by means of diffusion. As we saw in Chapter 2, diffusion is the simplest method of exchanging molecules between the inside and the outside of cells. Molecules that are needed by the cell diffuse from areas of high concentration outside the cell to areas of low concentration in the cell's cytoplasm. Similarly, other molecules inside the cell are never too far from the external environment to diffuse from high concentration areas inside to low concentration areas outside the cell (Fig 6.1).

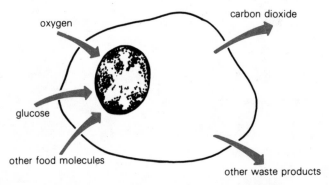

Fig 6.1 *Movement of molecules directly into and out of a unicellular animal; there is no need for a transport system*

All cells of small multicellular animals can be serviced by diffusion

The same simple processes of diffusion are also sufficient for some small multicellular animals. Even though some of the cells in the centre of the animal may have no part of their cell membrane in contact with the external environment, molecules can still be exchanged between all the cells and the outside environment by diffusion through the fluid spaces between cells (Fig 6.2).

In larger multicellular animals, many central cells may be starved of food and oxygen or swamped with wastes

However, if we increase the size of our hypothetical multicellular animal, problems begin to arise. Every cell in the animal requires constant exchange of waste molecules for more food molecules. Diffusion along the little fluid channels between the cells occurs only slowly. The cells at the centre of the mass would soon be starved of their vital food and oxygen molecules, and, in addition, would accumulate damaging or toxic waste-products (Fig 6.3a). A means must be found to speed up diffusion for these central cells. In any large multicellular animal, there must be a

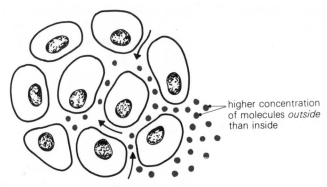

Fig 6.2 *In a small multicellular animal, molecules can diffuse through fluid spaces between cells; all cells have adequate contact with the external fuel supply*

transport system to provide rapid delivery of molecules to all cells and to remove waste products.

The simplest form of transport system is a series of *tubes*, running from the outside to the centre of the organism (Fig 6.3b). These tubes rapidly carry fluid with its dissolved molecules to all cells. Diffusion of molecules can then occur directly between the fluid in the cells and the fluid in the transport tubes.

Simple tubes like those described are called **capillaries**. *Capillaries are the basis of all transport systems in animals.* They are simply a means of speeding up the movements of molecules to all parts of a many-celled organism. Diffusion need then occur over only short distances. However, the larger the organism, the more complex the transport system in the organism. For example, the transport system in a large animal like a human being is much more complex and refined than a set of capillary tubes. Special systems like the respiratory and digestive systems bring the necessary foods and gases inside the body. They are then transferred to

Rapid delivery of food and oxygen molecules and removal of wastes are carried out by a transport system in large multicellular animals

Capillaries are the basis of all transport systems in animals

Large animals require more complex transport systems

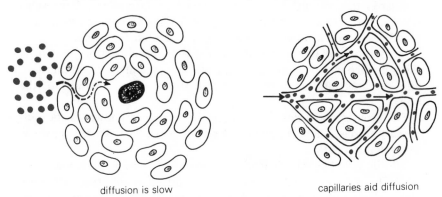

diffusion is slow

capillaries aid diffusion

Fig 6.3 *Capillaries supply food and remove water from all cells*
(a) Absence of capillaries results in death of central cells
(b) Even cells that are deep in body tissues can be supplied adequately by capillaries

the transport or circulatory system. The circulatory system delivers all these molecules to the cells. We shall see, now, how the human circulatory system is built around the tiny tubes or capillaries which feed and remove wastes from all cells in the body.

Building a transport system

The circulatory system is basically a system of closed tubes. Inside these tubes is a special carrier fluid known as **blood** which circulates through the tubes around the body. All the substances supplied to or leaving the cells are carried in the blood. A system of tubes containing blood, however, is not enough to make up a circulatory system. There must be a means of creating a flow of blood along the tubes. In a system of closed tubes flow can be produced by changes in pressure. To provide changes in pressure our transport system requires a pump.

You have probably already guessed that the pump in the circulatory system is the **heart**. When the heart contracts, its volume is reduced, pressure is increased, and blood is forced out into the tubes or vessels of the circulatory system. You probably also know already that not all the vessels of the circulatory system are the same. Although they form one continuous network, they vary according to their location in the body and their function.

The vessels through which blood flows away from the heart to the tissues and organs are called **arteries**. These large strong vessels branch to supply the limbs and organs. As they do so their diameter becomes smaller. Finally, within the tissues, they branch to form a network of very fine tubes—the capillaries, which run close to all the cells. Only from the capillaries can the cells receive their food and oxygen. The capillaries then rejoin to form small and then increasingly large **veins** which return blood to the heart. Figure 6.4 shows how the heart and blood vessels are arranged to make up the circulatory system.

As is shown diagrammatically in Fig 6.4, the circulatory system is easily divided into two quite distinct parts: one system of vessels that supplies the lungs and another system that supplies the remainder of the body.

The arteries and veins that supply the lungs are known as the **pulmonary vessels**. Those supplying the remainder of the body are known as the **systemic vessels**.

Why do we make this distinction between systemic and pulmonary vessels? The pulmonary vessels have a very different role from all other blood vessels in the body. After passing through systemic tissue capillaries, blood in the systemic veins is short of oxygen but loaded with carbon dioxide. It flows back to the right side of the heart (see the next

---

Margin notes:

The circulatory system includes
• a system of closed tubes
• a carrier fluid (blood)
• a pump

The heart is a pump which produces pressure changes in the closed system of tubes

Arteries carry blood from the heart to the tissues

Arteries
↓
small arteries (arterioles)
↓
capillaries
↓
small veins (venules)
↓
veins

Circulatory system:
• pulmonary vessels (arteries and veins leading to and from lungs)
• systemic vessels (arteries and veins leading to and from remainder of the body)

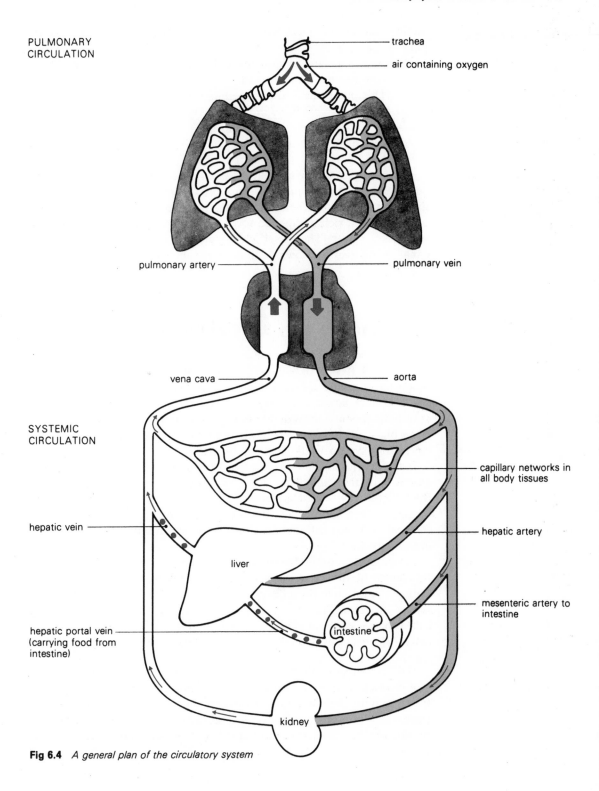

PULMONARY
CIRCULATION

trachea

air containing oxygen

pulmonary artery

pulmonary vein

vena cava

aorta

SYSTEMIC
CIRCULATION

capillary networks in
all body tissues

hepatic vein

hepatic artery

liver

mesenteric artery to
intestine

hepatic portal vein
(carrying food from
intestine)

intestine

kidney

Fig 6.4 *A general plan of the circulatory system*

Blood that is high in carbon dioxide and low in oxygen flows to the right side of the heart

The right heart-pump pumps blood to the lungs. Here it picks up oxygen and gets rid of carbon dioxide

Blood that is high in oxygen and low in carbon dioxide returns to the heart from the lungs. The left heart pump pushes this blood into the systemic arteries

Food entering the capillaries in the intestine is transferred to the liver via the portal vein

section, below). The right heart-pump then pushes the blood through the pulmonary arteries to the lungs, where carbon dioxide is transferred from blood to air and oxygen from air to blood (see Chapter 8). Blood loaded with oxygen then flows in the pulmonary veins to the left heart-pump. This pump then pushes the blood into the systemic vessels. *The blood leaving the left heart in the systemic arteries is therefore always loaded with oxygen. In contrast, that in the pulmonary arteries is low in oxygen and high in carbon dioxide.*

Figure 6.4 illustrates a special area of the systemic circulation. This is the blood supply of the alimentary canal. The arrangement of the blood vessels here is an exception to the normal pattern. Instead of flowing directly back to the large veins and the heart, blood leaving the stomach and intestines, rich in digested foodstuffs, enters a second capillary network in the liver. The vessel which carries blood from the alimentary canal to the liver is known as the **portal vein**.

The heart—a very special pump

In the course of a lifetime, the heart performs a staggering amount of work. The left side of the heart, alone, pumps on average 5 litres of blood into the arteries each minute, and this amount can be increased five-fold in response to increased demand by the tissues. All the blood in your body (about 5 litres or 12 pints) passes through the heart every 60 to 90 seconds. Without a heart to maintain the constant flow of blood, the circulatory system would cease to function.

In the developing embryo, the heart forms as a thickening of the muscle layer of the wall of an artery. As the walls of the vessel become thicker, the cavity or chamber inside the heart increases in size, too. Structures then form which ensure that the contractions or squeezing of the heart muscle push the blood in one direction only. These structures are called valves.

The heart is a muscular pump which lies in the centre of the thoracic cavity

The pericardium is a tough bag of connective tissue which surrounds the heart

Let us look, now, at the structure of the human heart. The heart lies in the centre of the chest or thoracic cavity. However, it is not placed symmetrically—one-third lies on the right side, and two-thirds on the left side of the chest (Fig 6.5). It is enclosed in a tough connective tissue bag called the **pericardium**. This bag is attached to the breast bone by strong cords (ligaments) which help to hold the heart in position inside the rib cage.

We have already said that the heart is composed of two pumps: a right pump which receives blood from the systemic veins and pumps it to the lungs, and a left pump which receives blood from the pulmonary veins (lungs) and pumps it to the organs and limbs. These two pumps lie side by side and together form the single organ. Refer again to Fig 6.4, and you will see how important the presence of the two pumps in the heart is.

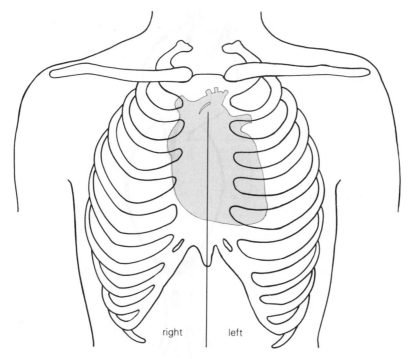

right   left

Fig 6.5 *Position of the heart in the thoracic cavity*

The blood in the left and right sides of the heart *never mixes*. Oxygen-rich blood returning from the lungs is pumped straight to the tissues where it is needed, never mixing with the oxygen-depleted blood returning to the heart from the tissues. This makes for a particularly efficient pumping system.

The structure of each side of the heart is basically the same. The arrangement of the two sides is shown in Fig 6.6. Each pump is divided into two chambers: a thin-walled **atrium** which receives blood from the veins, and a thicker-walled **ventricle** which propels blood forward into the arteries. The muscle walls of the left heart are thicker than those of the right heart—the left heart must develop sufficient pressure to pump blood around the entire body.

Figure 6.7 is a diagram of the heart, cut in longitudinal section. Let us now see how blood flows through the heart. Blood, low in oxygen and laden with carbon dioxide collected from all parts of the head, limbs and trunk, flows through two large veins, the **superior** and **inferior venae cavae**, into the right atrium. From there, blood passes into the right ventricle and is then pumped into the pulmonary arteries and to the lungs. From the lungs blood rich in oxygen returns to the heart in the pulmonary veins and enters the left atrium. It passes next into the left ventricle. From here it is pumped into the aorta, the largest artery in the body, for circulation around the body.

Blood from the right side of the heart never mixes with blood from the left side of the heart. Thus oxygen-rich blood never mixes with oxygen-depleted blood

Each pump consists of
• a thin-walled chamber (atrium), which receives blood from the veins
• a thicker-walled chamber (ventricle), which pumps blood into the arteries

The superior and inferior venae cavae lead blood into the right atrium

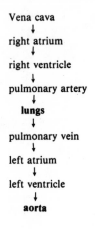

Vena cava
↓
right atrium
↓
right ventricle
↓
pulmonary artery
↓
lungs
↓
pulmonary vein
↓
left atrium
↓
left ventricle
↓
aorta

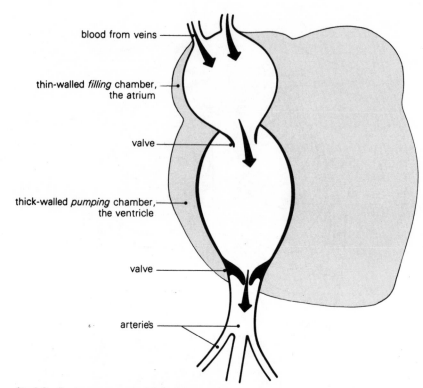

blood from veins

thin-walled *filling* chamber, the atrium

valve

thick-walled *pumping* chamber, the ventricle

valve

arteries

Fig 6.6 *Basic arrangement of the heart pump*

This one-way flow of blood through the heart is made possible by the presence of the **heart valves** (refer again to Fig 6.7). There are two types of valves, those separating the atria and ventricles—atrio-ventricular valves—and those separating the ventricles and the arteries—the pulmonary and aortic semilunar valves. The atrio-ventricular valves are attached to the walls of the ventricles by thin tendons called **tendinous cords.** Figure 6.8 shows how the flaps of the atrio-ventricular valves prevent back-flow of blood. When the pressure of blood in the atrium is greater than that in the ventricles, blood flows forward into the ventricle. The tendinous cords of the flap valves are slack. When the ventricles contract, pressure inside the ventricles increases and the flap valves close tightly over the opening between the two chambers. The strong tendinous cords become taut and prevent the valves from turning inside out. The semilunar valves operate in a similar way. After the ventricles contract, blood is prevented from flowing back from the arteries into the heart by pocket-like valves which close as blood pushes back into the heart.

The regular and rhythmic pumping action of the heart is what we know as the **heart beat.** The contractions of the heart beat occur as an organised sequence of events, called the **cardiac cycle.** The actual contraction period of the heart is called **systole**, and the period of relaxation is called **diastole.**

Atrio-ventricular valves prevent back-flow of blood from the ventricles into the atria

Semilunar valves prevent back-flow of blood from the arteries into the heart

Systole—the time when the heart muscle contracts

Diastole—the time when the heart muscle relaxes

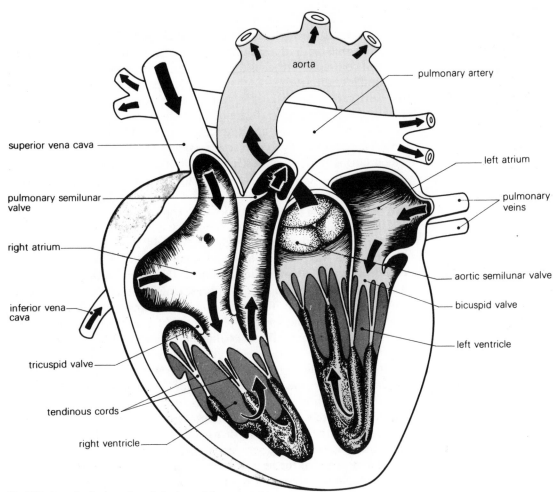

Fig 6.7   *Longitudinal section of the heart (diagrammatic)*

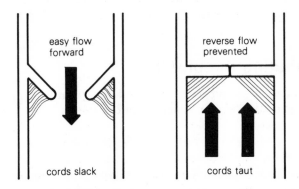

easy flow
forward

cords slack

reverse flow
prevented

cords taut

Fig 6.8   *Valves between the atria and the ventricles of the heart prevent back-flow of blood*

Each cycle begins with a wave of muscle contraction which sweeps across both atria, almost at the same time. At this stage, the ventricles are still relaxed (ventricular diastole) and blood flows into the ventricles. Less than one-tenth of a second later (just as the atria start to relax), the wave of contraction reaches the ventricles. These contract to force blood forward into the arteries. Both the ventricles and the atria then relax until the next cardiac cycle begins. (Each cardiac cycle lasts on average 0.8 seconds, producing a heart rate of 70–75 beats per minute.)

Cardiac cycle:
- atria contract (ventricles are relaxed)
- ventricles contract (atria are also contracted)
- both atria and ventricles relax

Figure 6.9 shows the appearance of the heart during ventricular relaxation (diastole) and contraction (systole). (It is worth noting that blood normally flows almost continually from the veins into the atria. Approximately 70 per cent flows directly into the ventricles, even before the atria contract. Atrial contraction boosts ventricular filling by 30 per cent and acts as a primer to make the ventricles more efficient pumps.)

The rhythmic contraction of the heart is basically automatic—even when a heart is entirely removed from the body, it will continue to beat in an organised way, as long as an adequate form of artificial circulation can be arranged. It owes this ability to the special properties of heart muscle cells—the cardiac muscle fibres. Unlike muscles of the limbs and trunk, cardiac muscle fibres can contract without nervous stimulation. They can produce their own impulses to start a contraction. Also, unlike skeletal muscle fibres, the cells that make up heart muscle are joined tightly together, so that waves of contraction which begin as an electrical impulse in one muscle fibre spread over the entire heart muscle mass. As we shall see later, the nervous system does control the rate of the heart beat. However, it is a small area of muscle within the heart, known as the pacemaker muscle, that sets the natural rhythm of the cardiac cycle.

Cardiac muscle fibres are able to contract by themselves

An impulse in one heart muscle fibre will automatically spread to others

Because of the constant work which the heart muscle performs, the heart requires far more nourishment and oxygen than any other organ. The muscle walls of the heart are far too thick for the muscle cells to obtain their supplies directly from the chambers of the heart. They obtain their supply from the aorta, via arteries known as the **coronary arteries**. The proper working of the heart depends entirely on the well-being of these coronary arteries (as we shall see later in the chapter).

The coronary arteries supply food and oxygen to the heart muscle

Distributing the blood

Arteries, capillaries and veins are all designed differently, in order to perform their particular job in the circulatory system (refer to Fig 6.10).

Arteries

The heart squirts blood into the large arteries at great pressure. The walls of the arteries must be thick and tough to withstand these pressures. These blood vessels possess a certain amount of elasticity. If they were

Arteries are
- thick and tough to withstand high blood pressures
- elastic to ensure continuous flow of blood

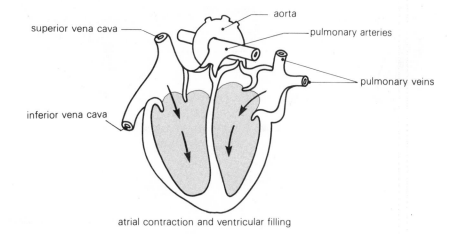

ATRIAL SYSTOLE
(lasts for 0.15 sec)

superior vena cava

aorta

pulmonary arteries

pulmonary veins

inferior vena cava

atrial contraction and ventricular filling

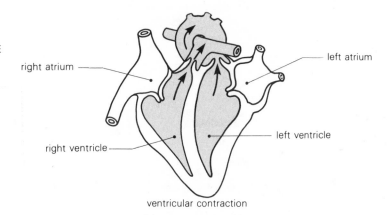

VENTRICULAR SYSTOLE
(lasts for 0.30 sec)

right atrium

left atrium

left ventricle

right ventricle

ventricular contraction

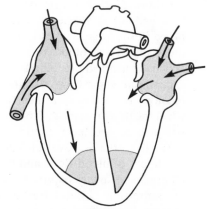

DIASTOLE
atrial and ventricular filling
(lasts for 0.60 sec in the resting heart)

atrial and ventricular filling

Fig 6.9 *Appearance of the heart during the cardiac cycle*

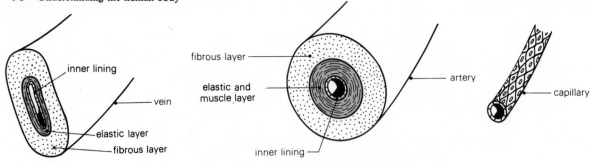

Fig 6.10 *Structure of veins, arteries and capillaries*

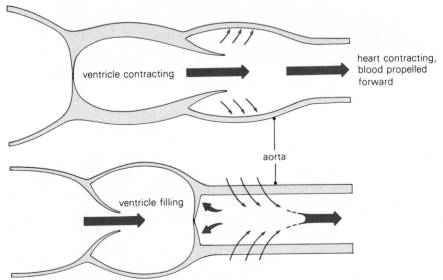

Fig 6.11 *Elastic recoil in the arteries helps to produce a continuous blood flow*

rigid tubes, blood would flow along them only during ventricular contractions. During ventricular relaxation blood pressure would drop to zero and blood would not flow at all. However, continuous flow of blood in the large arteries is made possible by a layer of elastic tissue in the walls of the blood vessels. Figure 6.11 explains how this occurs. When the heart squirts blood into the aorta, some of it forces the aorta to expand and some flows straight on towards the smaller arteries. Elastic recoil of the artery wall then forces some blood along the artery, even when the heart is resting. Blood flow therefore becomes continuous—not stopping between each contraction of the ventricles.

Smaller arteries have less elastic tissue in their walls, but possess a layer of muscle which can regulate blood flow

Smaller arteries have less elastic tissue in their walls. They are the regulators of blood flow, and have a layer of muscle in their walls. Not all organs or tissues require a maximum amount of blood (or oxygen) at the same time. Contraction of muscles in the walls of small arteries reduces blood flow as required. The smallest muscular arteries are known as **arterioles**. The arrangement of the major arteries of the body is shown in Fig 6.12.

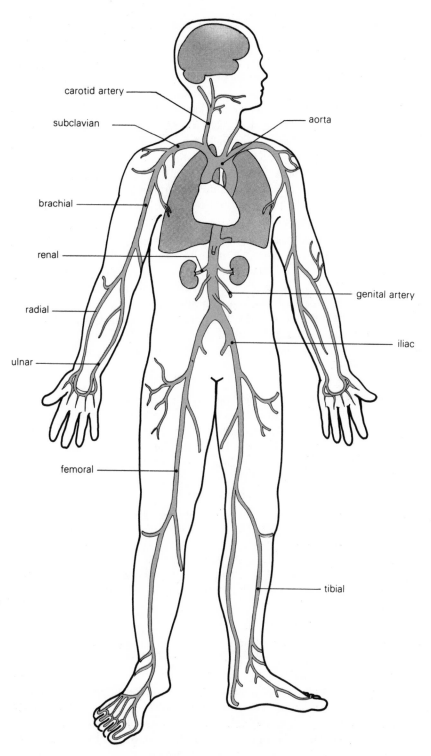

Fig 6.12   *The major arteries of the body*

Capillaries

The capillaries are responsible for the collection and delivery of materials to the tissues. They must therefore be in very close contact with all the tissues of the body. To make this possible, arterioles branch in the tissues into a very dense network of very fine capillaries. The diameter of capillaries is extremely small—an average of one-hundredth of a millimetre. This means that the blood cells must be squeezed flat, or folded in two, while passing through them. Movement of blood is thus slowed, and this helps diffusion of materials to the tissues.

The walls of capillaries are also extremely thin—just a single layer of flattened cells keeps the blood inside the capillary walls (see Fig 6.10).

Formation of tissue fluid

The thin capillary walls allow water and dissolved substances (except for very large protein molecules) to move in and out of the circulation. At the arterial end of the capillary the blood pressure is high, and fluid with dissolved substances is forced through the capillary wall. This fluid is similar to the blood plasma—it contains glucose, amino acids, fatty acids, glycerol and mineral salts, but only low concentrations of the large blood proteins. This fluid fills all the spaces between the cells and is called tissue fluid. From it the cells extract all the molecules they need, oxygen, glucose etc, and into it pass their waste products: carbon dioxide, urea etc.

Since plasma proteins cannot pass readily through the capillary wall from the blood plasma to the tissue fluid, blood plasma contains more proteins than tissue fluid. This produces an osmotic force which tends to draw water from the tissue fluid back into the blood. We call this force osmotic pressure (Chapter 2, p 24). At the arterial end of the capillary, blood pressure is greater than this osmotic pressure, so fluid is forced outwards. Because of the resistance to flow in the capillary, blood pressure drops along the capillary. At the venous end, where blood pressure is almost zero, osmotic pressure is the main force operating and water enters the capillary. This is summarised in Fig 6.13.

Not quite all the fluid that leaves the capillary at the arterial end re-enters at the venous end. A small amount (approximately 10 per cent) returns to the circulation through lymph vessels. These will be discussed in Chapter 7.

Veins

The capillaries rejoin to form small, and then increasingly larger, veins, which return blood to the heart. Most of the force of the heart beat or blood flow has been lost by this stage and pressure in veins is low. For this reason the space within veins is relatively large, and vein walls are thin, so there is little resistance to blood flow (see Fig 6.10).

The body tissues are supplied by dense networks of capillaries

Red blood cells have to be squeezed flat or folded in two in order to fit through a capillary. This slows blood flow

Capillary walls have only a single layer of flattened cells

Capillary walls allow movement of water, glucose, amino acids, mineral salts, fatty acids and glycerol

Proteins do not pass easily through capillary walls

The fluid and nutrients filling the space between cells is tissue fluid

At the arterial end, fluid leaves the capillary

At the venous end, fluid re-enters the capillary

Lymph vessels return some tissue fluid to the bloodstream

Veins have thin walls and large internal spaces to reduce resistance to blood flow

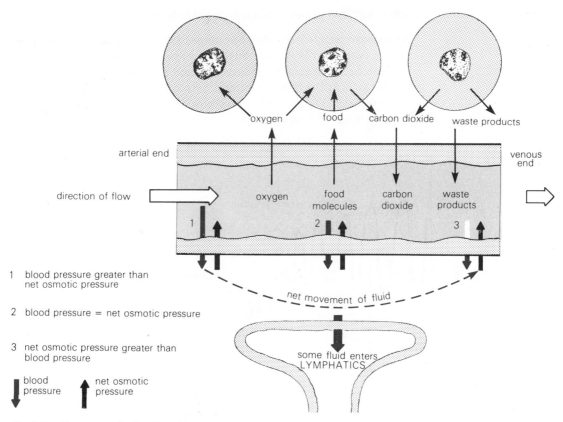

Fig 6.13 *Movement of substances across the capillary wall*

1 blood pressure greater than net osmotic pressure

2 blood pressure = net osmotic pressure

3 net osmotic pressure greater than blood pressure

↓ blood pressure   ↑ net osmotic pressure

The movement of blood in the veins (particularly in the limbs) is very much assisted by the contraction of the skeletal muscles which surround them. Contraction of muscles during exercise squeezes blood forward in the veins. As in the heart, the back-flow of blood in the veins is prevented by the presence of valves (Fig 6.14).

Blood flow in the veins is assisted by contraction of muscles which surround the veins

Valves in the veins direct blood flow towards the heart

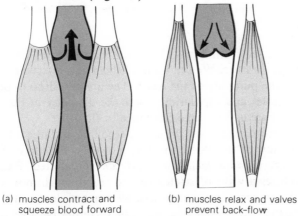

(a) muscles contract and squeeze blood forward

(b) muscles relax and valves prevent back-flow

Fig 6.14 *Skeletal muscles assist the flow of blood in veins*

The pulse and blood pressure

As we have seen, blood must be pumped through the vessels under pressure to reach all the organs. Just like a town water supply, the greatest pressure in the circulatory system is found as it leaves the pumping station (heart). As the blood is pumped into smaller and smaller vessels, the pressure falls. Figure 6.15 shows how the blood pressure falls in the different types of blood vessels.

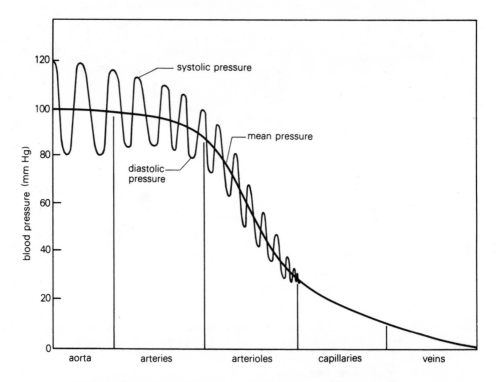

Fig 6.15 *Changes in blood pressure in different types of blood vessels*

As you can see from Fig 6.15, all the main arteries have about the same average pressure. We can think of them as a reservoir kept at high pressure by the pumping of the heart. The greatest drop in pressure occurs in arterioles and capillaries, where the diameter of the vessels decreases and there is very large resistance to flow.

The greatest drop in blood pressure occurs in the arterioles and capillaries

We have already seen how the elastic recoil of the large arteries makes continuous flow of the blood possible. However, the surge of blood entering the arteries with each heart beat *can* be detected. Each spurt of blood produces a wave of stretching and recoil which moves along the walls of the arteries. In places where arteries are close to the skin, this pressure change can be felt as a pulsation or pulse. Because there is one pulse every time the heart beats, the pulse can be taken as a measure of how fast the heart is beating.

The pressure in the arterial reservoir varies during the day. It is lowest when we are asleep and highest when we are exercising vigorously or excited. Two things govern the amount of blood in the arterial reservoir (and therefore the blood pressure). These are shown diagrammatically in Fig 6.16. They are:

- Cardiac output—the amount of blood pumped into the arteries per minute. Cardiac output depends on the strength of the heart beat and the rate of the heart beat.

- Outflow into capillaries—controlled by the presence of muscle bands in the walls of arterioles (small arteries). These muscle bands cause the arterioles to constrict or dilate, allowing less or more blood into the capillaries. The constriction and dilation of the muscle bands are controlled by nerves and hormones. They are also affected directly by lactic acid and carbon dioxide. If carbon dioxide and lactic acid build up in the tissues, the blood vessels supplying these tissues dilate. In this way blood flow is increased to tissues in need.

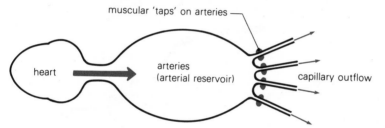

muscular 'taps' on arteries

heart

arteries (arterial reservoir)

capillary outflow

Fig 6.16 *How cardiac output and capillary outflow affect the amount of blood in the arterial reservoir*

Although blood pressure varies quite considerably with normal changes in activity, many people have high blood pressure all the time. This is called **hypertension**. It is estimated that, in Australia, as in many other Western nations, one person in every six is affected by hypertension.

Scientists are still not sure of the cause of high blood pressure. The body's nervous system is important in controlling blood pressure, as is a substance produced by the kidneys. Too much salt in the daily diet seems to aggravate high blood pressure. A small proportion of cases of high blood pressure are caused by kidney disease.

High blood pressure is a serious condition, however, because over a period of time it causes damage to arteries. This may lead to stroke, heart attack or other complications (p 105). Although we do not know much about the causes of high blood pressure, there are a number of effective ways of treating it. For this reason, and because of the danger of long-term high blood pressure, the National Heart Foundation recommends that all adults should have their blood pressure checked every year.

Blood pressure is measured
using a
sphygmomanometer

Blood pressure can be measured using an instrument called a sphygmomanometer (Fig 6.17). This is a fairly simple instrument, consisting of a rubber cuff, into which air can be pumped, and a gauge filled with mercury, which shows the pressure inside the cuff. The cuff is wrapped around the arm and inflated to a pressure well above arterial pressure. This squeezes the artery and stops blood flow. Then the pressure in the cuff is gradually released and the doctor listens with a stethoscope placed over the artery, below the cuff, for the sound of the pulse returning to the artery. The doctor can actually record two pressure readings: one at the point of systole, when blood is first forced past the obstruction, and the other at diastole, when no obstruction remains to blood flow at all.

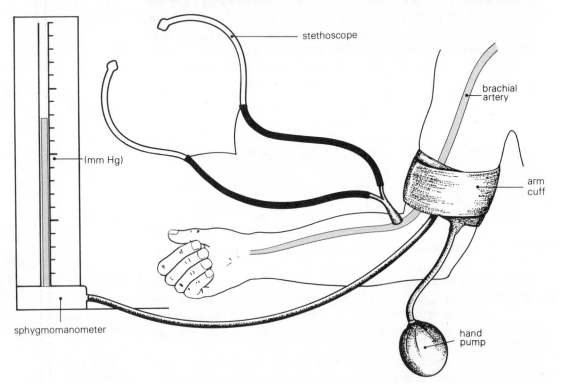

Fig 6.17 *Measuring blood pressure with a sphygmomanometer*

Control of the heart rate

We have already said that the rhythmic beating of the heart is basically automatic—it needs no nervous stimulation to keep it going. However, the heart must be able to respond to huge changes in the needs of the tissues in different situations. When we exercise, the heart can pump five times as much blood, per minute, as it does when we rest. This is made possible because the rate at which the heart beats is controlled by nerves.

The heart is supplied with two types of nerves: one type that speeds up the heart, the other that slows it. When we exercise, the tissues (and particularly the muscles) need more oxygen. Messages are sent from the brain to the heart to increase the heart rate. The increased heart beat increases the speed with which blood is supplied to the tissues. When we rest, the demands of the tissues are lowered. Messages are sent to the heart, along other nerves, which slow the pulse and lower blood pressure to resting levels.

The heart beat is controlled by two types of nerves:
• one that speeds up the heart rate
• the other that slows the heart rate down

Atherosclerosis

The most common arterial disease found in people today is known as atherosclerosis. In this disease, patches of fatty or fibrous material build up on the inner walls of the arteries (Fig 6.18). (They do this in much the same way as rust or lime deposits build up on the inside surfaces of water pipes.) In the human body, the fatty deposits may restrict blood flow in the arteries. If these fatty deposits continue to build up, a complete blockage in an artery supplying blood to a vital organ such as the heart, brain or kidneys may occur.

Atherosclerosis—arterial disease in which fat deposits build up on the inside of arteries

Atherosclerosis is the cause of two severe conditions: coronary heart disease and strokes. These two diseases are responsible for approximately half of all deaths in Australia, the United States and Great Britain.

Atherosclerosis is responsible for
• coronary heart disease
• strokes

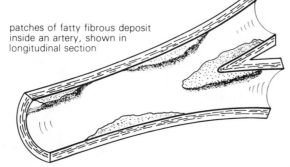

patches of fatty fibrous deposit inside an artery, shown in longitudinal section

Fig 6.18 *Cross-section of a diseased artery showing the buildup of fibrous and fatty deposits on the inner lining*

Coronary heart disease

The most common form of coronary heart disease is angina. This occurs when one of the arteries supplying blood to the heart (coronary artery) becomes partly blocked by fibrous or fatty material. Thus, under conditions of stress or strenuous exercise, the amount of blood flowing through the coronary arteries may not be sufficient to provide enough

Angina occurs when one of the coronary arteries becomes partly blocked

Reduced oxygen to the heart muscle may cause pain

oxygen for the rapidly contracting heart muscle. Oxygen is necessary for energy production, and without sufficient energy, muscular cramp may occur. This in turn causes pain in the chest. When this occurs, it is important that the person rests immediately. This allows the muscle to recover, and no damage results.

A serious blockage in a coronary artery may stop blood flow to part of the heart completely. This results in heart attack

If one of the coronary arteries is seriously blocked with atherosclerosis, blood flow to one particular part of the heart may suddenly be totally stopped, and a heart attack results (Fig 6.19). Severe, sudden chest pain is felt by the person. In this case, there will be a complete lack of oxygen in the area fed by the coronary artery, causing muscle damage. How much damage occurs depends on which artery is blocked and whether other arteries nearby can form new branches to take over the blood supply to the oxygen-starved area of muscle. The damaged area, which is left unsupplied by blood, will form a scar within about eight weeks. If the area of scarred muscle is not large and does not interfere with the heart's ability to pump, the person usually recovers and can resume normal activities.

During heart attack, damage to the heart muscle is caused by severe lack of oxygen

Scar tissue may develop in the damaged heart muscle

If the area of scar tissue is not large, the person usually recovers

However, some heart attacks are fatal. This occurs when the oxygen-starved muscle disturbs the heart's rhythmic beat, leading to the stopping of the heart, ie cardiac arrest.

Stopping of heart—cardiac arrest

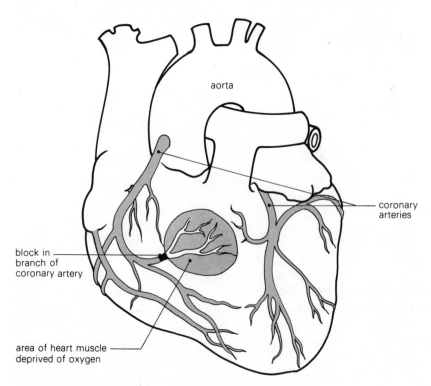

Fig 6.19 *Sequence of events in a heart attack*

Stroke

Atherosclerosis may also result in a stroke. This occurs when the blood supply is cut off from part of the brain. Such a block is often caused by a blood clot which forms amongst fatty deposits in an artery diseased with atherosclerosis. Once blood flow is stopped, the cells in the affected area rapidly die. The most common effects of a stroke are weakness or paralysis of the arms or legs. If the area of the brain that has been damaged controls speech, vision or hearing, the person will lose some of the ability to speak, see or hear. Some strokes are mild and recovery occurs quickly. When they are severe, recovery may never be complete.

A stroke occurs when the blood supply to part of the brain is cut off

A blood clot settling amongst fatty deposits in blood vessels often cuts off blood supply to the brain

Causes of atherosclerosis

How is atherosclerosis caused? There are two factors that seem to contribute most to this disease. One of these is the presence of high concentrations of fats such as cholesterol and lipids in the blood. Eating a lot of foods containing these fats is now considered to be the major cause of high blood fats (see Chapter 10). The higher the fat concentration, the more readily fatty deposits seem to form along the artery walls. The second factor that contributes to atherosclerosis is high blood pressure. The inner surfaces of arteries that have been damaged by high blood pressure seem to attract deposits of fatty material.

Two facts seem to contribute to atherosclerosis:
• high concentrations of cholesterol and lipids in the blood
• high blood pressure (hypertension)

In time, areas of an artery in which fatty material has been laid down may form tougher fibrous tissues. As a result, the artery begins to lose some of its elasticity and is described as becoming 'hardened'. In fact, the term atherosclerosis literally means 'hardening of the arteries'.

Atherosclerosis: damage to artery wall
↓
tough fibrous tissue forms in artery wall
↓
artery loses some elasticity and becomes hardened

One further result of atherosclerosis is a stressed heart. As the space inside arteries decreases, and as their elasticity disappears, blood pressure increases, and the heart is forced to work harder to pump the blood around the body. Under these conditions the heart may become enlarged, a condition known as hypertensive heart disease.

Atherosclerosis may cause enlargement of the heart. This condition is known as hypertensive heart disease

Blood—the carrier for the transport system

We have now described the system of tubes and the pump of the circulatory system. It remains to examine the carrier itself—blood.

Blood consists of a fluid—**plasma**—in which are suspended **blood cells**: red blood cells, white blood cells and platelets. A 70 kg man has approximately 5 litres of blood, roughly 8 per cent of his body weight. The fluid part of blood (plasma) amounts to 55 per cent of the total blood volume; the remaining 45 per cent is blood cells. Any particular red blood cell passes through the heart, on average, once every 45 seconds.

Blood =
plasma
+ blood cells
+ platelets

Blood has a large variety of very specific functions:

• Transport of gases; this applies particularly to oxygen and carbon dioxide.

Functions of the blood:
• transport of gases
• transport of food
• transport of wastes
• transport of messengers and regulators
• distribution of heat

- Transport of foods—all the products of digestion (sugars, fats, proteins, amino acids, glycerol, fatty acids, vitamins and minerals) are carried in the blood from the small intestine to the liver and then to the tissues.

- Transport of wastes—excretory products of the cells are carried in the blood to the kidneys, lungs and liver.

- Transport of messengers and regulators—hormones (the messengers of the body), vitamins and some enzymes are carried to the tissues in the blood.

- Distribution of heat—muscle contraction and chemical activity produce heat. The heat produced in localised areas of the body is spread all around the body by the blood. In this way an even temperature is maintained. In addition, diversion of blood to or away from the skin controls overall heat loss from the body.

Which parts of the blood are responsible for the transport of the different substances? Table 6.1 summarises this information. In broad outline, oxygen and some carbon dioxide are carried by the red blood cells, while the blood plasma carries all other substances.

Table 6.1 *Functions of the blood*

Substances transported	From:	To:	How carried
Oxygen	Lungs	All tissues	Red blood cells (haemoglobin)
Carbon dioxide	All tissues	Lungs	Mainly as bicarbonate ions in the plasma. (Small amounts are carried in the red blood cells as carboxy-haemoglobin, or as dissolved gas in the plasma)
Products of digestion	Small intestine	All tissues	Plasma
Hormones	Ductless glands	All tissues	Plasma
Urea	Liver	Kidney	Plasma
Heat	All tissues	All tissues	All parts of the blood

In addition, the blood cells have other specific functions:

White blood cells are responsible for defending the body against disease

- White blood cells are responsible for defence against disease. White blood cells help to limit the spread of disease in the body by a number of means. Their function will be discussed in detail in Chapter 7.

Platelets are necessary for blood to clot

- Blood platelets have a special task in the control of blood loss by the formation of clots.

The composition of the blood is summarised in Fig 6.20.

Plasma

Plasma =
  water
  + dissolved substances
  + large proteins

Plasma consists mainly of water in which a variety of substances is dissolved. Most of these are substances that are being transported from one part of the body to another: food materials, hormones, mineral salts and carbon dioxide as dissolved gas or bicarbonate ions.

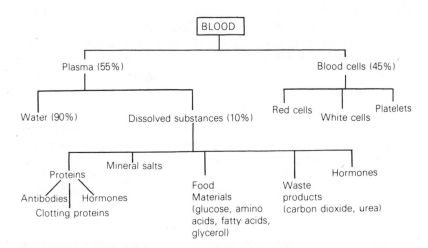

Fig 6.20 *Composition of the blood*

The plasma also contains large **plasma proteins**. Some of these are involved in blood clotting, others are the antibodies of the defence system. As we saw earlier, it is from the blood plasma that tissue fluid forms. Plasma therefore provides for the continual exchange of substances between all the tissues and the blood.

Red blood cells

The red colour of blood is due to the presence of red blood cells (**erythrocytes**). There are about 5 million cells per cubic millimetre of blood. Of these, only about 9000 are white—the remainder are red. Red blood cells are formed in the bone marrow. The main function of red blood cells is to carry oxygen from the lungs to the tissues. (They also carry some carbon dioxide in the reverse direction.) The chemical structure and composition of the red blood cell make it an excellent example of a cell designed to perform a particular job. Its special features are as follows:

Red blood cells
- carry oxygen
- carry some carbon dioxide

- Figure 6.21 shows the appearance of a red blood cell, as seen with a scanning electron microscope. Look at its shape. Red blood cells are relatively small cells, and their shape is described as being a biconcave disc. In other words, they are round and flat—thick around the edge and thin in the middle, rather like a doughnut without a hole. This shape greatly increases the surface area available for movement of gases into and out of the cell. A red blood cell spends less than a second in the capillaries of the lungs where gas exchange takes place. If the cells were spherical, many more would be needed to pick up and distribute oxygen with the same speed.

The biconcave disc shape of the red blood cell increases the surface area available for the movement of gases into and out of the cell

- Red blood cells have particularly elastic cell membranes. This allows them to be greatly deformed as they squeeze through tiny capillaries.

Elastic membranes of red blood cells allow them to be squeezed through capillaries

Red blood cells contain haemoglobin, which is a very efficient carrier of oxygen

Haemoglobin: the oxygen container molecule

• Red blood cells have no nucleus. Instead, the cytoplasm is filled with a special pigmented protein called **haemoglobin**. Haemoglobin is the oxygen carrier protein. Oxygen is not very soluble in water—one litre of blood carries only 3 mL of dissolved oxygen. Blood containing red blood cells can transport seventy times as much oxygen as the same volume of blood plasma. It makes the whole gas exchange system possible.

It is the haemoglobin that gives red blood cells their red colour. The haemoglobin molecules consist of a protein molecule or globin combined with an iron-containing haem group. The iron attached to the haem molecule gives haemoglobin its bright red or red-purple colour. Haemoglobin is an unusual molecule, because in tissues with a high oxygen

Fig 6.21   *Red blood cells (as seen with a scanning electron microscope)*

concentration (eg lungs) it very rapidly picks up oxygen. In this state, it is called **oxyhaemoglobin**. The oxygen remains bound to the haemoglobin until it reaches tissues where the oxygen concentration is low. Oxygen is then released from haemoglobin and diffuses out of the red blood cells and through the capillary walls to the cells. Oxyhaemoglobin is bright red; haemoglobin is dark, almost purplish, red.

Haemoglobin + oxygen - = oxyhaemoglobin (red colour)

Haemoglobin without oxygen is purplish-red

Having a carrier molecule like haemoglobin increases the *speed* of oxygen movement into red cells, as well as the amount which can be carried. As soon as it enters the red blood cell, oxygen combines with haemoglobin. It is therefore removed from solution inside the cell. The concentration of dissolved gas inside the cell is thus kept very low, and a steep diffusion gradient is maintained between the cytoplasm of the red blood cells and the blood plasma.

Haemoglobin increases
• the speed of oxygen movement into the red cells
• the amount of oxygen which can be carried by the red cells

Red blood cells are also important in the transport of carbon dioxide. A small amount of carbon dioxide gas dissolves and is carried in the blood plasma. The remainder enters the red blood cells. Here it is rapidly converted by an enzyme into bicarbonate ions. Once formed, most of these bicarbonate ions diffuse back into the plasma. Thus most carbon dioxide is carried as bicarbonate in the blood plasma. A smaller proportion is carried bound to haemoglobin molecules. In this case, the compound formed is called **carboxyhaemoglobin**.

Most carbon dioxide is carried as bicarbonate ions in the blood plasma

Figure 6.22 summarises the important features of the red blood cell.

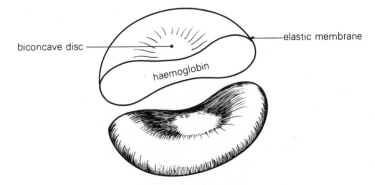

biconcave disc

haemoglobin

elastic membrane

Fig 6.22   *Important features of a red blood cell (diagrammatic)*

Life history of red blood cells

The red blood cells are produced in **red bone marrow**. In the adult, red bone marrow is found in the marrow cavity of short bones, for example ribs, sternum (breast-bone) and vertebrae. (In the young child red bone marrow is also found in the upper parts of the long bones of the limbs—see Chapter 18.) As the red blood cells mature in the bone marrow, their cytoplasm becomes more and more packed with haemoglobin and their nuclei disintegrate and disappear. At about this time the cells pass out of the bone marrow and enter the circulation.

Red blood cells are produced in the red bone marrow

As red cells mature, they lose their nuclei and become packed with haemoglobin

Red blood cells have an average life span of 4 months

On average, a red blood cell has a life span of about 4 months. From calculations based on the number of red blood cells per cubic millimetre (about 5 million/mm^3) and an average blood volume of 5 litres, it can be estimated that 1½ million red cells are destroyed (and new ones manufactured) every second. Damaged and broken red blood cells are removed from the circulation mainly in the liver and spleen. Special cells in these organs engulf the worn-out cells and break down their haemoglobin. In the spleen haemoglobin is broken down to iron-containing haem and globin. These breakdown products are then transferred to the liver via the bloodstream. In the liver, the haem portions are converted into **bile pigments** which are excreted, in the bile, into the small intestine. The iron from the haem is stored in the liver until it is recycled to the bone marrow. It is then used again to form more haemoglobin and red blood cells.

Red blood cells are broken down in the spleen and liver

White blood cells

The other group of blood cells are the white cells. White blood cells are frequently called **leucocytes** (from the Greek *leukos*, meaning white). They appear white, however, only when they are closely packed in a test-tube. If they can be viewed individually, they are transparent and colourless.

White blood cells are not nearly as numerous in the blood as red blood cells. (There are approximately 500 red blood cells to every one white blood cell.) It is quite easy, however, to recognise white blood cells in a blood smear prepared for examination under the microscope. This is because all white blood cells differ from red blood cells in two quite distinct ways:

All white blood cells contain nuclei

- All white blood cells have nuclei.
- No white blood cells have haemoglobin.

If we take our microscopic examination of the blood smear further, we can see also that there are several different types of white blood cells. Basically, white blood cells fall into two groups:

Two groups of white blood cells:
- granular leucocytes
- non-granular leucocytes

- One group whose cytoplasm appears dotted with tiny granules; these are called **granular leucocytes**.

- The other group whose cytoplasm does *not* contain these granules; these are called the **non-granular leucocytes**.

The most numerous (65 per cent of white blood cell population) and best understood of the granular leucocytes are the **neutrophils**. They are distinguished by the way in which their granules stain with particular chemical dyes. As we shall see in Chapter 7, neutrophils are scavenger cells—they have an important job moving to the site of an infection, and there engulfing and destroying foreign particles and organisms. This process is called **phagocytosis**.

Neutrophils engulf and destroy foreign particles and organisms

Much less is known about the other types of granular leucocytes—the **eosinophils** and **basophils**. These are much less numerous (only 1 to 2 per cent of the white blood cell population). They are recognised by the characteristic staining of their granules with particular dyes. Like the red blood cells, all the granular leucocytes are formed in the bone marrow.

The non-granular leucocytes are also important in the body's defence system. There are two types of non-granular leucocytes: **lymphocytes** and **monocytes**. Like the neutrophils, monocytes are scavenger cells. They engulf and destroy foreign organisms by the process of phagocytosis. Lymphocytes have a different and more complex role. They are the immune cells of the body's defence system. How they protect the body will be discussed in detail in Chapter 7. (A sub-type of the lymphocyte group of cells is the **plasma cell**, whose job is to produce antibodies.)

In contrast to the granular leucocytes, both lymphocytes and monocytes are formed in lymphatic tissue. (Table 6.2 summarises some distinctive characteristics of the different types of white blood cells and their functions.)

Granular leucocytes are formed in the bone marrow

Monocytes engulf and destroy foreign organisms

Lymphocytes
↓
plasma cells (produce antibodies)

Lymphocytes and monocytes are formed in the lymphatic tissue

Table 6.2   *Characteristics and functions of white blood cells*

Cell type	Name	Appearance	Where formed	Function (Chapter 7)
Granular leucocytes	Neutrophil		Bone marrow	Scavengers— phagocytosis
	Eosinophil		Bone marrow	Unclear—involved in immune processes
	Basophil		Bone marrow	Stores histamine (unclear)
Non-granular leucocytes	Lymphocyte		Lymphatic tissue	Immune responses
	(sub-type plasma cell)		Lymphatic tissue	Antibody production
	Monocyte		Lymphatic tissue	Scavengers— phagocytosis (may be involved in immune responses)

Platelets and blood clotting

Platelets are really just tiny cell fragments (roughly half the diameter of red blood cells) which have budded off from special very large cells in the bone marrow. They play an important part in blood clotting. The sequence of events in the clotting process can be summarised, in simple terms, as follows:

Platelets have an important role to play in blood clotting:
• platelets form an initial plug for the wound
• clotting activators are released from damaged tissue cells and from platelets
• clotting activators convert soluble plasma protein fibrinogen to fibrin

● Platelets stick to the damaged area and help to form an initial plug. (By this process alone, platelets can stop blood loss from small vessels.)

● When a blood vessel is cut open, or its lining damaged, special chemicals—**clotting activators**—are released from damaged tissue cells. Clotting activators are also released from platelets, which break up when they make contact with air, or any rough surface.

● Through a series of chemical reactions in the blood plasma these activators help to convert the soluble plasma protein **fibrinogen** to an insoluble protein **fibrin**.

Fibrin forms a network of threads across the wound

Platelets, red cells and white cells become trapped in the network

The whole complex = a clot

● Fibrin forms a network of threads across the wound.

● Platelets, red cells and white cells all become trapped in this meshwork—the whole complex forms a clot, which prevents further blood loss.

Chapter 7

Defending the body against disease

- Causes of disease
- Defence barriers on the body surface
- Lines of defence inside the body
- Immune memory and vaccination
- Rejection of foreign grafts
- 'Self' and 'non-self'
- Blood groups and transfusions
- The Rh factor

Our bodies are constantly under attack from factors in the environment. These factors are of two types—physical and biological. The physical factors are such things as heat, cold, dehydration and poisonous chemicals. The biological factors are living organisms, such as microorganisms, which are always trying to invade our bodies. We have a variety of mechanisms to help us cope with the physical factors we are exposed to. For example, special processes in our kidneys help us to conserve water and prevent dehydration; our skin forms a barrier to penetration of poisonous chemicals; special processes operate to control heat loss and maintain a constant body temperature. The biological factors present an equally great, if not greater, threat than the physical factors. Because of this we have a complex and varied system in our bodies to protect us from microbial invasion. This defence system is the subject of this chapter.

Our bodies are under attack from
- *physical factors*
- *biological factors*

Causes of disease

In a healthy individual, all the systems and organs of the body are working normally. If, for any reason, part of the body fails to work as it should, that organ is said to be diseased. In other words, a disease is any condition that prevents any part of the body from functioning normally.

Disease—any condition that prevents part of the body from functioning normally

All sorts of things can cause disease, but the body can defend itself against only some types of diseases. In this chapter, we shall discuss how the body defends itself, particularly against invading microorganisms. (Recently, scientists have also discovered that the body probably has special systems to protect itself from the growth of cancer cells.) Most other forms of disease, however, are beyond the scope of the body's defence system. Without medical intervention, these diseases are essentially irreversible. Table 7.1 shows the range of diseases classified according to their cause.

Infectious diseases

Like all living things, humans do not 'live alone'. A host of tiny organisms is always present in their environment—on the skin, the surfaces lining the digestive system, the respiratory passages and so on. Many of these organisms are a normal part of the human make-up. Under normal circumstances they cause no damage to their host.

Tiny organisms are a natural part of man's environment

Some organisms, though, invade the body and interfere with the way the body works, causing disease. These organisms that cause disease are called **pathogens**. The animal (or plant) in which they normally live is called their host. We shall see, later, some of the ways in which pathogens cause damage to their host.

Organisms that invade the body and cause disease are called pathogens

All diseases caused by living organisms are called **infectious diseases**. Obviously, if the organism that causes a disease can be transferred from

Infectious diseases— diseases caused by living organisms

Table 7.1 *Causes of disease*

Type of disease	Cause	Examples
Infectious disease	Viruses	Influenza, mumps, measles
	Bacteria	Tetanus, syphilis, tuberculosis
	Fungi	Thrush, tinea
	Animal parasites: protozoa, worms, arthropods	Malaria Hydatids, roundworms Fleas, lice
Cancer (tumour)	Abnormal multiplication of certain groups of cells	Lung cancer (Chapter 9)
Degeneration (ageing diseases)	Gradual breakdown of particular tissue structure	Atherosclerosis of blood vessels (Chapter 6)
Nutritional disease	Imbalance of dietary factors or deficiency of a dietary factor	Obesity (Chapter 10) Rickets, scurvy
Birth defects and genetic abnormalities	Errors in development of foetus in uterus	Cleft palate, thalidomide deformities (Chapter 17)
	Errors in structure of gene or chromosome (may be inherited)	Haemophilia
Chemical (metabolic) disease	Absence of enzyme or hormone	Diabetes (Chapter 13)
Physical and chemical damage	Heat, radiation, mechanical force (trauma)	Burns, cuts, fractures
	Poisoning	Alcoholism (Chapter 16) Drug overdose (Chapter 14)
Mental illness	Many factors may contribute	Depression, anxiety, tension (Chapter 14)

an infected person to somebody else, that disease can be spread, or passed on. Some diseases are passed on more easily than others. Those diseases that are passed on most easily are diseases that are spread directly from one person to another. For example, the influenza virus is spread directly from the nasal passages of an infected person, in the droplets of a sneeze, to the nasal passages of another person. Infectious diseases that are spread directly from person to person are called **contagious diseases**.

Other infectious diseases are not contagious. For example, the blood disease malaria cannot be spread directly from one person to another. It is spread by a mosquito which sucks blood from an infected person and then carries the malaria organisms in its mouthparts. Another person may be infected when bitten by the disease-carrying mosquito. In this situation, the mosquito is called a **vector** (carrier) of disease.

Infectious diseases may be caused by several different types of pathogens.

Contagious diseases—diseases that are spread directly from one person to another

Malaria (spread by mosquito) is an infectious, but not a contagious, disease

Vector—carrier of disease

Bacteria

Bacteria are microscopic, single-celled organisms. They are neither plants nor animals, but form another group of organisms called protists. They are able to extract material from their surroundings to make the energy required for living.

Many bacteria are useful to man and other organisms

There are many different types of bacteria, and only a relatively small number of them cause disease. Most bacteria are, in fact, useful. Some live in the soil and break down dead animal matter, leaves and litter into simple chemicals which can be used again by plants. Others make certain vital chemicals which are needed by plants. We make use of bacteria in the manufacture of foods such as cheese and vinegar.

Pathogenic bacteria usually depend on their host for ready-made food substances, which they need for growth and division

Disease-causing bacteria are pathogens. Some pathogenic bacteria can survive for quite long periods outside the body, but all of them normally depend on their host for ready-made food substances, which they require for growth and division. There are many types of disease-causing bacteria. Some of these can be recognised under the microscope by their distinctive size and shape. Figure 7.1 illustrates a few bacteria that cause disease in humans.

Disease-causing bacteria enter the body through
• epithelial surfaces of the digestive and respiratory systems
• broken skin

How do bacteria cause disease? To cause disease, bacteria must first enter the body. Most of them do this through the mouth or nose, and then through the epithelial surfaces of the digestive or respiratory systems. If the skin surface is cut or broken, bacteria may gain entry this way, too. Different bacteria often prefer to live in different particular organs of the body. This may be because they need certain chemicals found only in particular tissues. Under ideal conditions bacteria reproduce very

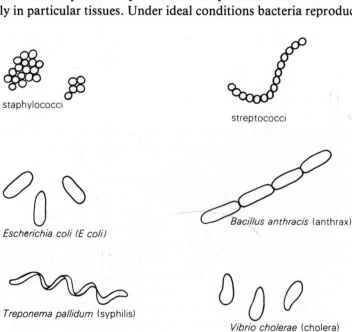

staphylococci

streptococci

Escherichia coli (E coli)

Bacillus anthracis (anthrax)

Treponema pallidum (syphilis)

Vibrio cholerae (cholera)

Fig 7.1   *Some disease-causing bacteria*

rapidly by simple fission. As a result, huge numbers of bacteria can be produced in the body in a matter of hours. There are two main ways in which bacteria cause disease in organs and tissues. First, they may produce chemicals, called **toxins**, which are poisonous to their hosts. (The bacterium that causes the disease tetanus produces a chemical, tetanus toxin, which paralyses all the muscles of the body.) Second, bacteria may actually invade and live in cells. When they do this, they interfere with the normal activities of the cell and may cause cell death. Large numbers of dead or injured cells in a tissue or organ will cause disease for the body as a whole. (The bacterium that causes tuberculosis is an example of one that invades and lives inside cells of the body.)

Bacteria cause disease by
- *producing toxins*
- *invading and living in cells*

Viruses

Viruses are entirely different from bacteria. They are very much smaller particles, which can be seen only with the help of an electron microscope. Viruses are thought to be on the border-line between living and non-living. They *can* reproduce themselves, but their chemical make-up is so simple that it is quite impossible for them to do so unless they are inside the living cell of a host. In the process of reproduction, thousands of new viral particles are produced, and as they burst out of the cell, they destroy their host cell. For this reason, unlike bacteria, viruses are always associated with disease—measles, mumps, rubella, poliomyelitis, smallpox, warts, influenza and the common cold are all viral diseases. Viruses also cause disease in plants.

Viruses are much smaller than bacteria

Viruses can reproduce themselves only when they are inside a living cell

Viruses always cause disease

Fungi

Fungi (simple plants) are much less important pathogens than bacteria and viruses. However, they do cause diseases such as thrush, tinea and ringworm.

Fungi and animal parasites may cause disease

Animal parasites

The larger pathogens, which are members of the animal kingdom, are generally called parasites. Their bodies are so adapted that they depend on their host for their source of food and shelter.

The smallest of the animal parasites are single-celled animals, members of a group of organisms known as protozoa. They are responsible for some serious diseases in humans, for example amoebic dysentery, malaria and sleeping sickness.

Amongst the larger animal parasites, many species of tapeworm, roundworm, and flukes may cause serious diseases in humans. Insects (fleas, mites and lice) can also cause skin diseases and anaemia.

Animal parasites:
- *protozoa*
- *tapeworm*
- *roundworm*
- *flukes*
- *fleas, mites, lice*

Treatment of infectious diseases

Until the introduction of sulphanilamide in 1936, attempts to combat infectious disease with chemical agents had met with only very limited success. As a result of the discovery and widespread use of sulphonamide drugs, there was a sharp drop in the death rate for the treatable infectious diseases.

Antibiotics are chemical substances, produced by bacteria or fungi, which suppress the growth of other microorganisms and eventually destroy them

This discovery was followed, in the 1940s, by the introduction of **antibiotics** into clinical medicine. Antibiotics are chemical substances, produced by various types of microorganisms (eg bacteria, fungi), which suppress the growth of other microorganisms and may eventually destroy them. The first antibiotic to be discovered was penicillin. It was discovered almost by accident, in 1929, by the British bacteriologist Alexander Fleming. Some mould spores floated into his laboratory through an open window and landed on an agar plate on which the bacteria staphylococci were growing. To his surprise, as the mould grew, the bacteria were quickly destroyed. The mould was subsequently identified as *Penicillium notatum* and, as a result, the active substance was called penicillin. However, it was not until more than ten years later that a group of biochemists at Oxford University, under the leadership of an Australian, Howard Florey, succeeded in isolating and purifying this chemical, so that it could be used in injections.

The number of known antibiotics now runs into hundreds, and more than forty are useful in treating infectious diseases. Different antibiotics are effective against different microorganisms, and the choice of antibiotic depends on the particular organism causing the disease, as well as on the site of the disease in the body.

The use of antibiotics has two short-comings:
• antibiotics do not destroy viruses
• some types of bacteria readily develop resistance to antibiotics

However, it must be understood that not all infectious diseases can be successfully treated with antibiotics. The range of antibiotics available today is reasonably effective against most bacterial and fungal diseases. However, antibiotics do not destroy viruses. There are, at present, no drugs in general use which effectively treat viral diseases. The control of viral diseases depends largely on preventive measures such as vaccination programmes (see later). Another drawback to the use of antibiotics is that some types of bacteria develop drug resistant strains very rapidly. Every time a new antibiotic is developed, new resistant bacteria develop, so that further drugs have to be developed. For this reason, antibiotics should always be used in a careful and limited way.

Defence barriers on the body surface

Microorganisms are constantly trying to invade our bodies. We survive only because we have a very effective defence system. The body's defence system has two major tasks. It prevents microbes from entering the body, and it kills or inactivates any microbes that do gain entry to the body.

First we shall see how the body surfaces prevent microbes from entering the body.

Skin

You are probably already aware that bacteria can gain entry to the body when the skin surface is cut or broken. (That is the basis for the practice of applying antiseptic preparations to cuts, scratches and grazes.) We shall now see how, under normal circumstances, the skin is able to prevent microorganisms from entering the body.

Figure 7.2 shows the structure of skin viewed under a light microscope. As you can see, skin is composed of two layers:

Skin = epidermis + dermis

- an outer layer, epidermis
- an inner layer, dermis.

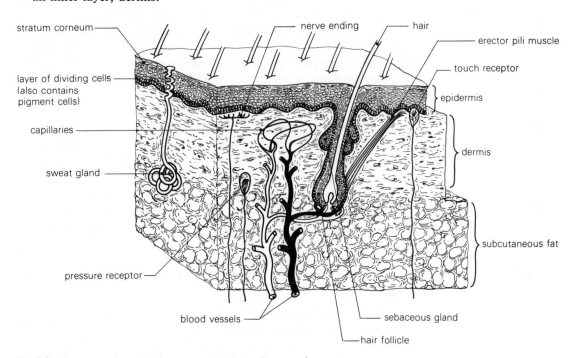

Fig 7.2 *Structure of the skin (as seen with a light microscope)*

Epidermis

The epidermis is principally responsible for protection of the body. It provides a tough, waterproof but flexible surface over all the body, protecting the tissues beneath from mechanical damage, ultraviolet rays in sunlight, and desiccation, as well as from bacterial infection.

The epidermis is made up of many layers of epithelial cells. (You will remember from Chapter 2 that epithelial cells cover all body surfaces.) The epithelial cells of the skin are specially arranged for their job of protecting the body. At the bottom of the epidermis is a layer of cells which are constantly dividing. The new cells produced by these divisions are

Epidermis:
- tough
- waterproof
- flexible
- protects lower tissues from mechanical damage, ultraviolet light, desiccation
- protects tissues from bacterial infection

pushed upwards towards the surface. As this happens they become flattened and begin to accumulate a tough protein called **keratin** in their cytoplasm. As they are pushed still closer towards the surface, the epithelial cells die. The dead cells, almost completely filled with keratin, form a horny, tough, water-repellant layer called the **stratum corneum**. In areas like the soles of the feet and the palms of the hands, the stratum corneum is much thicker than it is in other parts of the body. Because of the constant wear on the body surface, the dead cells of the horny outer layer are constantly being shed. The division of cells at the base of the epidermis replaces those cells that are shed.

Another type of epidermal cell is the pigment cell, which is responsible for producing the pigment **melanin**. All people have some melanin in their skin—the content of melanin in the epidermis gives different races of people different skin colour, black, brown, yellow and white. When white skin is exposed to the ultraviolet rays of sunlight, the pigment cells make more melanin pigment. This is what gives skin a tan.

Dermis

The dermis has quite a different role from the outer epidermis. It is a loose connective tissue layer with a variable number of fat cells which provide padding and help to reduce heat loss from the body. Some important structures are embedded in this connective tissue:

- Capillaries, which supply the skin with its necessary food and oxygen and remove waste products. In addition, they have a very important role in heat regulation. When muscles in the walls of the arterioles relax, more blood flows through the capillaries, and more heat is radiated or lost from the body. When body heat must be conserved, the muscles of the arterioles contract, blood flow is reduced and less heat is lost.

- Sweat glands, which are another special structure designed to regulate heat loss. Sweat glands are coiled tubes lined with special epithelial cells. These cells take up fluid (and some salts, particularly sodium chloride) from the tissue fluid and secrete it into a duct which leads to the skin surface. The evaporation of this fluid (sweat) on the surface of the skin cools the skin. (Sweat glands are also richly supplied with capillaries, which aid in heat loss.)

- Sensory nerve endings ('sense organs'), which send impulses to the brain, resulting in sensations of touch, pain, heat and cold, thus keeping us informed of changes in our environment. Some of these 'sense organs' are shown in Fig 7.2. Their function is explained more fully in Chapter 15.

- Hair follicles. Humans have relatively very little hair. However, the thin layer of body hair they have does play a minor role in temperature control. Hair follicles are made up of epidermal cells that have invaded the dermis and the subcutaneous tissue (tissue under the skin

Surface cells in the epidermis accumulate keratin

Stratum corneum—dead epithelial cells filled with keratin

Dead cells are constantly being shed from the skin surface

Other types of cells in the epidermis produce the tan pigment, melanin

Dermis:
- provides padding
- reduces heat loss

Capillaries regulate heat loss from the body

Sweat glands aid heat loss from the body

Sensory nerve endings keep us informed of changes in our environment

Hair follicles produce hairs, which help to regulate heat loss

layer). Inside the follicle, the epidermal cells divide, become impregnated with keratin and die, to form the **hair shaft**. The continuous addition of new cells at the base of the follicle causes the hair to grow. Associated with each hair follicle is a muscle which raises the hair when it contracts. When a large number of hairs become erect, a layer of air is trapped just above the surface of the skin. This reduces the amount of heat lost from the body surface.

● Sebaceous glands, which open into the hair follicle. They produce an oily secretion which lubricates the hair and helps to keep the skin surface flexible and water repellent. It is thought that the oily secretions also have antiseptic properties; that is, they can rid the skin of pathogenic bacteria. Exactly how this antiseptic ability operates is not known, but it is clear that these secretions help to form a chemical barrier to bacteria, in addition to the physical barrier of skin structure.

Sebaceous glands produce an oily secretion which
● lubricates the hair
● helps to keep the skin surface flexible
● makes the skin surface water repellent
● provides an antiseptic barrier to bacteria

Mucous membranes

As long as it remains unbroken, the skin forms a very effective barrier to invading bacteria. The other 'external' surfaces of the body—the respiratory and alimentary tracts, and the urinary and reproductive systems—are far more common pathways of entry of microorganisms into the body. They too, however, have some mechanisms to reduce the entry of foreign particles and remove those which do gain entry. These mechanisms are of two types: physical barriers and chemical barriers.

Physical barriers   One of the most common pathways of entry into the body for bacteria is via the respiratory passages. As we shall see in Chapter 8, the respiratory system has its own special traps to reduce infection. First, the air passages in the nose are narrow and curved, so that the movement of air is slowed as it enters the body. Second, the lining of the nasal passages is covered with sticky mucus and nasal hairs. Over 90 per cent of microorganisms entering the nose are trapped by these processes and later expelled in the mucus.

External surfaces of the respiratory, urinary, reproductive and digestive systems are protected by
● physical barriers
● chemical barriers

Physical barriers in the respiratory system:
● air passages in nose are narrow and curved
● lining of nasal passages is covered with sticky mucus and nasal hairs
● trachea is covered with beating cilia and mucus

Microorganisms and other foreign particles that escape these barriers may be caught by other traps further along the respiratory passages. As we shall see, again in Chapter 8, the surfaces of the trachea (wind-pipe) and bronchi have a covering of fine hair-like projections called cilia. The cilia beat in an organised way, creating waves of movement in the mucus which covers the lining of the respiratory passages. Particles that become trapped in the surface mucus are thus swept upwards towards the mouth, from where they can be expelled from the body or swallowed.

Another very important way in which all the epithelial surfaces are kept clean is by washing or flushing processes. Tears, saliva, bile and even urine and the contents of the alimentary canal remove organisms lodging on the surfaces of organs by their flushing action. When the flow of any of these fluids is stopped, infection develops remarkably

All epithelial surfaces are cleaned by washing processes

quickly—particularly in the eyes if tears are not produced, and in the bladder if urine is not produced or if the bladder is not emptied at regular intervals.

In addition to these barriers, sneezing, coughing and vomiting all help to eliminate foreign objects from the respiratory passages and the stomach.

Sneezing, coughing and vomiting help to clear the respiratory passages and stomach of foreign material

Chemical barriers We have seen already that the skin possesses chemical properties which help to destroy pathogenic bacteria. Other body surfaces have similar properties. The acid secretions of the stomach destroy most bacteria—few survive to reach the intestine. The vagina, too, is an acid environment which reduces the growth of bacteria. Tears and saliva contain special proteins called lysozymes, which make it easier for white blood cells to engulf foreign particles (see the next section). The important barriers of defence on the body surfaces are summarised in Fig 7.3.

Chemical barriers:
- antiseptic oils in the skin
- tears in the eyes
- saliva in the mouth
- acid in the vagina and stomach

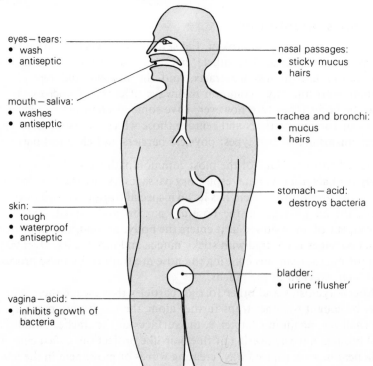

eyes — tears:
- wash
- antiseptic

mouth — saliva:
- washes
- antiseptic

skin:
- tough
- waterproof
- antiseptic

vagina — acid:
- inhibits growth of bacteria

nasal passages:
- sticky mucus
- hairs

trachea and bronchi:
- mucus
- hairs

stomach — acid:
- destroys bacteria

bladder:
- urine 'flusher'

Fig 7.3 *Barriers of defence on the body surfaces*

Lines of defence inside the body

If microorganisms do penetrate one of the body surfaces, the special defence systems inside the body can mount a very organised and systematic attack to destroy them. In the battle with the invading microorganisms, the body has a number of lines of defence. These are summarised in Fig 7.4.

As you can see from Fig 7.4, the body's defence processes are basically of two types, general or non-specific processes and specific processes. Non-specific processes are designed to combat *any* invading microorganisms. They include the white blood cells which engulf bacteria as they enter the tissues, the lymphatic system with its lymph nodes, and the spleen.

Non-specific defence processes—processes designed to defend the body against any invading organism

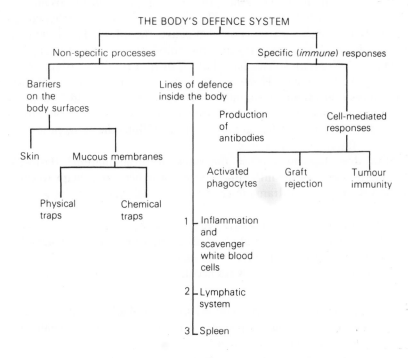

Fig 7.4 *Summary of the body's lines of defence*

Some very powerful microbes can overwhelm the general defence processes and so survive in the body. Often, however, the body develops special defence mechanisms to combat these particular microbes. These special processes are called **immune responses**. The best-known immune responses are those that involve the production of antibodies. There are also immune cells, which can recognise and destroy foreign organisms or cells. We shall consider the non-specific processes first.

Specific defence processes—immune responses specifically designed to combat particular microorganisms

Non-specific processes

To understand how some of the non-specific processes work, let us examine what may happen when common skin bacteria gain entry to the body through a wound.

The inflammatory response

When the skin is broken and bacteria enter the body, cells and tissues are injured. As a result of this injury, the tissues in the affected area become inflamed. We are all familiar with the signs of inflammation—the affected area becomes hot, reddened, swollen and painful, and as a result of these changes normal function may be impaired. But these uncomfortable signs of inflammation are actually a vital part of the body's repair and defence system. Let us see why this is so.

When cells are injured or killed, they release special chemicals into the tissue fluid which bathes them. The chemical substances released are probably the same, regardless of what causes the injury. This is why the signs of inflammation are the same, regardless of the cause of the injury.

Many different chemicals have been shown to produce inflammation when applied to tissues. However, probably the most important of these substances is **histamine**. Histamine is present in a loosely held form in the cells of many tissues, and it is released from these cells in response to injury. Tiny amounts of histamine, if scratched into the skin, produce a typical inflammatory response.

How does histamine cause the signs of inflammation? Basically, histamine produces the inflammatory response because it helps to cause some very rapid and dramatic changes in blood vessels in the affected area:

(i)   First, blood vessels in the affected area dilate, so that blood supply to the injured area is increased. (This is the cause of the redness and heat we experience in inflammation.)

(ii) Second, the blood vessel walls become more permeable. This results in:

- Passage of plasma proteins across the wall and into tissue spaces (some of the plasma proteins are very important in repair processes, as well as in defence)
- Movement of scavenger white blood cells out of blood vessels and into tissue spaces.

Scavenger white blood cells, which squeeze their way out of the blood vessels in the inflamed area, have a very important role. In the initial stages of the response, the white blood cells are mainly neutrophils. Two properties of neutrophils make them particularly important if the inflammation results from bacterial infection. First, neutrophils can move towards the site of an infection. They move through the tissue spaces by a gliding motion called amoeboid movement. (This was discussed in Chapter 1.) They are attracted towards the site of the infection by chemicals released from bacteria or from dead or injured cells. This movement in the direction of particular chemicals is known as **chemotaxis**.

Second, neutrophils can engulf foreign organisms and destroy them inside their cytoplasm. This ability to engulf foreign particles is called **phagocytosis**. Because of these two properties, neutrophils are sometimes called scavenger cells. They circulate in the blood until they reach an infected area, and then leave the blood vessels and move through the tissues, engulfing any foreign particles they encounter. Figures 7.5a and 7.5b show how neutrophils and other phagocytic white blood cells engulf and destroy foreign particles.

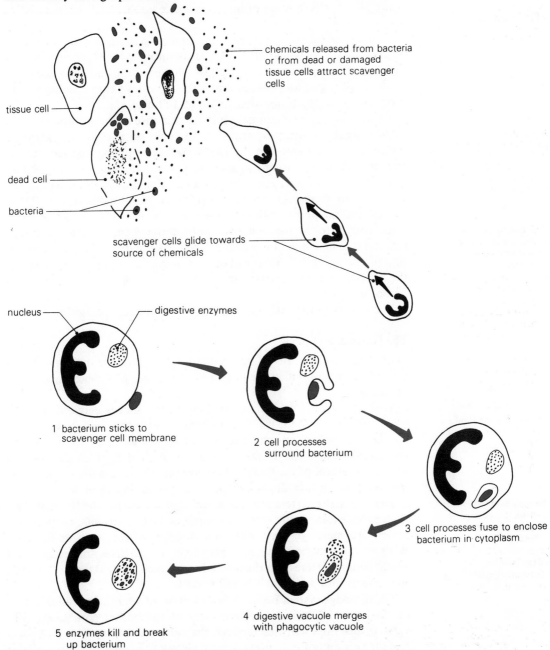

Fig 7.5 *How phagocytic white blood cells engulf and destroy foreign particles*
(a) Chemotaxis — movement of scavenger cells towards invading bacteria
(b) Scavenger cells engulf and destroy invading bacteria

As neutrophils and monocytes digest the bacteria they have engulfed, they also are destroyed

Accumulations of dead white blood cells form pus

Inflammation may be harmful to the body

Generally, inflammation is an important mechanism of defence

First line of defence—protection of body by white blood cells:
• neutrophils
• monocytes

The lymphatic system transports tissue fluid back into the circulatory system

The lymphatic system removes
• fluid
• protein
• fats
• dead cells
• foreign objects
from the tissue spaces

Inside the neutrophil, the bacteria may continue to multiply and destroy the neutrophil, or the enzymes of the neutrophil may completely destroy all the bacteria. However, in the process of killing the bacteria, the white blood cells are usually destroyed too. Accumulations of dead white blood cells in areas of infection make up much of the material we know as pus.

In the later stages of an infection, another scavenger white blood cell appears in the inflamed area. This is the monocyte. Monocytes behave in much the same way as neutrophils—they move towards the site of infection and engulf and destroy any foreign particles they encounter. One monocyte can engulf and destroy up to 100 bacteria.

As we have said, inflammation is the response of the connective tissue of any organ to injury of any sort. In some situations this reaction is harmful—inflammation in the joints may be crippling and painful; inflammation in vital organs such as the brain, kidneys or heart may even cause death. However, generally, inflammation is a helpful reaction, and it acts as an important mechanism of defence. By increasing the blood supply and the permeability of blood vessels, not only are white blood cells brought to the site, but also antibacterial chemicals and antibodies (see later). The white blood cells of the inflammatory reaction form the first line of defence. The spread of most bacterial infections is limited by the activity of the monocytes and neutrophils which operate in this first line of defence.

The events in the inflammatory response are summarised in Fig 7.6.

The lymphatic system

Should the bacteria of an infected wound overwhelm the white blood cells at the site of entry, the body has other lines of defence against the invaders.

You will recall from Chapter 6 that all the spaces between cells are filled with tissue fluid, which is in balance with the fluid which makes up blood plasma. You may also recall that not all tissue fluid re-enters the circulation through the capillaries. Although it carries only a small proportion of the body's fluid volume, the lymphatic system is extremely important in the body's defence system. We shall now see why.

The lymphatic system is really a drainage system for the tissue spaces. It removes excess fluid, as well as particles such as protein and fat molecules, fragments of dead cells, and foreign objects such as bacteria. Without the lymphatic system, these types of particles and excess fluid would soon interfere with the normal movement of fluid (and other vital substances) into and out of blood vessels.

The drainage system begins as a fine mesh of small thin-walled lymph capillaries which branch through most of the body's soft tissues (Fig 7.7). Tissue fluid diffuses through the walls of the capillaries to form lymph. Lymph is a colourless or pale yellow fluid, which is very similar in composition to tissue fluid and blood plasma. Lymph also contains a certain type of white blood cell, the lymphocytes (see later).

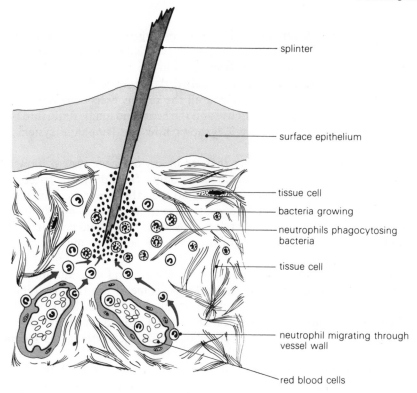

Fig 7.6 *White blood cells form the first line of defence against invading microorganisms*

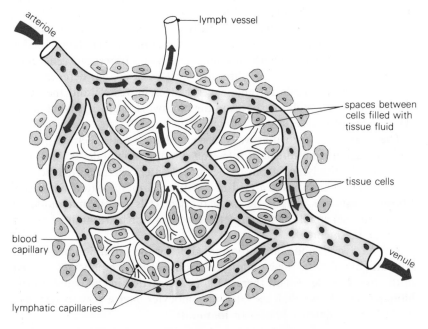

Fig 7.7 *Relationships between cells, capillaries, tissue fluid and lymph*

The tiny lymph capillaries join to form larger vessels, which receive other branches all along their length. They finally join up to form two main ducts which empty into large veins in the lower part of the neck. The larger of these main ducts is called the thoracic duct—it receives lymph from most of the body and all the organs except the heart and lungs. The remainder of the body, and the heart and lungs, drain into the right lymphatic duct. Figure 7.8 shows how the lymphatic system is arranged.

It is important to remember that, as in any drainage system, flow in the lymphatic system is in one direction only—from the tissue spaces to the large veins and the heart. There is no special pump in the lymphatic system. Lymphatic vessels, like veins, have thin walls and many valves. Lymph moves along lymph vessels as a result of tissue fluid pressure and, more importantly, as a result of the pumping action of muscles of the limbs and trunk.

Bacteria that cannot be destroyed by white blood cells multiply and spread in the fluid spaces between cells. As some of this fluid is drained into the lymph capillaries, bacteria, too, enter the lymphatics. However, their passage into the bloodstream and spread around the entire body is often prevented by a second barrier in the defence system, the **lymph nodes**.

There are clusters or chains of lymph nodes along all the larger lymphatic vessels. They are particularly numerous in regions like the groin, the armpit and the neck, where they guard the organs of the trunk from entry of bacterial infection. Almost without exception, tissue fluid picked up by the lymph capillaries passes through at least one (and often many) nodes before entering the circulation.

Figure 7.9 shows the structure of a lymph node and helps to explain how it serves its particular role in defence. As you can see, lymph nodes are made up of a meshwork of connective tissue fibres and cells. Suspended in this meshwork of fibres are clusters of special defence cells. Lymph enters the node through several afferent vessels and then percolates slowly through the spaces in the meshwork, before leaving in the efferent lymphatic vessels.

There are three particular ways in which lymph nodes help to protect the body against the spread of infection. First, lymph nodes act as filtering beds. As the lymph from tissue spaces enters the node, particulate matter and bacteria are trapped in the fibrous mesh. Attached to this fibrous mesh are phagocytic or scavenger cells called **macrophages**. These cells can engulf and destroy the particles which are strained out by the node meshwork.

Second, lymph nodes are important sites for the formation of particular white blood cells, the lymphocytes. Some of the lymphocytes formed in the lymph node remain there. Others are carried in the lymph to the bloodstream. As we shall see later, lymphocytes have a very special task in the specific defence system or **immunity**.

The thoracic duct receives lymph from most of the body and all organs except the heart and the lungs

Flow in the lymphatic system occurs in only one direction—to the large veins and the heart

Lymphatic vessels have
• thin walls
• many valves

Bacteria in the tissue spaces may enter the lymphatic vessels. Here the lymph nodes act as a second barrier

Lymph nodes are particularly numerous in the groin, armpit and neck

Lymph nodes contain
• clusters of special defence cells
• a network of connective tissue fibres

Lymph nodes protect the body against infection by
• trapping particles and bacteria in the fibrous mesh of the lymph nodes and engulfing them

• producing white blood cells (lymphocytes) which act to defend the body in specific ways

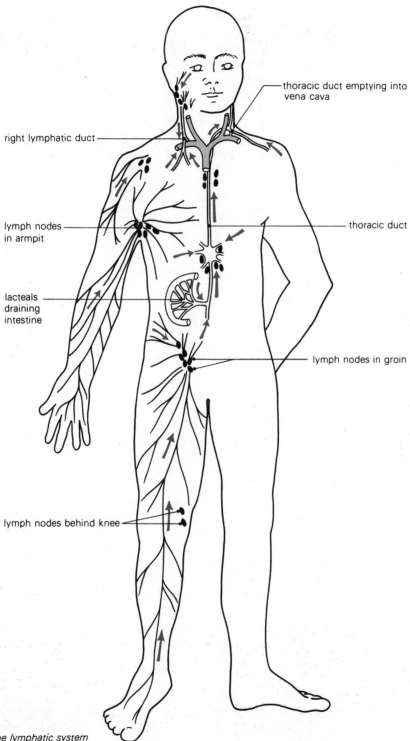

thoracic duct emptying into
vena cava

right lymphatic duct

lymph nodes
in armpit

thoracic duct

lacteals
draining
intestine

lymph nodes in groin

lymph nodes behind knee

Fig 7.8 *The lymphatic system*

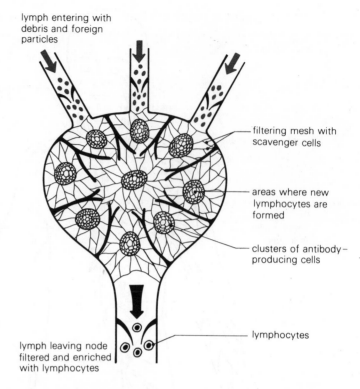

lymph entering with
debris and foreign
particles

filtering mesh with
scavenger cells

areas where new
lymphocytes are
formed

clusters of antibody-
producing cells

lymphocytes

lymph leaving node
filtered and enriched
with lymphocytes

Fig 7.9 *Structure of a lymph node*

- allowing direct contact between invading microorganisms and immune cells lining the channels of the nodes

Third, lymph nodes are very important in the body's defence system because they allow direct contact of the special immune or defence cells with any invading microorganism. Clusters of immune cells line the channels through which lymph (and any foreign matter) must pass in the node. When particular microorganisms reach the node, some of these immune cells respond by producing **antibodies** (chemicals which help to destroy the pathogens). We shall see, soon, why these special processes are the most efficient of any of the body's defence systems.

Performing all these vital tasks, the lymph nodes are an important second line of defence in the protection of the body. Perhaps now you can understand the significance of swollen and painful glands in the armpit, which may accompany an infected finger; or in the neck, accompanying a sore throat.

Bacteria can be destroyed in the spleen, which acts as a blood filter

Even if bacteria survive their passage through numerous lymph nodes and reach the bloodstream, another system exists for their removal in the spleen.

The spleen

The spleen is a poorly understood organ—it can be removed without any apparent harm to the patient. Its structure is similar to the lymph nodes, but with the difference that its special task is to filter blood. Scavenger cells called macrophages in the spleen capture and destroy any foreign matter they detect, and, in addition, they assist the liver in removing worn-out red blood cells from the circulation.

Macrophages in the spleen
- engulf and destroy foreign particles
- remove worn-out red blood cells

Specific processes

Up to this stage, we have been discussing the non-specific or general system of defence. This system is normally quite effective in controlling the more common and relatively mild pathogens which invade the body. However, some invading organisms are far more powerful and damaging. This may be because they produce toxins which kill phagocytes and prevent them from engulfing the invader, or because they have special properties which allow them to survive and multiply, even inside the phagocytic or scavenger cells which engulf them. When these sorts of aggressive pathogens threaten the body, the non-specific processes are often overwhelmed. Other special defence processes exist, however, which can provide specific protection against many of these agents. These processes are known, in general terms, as immune responses.

Some invading organisms
- produce toxins which kill phagocytes
- have properties which allow them to survive and multiply inside phagocyte cells

The body is protected against more damaging pathogens by specific processes

Specific defence processes are called immune responses

Two special features of immune responses make them effective in combating attack by very harmful bacteria:

Immune responses
- are individually designed to combat particular pathogens
- have a memory

- Immune responses are individually designed to be effective against a particular pathogen.

- Immune responses have a *memory*. This means that we rarely suffer twice from diseases such as measles, mumps or chickenpox. On its first encounter with a particular pathogen, the immune system becomes 'programmed' to resist infection with that pathogen. It then retains this ability in its immune memory. If the same pathogen attacks the body at a later stage, the immune system is prepared to provide protection much more rapidly, often before the pathogen has been able to multiply sufficiently to overwhelm the host's defence system.

Let us now see how these special immune processes work. We have already said that immune responses are specific. For example, after an attack of measles, we are resistant to further measles infections, but have no protection from other virus infections such as mumps or polio. Why is this so? How does the immune defence system distinguish between such apparently similar microorganisms?

The immune defence system can distinguish between apparently similar organisms that cause different diseases

The body is able to distinguish between different invading pathogens because all microorganisms (and cells) have, on their surfaces, particular large molecules. These molecules are called **antigens**. An antigen is any substance that can cause an animal to produce antibodies. Each different microorganism has different antigens. Antigens are usually large protein or carbohydrate molecules. In an infection, antigens of the invading organism cause the immune system to produce antibodies. Antibodies combine with antigen, but only with the antigen that caused their production. We can say, then, that each antibody is specific to its antigen.

An antigen is any substance that can cause an animal to produce antibodies

Each antibody produced in the body is specific to a particular antigen

Microorganisms are recognised in the body by their surface antigens

How do antibodies act?

We have already said that antibodies combine with the antigen that stimulated their production. Antibodies are very large protein molecules. They combine with their antigens in a way similar to that in which enzymes combine with their substrates (see Chapter 3).

The combination of antibody with antigen interferes with the spread of the pathogen in one of a number of ways. If the organism is one that causes disease by producing a toxin, the antibody may combine with the toxin and so inactivate it. (An antibody that acts in this way is called an **antitoxin**.) Other antibodies combine with antigens on the surface of bacteria or viruses. This may result in one of a number of outcomes. First, antigen–antibody combination may cause numbers of microorganisms (or cells) to clump together (or agglutinate). This may make the clump of microorganisms easier for the phagocytes to engulf. (How this clumping together may occur is shown diagrammatically in Fig 7.10.) Second, antibodies which combine with particular antigens on the surface of bacteria may cause the bacteria to stick more readily to the cell membrane of phagocytic cells. As we saw earlier, bacteria must first stick to the membrane of a phagocyte before they can be engulfed and destroyed. These antibodies therefore help phagocytosis. Third, some antibodies, when they combine with surface antigens or bacteria, can actually cause weakening or damage to the wall of the bacterium. It seems that in this case the combination of antibody with antigen stimulates special enzymes which digest tiny holes in the membrane of the invading organisms. As a result, the bacteria are killed and fall apart.

How are antibodies made?

The existence of antibodies in blood plasma, which can provide protection against infectious diseases, has been accepted for many decades. Exactly *which* cells produce the antibodies has been discovered only much more recently. There is still tremendous debate about *how* these cells are instructed to make particular antibodies.

The human body is capable of producing antibodies to literally thousands of antigens, even to artificial or experimental ones—chemicals to which the body could never expect to be exposed in normal life. It is clear, therefore, that the production of antibodies to a particular antigen involves several steps:

- First, the antigen must somehow be recognised as foreign by the body's immune system.
- Second, the antibody-producing cells must be stimulated to produce the corresponding antibody.
- Third, the antibody-producing cells must produce and release this antibody.

More is now known about the last of these steps, so we shall start by discussing this one. By a variety of experimental techniques it has been

Antibody–antigen complexes are similar to enzyme–substrate complexes

Antibodies may
- combine with toxins produced by bacteria
- combine with the surface antigens of bacteria or viruses

Antibodies may
- cause organisms or cells to clump together (agglutination)
- bind to the surface of bacteria so that the bacteria stick more readily to phagocytic cells
- bind to the surface of bacteria and damage or weaken the bacterial wall

Steps in antibody production:
- the antigen must be recognised as foreign to the immune system
- the antibody-producing cells must be stimulated to produce antibody
- antibody-producing cells produce and release antibody

1 antibody may combine with a toxin and inactivate it

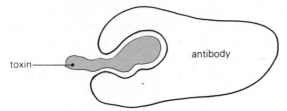

2 antigen–antibody combinations may cause numbers of microorganisms (or cells) to clump together (agglutinate)

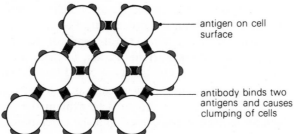

antigen on cell surface

antibody binds two antigens and causes clumping of cells

3 combination of antibody with antigens on the surface of bacteria may cause them to stick more readily to the cell membrane of phagocytes

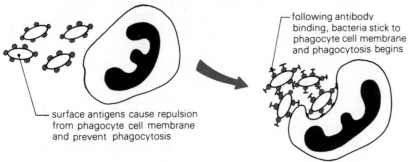

following antibody binding, bacteria stick to phagocyte cell membrane and phagocytosis begins

surface antigens cause repulsion from phagocyte cell membrane and prevent phagocytosis

4 antibody combines with surface antigen on foreign cell

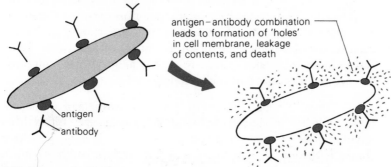

antigen–antibody combination leads to formation of 'holes' in cell membrane, leakage of contents, and death

antigen

antibody

Fig 7.10 *How antibodies act*

Antibodies are produced
by plasma cells

Plasma cells are present in
the blood, lymph nodes
and spleen

proved beyond reasonable doubt that antibodies are made by a special
type of white blood cell called the **plasma cell**. Plasma cells circulate in
the blood as well as in the lymph nodes and spleen, where they are present in large numbers. They are fairly large cells and are easily recognised
under a light microscope or an electron microscope because they are
specially designed for their task of antibody production. (Antibodies are
proteins, so, as you would expect, plasma cells are very richly supplied
with endoplasmic reticulum in which the proteins are made; see Chapter
2. Viewed under an electron microscope, it is often possible also to see
granules composed of antibody awaiting secretion.)

How antigen is recognised in the body, and how plasma cells are
stimulated to produce antibody, are much less well understood. Some
important facts about the process have been established, however, by a
huge variety of experiments. On the basis of these, a general theory was
developed by Sir MacFarlane Burnet, at the Walter and Eliza Hall In-
stitute in Melbourne. His theory is called the 'clonal selection theory'.

Clonal selection theory
attempts to explain the
sequence of events in
which antigens are
recognised and the
corresponding antibody is
produced

The clonal selection theory is really an hypothesis based on established
scientific knowledge. It attempts to explain the sequence of events in
which an antigen is recognised and the corresponding antibody is produced. No hypothesis can really be *proved* correct, but nearly all the
experiments conducted since the theory was first proposed in 1960 have
added support to the theory, and none have been able to disprove it.

As we have already said, antibodies are formed in plasma cells. However, many experiments have shown that antigen does not stimulate the
plasma cell directly to produce antibody. The antigen cannot, therefore,
instruct the plasma cell to make an antibody to fit it exactly. Another
white blood cell in the immune system, the lymphocyte, recognises (or is
sensitive to) the antigen and sets off the production of the required
antibody.

Lymphocytes recognise the
antigen and set off the
production of the antibody

The sequence of events in the formation of antibodies, based on the
widely accepted clonal selection theory, is summarised in Fig 7.11. The
following points are numbered to match those in the illustration:

Each lymphocyte has
DNA, which codes for one
particular antibody

Some of the antibodies
produced by each
lymphocyte are attached to
the surface of the
particular lymphocyte

1 The basis of the clonal selection theory is that each lymphocyte has the
   information stored in its genes (DNA) to make only one particular
   antibody. As you can imagine, however, there are many millions of
   lymphocytes in the body. There are, therefore, many different small
   populations of lymphocytes (sometimes called clones) in the body,
   each equipped to make one of a huge variety of antibodies. Some of
   the antibody molecules specific to each lymphocyte are built into the
   surface cell membrane of the lymphocyte.

When an antigen filters
through a lymph node, it
contacts lymphocytes with
different antibodies. When
the antigen fits an anti-
body, it combines with the
antibody

2 As we saw earlier, populations of lymphocytes reside in all the lymph
   nodes and also circulate in the blood. When an antigen filters through
   a lymph node, it comes into contact with many lymphocytes. In due
   course it encounters lymphocytes with its specific antibody on their

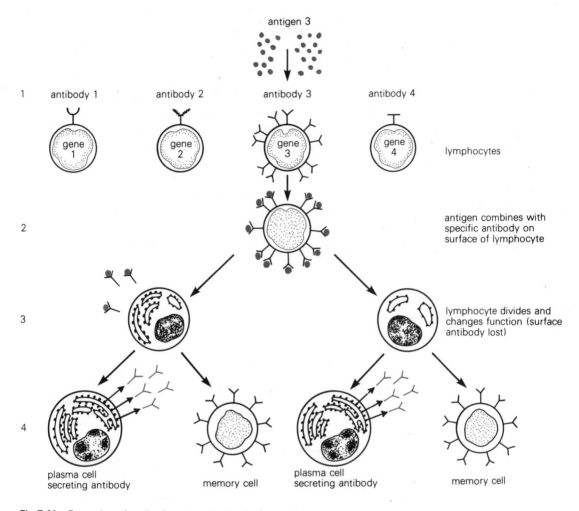

Fig 7.11 *Formation of antibodies – the clonal selection model*

surface. When the antigen contacts a lymphocyte whose antibody is a good fit, the antigen combines with the surface antibody.

3 The combination of antigen with lymphocyte surface antibody gives the lymphocyte the signal to divide and change its function.

4 Some cells change into plasma cells and begin to produce antibodies.

5 Other cells remain as lymphocytes and become memory cells, ready to respond, like their parent cells, if the antigen reappears at a later date.

A lymphocyte with an antigen attached to a surface antibody may change into a plasma cell which produces antibodies

Some recognised lymphocytes do not become plasma cells but remain as memory cells

You can see, then, that this selection theory explains how an antigen can select, out of a huge range of antibody-producing cells, just those cells that can trigger off production of the one correct antibody. In other words, it explains how immune defence responses are specific. The clonal selection theory can also explain the other basic feature of all immune responses—the fact that they have a memory.

The key to immune memory

Up to this stage, we have been discussing the response of the body's immune system on its first contact with an invading organism. This first response is called the **primary response**. As we have outlined, the response involves the production of antibodies, their combination with the antigen, and finally the elimination of the invading organisms from the body. It is possible to measure the change in the concentration of antibodies in blood plasma in the course of this response. Figure 7.12 shows the result of such an experiment, in which a bacterial toxin was injected into a rabbit. As you can see, antibodies are first detected in the blood about 5 days after injection of the antigen. The antibody concentration then rises fairly slowly to a peak, 18 to 20 days after injection. After this time it gradually falls as formed antibodies are broken down and eliminated and plasma cells cease production of new antibodies.

Primary response, the body's first response to an invading antigen results in
• formation of plasma cells and production of antibodies
• formation of memory cells

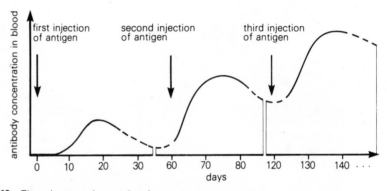

Fig 7.12   *The primary and secondary immune response*

Secondary response After a second injection of toxin:
• antibody is detached in the blood more rapidly
• much higher concentrations of antibody are produced
• antibody persists longer in the blood

If, then, at some later date the animal is given a second injection of the toxin, the immune response is dramatically different. Look again at Fig 7.12. As you can see, it differs in several ways:

● Antibodies are detected in the blood much more rapidly.

● Much higher concentrations of antibodies are produced.

● The antibodies persist longer in the blood. These features are all typical of the **secondary response** to any invading antigen. They are in fact the events which make up immune memory and prevent us suffering more than once from diseases such as mumps, measles or chickenpox.

If you refer back to Fig 7.11, you may gain some clue as to how this immune memory works. As we have seen, antibody production by

stimulated plasma cells stops relatively soon after contact with an antigen. Plasma cells play no part in immune memory. The memory cells in
the immune system are the lymphocytes. During the primary response to
an antigen, the particular antigen-sensitive lymphocytes divide, so that
an enlarged population of memory cells exists. Should a second infection
occur, a large population of cells is already primed to change rapidly into
increased numbers of plasma cells, capable of producing higher concentrations of antibody.

During primary response:
lymphocytes

↓

large population of
memory cells

Immunity without antibodies

The production of antibodies, and antigen–antibody combinations, is
only one part of the immune defence system; there is another equally
important part. Like the antibody system, this system is specific and
exhibits an immune memory. However, it involves no antibodies. Instead, the agents of this part of the immune system are specially equipped
lymphocytes. As a result, this part of the immune system is called **cell-
mediated immunity**.

Another part of the
immune defence system is
cell-mediated immunity

For many years it has been known that cells, as well as antibodies, are
important in immune processes. Antibodies from plasma alone cannot
confer immunity to all infectious diseases. Just which cells are involved
in the immune processes, and how they help in these processes, has been
much more difficult to establish.

It is now known that there are two populations of lymphocytes in the
body. One of these we have discussed already. This population consists
of the cells that recognise antigens and can change into antibody-
producing plasma cells. Scientists refer to these cells as B-lymphocytes.
The others, although they look identical, have a quite different job. They
are responsible for a variety of other immune reactions in the body.
Some of them, when triggered by specific antigens, produce chemicals
which activate phagocytes and so help them to digest very resistant
bacteria. The role of these cells is very important, particularly in diseases
like tuberculosis, where the bacteria may survive inside cells, out of reach
of plasma antibodies, for many months. Others, as we shall see later, become the 'killer' cells which are responsible for the phenomenon of graft
rejection—the special immune reaction that follows the transplanting
of an organ or tissue from one person to another. Because these lymphocytes are thought to develop in the thymus gland, they are referred
to by scientists as T-lymphocytes. The role of T-lymphocytes and cell-
mediated responses in the body's immune system is summarised in
Fig 7.13.

Two populations of
lymphocytes are involved
in immune processes:

• B-lymphocytes—cells
that recognise antigens
and can change into
antibody-producing cells
• T-lymphocytes—cells
that produce chemicals
which activate
phagocytes
or
killer cells which attack
graft cells

T-lymphocytes are thought
to develop in the thymus

As more is learned about the mechanisms of immune responses, it is
becoming clear that in many responses both antibody *and* cell-mediated
responses are involved. Only when there is cooperation between the two
populations of lymphocytes and other related cells—phagocytes and
plasma cells—can full immunity be provided.

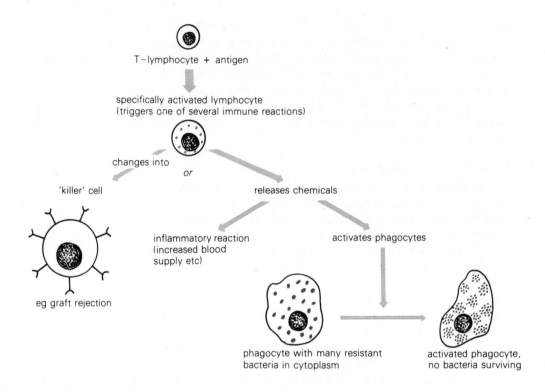

T–lymphocyte + antigen

specifically activated lymphocyte
(triggers one of several immune reactions)

changes into
or

'killer' cell

releases chemicals

inflammatory reaction
(increased blood
supply etc)

activates phagocytes

eg graft rejection

phagocyte with many resistant
bacteria in cytoplasm

activated phagocyte,
no bacteria surviving

Fig 7.13 *T-lymphocytes and cell-mediated immunity in defence of the body*

Immune memory and vaccination

For centuries it has been known that people rarely suffer more than once
from an infectious disease. Long before scientists had any understanding
of how immune memory worked (or even of what caused infectious
diseases), people were trying to produce artificially the type of protection
from further disease which an infection produced. Some individuals
allowed themselves to be inoculated with pustule material obtained from
mild cases of smallpox, in the hope that they themselves might be protected against later fatal attacks. However, the technique was far too
dangerous for general use—frequently the inoculation proved fatal!

A safe means of developing immunity (immunisation) was first developed by an Englishman, Edward Jenner, in 1796. He was aware of a
popular belief that persons who had recovered from the mild disease
cowpox were in some way protected against the more serious smallpox
disease. He therefore inoculated a person deliberately with cowpox, using material from pustules from an infected cow. When he later inoculated his patient with true smallpox material, he found him to be
completely immune! Jenner called his process vaccination (from the
Latin *vacca*, meaning cow). His process eventually became widely accepted for the prevention of smallpox.

Vaccination—the artificial
introduction of dead,
inactivated or harmless
bacteria or viruses into the
body, in order to produce
immunity

Today we understand far more about the organisms that cause infectious disease—bacteria and viruses—and about the body's immune response to them. It is possible to immunise people against a large number of infectious diseases. Immunisation or vaccination is based on an understanding of how the body's immune system works. It involves using the antigen, prepared in a relatively harmless form, as the primary stimulus to develop immune memory. In the event of a subsequent infection with the pathogen itself, the person then has the ability to produce large quantities of the appropriate antibodies or activated cells very rapidly, without having previously suffered the symptoms of the disease.

Types of vaccines

The preparation of antigen that is used in immunisation is called the vaccine. There are three basic types of vaccines. Which one is most effective in developing immunity against a particular disease depends on the organism involved—how it causes disease, and how the body can best defend itself against it.

Toxoids   When organisms cause disease by producing toxins, the body protects itself by making antibodies which inactivate the toxin. These antibodies are called antitoxins. Many bacterial toxins can be inactivated by chemical procedures in the laboratory that do not interfere with the antigen part of the toxin molecule (Fig 7.14). Such inactivated toxin can therefore be used in vaccines to stimulate formation of the appropriate antitoxin, without itself producing the signs of disease. A toxin inactivated in this way is called a **toxoid**. Preparations of toxoids are used in vaccination against tetanus and diphtheria.

Killed organisms   Preparations of dead microorganisms make very safe vaccines. However, the immunity that develops in response to 'dead' vaccines is often not as strong or as long-lasting as that resulting from infection with live organisms. Typhoid and cholera vaccines are killed vaccines.

'Modified' living organisms   For diseases caused by organisms that do not produce toxins, living vaccines produce the strongest immune response. The multiplication of the microbes in the vaccine confronts the body's immune system with a larger and longer-lasting dose of antigen.

The prepared antigen used in immunisation is called the vaccine

Three types of vaccines:
- toxoids—inactivated toxin. This causes the body to produce antibodies, which are called antitoxins (eg used in vaccines against tetanus and diphtheria)

- killed organisms (eg used in vaccines against typhoid and cholera)

- modified or neutralised living organisms (eg used in vaccines against poliomyelitis, tuberculosis and German measles)

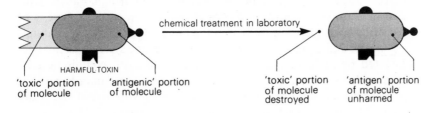

chemical treatment in laboratory

HARMFUL TOXIN

'toxic' portion of molecule

'antigenic' portion of molecule

'toxic' portion of molecule destroyed

'antigen' portion of molecule unharmed

Fig 7.14   *Preparation of a toxoid from a toxin*

Scientists have now been able to modify many of the microorganisms that cause disease, so that they can be inoculated into people and stimulate the immune system, without causing signs of disease. The Sabin (oral) vaccine for poliomyelitis is one such vaccine. It contains a modified form of the poliomyelitis virus, which can enter the body by the natural route of infection (the alimentary canal) and stimulate an immune response, without causing disease. Being a living vaccine, it is more effective than the dead (Salk) vaccine which it replaced. Other important modified live vaccines are BCG vaccine for tuberculosis and rubella or German measles vaccine.

Vaccination schedules and boosters

You may be aware that very early in your childhood you received a course of vaccinations against a number of serious diseases. The course probably consisted of three doses of appropriate vaccines spaced over six or nine months. Since then you may have received booster doses of one or more of these vaccines. Why is a course of vaccinations necessary, and what does a booster dose do?

Look again at Fig 7.12. You will remember that with the second dose of antigen, more antibody was produced, and it persisted for longer. In other words, greater protection against the disease was provided. Although, in theory, immune memory lasts for a lifetime, in practice, the immunity produced by vaccines may not. Booster doses help to make the protection last longer. With successive doses of vaccine, progressively higher antibody concentrations are produced, and the memory and protection appear to last longer.

Boosters are necessary to prolong the effect of a vaccine

Passive immunity

We have been talking so far about situations in which the body makes its own immunity. We can call this active immunity. In some situations (both natural and artificial), a person can be given ready-made immunity. This situation is called passive immunity.

So-called natural passive immunity is important in protecting the newborn baby against disease. The baby receives ready-made antibodies from its mother both across the placenta and in breast milk. These antibodies help the baby to fight off disease in the first months of life. Artificial passive immunity is provided when ready-made antibodies are injected directly into the blood of a person in immediate danger from a disease. Passive immunity provides *immediate* protection (there is no delay while antibodies are formed in the body). However, the immunity does not last and there is no memory, as the immune system has not been stimulated by antigen. (Preformed tetanus antitoxin, containing antibodies made by a horse against tetanus toxin, may sometimes be given to a patient who has not previously been vaccinated with toxoid and is suspected of having contracted the disease tetanus; see Fig 7.15.)

Active immunity—body makes its own immunity

Passive immunity—body is given ready-made immunity

Natural passive immunity—antibodies enter baby's bloodstream from the mother

Artificial passive immunity—ready-made antibodies are injected into a person's bloodstream

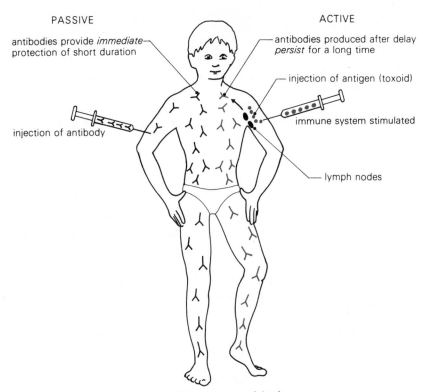

PASSIVE

antibodies provide *immediate* protection of short duration

injection of antibody

ACTIVE

antibodies produced after delay *persist* for a long time

injection of antigen (toxoid)

immune system stimulated

lymph nodes

Fig 7.15 *Active and passive immunity to a tetanus infection*

Rejection of foreign grafts

It would often be very useful to be able to transplant a piece of tissue or organ from one individual to another, and from a surgical point of view, this may be quite a straightforward procedure. However, unless special steps are taken to avoid such a reaction, transplanted tissue is usually rejected and killed by its new host within about ten days of grafting. This response is a by-product of the body's immune system.

In the process of graft rejection, special lymphocytes recognise the foreign antigens on the surface of the graft cells. Because of their special surface-bound antibodies, these so-called killer lymphocytes bind themselves to the foreign graft cells. This damages the membranes of the graft cells and brings about their destruction.

That graft rejection is, in fact, an immune response has been demonstrated by a number of experiments. First, graft rejection exhibits memory. If a second graft from the *same* donor is transplanted, it is rejected much *more quickly* than the first. However, if the second graft is from an unrelated donor, it is rejected at the same rate as the first graft. This highlights the second feature of all immune responses—that the response is specific to a particular antigen.

Transplanted tissue is usually rejected by an organism within ten days of grafting

Killer lymphocytes bind themselves to foreign graft cells. This damages the graft cells and finally destroys them

If a second graft is from an unrelated donor, it is rejected at the same rate as the first graft. If the second graft is from the same donor as the first, it is rejected more quickly, ie the response is specific to a particular graft antigen

The ability of the body's defence system to recognise cells bearing foreign antigen may have significance far beyond the problem of graft rejection. Some cancer cells, too, have been shown to have different or foreign antigens on their surface. It may well be that the lymphocyte killer cells, which are such a nuisance to the transplantation surgeon, have a vital role in policing all the body cells, detecting and destroying possible cancer cells as they appear in the body. A better understanding of the mechanisms of graft rejection may well improve our knowledge of the treatment and prevention of cancer.

'Self' and 'non-self'

We have now examined the range of immune processes in the body. We have seen how lymphocytes can recognise and respond to foreign chemicals, microorganisms and cells. One important question remains yet to be answered. How does the body distinguish between what is foreign, 'non-self', and 'self'? Why is it that our bodies reject a heart transplanted from another person but do not reject our own heart, kidneys, skin and so on?

The clonal selection theory also helps to explain this ability of the body to distinguish self antigens on cells from non-self antigens. You will remember that the clonal selection theory proposes that there are many different small populations of lymphocytes in the body. Each of these clones is equipped to make only one of a huge variety of antibodies. Burnet proposed that these clones of cells with different antigen-recognising capacities form during divisions of lymphocytes in the foetus (and possibly early in post-natal life). At this stage, almost all the antigens with which the developing lymphoid system has contact are body components, that is, self. He proposed that, during development, the immune system could learn that these antigens were self, and as a result learn not to produce antibodies to them. This knowledge of what is self then persists through life and is known as **immune tolerance**. In other words, the immune system is 'tolerant'. It does not produce antibodies against its own tissues (self).

(How this learning process operates is not clear. It seems that during cell divisions in the developing individual lymphocytes with the capacity to produce antibodies to all sorts of antigens are formed. However, lymphocytes capable of producing antibodies to self are rapidly destroyed, so that none persist when development is complete.)

Although this explanation is rather theoretical, experiments have been conducted which provide support for it. One of these is shown in Fig 7.16. In this experiment, Medawar and his co-workers found that they could produce tolerance in mice artificially. New-born strain A mice were injected with cells from foreign strain B mice. After they had grown to maturity, they were then given skin grafts from the foreign strain B mice. In littermate control mice that had not received foreign cells at

The clonal selection theory proposes that
• many different kinds of lymphocytes, each capable of producing a different antibody, develop in the foetus
• lymphocytes capable of producing antibodies to self tissues are destroyed during development

Immune tolerance— absence of production of antibodies against self tissues

Adult strain A mice injected with strain C cells at birth did not reject strain C graft tissue

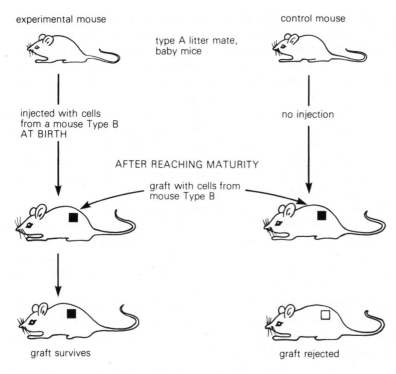

experimental mouse

type A litter mate, baby mice

control mouse

injected with cells from a mouse Type B AT BIRTH

no injection

AFTER REACHING MATURITY

graft with cells from mouse Type B

graft survives

graft rejected

Fig 7.16   *Treatment that allows mice to accept foreign graft tissue*

birth, the grafts were rapidly rejected. In the mice that received strain B cells at birth, the grafts were not rejected and grew to form healthy skin tissue. Presumably, because of their treatment at birth, there were no lymphocytes in the tolerant mice capable of recognising the skin graft as foreign—non-self.

Occasionally the system which recognises self and non-self breaks down. When this happens, antibodies capable of reacting with self antigens are produced. These antibodies are called **auto-antibodies**. When auto-antibodies are produced in the body, they may cause serious damage to cells of particular organs or tissues. Diseases that result from damage of this sort are called **auto-immune diseases**. A variety of diseases is now thought to be auto-immune; that is, due to a breakdown in the normal functioning of the immune system. One of the most common of these diseases is rheumatoid arthritis.

Auto-antibodies— antibodies produced against self tissue

Blood groups and transfusions

Blood transfusions are, in essence, tissue grafts. 'Foreign' cells and blood plasma are introduced into a patient's circulatory system. However, the transfusion reaction which may follow this procedure is different from the normal graft rejection response. Let us see why this is so.

From an immunologic point of view, red blood cells are rather a special case. Like all other cells, they possess large molecules on their surfaces which can act as antigens. However, unlike other graft rejection responses, the recipient of blood transfusions does not actually have to form antibodies following a transfusion. *Antibodies to foreign red blood cells may already be present in the blood plasma.*

Antibodies to foreign red blood cells may already be present in the blood plasma

The entire human population can be divided into four groups, on the basis of the reaction that follows when blood from different individuals is mixed. The group an individual belongs to depends on which particular antigens are present on the surface of his red blood cells. Only two antigens are important in this blood grouping system. These are called type A antigens and type B antigens.

All people in the population belong to one of four blood groups: A, B, AB, O

The combinations of the A and B antigens on the surfaces of red blood cells give rise to four blood types: A, B, AB and O. An individual with blood type A has red blood cells with the A antigen on the surface of their cell membranes. B has the B antigen on his red blood cells. An individual with type AB blood has *both* A and B antigens, and one with blood type O has *neither* A *nor* B antigens.

The blood group an individual belongs to depends on which antigens are present on his red blood cells

Remember our discussions of self and non-self. Obviously, an individual will not have antibodies in his blood to his own (self) blood type. (If he did, the antigen–antibody reaction would cause clumping (agglutination) of red blood cells and severe illness.) However, most people do have antibodies to other (non-self) red blood cell antigens.

Antigens are of two types: A and B

In other words, somebody with type A red blood cells will have B antibodies but not A antibodies. An individual with type B red blood cells will form only A antibodies. People with type AB blood form neither A nor B antibodies in their blood. This information is summarised in Table 7.2.

An absence of an antigen corresponds with the presence of the corresponding antibody

Table 7.2

Blood type	Proteins on the membranes of red blood cells		Antibodies present in blood	
A	Protein A		B antibodies	
B	Protein B		A antibodies	
AB	Proteins A and B		Neither A nor B antibodies	
O	Neither proteins A nor B		Both A and B antibodies	

You can probably see now why it is so important to know which blood group a patient belongs to, before he receives a blood transfusion. (It is equally important, of course, to know the donor's blood type.) If blood serum containing A antibodies is mixed in a test tube with blood type A cells, the cells and antibodies bind to one another. This results in ag-glutination or clumping of the red blood cells (Fig 7.17). If the same reaction occurs in the body as a result of a mis-matched transfusion, red blood cells clump and then break up and are destroyed. Severe illness and even death may follow.

Using Table 7.2 we can work out when such a reaction might occur. If a patient with blood type B (who has A antibodies) receives blood from a donor with blood type A, the A antibodies will bind with the donor A cells and cause clumping and illness. In the same way, if a patient with blood type A (the receiver) receives blood from a blood type B donor, the B antibodies in the receiver's blood will cause clumping of the type B donor cells.

A person with blood type AB has *neither* A *nor* B antibodies in his blood. Thus any of the four blood groups can be given to this person and agglutination will not occur. Because of this, people with blood type AB are called **universal receivers**.

A person with blood type O produces both A and B antibodies. As a result, this person cannot receive blood from people with blood types A, B or AB. However, because type O red blood cells lack both A and B antigens, type O blood can be given to people with any of the four blood types. Thus, people with blood type O are called **universal donors**.

In this discussion of blood transfusions we have considered only the red blood cells of the donor and the antibodies of the receiver. One might

Agglutination—clumping of red blood cells

Combination of antibodies with corresponding antigens on red blood cells results in clumping of red blood cells and serious illness

People with type AB blood are called universal receivers because they have neither A nor B antibodies in their blood

People with blood type O are called universal donors because their blood cells have neither type A nor B antigens

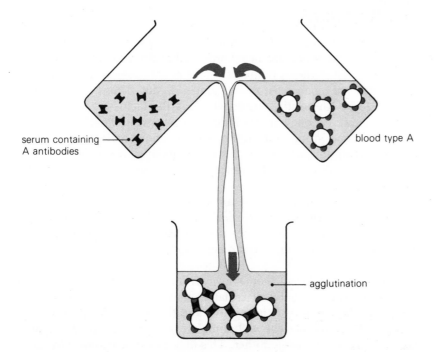

serum containing A antibodies

blood type A

agglutination

Fig 7.17 *Agglutination, eg the result of mixing serum containing A antibodies with blood type A*

WINDSOR & MAIDENHEAD COLLEGE
CLAREMONT ROAD
WINDSOR

well ask about the donor's antibodies. How do they react with the receiver's red blood cells? In theory, they too could cause clumping of red blood cells, but in practice they do not. The antibodies in the donor blood very rapidly become too dilute in the receiver's bloodstream to cause any significant clumping of red blood cells. This information about reactions to blood transfusions is summarised in Table 7.3.

Table 7.3

Blood group of receiver	Antibodies in receiver	Donor blood type			
		Blood type O universal donor	Blood type A	Blood type B	Blood type AB
O	A, B	✔	✕	✕	✕
A	B	✔	✔	✕	✕
B	A	✔	✕	✔	✕
AB universal receiver	none	✔	✔	✔	✔

✔ = satisfactory blood transfusion

✕ = dangerous transfusion

The Rh factor

People whose red blood cells carry the rhesus antigen are said to be rhesus (Rh) positive

Rh negative individuals do not, under normal circumstances, possess Rh antibodies

The rhesus factor becomes important if an Rh negative mother gives birth to an Rh positive baby

The firstborn baby is usually not affected, but subsequent babies may suffer haemolytic disease (splitting of red blood cells) shortly after birth

Another important antigen is found on the surfaces of red blood cells. This is called the **rhesus factor** (abbreviated as Rh factor) because it was first discovered in rhesus monkeys. Some people possess the rhesus factor on their red blood cells, the remainder do not. Those who possess it are said to be Rh positive, those who lack the factor are Rh negative. There is, however, one important difference between the Rh system and the ABO blood group system. Rh negative individuals do *not*, under normal circumstances, possess the Rh antibodies. (In the ABO blood group system, absence of the antigen corresponds with presence of the antibody.)

The Rh factor becomes important where an Rh negative mother gives birth to an Rh positive baby. Normally an Rh negative mother lacks any Rh antibodies (as does an Rh positive mother). However, if Rh positive red blood cells are introduced into her bloodstream, she will produce Rh antibodies.

At birth, as the placenta comes away from the wall of the uterus, a few blood cells from the baby's circulation may enter the mother's bloodstream. If the mother is Rh negative and the baby is Rh positive, the introduced red blood cells will stimulate the production of Rh antibodies in the Rh negative mother. This in itself is not serious. However, problems will arise if the mother has a second baby which is also Rh positive. Late in pregnancy, Rh antibodies from the mother's blood can move across the placenta and enter the baby's bloodstream. They will then bind with the Rh positive red blood cells of the baby. This causes the red blood cells to be split open and destroyed. The splitting of red blood cells is called **haemolysis**. As a result of haemolysis, the baby is born seriously ill. Unless a blood transfusion (with Rh negative cells) is given shortly after birth, the condition may be fatal. (In more severe cases, when large numbers of red blood cells are destroyed, the baby may die in the uterus.) These events are summarised in Fig 7.18.

Haemolysis—splitting and destruction of red blood cells

Modern medical research has developed a method for ensuring that the above sequence of events does not occur. A few days after an Rh negative mother has given birth to her first baby, she is injected with Rh antibodies. Any red blood cells possessing the Rh antigen are immediately destroyed and are not available to stimulate formation of Rh antibodies which could harm future babies.

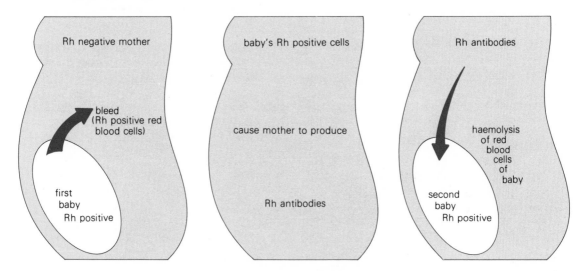

Fig 7.18 *Possible dangers for the second baby of an Rh negative mother*

Chapter 8

The lungs—a two-way diffusion unit

As we saw in Chapter 4, every cell in the human body must generate its own supply of energy to enable it to perform its particular work. This energy is obtained from chemical fuels, which are delivered to the cell from the bloodstream. These fuels are broken down or oxidised in the cell to release energy in the process known as cellular respiration. Remembering the general equation for cellular respiration:

Cellular respiration provides energy for cells

$$\text{Glucose} + \text{oxygen} \rightarrow \text{carbon dioxide} + \text{water} + \text{energy}$$

Oxygen must be supplied to cells and carbon dioxide removed

it becomes obvious that the survival of all cells depends on both a continuous supply of oxygen and a means of removing the carbon dioxide produced during cellular respiration.

In Chapter 6 we saw how the circulatory system provides this life-line for the cells, constantly supplying oxygen and removing carbon dioxide. As carbon dioxide accumulates in a cell through respiration, its concentration in the cell becomes greater than its concentration in the blood. Thus carbon dioxide diffuses into the bloodstream.

Carbon dioxide is removed from cells by diffusion

Oxygen is supplied to cells by diffusion

The supply of oxygen to the cell occurs in the reverse way. As oxygen is used in the cell, its concentration in the cell compared with the concentration in the blood drops. Thus diffusion of oxygen occurs from the bloodstream into the cell.

The problem of gas exchange

How does the circulatory system release its carbon dioxide from the body into the outside atmosphere? And by what means is oxygen replenished in the blood? Both oxygen and carbon dioxide are soluble in water, so, for small aquatic animals like the amoeba, gas exchange does not present many problems. It occurs by means of simple diffusion from the fluid outside to the fluid inside the cell.

Lungs are the structures in which oxygen is supplied to the blood and carbon dioxide is removed from the blood by gaseous exchange

In Chapter 6 we saw that our multicelled bodies require a special transport or circulatory system. In the same way, a special method for supplying oxygen to the blood and removing carbon dioxide from the blood is also necessary. The process by which oxygen is supplied to, and carbon dioxide is removed from, the bloodstream is called **gaseous exchange**. The special area within the body where gaseous exchange occurs is the **lungs**. The lungs, and the structures that help the lungs to operate, are all part of the respiratory system. Figure 8.1 shows in schematic form the exchange of gases between the tissues, the bloodstream and the air in the lungs.

Gaseous exchange and lung structure

Gaseous exchange between the bloodstream and the outside atmosphere takes place in the lungs, which are situated in the **thoracic cavity**. This gaseous exchange relies on a simple process of diffusion. Many thousands of cubic centimetres of oxygen per minute are taken into the

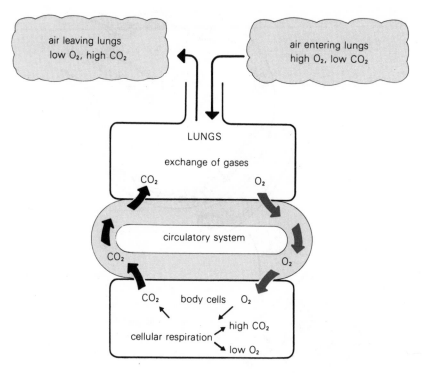

Fig 8.1 *Exchange of respiratory gases (diagrammatic)*

lungs of an adult. Similar volumes of carbon dioxide are removed each minute. To cope with such huge volumes of gas exchange, the lungs must be specially structured. Let us consider how the structure of the lungs assists the exchange of gases.

The lungs consist of millions of tiny sacs called **alveoli** (Fig 8.2). If you examine the cut surface of a piece of lung tissue, these structures are just visible to the naked eye. Each alveolus is connected with the outside air through a number of tubes called **respiratory passages**. Like all structures in contact with the outside environment, alveoli are lined with epithelial cells. These cells are flattened or thin in cross-section. Even under the light microscope, their cytoplasm is scarcely visible. Immediately beneath the epithelial cells lie the **alveolar capillaries**.

The alveolus has a number of important properties which fit it for efficient gas exchange; these are discussed below.

Thin walls   In an efficient lung, carbon dioxide and oxygen must be able to diffuse rapidly between the alveolar spaces and the bloodstream. The barrier between the space inside an alveolus and the blood in the surrounding capillaries consists of two cells—the single cell of the capillary wall and the epithelial cell of the alveolus. In order to ensure that the path through these two cells is as short as possible, and that diffusion can occur as rapidly as possible, both these cells are thin or flattened.

The lungs are specially structured to cope with the large volumes of carbon dioxide and oxygen which must be exchanged

An alveolus is a small air sac

Alveoli are lined with epithelial cells

Efficient gas exchange in the alveoli depends on
• thin walls of the alveoli

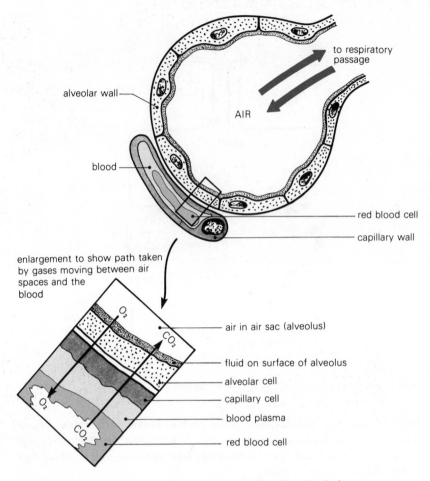

to respiratory passage

alveolar wall

AIR

blood

red blood cell

capillary wall

enlargement to show path taken by gases moving between air spaces and the blood

O_2

CO_2

O_2

CO_2

air in air sac (alveolus)

fluid on surface of alveolus

alveolar cell

capillary cell

blood plasma

red blood cell

Fig 8.2 *An alveolus (air sac) and its associated capillary (line drawing)*

Thus the barrier between the alveolar space and the bloodstream is as thin as possible (Fig 8.3).

Large surface area   In order to cope with the large volume of carbon dioxide and oxygen that needs to be exchanged in the lungs, there must be a large surface area of lung tissue between the external air and the blood supply. Two sacs the size of the lung would not provide sufficient surface area for the necessary gas exchange to occur. However, since the lung is divided into large numbers of alveoli, the required surface area is present within the lungs. The 300 million alveoli provide a surface area of some 90 square metres.

Large numbers of capillaries   If large volumes of carbon dioxide and oxygen are to be exchanged through the surfaces of the alveoli every minute, large volumes of blood must flow near these surfaces to deliver

• large surface area of the alveoli

• large numbers of capillaries surrounding the alveoli

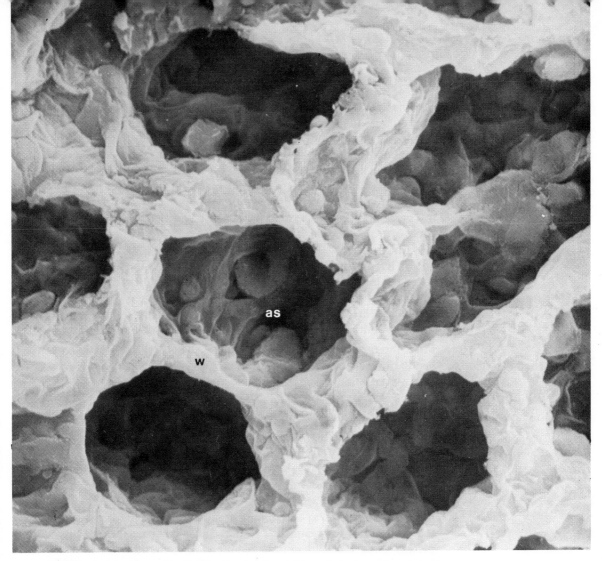

Fig 8.3 *A cut surface of lung, showing alveoli and thin walls between them (scanning electron micrograph). (as = air space, w = alveolar wall)*

carbon dioxide and pick up oxygen. As explained earlier, capillaries carry blood close to the alveolar walls. In order to supply the alveoli with sufficient blood, a large number of capillaries supply each alveolus. In fact, so extensive is the network of capillaries in the lungs, that almost 20 per cent of the total volume of blood in the body is found in the lungs at any one time.

Moist internal surfaces   The diffusion of gases through a membrane is helped considerably if a thin layer of fluid covers the surface of the membrane. For this reason, the surfaces of the alveoli are always covered with a thin layer of moisture to aid diffusion. However, in order to avoid rapid evaporation from these surfaces, and water loss from the body, these alveolar surfaces are housed well inside the body.

• moist surfaces of the alveoli

Diffusion in the alveoli

Blood arriving in the capillaries of the alveoli has
• higher concentration of carbon dioxide
• lower concentration of oxygen
than the alveolar air

You will recall from Chapter 2 that diffusion is the movement of particles from an area of high concentration to an area of low concentration. Blood entering the capillaries of the alveoli from the rest of the body contains high carbon dioxide concentrations and low oxygen concentrations, when compared with fresh air in the alveolar spaces. As a result, oxygen diffuses from the alveolar spaces into the capillaries, while carbon dioxide diffuses from the capillaries into the alveolar spaces (Fig 8.4). Thus blood leaving the lungs is replenished with oxygen and cleared of excess carbon dioxide. In this state it is ready to serve the respiring cells of the body.

Oxygen diffuses from the alveoli into the capillaries; carbon dioxide diffuses from the capillaries into the alveoli

The difference in the concentrations of particles in the areas of high and low concentration is known as the **diffusion gradient**. The greater the diffusion gradient, the greater is the rate of diffusion of the particles. In the lungs, three factors cause the diffusion gradient to remain high, resulting in continued rapid diffusion of carbon dioxide and oxygen:

The diffusion gradient in the lungs remains high because

• ventilation causes alveolar air to be replenished regularly

• First, the regular replenishment of air in the alveoli by **breathing** or **ventilation** keeps the concentration of oxygen in the alveoli high and the concentration of carbon dioxide low.

• continuous blood flow removes blood with high oxygen and low carbon dioxide concentrations

• Second, the continuous flow of blood in the capillaries surrounding the alveoli continually removes blood with high concentrations of oxygen and low concentrations of carbon dioxide, and replaces it with blood of low oxygen and high carbon dioxide concentration.

• the presence of haemoglobin in the red blood cells keeps the concentration of oxygen in the plasma low

• Third, the presence of the special carrier molecule haemoglobin in the red blood cells (Chapter 6) keeps the oxygen concentration in plasma low. Haemoglobin rapidly binds oxygen to itself, thus removing it from the blood plasma and binding it inside the red blood cells. Since the diffusion of oxygen occurs from the alveolar space into the blood plasma, and from there into the red blood cells, the diffusion gradient between the alveolar air and plasma remains high. This allows diffusion to continue rapidly.

As a result of the gas exchange which occurs in the alveoli, the air breathed in has quite different concentrations of oxygen and carbon dioxide from air breathed out, as shown in the following table:

Table 8.1 *Exchange of gases in the alveoli*

	Percentage of gas in inspired air	Percentage of gas in expired air
Oxygen	21	16
Carbon dioxide	0.03	4
Nitrogen	79	79
Water vapour	depends on atmosphere	saturated

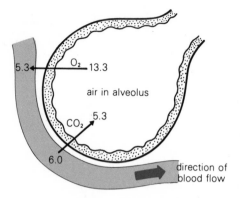

Fig 8.4 *Diffusion of gases between an alveolus and the blood. The figures given are the partial pressures (in kilonewtons per square metre) of oxygen and carbon dioxide in the alveolus and blood arriving in the alveolar capillary*

Conveying air to the lungs

The respiratory system can be divided into two working parts: the alveoli, whose function is gas exchange, and the conducting system or respiratory passages, whose role is to convey air to the alveoli. Figure 8.5 outlines the main structures that make up the respiratory passages.

Air enters the respiratory passages through the nostrils and nasal cavity, or through the mouth. (The nasal passages are responsible for humidifying air before it reaches the lungs.) It then passes to the **pharynx**, an area at the back of the mouth and nose through which both food and air pass. The combined actions of the epiglottis and larynx prevent the entry of food into the respiratory passages during swallowing (see Chapter 10).

From the pharynx, air passes into the **larynx** (or voice box), which is composed of cartilage plates and small muscles. It then flows into the **trachea** (or wind pipe), and through to the **bronchi** (singular **bronchus**) and **bronchioles**.

Because of its branching structure, this system of conducting tubes is sometimes referred to as the respiratory 'tree' (Fig 8.6a). The trachea forms the 'trunk' and descends from the larynx to the middle of the thorax, where it divides above the heart into two bronchi which supply the right and left lungs. It is a tube approximately 3 cm in diameter in the adult, composed of cartilage rings, enclosed and joined together by elastic connective tissue. The presence of cartilage rings ensures that the air passages remain open at all times, whilst the elastic fibres connecting the rings allow for some stretching of the trachea and bronchi during breathing.

Each bronchus enters the lung and continues to branch into smaller bronchi, then into small tubes called bronchioles. Unlike the bronchi and the trachea, the walls of bronchioles are not supported by cartilage. Bronchioles divide again and terminate in alveoli (Figs 8.6b and 8.6c).

Two working units of the respiratory system:
• alveoli
• respiratory passages

The passage of air:
nostrils and mouth
↓
pharynx
↓
larynx
↓
trachea
↓
bronchus
↓
bronchioles
↓
alveoli

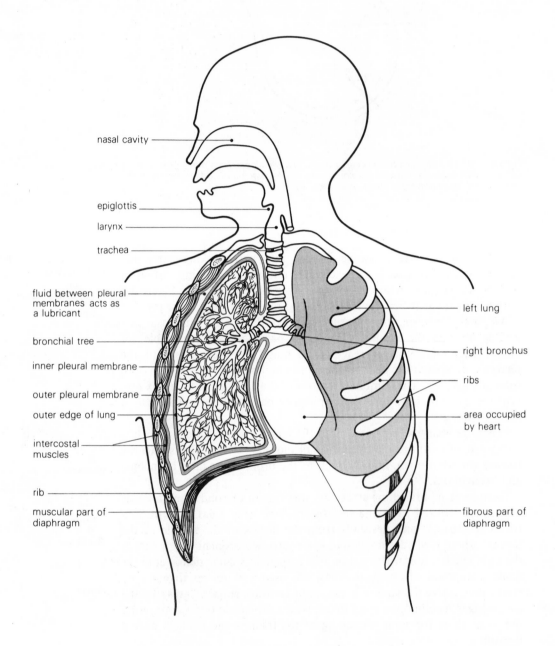

nasal cavity

epiglottis

larynx

trachea

fluid between pleural
membranes acts as
a lubricant

bronchial tree

inner pleural membrane

outer pleural membrane

outer edge of lung

intercostal
muscles

rib

muscular part of
diaphragm

left lung

right bronchus

ribs

area occupied
by heart

fibrous part of
diaphragm

Fig 8.5   *The respiratory system. On the right, the ribs and lungs remain intact. On the left, the ribs have been cut away, and the contents of the thoracic cavity are seen in vertical section (diagrammatic)*

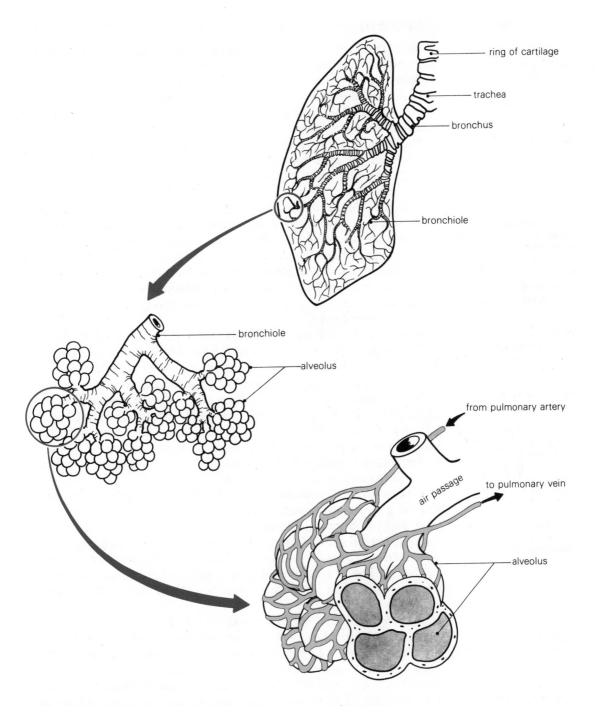

ring of cartilage

trachea

bronchus

bronchiole

bronchiole

alveolus

from pulmonary artery

to pulmonary vein

air passage

alveolus

Fig 8.6 *Relationships between the alveoli and the air passages of the lungs*
(a) Parts of the respiratory 'tree'
(b) Air passages terminating in alveoli
(c) Relationship between the blood vessels and the alveoli

Supplying fresh air to the alveoli

Breathing = inspiration + expiration

As already explained, the diffusion of gases in the alveoli depends to a large extent on regular replacement of air in the alveoli with fresh atmospheric air. The process by which air is supplied to and removed from the lungs is known as ventilation or breathing. Ventilation has two phases—**inspiration**, during which air enters the lungs, and **expiration**, when air leaves the lungs.

The lungs are soft and expansive

The lungs themselves are very soft, spongy and elastic, because they do not contain any rigid connective tissue, such as cartilage. If removed from the thoracic cavity, the lungs collapse to a fraction of their normal size.

Pleural membranes are attached to the outer surface of the lungs and the inner surface of the thorax

A thin layer of fluid lies between the two pleura

The outer surface of the lungs and the inner surface of the thoracic cavity are each covered by a membrane called the **pleural membrane**. Together the two pleural membranes are known as the **pleura**. It is important to realise that the pleura not only cover the thorax and lung surfaces, but are actually attached to these surfaces (Fig 8.5). Both pleural membranes produce a very small amount of fluid, the **pleural fluid**. This lubricates the very small space between the two pleural membranes, called the **pleural cavity**.

The thin layer of fluid causes the two pleural membranes to stick together

The wall of the thorax expands outwards

Outer pleural membrane is drawn out with the wall of the thorax

Inner pleural membrane is drawn out with the outer membrane

Outer surface of the lungs is drawn out with the inner pleural membrane

When the thoracic cavity expands, the outer surface of the lungs clings closely to the inner surface of the thoracic wall. Yet the two surfaces are not connected. Why do they move together? Recall that the two pleural membranes lie between the lung and thoracic surfaces, one being connected to the thoracic surface and one being connected to the lung surface. The key point is that there is a 'sticking' force, or force of adhesion, between the two pleural membranes. As a result, when the outer pleural membrane is drawn outwards by the wall of the thoracic cavity, the inner membrane moves with it. This in turn causes the outer surface of the lungs to move outwards.

A good analogy to illustrate how the pleural membranes and fluid operate is to take two plates of glass with a thin film of water between them and try to separate them. The two plates can be slipped off one another, but it is almost impossible to separate the plates by pulling them apart. Similarly, the two pleural membranes are held close to each other by the thin film of pleural fluid—they can be slipped across each other but not pulled apart. They thus ensure that the thoracic wall and lungs are in contact at all times.

Inspiration:
thoracic cavity expands
↓
volume of lungs increases
↓
air pressure in lungs decreases
↓
air rushes into lungs

To understand how ventilation takes place, the thorax can be visualised as an air-tight box, with a single entrance at the top, which is a tube, the trachea. The lungs are inside the box and, because of the pleural membranes, remain in contact at all times with the inner surface of the box (Fig 8.7a). The volume of the box can be increased by increasing the length of all or any of its sides. An increase in the volume of the box causes the volume of the lungs to increase. This in turn causes a decrease in pressure within the lungs. This pressure will now be less

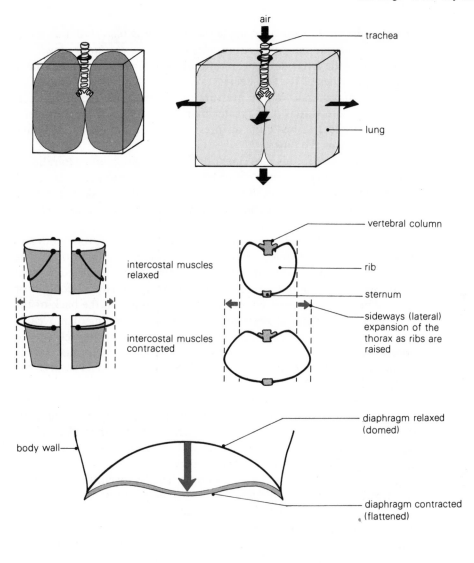

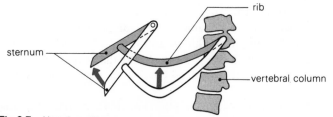

Fig 8.7 *How breathing occurs*

(a) The lungs can be visualised as a box with expanding sides

(b) The action of the ribs can be likened to bucket-handles. As the intercostal muscles contract, the ribs swing up and out

(c) Contraction of the diaphragm causes flattening and lowering of the floor of the thoracic cavity

(d) As the ribs are raised, the sternum is pushed forward

than the pressure of the air outside the box. *Air is therefore drawn into the lungs to make the pressures inside and outside the lungs equal.*

Expiration—air is forced out of the lungs by the reverse process:
thoracic cavity decreases in volume
↓
volume of lungs decreases
↓
air pressure in lungs increases
↓
air is pushed out of lungs

Air leaves the lungs during expiration by the reverse sequence. One or more of the sides of the box decreases in length. Thus the volume of the lungs is reduced, causing the pressure of the air inside the lungs to increase. This pressure is now greater than the pressure of the air outside the box. In order to make the air pressures inside and outside the lungs equal, air leaves the lungs.

In summary, then, air movement during inspiration and expiration is the result of changes in the volume of the thoracic cavity (or box) which cause pressure differences between the air in the lungs and the atmosphere. How do the structures in the wall of the thorax cause a change in its volume?

Thorax:
• roof
  −organs at top of thorax
• sides
  −ribs
  −sternum
  −vertebral column
• floor
  −diaphragm

As we have said, the thorax is like a box, having a roof, four sides and a floor. The roof is formed by the organs at the top of the thorax. The walls of the thoracic cavity are formed by pairs of **ribs**, attached in front to the **sternum** or breast-bone, and behind to the **vertebral column** or spine. The ribs are connected to the vertebral column at the back of the body and the sternum at the front of the body by means of moveable joints. The ribs are joined to one another by two layers of muscles called **intercostal muscles**. The floor of the thoracic cavity is formed by the **diaphragm**. This is a domed sheet of muscle connected to all sides of the body wall (see Fig 8.5).

Ribs raised—volume of thorax increases

Ribs lowered—volume of thorax decreases

How does the volume of the thoracic cavity change? Four structures are involved: the ribs, the intercostal muscles, the diaphragm and the sternum. Look at Fig 8.7b. The ribs are shaped rather like bucket handles. If they are raised, the volume of the thorax increases. If the ribs are lowered, the volume of the thorax decreases.

Intercostal muscles contract—ribs raised

Intercostal muscles relax—ribs lowered

How are the ribs raised and lowered? Their movement is brought about by the intercostal muscles. The arrangement of ribs and intercostal muscles is shown in Fig 8.8a. When the intercostal muscles contract, the ribs are raised (Fig 8.8b). When the muscles relax, the ribs are lowered. The first rib is fixed—it does not move—and the top of the first row of intercostal muscles is attached to this fixed rib.

Diaphragm contracts—volume of thorax increases

Diaphragm relaxes—volume of thorax decreases

Contraction and relaxation of the diaphragm can also cause the volume of the thoracic cavity to change. As the diaphragm muscle contracts, it causes the diaphragm to flatten and lower. This increases the volume of the thoracic cavity (see Fig 8.7c). As the diaphragm relaxes, it lifts and again becomes domed. This decreases the volume of the thoracic cavity.

Sternum pushed forward—volume of thorax increases

Sternum moves back—volume of thorax decreases

Finally, the sternum plays a small role in changing the volume of the thoracic cavity. As the ribs are raised, the sternum is pushed forward, helping to increase the volume of the cavity. Lowering the ribs allows the sternum to move back to its original position, helping to decrease the thoracic volume (see Fig 8.7d).

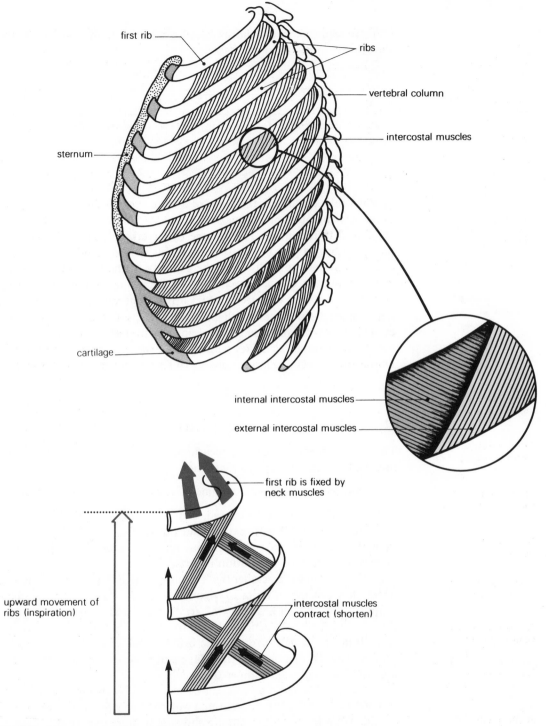

Fig 8.8 *Arrangement of ribs and intercostal muscles*
(a) The bony structures and the muscles
(b) The ribs are raised when the muscles contract

The movements in the thorax causing inspiration and expiration are summarised in the following table:

Table 8.2 *Movements of the thoracic wall during breathing*

Inspiration	Expiration
• Intercostal muscles contract	• Intercostal muscles relax
• Ribs rise and move out	• Ribs lower and move in
• Diaphragm contracts	• Diaphragm relaxes
• Sternum is pushed forward	• Sternum moves back

Tidal volume is the volume of air a person at rest takes in and expels with each breath

When fully expanded, the lungs of an adult man hold about 5½ litres of air. During quiet breathing only about 500 cm³ of air per breath are exchanged in the lungs. The volume of air taken in and expelled with each breath by a person at rest is known as the **tidal volume**.

It is important to realise that the capacity of the lungs is far greater than the amount of gases exchanged under resting conditions. During periods of vigorous exercise, up to 3 litres of air can be drawn into the lungs. Since the lungs never collapse completely, some air remains in them even after forced expiration. This is known as the **residual volume**. At each inspiration inspired air mixes with the residual air present in the alveoli. During quiet breathing larger volumes of residual air remain in the alveoli.

Control of ventilation rate

The rate of breathing can be measured in terms of the volume of air breathed per minute, or the ventilation rate.

Ventilation rate = tidal volume × number of breaths/minute

The ventilation rate can be altered, depending on how quickly the body needs to supply itself with oxygen and rid itself of carbon dioxide. For example, during periods of strenuous muscular exercise, both the frequency and depth of respiration increase.

It is important to remember that the lungs have a large reserve volume, which they can use in times of vigorous exercise. At rest, only a small proportion of alveoli are receiving fresh inspired air with each inspiration. The number of alveoli receiving fresh air is controlled by layers of smooth muscle which surround the bronchi and bronchioles leading to these alveoli. During exercise these layers of muscle relax and fresh air is able to reach a greater number of alveoli.

The number of alveoli receiving fresh air is controlled by layers of smooth muscle surrounding the bronchioles

Gas exchange in the alveoli can be increased by
• more rapid breathing rate
• deeper breathing
• more rapid blood flow through capillaries

Gaseous exchange in alveoli can be increased by two methods. First, increased rate and depth of breathing will obviously remove more carbon dioxide from the lungs per minute and supply more oxygen per minute. Under these conditions a greater diffusion gradient is maintained, and diffusion of gases across the alveolar walls becomes more rapid. Thus, more favourable levels of oxygen and carbon dioxide are maintained in the blood. Slower breathing rates will produce the opposite effect and result in the blood containing an excess of carbon dioxide and a deficiency of oxygen.

Second, increased blood flow through the alveolar capillaries increases the amount of carbon dioxide delivered to, and oxygen picked up from, the alveoli per minute. Blood flow in the capillaries is controlled by the diameter of arterioles in the lungs. This is controlled by layers of smooth muscle in the arterioles (Chapter 6, p 96). When these layers of muscle relax, more blood is able to flow through the arterioles and enter the capillaries. This results in greater diffusion of gases.

During strenuous exercise rapid use of oxygen and production of carbon dioxide by muscle cells results in the blood being deficient in oxygen and laden with carbon dioxide. To overcome this, the rate of exchange of gases in the lungs must be increased. As we have explained, this is achieved by rapid, deep breathing and increased blood flow through the alveolar capillaries.

How does the body control the rate of ventilation and thus the levels of carbon dioxide and oxygen in the cells? The rate of ventilation is controlled by an area in the brain known as the **respiratory centre**. The respiratory centre is sensitive to changes in carbon dioxide concentration in the blood. Nerves from the respiratory centre supply both the diaphragm and the intercostal muscles. The respiratory centre can, therefore, alter both the rate and the depth (tidal volume) of breathing.

The respiratory centre is informed of changes in the concentration of carbon dioxide in the blood by means of special receptor cells. The most important receptor cells are located in the respiratory centre itself. Others are specialised nerve cells located in the base of the carotid arteries in the neck and in the wall of the aorta, close to the heart.

When the carbon dioxide level in the blood rises, nerve impulses from the carbon dioxide receptor cells are relayed to the respiratory centre. The respiratory centre responds by sending an increased number of nerve impulses per second to the diaphragm and intercostal muscles. This causes greater expansion of the thoracic cavity (increased tidal volume) and/or more inspirations per minute. As a result, carbon dioxide is removed more rapidly from the lungs, and the concentration of carbon dioxide in the blood returns to normal. Figure 8.9 shows how this system operates.

If the carbon dioxide concentration in the blood falls, the reverse occurs. Fewer nerve impulses are transmitted from the receptor cells to the respiratory centre. The respiratory centre therefore relays fewer impulses to the diaphragm and intercostal muscles, causing a decrease in ventilation rate and tidal volume.

These adjustments are being made in the body all the time, in response to changes in demand for carbon dioxide removal and oxygen supply to the cells of the body. For example, during periods of physical activity muscle cells produce more carbon dioxide and use more oxygen. The levels of carbon dioxide and oxygen in the blood are therefore altered.

Receptor cells in the respiratory centre and two main arteries are sensitive to carbon dioxide concentration

Carbon dioxide concentration rises:
↓
detected by receptor cells
↓
more nerve impulses relayed to respiratory centre
↓
more nerve impulses relayed to intercostal muscles and diaphragm

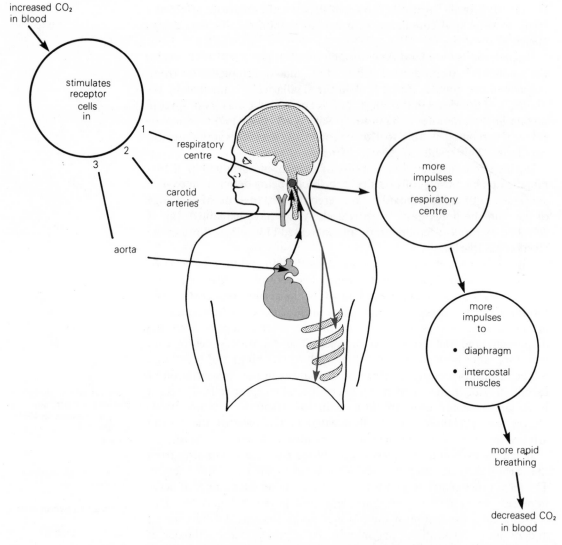

Fig 8.9 *Effect of increased carbon dioxide concentration in the blood on breathing rate*

The receptor cells detect these changes, and the respiratory centre adjusts the ventilation rate accordingly.

It is important to note that at normal working concentrations of blood oxygen and carbon dioxide, it is the carbon dioxide concentration only that regulates ventilation rate. The receptors of the aorta and carotid arteries are sensitive to the concentration of oxygen in the blood, but only when oxygen concentration falls to exceptionally low levels.

This fact is important in a number of situations in everyday life. It has been found that during some operations under general anaesthesia, it is necessary to add 5 per cent carbon dioxide to the oxygen supplied to the

Carbon dioxide concentration in the blood controls rate of ventilation

patient. If no carbon dioxide were present in the gas supply, the concentration of carbon dioxide in the alveoli and blood would fall to very low levels. The respiratory centre would detect the low carbon dioxide concentrations in the blood and respond by decreasing the breathing rate. As a result, the cells of the body would be deprived of vital oxygen supplies.

Similarly, every year a number of people almost drown. In an effort to take in more oxygen, a swimmer may breathe very deeply and rapidly, or **hyperventilate**, before attempting an underwater swim. Although this may increase the concentration of oxygen in the alveoli and blood slightly, it has the more dangerous effect of decreasing carbon dioxide levels in the alveoli and blood. Because the carbon dioxide level in the blood is so low, the respiratory centre is not stimulated to send impulses to the respiratory muscles, forcing the swimmer to breathe or come up for air. However, the muscular activity of swimming does use up the reserves of oxygen in the bloodstream. Without the warning system of increased carbon dioxide concentration to stimulate the desire to breathe, the swimmer may faint or 'black out' under water, before feeling the need to come up for air. Once unconscious under the water, he may later be stimulated to breathe by rising carbon dioxide levels in his blood. But in doing so, he may take water into his lungs and drown.

The larynx and vocal cords

The larynx is a structure at the top of the trachea; it has two important functions. It prevents anything other than air from entering the trachea and bronchi. It also contains the vocal cords which produce the sound in speech.

Larynx:
• allows only air to enter the trachea
• contains vocal cords

The larynx is made up of cartilage plates connected to one another by muscles or ligaments. The vocal cords are folds of the lining of the larynx, which hang into the cavity of the larynx. The vibration of the vocal cords during passage of air through the larynx produces sound. By contraction of the muscles of the larynx, the tension of the vocal cords can be altered, thus causing variations in the pitch and quality of the sound produced.

Sound is produced by vibrating vocal cords

Keeping the lungs clean

Obviously, efficient gaseous exchange cannot occur unless the surfaces of the alveoli are kept clean, and the air passages are not blocked by foreign objects of any sort. A number of mechanisms operate to ensure these things.

As we have mentioned, the larynx has a very important role in preventing anything other than air from entering the lungs. It is sometimes called the 'watchdog' of the lungs. The muscles of the larynx can contract to prevent entry of foreign objects into it. If, in spite of this, solids do enter the larynx, receptors in the walls of the larynx cause coughing, which normally returns the objects to the mouth.

In addition to these mechanisms, the linings of the nasal cavity, trachea and bronchi are equipped with their own cleaning system, to remove smaller, airborne dust particles and bacteria. The surfaces of the epithelial cells lining these parts of the respiratory passages are covered with tiny hair-like projections called cilia. The cilia beat to and fro constantly.

Other epithelial lining cells produce mucus, which forms a thin layer on the surface of the air passages (Fig 8.10). Dust and bacteria are caught in this mucus as they pass through the nasal cavity, trachea or bronchi. The regular upward beating motion of the cilia on the surface of the trachea or bronchi (Fig 8.11) ensures that any dust or bacterial particles arriving on these surfaces are swept, together with the surface mucus, back towards the pharynx. The mucus, with its suspended dust and bacterial particles, is then swallowed or coughed out. The beating of the cilia in the nasal passages transports particles backwards to the pharynx. The action of the cilia in the trachea, bronchi or pharynx is rather like that of an escalator. Foreign particles in the nasal passages can also be eliminated by sneezing.

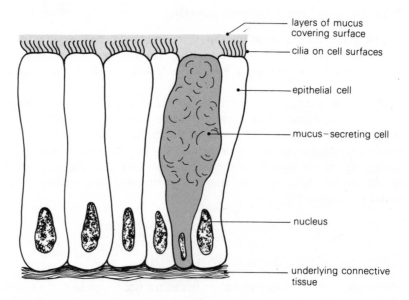

Fig 8.10 *Epithelial cells lining the respiratory passages*

Fig 8.11 *Scanning electron micrograph of the surface of the trachea. Two types of cells can be seen: mucous cells (mc) and ciliated cells whose surface is obscured by a thick covering of cilia (c)*

Chapter 9

Tobacco—more than a health hazard

- The effects of nicotine
- Smoking and heart disease
- Smoking and cancer
- Other substances in tobacco smoke
- Further ill effects of tobacco smoke

Tobacco is composed of dried leaves of the tobacco plant, a plant originally cultivated for smoking by the American Indians. In the early 1600s, European explorers and colonial settlers quickly acquired the habit and took tobacco smoking back to their home countries. They found that inhaling tobacco smoke seemed to produce a feeling of tranquillity and, in some instances, excitement. Since then, it has been found that tobacco smoke contains a drug called nicotine which is responsible for these effects.

During the past fifty years much has been learned about the effects of tobacco smoke on the human body. Tobacco smoke contains a number of chemicals in addition to nicotine. Some of these, like nicotine, produce their effects on the body immediately. Others have an effect over a long period and can lead to diseases such as lung cancer, bronchitis, heart disease and emphysema. It is now believed that tobacco smoking is responsible for more deaths each year than any other single agent.

Smoking is a health hazard

The effects of nicotine

Nicotine reaches the bloodstream when tobacco smoke is inhaled. The smoke is taken into the lungs with inspired air, and the nicotine vapour molecules diffuse from the alveoli, across the layer of alveolar epithelial cells and into the bloodstream. The amount of nicotine reaching the blood from individual puffs of a cigarette is relatively small.

Nicotine diffuses from the alveoli into the bloodstream

Experiments with radioactive nicotine have shown that smokers who inhale absorb more than 95 per cent of the nicotine in the smoke passing through their mouths into their lungs. Figure 9.1 shows the blood levels of radioactive nicotine resulting from smoking a single cigarette. Nicotine concentration rises rapidly when smoking begins and falls off equally rapidly when smoking ceases. Smokers who do not inhale have much lower concentrations of nicotine in their blood.

Nicotine is a powerful drug—the amount from one cigar injected intravenously would kill a man

Nicotine is one of the most poisonous of all drugs. The amount from one small cigar injected intravenously would be enough to kill an adult man. A smoker who inhales can absorb up to 10 per cent of the total amount of nicotine present in a cigar. However, the effect may be spread over 30 minutes, which is long enough for the chemical processes of the

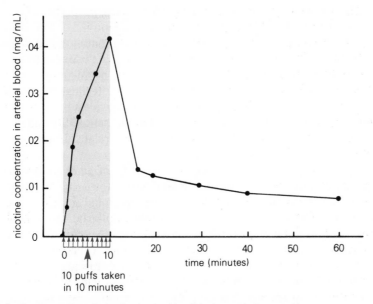

Fig 9.1 *Concentration of nicotine in the blood during and after smoking*

body to inactivate some of the drug. If tobacco is swallowed, the absorption of nicotine is fortunately slow enough for vomiting to empty the stomach before the blood becomes overloaded with the drug.

Nicotine has a number of effects on the individual:

- It stimulates nerves of the brain and some of the nerves leading to muscles and organs. It does this by assisting the passage of impulses from one nerve cell to another.

- It causes muscles to relax.

- It causes the release of the hormone adrenalin, which increases both blood pressure and heart rate.

- It decreases urine output, owing to an increase in the amount of antidiuretic hormone in the blood (see Chapter 12).

- It causes fatty acid concentrations in the blood to rise.

- It causes platelets to stick more readily to each other and to the walls of blood vessels.

Effects of nicotine:
- stimulates brain
- relaxes muscles
- increases blood pressure and heart rate
- decreases urine output
- increases fatty acid concentration in blood
- causes platelet stickiness

The smoking habit

Despite all the publicity given to the dangers of smoking, surveys of all those people who have ever smoked showed that only about 20 per cent of smokers managed to stop smoking, even for short periods. Other studies, in England, have shown that three out of four current smokers either wish to stop smoking or have tried but failed. Why is it that smoking becomes such a compulsive habit?

Dependence on nicotine

It is now widely believed that the habit-forming properties of smoking are due to the presence of nicotine in tobacco smoke. People begin to smoke for a large variety of reasons, which are mainly social. These include such reasons as curiosity, rebelliousness, or the desire to conform to particular social group behaviour. However, people may continue to smoke for other reasons. Smoking may produce feelings of satisfaction and pleasure; it may ease tension; it may also provide a boost to thinking and concentration. The feelings of satisfaction, tranquillity and alertness which are obtained from smoking cigarettes are related largely to the effects of nicotine on their bodies.

People may begin smoking for social reasons

Continued smoking may be due to the pleasures and benefits of smoking:
• feelings of satisfaction and tranquillity
• increased alertness

There is now little doubt that the majority of smokers become dependent on nicotine. (Studies in England have shown that less than 2 per cent of smokers can limit themselves to an occasional cigarette on special occasions. The majority of smokers smoke regularly, rarely going for more than an hour or two without a cigarette.) Another feature of dependence on nicotine is that smokers are found to become tolerant to nicotine. That is, the more they expose themselves to cigarette smoke, the less the nicotine in the smoke appears to affect them. In order to overcome this, most smokers smoke progressively more cigarettes each day, or change to brands containing higher concentrations of nicotine.

Smokers become dependent on nicotine

Smokers become tolerant to nicotine

Dependence on nicotine makes it hard for smokers to give up the habit. In some, the dependence is purely psychological, causing intense craving, tension, irritability and restlessness. In others, a true physical dependence on nicotine may develop as well, with withdrawal symptoms developing when nicotine intake stops (Chapter 14). These symptoms include a fall in pulse rate and blood pressure, disturbance of sleep and impaired performance at tasks requiring skill. Many of these effects have been observed in experimental animals as well as in humans.

Nicotine dependence may be psychological and physical

Withdrawal symptoms may develop when nicotine intake stops:
• fall in pulse rate and blood pressure
• disturbance of sleep
• impaired performance of tasks requiring skill

Giving up smoking may, therefore, not be easy. However, immediate rewards, such as improved fitness and loss of smoker's cough, as well as the long-term benefits of better health and less risk of serious disease, soon outweigh the discomforts of the absence of nicotine.

Smoking and heart disease

Research workers have found that a definite relationship exists between coronary heart disease and smoking. Compared with non-smokers, the risk, for all smokers, of dying from coronary heart disease is increased by one and a half to two and a half times, and up to three and a half times for heavy smokers. Figure 9.2 shows how the risk of death from coronary heart disease increases as the number of cigarettes smoked daily increases, for different age groups.

Smoking is connected with heart disease

Why might smoking cause heart disease? As already seen, nicotine causes an increase in blood pressure both by constricting arteries and increasing the rate of heart beat. Nicotine also raises blood fatty acid concentrations and causes platelets to stick more readily to arterial walls. All

Smoking causes heart disease by
• increasing blood pressure
• raising concentrations of fatty acids in the blood
• causing platelets to stick to arterial walls

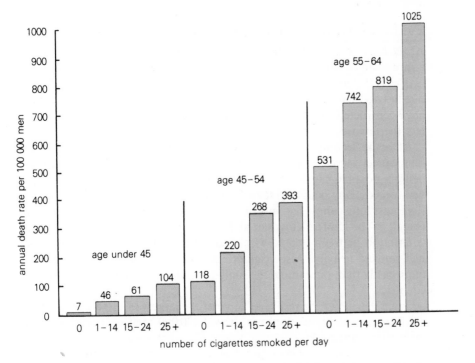

Fig 9.2 *Relationship between number of cigarettes smoked daily and the annual death rate from coronary heart disease*

these factors contribute to the process of atherosclerosis (Chapter 6), and, as a result of this, coronary heart disease may occur. Coronary heart disease has been discussed in greater detail in Chapter 6.

Smoking and cancer

Cancer is a disease in which a particular cell type in the body begins to divide and multiply uncontrollably. The cell type is usually a general or undifferentiated type which cannot perform the work of the normal cells of the organ or tissue. Because of their more rapid rate of division, these cells crowd out and replace the cells of normal body tissues, forming a mass of non-functioning tissue called a tumour. A tumour may be either *benign* or *malignant*. Benign tumours are ones that remain and grow at the site at which they are first formed. They may become life-threatening as they enlarge, because of the space they occupy. For example, a benign tumour of the intestine may cause a serious blockage. They may also produce chemicals that are damaging to the body.

In contrast to this, malignant tumours may spread to other regions of the body. Tumour cells break off from the original growth and may travel in the blood or lymph. They settle in other organs, particularly the liver or lungs. These cells divide to produce further growths known as secondary tumours.

Cancer is produced by uncontrollably dividing cells

Cancer cells crowd out and replace cells of the normal body tissues

Benign tumours remain and grow at the site where they first form

Malignant tumours spread to other parts of the body

Evidence from medical records

At the beginning of this century, cancer of the lung was considered to be a rare form of cancer and seldom appeared on death certificates. Now it is one of the commonest forms of cancer in developed countries. This is due to two factors: first, to a real increase in the numbers of people who have contracted the disease, and second, to our improved ability to detect the disease.

After the Second World War it was noticed that the number of cases of lung cancer increased dramatically. Cigarette smoking was suggested as being a possible cause of this epidemic, as the stresses of war-time life had forced many people to take up the habit. Later on it was pointed out that most lung cancer patients in Germany had been smokers. It was also found, in the United Kingdom and United States, that there was a clear connection between people who died from lung cancer and those who had smoked heavily. Also, cigarette smokers seemed to develop cancer more easily than pipe smokers. Similar results were found in many other countries.

Surveys have found that the risk of dying from lung cancer increases with the number of cigarettes smoked per day

Figure 9.3 shows the results of three of the largest of these surveys, giving information about approximately 1 430 000 men who were studied for periods ranging from 4 to 20 years. This shows how much the risk of dying from lung cancer is multiplied in those who smoke various numbers of cigarettes per day, compared with the risk to non-smokers.

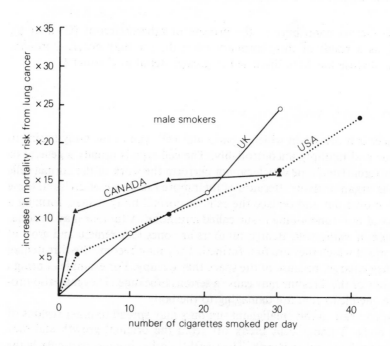

Fig 9.3 *Relationship between number of cigarettes smoked daily and the risk of death from lung cancer (males only)*

The steady rise in death from lung cancer with increased smoking, found in the British and American studies, is striking. The slightly higher British rate may be due to the British habit of smoking cigarettes to a shorter stub length than the Americans, and perhaps to the fact that British men are more exposed to air pollution from domestic and industrial smoke.

Further survey work has shown how variations of the smoking habit may decrease the risk of death from lung cancer. Smokers who do not inhale smoke have been found to be at less risk than those who take smoke into their lungs. Those who take fewer puffs per cigarette, or who smoke filter-tipped cigarettes, also have less chance of developing lung cancer. Several large surveys have also shown that the risk decreases for those who stop smoking—the risk for those who remain smokers increases with age whilst the risk for those who give up smoking remains the same.

People who take fewer puffs per cigarette, or who smoke filter-tipped cigarettes, have less chance of developing cancer

The lungs are not the only organs in which cigarette smoke causes cancer. Cancer of the mouth, throat and oesophagus are all connected with smoking. The risk of smokers getting these forms of cancer is thought to be 5 to 10 times greater than the risk to non-smokers. Cancer of the pancreas and the urinary system have also been shown to be connected with cigarette smoking.

Cancer of the mouth, throat, oesophagus, pancreas and urinary system also seems to be connected with smoking

Experiments with animals

In many experiments, animals have been exposed to cigarette smoke for long periods. Most of the same effects have been observed in man, although we are not able to carry out direct experiments using human 'guinea pigs'. When golden hamsters were placed in an atmosphere of cigarette smoke for most of their life, some of the cells in the larynx were found to change in appearance and function. Some of these cells developed into cancer tissue. In the same types of experiments performed on rats, it was found that the smoke caused changes in the cells lining the alveoli of the lungs. Scientists think that such changes in cells are the first stages of cancer. Experiments in which mice and dogs were allowed to breathe a mixture of cigarette smoke and air showed that these animals developed lung cancers more frequently than animals living in normal conditions.

Much evidence for the cancer-producing effects of tobacco smoke is gained from animal experiments

The carcinogenic (cancer-producing) action of tobacco smoke in animals depends on the type of tobacco, the way it is burned, and the filters used. Different varieties of tobacco seem to differ in their ability to produce cancer. Filters seem to be able to remove some of the cancer-producing substances from cigarette smoke, since they reduce the number of cancerous growths in experimental animals.

Cancer-producing substances in tobacco smoke

Many chemical compounds have been isolated from tobacco smoke and tested for their ability to produce cancer. This has been done using the

Polycyclic aromatic
hydrocarbons in tobacco
smoke produce cancer

skin of mice, where the compound in question is rubbed onto the skin and any reaction observed. A number of conclusions regarding cancer-producing substances have been drawn from these experiments.

The substances chiefly involved in producing cancer are chemicals known as **polycyclic aromatic hydrocarbons**. The simplest aromatic hydrocarbon is benzene, in which there is a ring of six carbon atoms, each of which is joined to a hydrogen atom (Fig 9.4a). Now two benzene rings can be joined together, as shown in Fig 9.4b, to form a compound called naphthalene. Other rings can be joined to naphthalene to give many-ringed or polycyclic compounds. These polycyclic hydrocarbons usually produce an odour—hence the term aromatic. Such compounds having four or more rings have been found to be carcinogenic. One of the best-known and most potent carcinogens of this type is 3,4-benzpyrene (Fig 9.4c).

Other substances in tobacco smoke can cause cancer. Among these are N-nitroso compounds (Fig 9.4d). Some of these chemicals are harmful in their unburned form. One such compound is N-nitrosonicotine, which is present in raw tobacco leaves. Its presence may explain the relationship between tobacco chewing and the development of cancer in the mouth.

Raw tobacco leaves can
cause mouth cancer

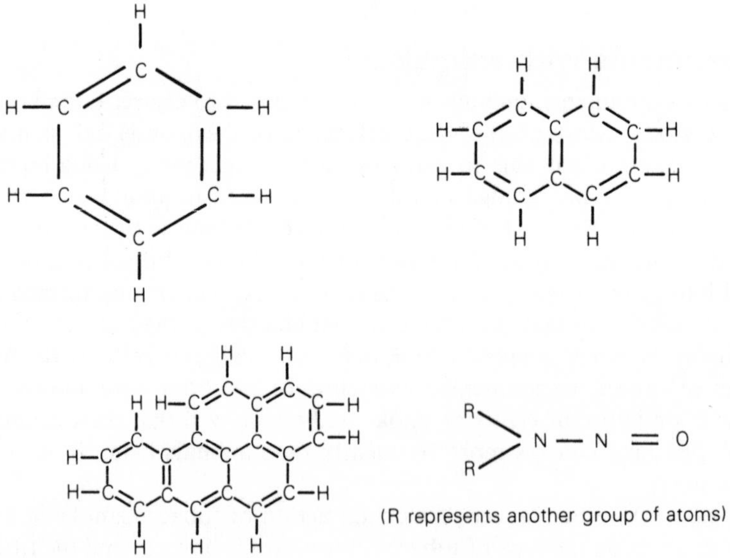

Fig 9.4 *Aromatic hydrocarbons*
(a) Single-ringed (benzene)   *(c) Polycyclic (3,4-benzpyrene)*
(b) Double-ringed (naphthalene) *(d) N-nitroso compound*

The cancer-producing substances in tobacco smoke fall into three categories:

- Complete carcinogens, chemicals which, when applied in certain quantities, can themselves cause cancer in animals.
- Tumour initiators, carcinogens that bring about the first stage of tumour formation.
- Tumour promoters, chemicals that are able to complete the formation of a tumour only after it has been begun by other substances.

Other causes of lung cancer

Studies show that the ingredients of tobacco smoke are not the only factors that cause lung cancer. Air pollution, particularly coal smoke, appears to raise the risk of lung cancer. However, its effect is small compared with that of cigarette smoking. Workers in certain jobs who are exposed to asbestos dust, radioactive materials, mustard gas and the products of coal distillation in the gas industry seem to be more likely to contract lung cancer. This is particularly the case if they are smokers.

One theory suggests that smoking may not cause lung cancer at all. It proposes that the link between smoking and lung cancer may be a matter of genetics. The idea is that the genes that make a person want to smoke are closely connected with the genes causing a person to be more vulnerable to lung cancer. This suggests that it is not the smoking that causes lung cancer, but a genetic property of the person himself. If this were the case, it would follow that neither smoking nor any agent outside the body causes the disease, so giving up smoking would provide no protection.

Other causes of cancer:
- asbestos dust
- radioactive materials
- mustard gas
- products of coal distillation

Genetic make-up may be linked with lung cancer

Other substances in tobacco smoke

Other substances present in tobacco smoke have ill effects on the body.

Irritant substances

As we saw in Chapter 8, the surfaces of the cells lining the respiratory passages have numerous cilia. The cells are covered with a fine film of mucus, in which dust particles, bacteria or other foreign particles are trapped as they make their way towards the air sacs of the lungs. The purpose of the cilia of the epithelial cells is to beat the mucus, with the unwanted material, towards the throat. This mucus is removed from the mouth as phlegm.

Some substances contained in tobacco smoke appear to hinder the process of mucus removal. They do this by increasing the secretion of mucus in the bronchial tubes and interfering with the action of the cilia lining them. As a result of this, increased amounts of phlegm accumulate in the respiratory passages. This causes a rasping cough known as 'smoker's cough'. Some irritants assist in the development of cancer.

Irritants in smoke increase mucus and decrease beating of cilia

Carbon monoxide

Carbon monoxide combines with haemoglobin and prevents it from carrying oxygen

The gas inhaled from a cigarette contains 1 to 5 per cent carbon monoxide. This results from the incomplete burning of tobacco. The carbon monoxide inhaled with cigarette smoke is diluted with air in the alveoli, where it reaches a concentration of about 400 parts per million. Although low, this concentration of carbon monoxide can combine with haemoglobin in the red blood cells about 200 times more easily than oxygen. Thus a large proportion of the haemoglobin in heavy smokers is made inactive by its combination with carbon monoxide. The inactive compound formed is called carboxyhaemoglobin, which in some smokers forms up to 15 per cent of the total blood haemoglobin.

Because haemoglobin is made inactive by carbon monoxide, there is less free haemoglobin to carry oxygen in the bloodstream. Thus, less oxygen can be carried to all tissues in the body, and peak performance of any physical activity becomes impossible. Heart pain may also result under conditions of severe physical exercise, owing to impaired transport of oxygen through the coronary arteries to the heart muscle (see Chapter 6).

Tar is composed of a large number of chemicals

Many other compounds are contained in tobacco smoke. Most of these are present in small quantities, and a number make up the brown viscous liquid residue from tobacco smoke known as tar (Fig 9.5). Non-carcinogenic polycyclic aromatic hydrocarbons, as well as an enormous range of organic compounds such as phenols, aldehydes, acids and esters, have been detected and identified. Some of these have been shown to be not harmful, but it is still possible that there are a number of yet undiscovered carcinogens among the array.

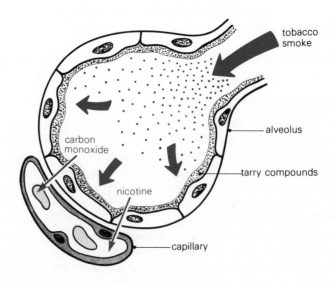

Fig 9.5 *Ingredients of tobacco smoke*

Further ill effects of tobacco smoke

On the lungs

Two other diseases of the respiratory system which may be caused by smoking are chronic bronchitis and emphysema. The first symptoms of chronic bronchitis are usually a grating cough and the accumulation of increased quantities of phlegm in the throat. In the case of the smoker, this is usually the result of the interference by tobacco smoke with the normal cleaning mechanisms of the respiratory passages, as we explained earlier. Later, the narrowing of bronchial tubes causes increased difficulty with breathing.

Two other results of smoking are bronchitis and emphysema

The continual coughing associated with chronic bronchitis may lead to the development of a more serious condition known as emphysema. In this condition, coughing causes the walls of the minute alveoli to break down to form larger air spaces. This results in a much reduced surface area of lung being available for the exchange of gases between the air spaces and the blood (Chapter 8, p 152). Damage caused to the alveoli of the lungs by the coughing of chronic bronchitis is permanent; it cannot be repaired in any way.

Emphysema involves the breakdown of the walls of alveoli, resulting in decreased gas exchange

In people with chronic bronchitis and emphysema, more rapid and strained breathing is necessary to keep the correct levels of oxygen and carbon dioxide in the lungs and bloodstream. This often causes a great deal of stress. In some people, the circulation of blood through capillaries in the lungs is also reduced. This causes reduced diffusion of gases into and out of the alveoli, and means that the lungs are unable to supply sufficient oxygen to the tissues during periods of exercise. Under these conditions the heart has to work harder to pump the necessary blood to the lungs. This may contribute to the onset of heart failure.

Rapid, strained breathing is a feature of people with chronic bronchitis or emphysema

On the digestive system

Gingivitis (see Chapter 11) and loss of teeth are more common in smokers than non-smokers. There is also evidence that gastric and duodenal ulcers are related to smoking. Relaxation of the stomach muscles during and after smoking allows acid to flow back into the oesophagus. This can cause severe indigestion.

Gingivitis, loss of teeth, gastric and duodenal ulcers are more common in smokers than non-smokers

On the immune system

Lung cells have been shown to shrivel and break up in the constant presence of cigarette smoke. White blood cells called macrophages, responsible for engulfing bacteria or viruses (see Chapter 7), have also been found to be reduced in number in lung tissue exposed to smoke. Lymphocytes, white blood cells responsible for defending the body against microbial invaders (Chapter 7), seem to become less active. All

Smoke reduces the number of macrophages in lung tissue and makes lymphocytes less active

these effects indicate that smoking may dramatically reduce the efficiency of the body's immune or defence system.

On physical fitness

Tar on the surface of alveoli decreases gas exchange

Tarry compounds and other particles from cigarette smoke, which collect on the surface of the alveolar epithelial cells, greatly reduce gas exchange. This further interferes with a smoker's ability to perform at peak efficiency in any physical activity.

Effects during pregnancy

Nicotine reduces growth in the baby and reduces the supply of food and oxygen through the placenta

A pregnant woman can cause harm to her baby through the nicotine and carbon monoxide of the smoke she inhales. Nicotine is carried from the mother to the baby via the placenta and seems to reduce tissue growth directly. It may also cause narrowing of the blood vessels of the placenta, resulting in a lower rate of food and oxygen supply to the baby (see Chapter 17). This interferes with the baby's normal growth.

Carbon monoxide combines with the baby's haemoglobin

The carbon monoxide carried in the mother's blood is also carried across the placenta to the baby's blood. In fact, the carbon monoxide concentration in a baby's blood is found to be higher than that in the mother's blood. Such a presence of carbon monoxide reduces the amount of haemoglobin available in the baby's blood for the transport of oxygen. This may also contribute to the lower birth weights of babies of smoking mothers.

The chances of still-birth and infant death increase if the mother smokes heavily

In other studies, heavy smoking by pregnant women after the fourth month of pregnancy has been shown to lead to an increased incidence of still-birth and infant death during the first week of life.

Figure 9.6 summarises the effects of the various substances present in tobacco smoke.

nicotine:
- increased risk of heart disease
- retarded growth of foetus
- dependence

carbon monoxide causes decreased oxygen-carrying capacity of blood, leading to:
- decreased physical fitness
- retarded growth of foetus

polycyclic aromatic hydrocarbons:
- risk of cancer development

other irritant substances:
- chronic bronchitis and emphysema
- gastric and duodenal ulcers
- gingivitis (inflammation of the gums)
- decreased resistance to disease

Fig 9.6 *Effects of tobacco smoke*

Chapter 10

The digestive system—a food refinery

Cells need a constant supply of fuel

We saw in Chapter 4 that all the cells of the body need a constant supply of fuel to produce the energy they require for living. In Chapter 6 the circulatory system was described as the 'lifeline' of the cell, delivering the chemical fuels to cells in all parts of the body.

Fuels are small molecules such as glucose, fatty acids, glycerol and amino acids

The fuels of cells are small molecules such as glucose, fatty acids, glycerol and amino acids. These molecules are carried in dissolved form in the blood plasma. From here they move into cells, through their membranes, by diffusion or active transport.

Food consists of complex organic substances:
• carbohydrates
• fats
• proteins
• nucleic acids
• vitamins
• mineral salts

However, as we saw in Chapter 3, most of the foods we eat are organic substances, formed in either animals or plants. Meat, vegetables, fruit, eggs, cereals, cakes and milk are all composed mainly of large complex organic compounds: carbohydrates, fats, proteins and nucleic acids, as well as vitamins, minerals and water. Table 10.1 shows the chemical composition of some common food substances.

Table 10.1 *The nutrient composition of foods*

Food	Protein	Fat	Carbohydrate	Vitamins	Minerals	Fibre
Meat	+ +	+ +	−	+ +	+ +	−
Fish	+ +	+	−	+ + +	+ +	−
Eggs	+ +	+	−	+ + +	+	−
Milk and cheese	+ +	+ +	+ +	+ +	+ +	−
Skim milk	+ +	−	+ +	+	+ +	−
Vegetables	+	−	+ +	+ + +	+	+ +
Fruit	+	−	+ +	+ +	+	+ +
Bread, cereals	+	−	+ + +	+	+	+ +
Fats, oils	−	+ + + +	−	+	−	−
Sugar/ honey	−	−	+ + + +	−	−	−

Source: Based on A Borushek, *The Complete Diet Manual for Australian Weight Watchers*, Diet Publications for Weight Watchers, 1315 Hay St, West Perth, Western Australia, 1978

Just as the crude oil from a deep sea bed must be refined to produce petrol for a car, or aviation fuel for an aeroplane, so these solid organic foods which we eat require refining. They must be broken down into their simple building-block molecules: monosaccharides (such as glucose), amino acids, fatty acids and nucleic acids. These building-block molecules are the purified simple fuel molecules for the cells. Because of their small size, they can dissolve in the blood plasma and travel through membranes into the cells.

Digestion is the breaking down of lumps of food into small molecules

The process by which the solid lumps of food we swallow are converted to building-block fuels for the cells is known as **digestion** (Fig 10.1). The organs responsible for digestion form the digestive system.

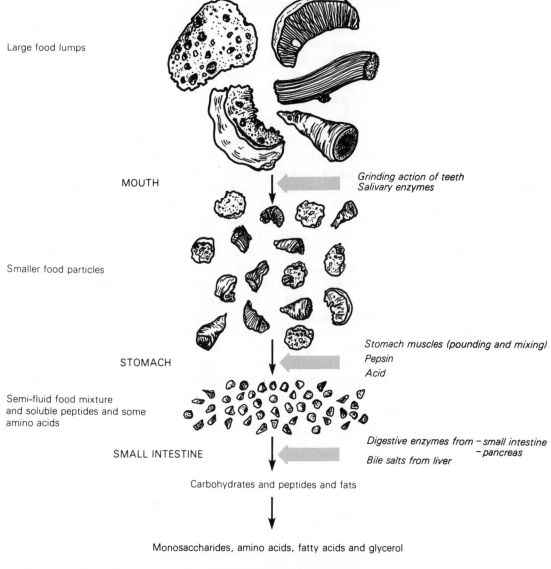

Large food lumps

MOUTH

Grinding action of teeth
Salivary enzymes

Smaller food particles

STOMACH

Stomach muscles (pounding and mixing)
Pepsin
Acid

Semi-fluid food mixture
and soluble peptides and some
amino acids

SMALL INTESTINE

Digestive enzymes from – small intestine
                                    – pancreas
Bile salts from liver

Carbohydrates and peptides and fats

Monosaccharides, amino acids, fatty acids and glycerol

Small soluble 'building block'
molecules

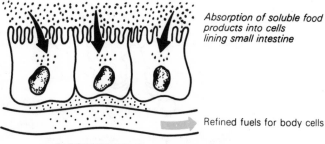

Absorption of soluble food
products into cells
lining small intestine

Refined fuels for body cells

Fig 10.1 *The process of digestion*   BLOODSTREAM

Terms and processes

The digestive system has many parts, specially designed to assist in the different stages of the refining or digestive process (Fig 10.2). These can be classified into three major groups:

- the mouth and pharynx
- the gut tube
- the glands outside the gut.

Food is taken into the digestive system by ingestion

In the first stage of the process, known as **ingestion,** food is taken into the digestive system. The structures concerned with this stage are the mouth, with its teeth and tongue, and the pharynx.

Food is swallowed

From here, food is then swallowed and enters the gut tube or alimentary canal. It is here that digestion occurs, converting the solid food lumps into simple soluble molecules which can then be absorbed from the alimentary canal into the bloodstream.

Food enters the alimentary canal where digestion occurs

Digestion occurs in two ways: **mechanical** (or physical) **digestion** and **chemical digestion.** The grinding action of the teeth and the muscular action of the walls of the alimentary canal are responsible for mechanical digestion. Mechanical digestion breaks down the solid food particles so that chemical digestion can occur. Chemical digestion is brought about by the action of digestive enzymes. These enzymes are secreted by the glands outside the gut tube, for example the salivary glands and pancreas, or by glandular cells situated in the gut wall itself. As we shall see later, different enzymes are involved in the different stages of the breakdown of organic compounds. These can be grouped and given general names, depending on the type of organic compound they act upon. Those acting on proteins are called proteinases, on fats—lipases, and on carbohydrates—carbohydrases.

Mechanical digestion—breakdown of food by the action of teeth and churning action of the alimentary canal

Chemical digestion—breakdown of food by enzymes

Mechanical digestion is performed by the teeth, and the muscles of the stomach and small intestine

Chemical digestion is performed in the mouth, stomach and small intestine by enzymes, acid and bile salts

Chemical and mechanical digestion go hand in hand. As the action of teeth and then muscles breaks down food into smaller particles, more surfaces are exposed on which the digestive enzymes can act.

Some of the food we eat cannot be broken down by the digestive enzymes or by muscular action. It continues on down the alimentary canal and is eliminated or egested from the body, through the anus.

Undigestable food is egested from the body

Structure of the gut tube

In smaller, simpler animals such as earthworms, the alimentary canal is a simple tube which looks much the same throughout its length. In the very early stages of the growth of the foetus (Chapter 17) the human alimentary canal is also a simple straight tube, connected with the outside at the mouth and the anus. Even at this stage, the cells of the gut tube wall are arranged into distinct tissue layers. (The arrangement of different cell types into tissues was discussed in Chapter 2.)

The alimentary canal begins in the foetus as a straight tube

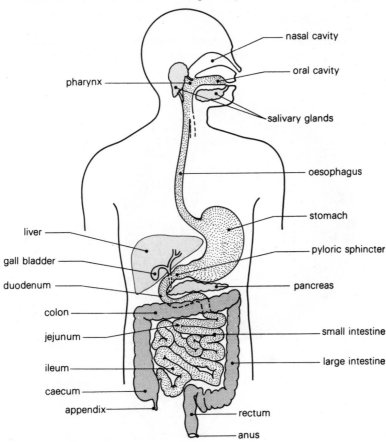

Fig 10.2 *Parts of the digestive system*

As the embryo grows and the digestive system develops, different segments of this simple tube enlarge and develop in different ways. By the time the alimentary canal is fully developed, the simple gut tube is made up of a number of specialised organs: the oesophagus, stomach, small and large intestines and associated glands.

Although these differentiated organs appear to be quite different from one another, they are all composed of the same tissue layers which were present in the simple gut tube. Depending on the particular digestive activity of each organ, their tissue layers have grown and developed in different ways. A brief look at the basic arrangement of the tissue layers of the gut wall will therefore help us to understand how the alimentary canal works.

Look at Fig 10.3, which shows the general structure of the alimentary canal, with its four tissue layers. These are the:

Four tissue layers of alimentary canal:
• mucosa
• submucosa
• muscle layer
• outer membrane

● mucosa

● submucosa

● muscle layer

● outer membrane.

The alimentary canal is in contact with the outside world through the mouth and anus. In a sense, therefore, the surface of the alimentary

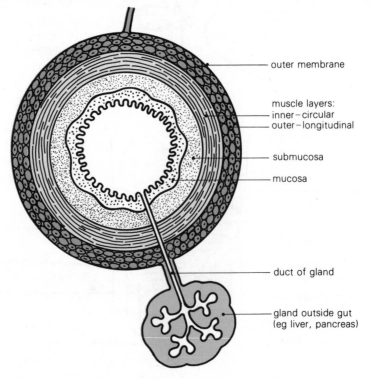

outer membrane

muscle layers:
inner – circular
outer – longitudinal

submucosa

mucosa

duct of gland

gland outside gut
(eg liver, pancreas)

Fig 10.3 *The tissue layers of the gut tube*

canal is an external body surface, even though it is inside the body. Like all body surfaces, it is covered by epithelial cells (see Chapter 2). These epithelial cells are supported by a thin layer of connective tissue. The epithelial cells and the thin layer of connective tissue are together called the **mucosa**.

The structure of the mucosa is different in different parts of the alimentary canal. It depends on the job of that particular part of the alimentary canal. For example, in the small intestine, which is responsible for absorbing digested food, the epithelial lining is only one cell thick. This permits easy absorption of the food molecules. In the oesophagus, which must be protected from hot liquids and the rough edges of food, the epithelium is made up of many layers of flattened cells. In this respect, the surface of the oesophagus is similar to that of the skin (see Chapter 7).

The structure of the mucosa varies along the alimentary canal, according to the role it has to play

Beneath the mucosa lies a layer of connective tissue called the **submucosa**. This supports the mucosa and provides it with blood and lymphatic vessels, and nerves.

The submucosa is connective tissue

Below the submucosa are the **muscle layers**. They are responsible for moving food through the alimentary canal, as well as for mixing food and mechanical digestion. The muscle of the gut tube is smooth or involuntary muscle. That is, we have no conscious control over its contraction or relaxation. It is arranged into two layers: an inner circular layer, whose fibres run around the gut tube, and an outer longitudinal layer, whose fibres run along the gut tube.

The muscle layers of the alimentary canal are responsible for mixing food and mechanical digestion

The outermost layer of the gut wall is a thin membrane which covers the alimentary canal and anchors it to the wall of the abdominal cavity.

Movement in the alimentary canal

The muscle layers of the gut wall play a very important part in the digestive process. They are responsible for:

Muscle layers also
• propel food along the alimentary canal
• separate the food digesting in different parts of the alimentary canal

- mixing of food and mechanical digestion
- propelling food along the gut tube
- separating the contents of different organs of the alimentary canal from one another.

Food is propelled along all parts of the gut tube by a process known as **peristalsis**. This is illustrated in Fig 10.4. Contraction of the circular muscle layer behind the food bolus and relaxation of the muscle layer in front of the bolus pushes food along the alimentary canal. These waves of muscle contractions may travel up to a metre along the alimentary canal or may die out after only a few centimetres. Waves of contraction begin when the wall of the gut is stretched by a lump of food. It is an involuntary process, over which we have no conscious control.

Contractions of circular muscle which push food along the alimentary canal—peristalsis

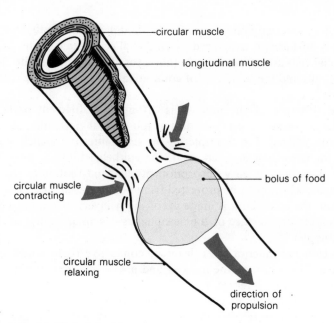

Fig 10.4 *Peristalsis (diagrammatic)*

In particular regions of the alimentary canal the circular muscle layer forms a much thicker layer. This area of thickened muscle is known as a **sphincter**. Sphincters are found where one organ joins with another in the alimentary canal; for example, between the oesophagus and stomach, and between stomach and small intestine, as well as at the end of the alimentary canal (anal sphincter). Sphincters act like a rubber band around the top of a bag. By their contraction or relaxation they control the passage of small quantities of digested food from one organ in the alimentary canal to the next.

Sphincters are muscular and control the passage of digesting food from one organ to another

Chemical breakdown of food

The muscle layers contribute to digestion by mechanically breaking down food into smaller particles and by mixing the food with digestive juices. Such digestive juices contain the agents responsible for the chemical breakdown of food. These agents are called **digestive enzymes**.

Muscle layers mix food with digestive juices

Enzymes carry out chemical digestion

As we saw in Chapter 3, enzymes are biological catalysts which allow chemical reactions to occur far more rapidly than would occur under normal circumstances. Almost all the chemical reactions taking place in the body depend on the presence of enzymes.

The digestive enzymes are extracellular enzymes. That is, they are released from the gland cells which manufacture them, and they catalyse reactions occurring outside the cells, in the alimentary canal. Like all enzymes, the digestive enzymes are specific in their activity (see Chapter 3).

Digestive enzymes are extracellular enzymes

Particular enzymes are needed for the breakdown of different types of organic compounds. Also, different enzymes may be needed for the different stages in the breakdown of one organic compound.

Digestive enzymes are manufactured in four parts of the alimentary canal: the salivary glands, the gastric glands, the intestinal glands and the pancreas. Table 10.2 shows the main fluids secreted in the different organs of the digestive tract and the functions of the digestive enzymes found in these secretions. In later sections of this chapter, we shall look in more detail at these organs and their secretions. At this stage we shall examine the step-by-step breakdown of the three main classes of food and the role of the digestive enzymes in this chemical digestion.

It is worth noting that in addition to the digestive enzymes, mucus is secreted by gland cells throughout the alimentary canal. This assists in mixing and lubricating food. The liver has an important role, too, in the secretion of **bile salts**, which, as we shall see, are necessary for the breakdown of fats.

Digestive enzymes are manufactured in
- salivary glands
- gastric glands
- intestinal glands
- pancreas

Mucus is secreted by cells in the alimentary canal

Table 10.2 *Secretions of the digestive tract*

	Gland	Secretion	Function
Mouth	Salivary glands	Saliva • amylase	Polysaccharides → disaccharides (starch and glycogen) (maltose)
Stomach	Gastric glands	Gastric juice • HCl • proteolytic enzyme (pepsin)	Acid environment for pepsin Proteins → polypeptides
Liver	Liver	Bile • bile salts	Emulsification of fats
Pancreas	Exocrine pancreas	Pancreatic juice • NaHCO₃ • amylase • lipase • trypsin	Neutralise HCl Polysaccharides → disaccharides Fats → fatty acids and glycerol Proteins → polypeptides
Small intestine	Intestinal glands	Intestinal juice • peptidase • maltase • sucrase • lactase	Peptides → amino acids Disaccharides → monosaccharides

Breakdown of carbohydrates

Many of the carbohydrates we eat are long chains of sugars, or polysaccharides. Others, such as sucrose, maltose and lactose, are disaccharides, with two sugar molecules joined together. All of these must be broken

**Breakdown of
polysaccharides by
enzymes:
polysaccharides**
↓
disaccharides
↓
monosaccharides

**Salivary and pancreatic
amylases break down
polysaccharides**
↓
disaccharides

**Pancreatic juices neutralise
the acid from the stomach**

**Disaccharides are broken
down to monosaccharides
in the intestine by**
• **maltase**
• **sucrase**
• **lactase**

down to simple monosaccharides before they can be absorbed from the intestine and carried in the bloodstream to the cells of the body.

This breakdown occurs in two stages (Fig 10.5). First, polysaccharides (long-chain sugars) are broken down to form disaccharides (double sugars). Then disaccharides are split to release the simple sugar molecules.

The first stage of the reaction is catalysed by enzymes called **amylases**. Digestion of carbohydrates begins in the mouth, when salivary amylase (produced by the salivary glands) comes into contact with food. Salivary amylase is made inactive once it reaches the stomach by the very acid gastric environment. Digestion of polysaccharides to disaccharides is completed in the intestine by pancreatic amylase. This enzyme can operate only after the acidic juices secreted in the stomach have been neutralised in the intestine by sodium bicarbonate. Sodium bicarbonate is also secreted by the pancreas.

The second stage of carbohydrate digestion is the breakdown of disaccharides to release monosaccharides. This is carried out in the intestine by enzymes manufactured by gland cells in the wall of the small intestine. These enzymes are named according to the type of disaccharide they act upon. For example, maltase catalyses the splitting of maltose to its glucose units; sucrase, the breakdown of sucrose to glucose and fructose;

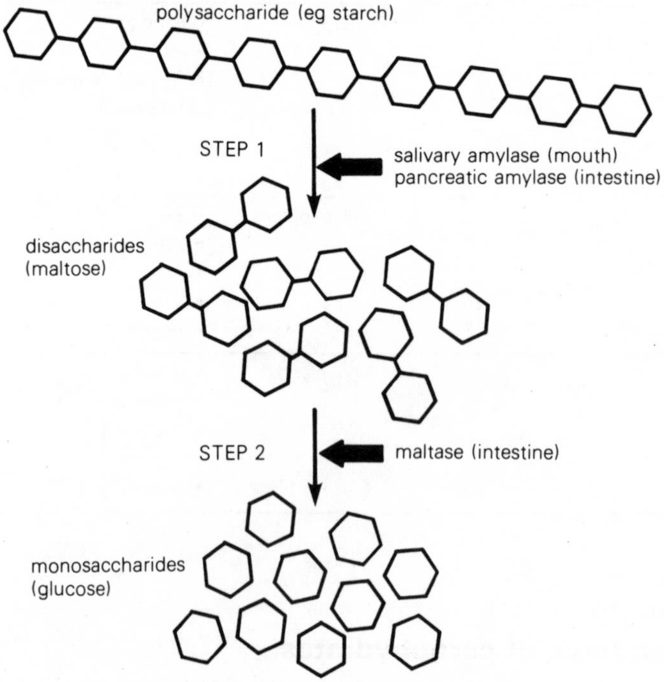

Fig 10.5 *Breakdown of carbohydrates*

and lactase, the breakdown of lactose to glucose and galactose. These monosaccharides are then readily absorbed.

Some carbohydrates, for example cellulose, which is responsible for the fibrous nature of vegetables and fruit, cannot be digested by humans. This is because the digestive enzyme cellulase, which is required for the breakdown of cellulose, is not secreted by any of the digestive glands. (Herbivorous or grass-eating animals are capable of digesting cellulose because of the presence of microbes in their alimentary canal, which manufacture the enzyme cellulase.) Despite its undigestible nature, however, the fibre or cellulose content of fruit and vegetables is an important part of our diet. It provides bulk or roughage, which aids in the movement of the waste products of digestion through the alimentary canal and their elimination from the body.

Undigested cellulose provides bulk or roughage, which aids movement of waste products

Breakdown of proteins

As we saw in Chapter 3, the basic subunits or building-block molecules of proteins are amino acids. These are joined together in long chains of amino acids called polypeptides. Proteins may contain up to three or four polypeptide chains, coiled together in particular ways. The refined products of protein digestion are amino acids, which, like the simple sugars, can be absorbed through the wall of the intestine into the bloodstream.

The breakdown of proteins in the digestive tract is illustrated in Fig 10.6. In the first stage, large protein molecules are broken up into chains of amino acids or polypeptides. The process begins in the stomach, where it is catalysed by the enzyme **pepsin**. Pepsin is produced by the gastric glands. Pepsin acts only to split bonds between particular amino acids so that a variety of polypeptides of varying lengths is produced. To prevent the gland cells of the stomach from being digested by the enzyme which they produce, pepsin is secreted in an inactive form, known as **pepsinogen**. Pepsinogen is converted to active pepsin in the stomach in the presence of **hydrochloric acid**. Hydrochloric acid is produced by other gland cells in the stomach wall. In addition to converting pepsin to its active state, it maintains the degree of acidity (pH) of the gastric contents at a level most favourable for pepsin to work (a pH of less than 2).

Breakdown of proteins by enzymes:
protein
↓ (pepsin)
polypeptides
↓ (trypsin)
smaller polypeptides
↓ (peptidases)
amino acids

Pepsinogen (inactive) is converted to pepsin (active) by acid

Protein and polypeptides are broken down further in the intestine (at neutral pH), catalysed by the pancreatic enzyme **trypsin**. (Like pepsin, trypsin is secreted in an inactive form, **trypsinogen**. It is made active by **enterokinase**, an enzyme secreted by the intestine.)

Trypsinogen (inactive) is converted to trypsin (active) by an enzyme, enterokinase

The final breakdown of peptides to amino acids occurs in the intestine. A variety of enzymes known as **peptidases** catalyses these reactions. Peptidases are secreted mainly by glands in the walls of the intestine and also by the pancreas.

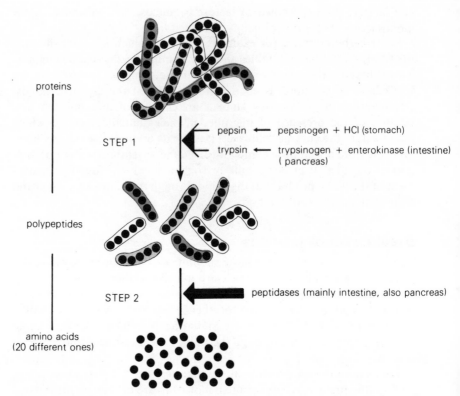

proteins

STEP 1

pepsin ← pepsinogen + HCl (stomach)

trypsin ← trypsinogen + enterokinase (intestine)
(pancreas)

polypeptides

STEP 2   peptidases (mainly intestine, also pancreas)

amino acids
(20 different ones)

Fig 10.6 *Breakdown of proteins*

Breakdown of fats

Pancreatic lipase breaks
down fats to fatty acids
and glycerol

The breakdown of fats to fatty acids and glycerol is catalysed in the intestine by **pancreatic lipase**:

$$Fat \xrightarrow{\text{lipase}} glycerol + 3\ fatty\ acids$$

Fatty acids and glycerol are absorbed into the mucosal cells of the intestine.

However, a special problem has to be overcome in fat digestion. Because fats are not soluble in water, they form large globules in the intestinal juices. These large globules are broken down by **bile salts**. Bile salts are not enzymes but chemicals which break up or **emulsify** the large fat globules to form many tiny fat droplets. The increased surface area of the tiny fat droplets then allows lipase to act more readily. If for any reason bile salts are not secreted into the intestine, almost all the fat passes into the faeces undigested. The secretion of bile salts by the liver is therefore very important in fat digestion. The stages in the breakdown of fats are illustrated in Fig 10.7.

Bile salts emulsify fats

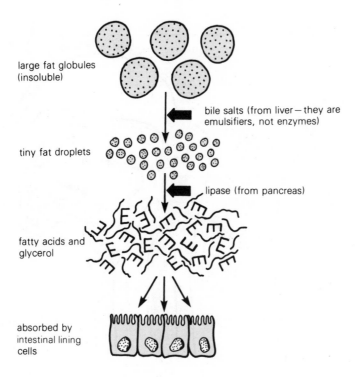

large fat globules
(insoluble)

bile salts (from liver — they are
emulsifiers, not enzymes)

tiny fat droplets

lipase (from pancreas)

fatty acids and
glycerol

absorbed by
intestinal lining
cells

Fig 10.7 *Breakdown of fats in the small intestine*

Organs of the alimentary canal

Look again at Fig 10.2, which illustrates the major organs of the alimentary canal, its associated glands and the mouth and pharynx.

Mouth, pharynx and salivary glands

Digestion of food begins in the mouth. The chewing action of the teeth—cutting by the incisor teeth and crushing by the premolars and molars—reduces the size of the lumps of food. At the same time this chewing mixes food with **saliva**. Saliva is secreted by the salivary glands, which are located in the tissues around the mouth. Their secretions travel from the gland cells along thin tubes called ducts, which open into the mouth. (Figure 10.8 illustrates the position of one of the salivary glands and its ducts entering the floor of the mouth.) In addition to the enzyme amylase, saliva contains water, minerals and some mucus, which helps to lubricate the food.

After chewing and mixing with saliva, the pellets of food are then swallowed. Once swallowing begins it is an automatic or reflex event, over which we have no conscious control. It occurs in four stages:

Teeth cut and crush food and mix food with saliva

Saliva travels to the mouth through ducts

Saliva helps to lubricate food

Swallowing is an automatic (reflex) event

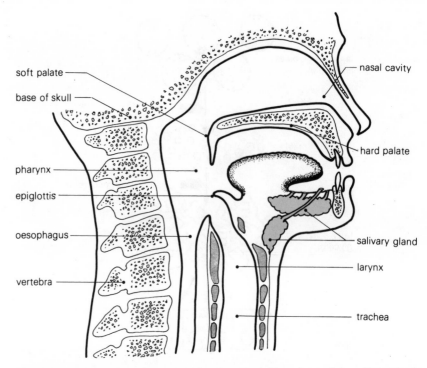

Fig 10.8 *Section through the head, illustrating the position of two of the salivary glands and their ducts entering the mouth*

- The tongue pushes against the top of the mouth and pushes food to the back of the mouth or pharynx.
- The soft palate is pushed upwards by the tongue, closing the opening to the nasal cavity.
- The larynx is pulled upwards against the **epiglottis**, preventing food from entering the respiratory passages.
- Food is then squeezed backwards and down, and guided through the pharynx to the oesophagus.

Figure 10.9 illustrates this process.

Oesophagus

Food is moved down the oesophagus by peristalsis

The oesophagus is a simple straight tube with very muscular walls. Solid foods are moved down the oesophagus by waves of peristalsis and reach the stomach in about 6 seconds. Liquids travel much more rapidly.

Stomach

The stomach is a large muscular sac which on first glance looks quite different from the other tube-like parts of the alimentary canal. In addition to its digestive role, the stomach acts as a reservoir area of the digestive

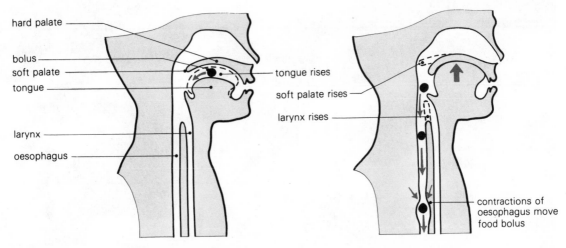

hard palate

bolus
soft palate
tongue

larynx

oesophagus

tongue rises

soft palate rises

larynx rises

contractions of
oesophagus move
food bolus

Fig 10.9 *Stages in the process of swallowing*

system. Its sac-like structure fits it for this role. After a heavy meal, foods may remain in the stomach for 3 to 4 hours, and its walls may stretch to hold over 2 litres of food and gastric juices.

> The stomach is a reservoir for the digestive system

The mechanical digestion of food, which began in the mouth, is continued in the stomach. The muscle layers of the stomach walls are very thick. Waves of peristaltic contractions spread rhythmically over the stomach wall, pounding and churning the contents. All the secretions of the stomach—acid, pepsin and mucus—are produced by special cells in the mucosa, the innermost tissue layer (Fig 10.10). The gastric secretions from these cells pass directly into the stomach. Figure 10.11 shows the arrangement of the tissue layers of the stomach.

> Peristaltic contractions of the stomach walls pound and churn the digesting food

> Special cells in the mucosa secrete the acid and enzymes

When digestion in the stomach is complete, food is converted to a semi-fluid mixture called **chyme**. From time to time, the **pyloric sphincter** (the ring of muscle separating the stomach contents from the intestine) relaxes and a small amount of fluid passes through to the small intestine.

> Chyme is the semi-fluid food mixture formed in the stomach

Small intestine

The small intestine is a very long tube—up to 7 metres in the adult. Because of its great length, it is coiled inside the abdominal cavity. The small intestine is divided into three parts: the **duodenum**, followed by the **jejunum**, and then the **ileum**. Although all three parts of the small intestine have a very similar structure, there are differences in their appearance.

> The small intestine consists of
> • duodenum
> • jejunum
> • ileum

The duodenum is the main site of chemical digestion in the gut tube. Digestive secretions enter the duodenum from:

> The duodenum is the main site of chemical digestion

- the liver, via a tube known as the bile duct
- the pancreas, via the pancreatic duct
- gland cells in the wall of the intestine.

> Digestive juices enter the duodenum from
> • liver
> • pancreas
> • mucosa of the intestine

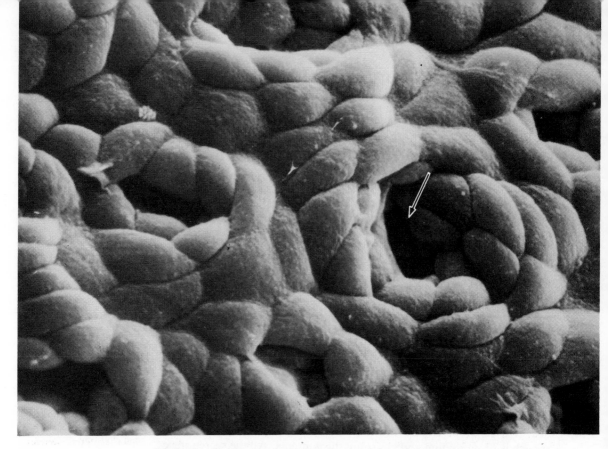

Fig 10.10 *The arrow indicates the opening of a gastric gland onto the surface of the stomach. Individual cells can be seen arranged around the openings*

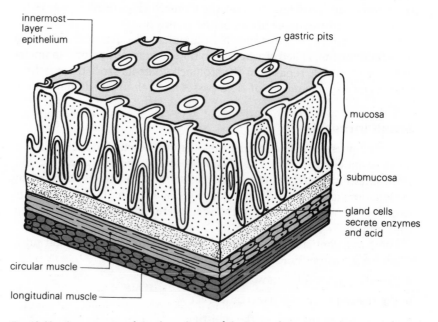

innermost layer – epithelium

gastric pits

mucosa

submucosa

gland cells secrete enzymes and acid

circular muscle

longitudinal muscle

Fig 10.11 *Arrangement of the tissue layers of the stomach*

The sodium bicarbonate of pancreatic juice soon neutralises the acid chyme from the stomach. The digestive enzymes, assisted by bile salts from the liver, can then complete the breakdown of food molecules to small soluble compounds. These products of digestion can pass through the intestinal lining and enter the bloodstream.

Digested foods are absorbed almost entirely in the ileum. (The structure of the ileum, and the process of food absorption, are discussed on p 197.)

Digested food is absorbed in the ileum

Large intestine

After all the digestible compounds are absorbed in the ileum, the material passes into the large intestine. Here the remaining materials consist of water and undigested matter: vegetable fibres and cellulose (roughage), bacteria and mucus.

The first part of the large intestine is the **caecum**. This is a relatively small sac with a small fingerlike projection of gut tube, called the **appendix**, at its 'blind' end. In humans, the caecum and appendix appear to have no specific function. In some plant-eating (herbivorous) animals, the caecum and appendix are very much more developed and are the site of cellulose digestion by microorganisms.

The large intestine secretes no enzymes and can absorb very little food. The **colon** absorbs a lot of water, however. As a result, the undigested residue which passes on to the **rectum** is in a semi-solid state, known as **faeces**. Remaining food material may spend up to 24 hours in the large intestine, before it is expelled through the **anus** after temporary storage in the rectum.

The large intestine consists of
• caecum
• colon
• rectum

The caecum and appendix are situated at the beginning of the large intestine. They have no special function in humans

The large intestine secretes no enzymes

Water is absorbed by the colon

Absorption of the refined food

After the food molecules have been broken down or digested in the stomach and small intestine, the final major role of the digestive system is to absorb the small refined food molecules. All the events in the digestive system before this stage are designed to convert food particles into molecules which are small enough to pass through the cells lining the intestine and enter the blood vessels. Once in the bloodstream, the molecules are transported to the cells of the body. This process of absorption takes place almost entirely in the small intestine.

Absorption of small molecules takes place in the small intestine

For absorption to be efficient and complete, a large area of contact between the digested food molecules and the intestinal lining is necessary. There are four ways in which the structure of the small intestine provides a huge surface area for absorption. First, the small intestine is very long (up to 7 metres in the adult). Second, it has circular folds, visible to the naked eye, on its inner surface. Third, this surface area is further increased by tiny finger-like projections of the mucosal lining called **villi** (singular **villus**), which can be seen under a light microscope. Finally, the

The large surface area of the intestine is due to four features:
• great length
• large circular folds
• villi (finger-like projections of mucosal lining)
• microvilli (tiny folds on surface of each cell)

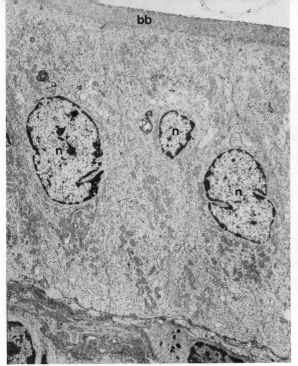

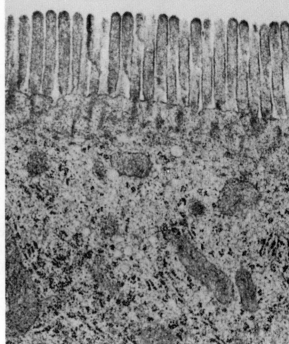

Fig 10.12 *Transmission electron micrograph of epithelial cells which cover the surfaces of the villi*
(a) The nuclei (n) of three absorptive cells can be seen. On the tops of these cells is the 'brush border' (bb)
(b) An enlargement of the brush border shows that it is made up of thousands of microvilli

surface of each cell capable of absorption is covered with tiny folds or projections called **microvilli**. The presence of villi and microvilli increases the surface area of the small intestine several thousand times. Figure 10.12a is a photograph of several intestinal absorptive cells, viewed with an electron microscope. The microvilli form a 'brush border' on the surface of the cells. An enlargement of this area of the cells (Fig 10.12b) shows that the brush border is in fact formed from tiny finger-like projections of the cell cytoplasm and membrane.

Figure 10.13 illustrates the folded structure of the intestinal lining (mucosa) and the cellular structure of a villus. (To convince yourself of the importance of these features in increasing surface area, try folding a piece of paper in a similar way.)

The lining of the small intestine is rich in capillaries

From the small intestine, absorbed molecules are carried in the hepatic portal vein to the liver

In addition to this specialised folding, the small intestine has a very large supply of blood vessels to transport the absorbed food molecules from the gut to the tissues of the body.

From inside the intestine, the products of digestion can pass through the epithelial lining cells and into the capillaries immediately below them. They are then carried away in veins, which eventually join to form one very large vein, the **hepatic portal vein**. The hepatic portal vein carries all the blood from the blood vessels of the intestine to the liver. Here the food molecules may be stored by the liver cells, or changed in the liver before joining the general circulation of the body.

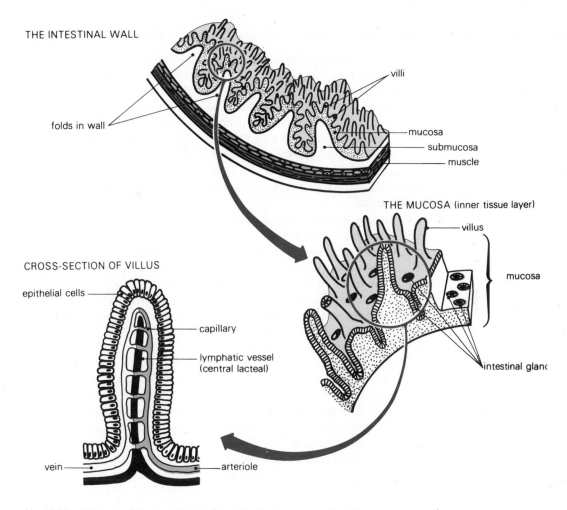

THE INTESTINAL WALL

villi

folds in wall

mucosa

submucosa

muscle

THE MUCOSA (inner tissue layer)

villus

mucosa

intestinal gland

CROSS-SECTION OF VILLUS

epithelial cells

capillary

lymphatic vessel
(central lacteal)

vein

arteriole

Fig 10.13 *Structure of the intestinal wall and detailed structure of a villus*

Some substances move through the intestinal walls by simple diffusion. Others, such as the monosaccharides and amino acids, are absorbed by active transport (see Chapter 2). This can take place against a concentration gradient, and is faster and more complete than diffusion. Large quantities of water are absorbed by osmosis.

The absorption of the breakdown products of fats differs from that of amino acids and monosaccharides. Most of the fatty acids and glycerol entering the epithelial cells are rejoined in these cells to form fats. Each villus has a central lymph vessel (see Fig 10.13). The re-formed fats, in the form of tiny white globules, pass into the lymph vessels and enter the lymphatic system. From here they flow into the bloodstream. The fat in the lymph vessels of the villi gives them a milky white appearance, for which reason they are known as **lacteals**.

Substances move through the intestinal wall by
• diffusion
• active transport

Water moves through the intestinal wall by **osmosis**

In the intestinal wall, fats enter lymph vessels called lacteals

The liver—dispatch centre for the refinery

The liver is the dispatch centre of the food refinery

We have described the digestive system as a food refinery—purifying the raw material foods to provide fuels and building materials for the cells. The liver has a role in this refinery too, as the dispatch centre for the digestive system—receiving from the alimentary canal the variety of refined products of digestion. Different engines require different and specific fuels. In the same way, the specialised cells of the body require particular fuels and particular building-block molecules for their special functions. The liver handles the final preparation of these molecules from the alimentary canal and controls their dispatch to those cells requiring them.

The liver handles the final processing of molecules from the alimentary canal

As we saw in Chapter 4, glucose is at the centre of the chemical network in the body. All the cells of the body use glucose. (Some, like the cells of the brain, rely on it entirely, except after long periods of starvation, when brain cells can then use other substances.) The level of glucose in the blood must be fairly constant at all times, to meet the cells' needs. The liver (in association with insulin produced by the pancreas) is responsible for maintaining a constant blood glucose concentration (see also Chapter 13). In this way, the liver controls the whole chemical network or metabolism of the body.

Glucose concentration in the blood must be kept fairly constant

Glucose reaching the liver may be
• broken down to provide energy for liver cells
• stored as glycogen
• converted to fats
• passed through the liver into general circulation

Let us briefly examine how the liver performs this function. Large quantities of glucose reach the liver from the alimentary canal via the hepatic portal vein. In the liver, three main things may happen to this glucose. First, it may be broken down as an energy source for liver cells, producing carbon dioxide and water. Second, it may be converted into an energy storage compound, glycogen, and stored in liver cells. Third, it may be converted into fats, which are then sent to fat depots in the body. Alternatively, glucose may pass through the liver to the general circulation.

Low level of blood glucose—glycogen is broken down and glucose is forced into the bloodstream

You can see how these different processes determine the concentration of glucose in the general circulation. When blood glucose concentration falls, glycogen stores in the liver are broken down and glucose is released to the circulation. After a meal, when blood glucose concentration is high, the liver removes glucose from the blood to form glycogen. If enough glycogen is present, extra glucose will form fat.

High level of blood glucose—glucose is stored in the liver as glycogen or fat

Amino acids, the products of protein digestion, are also processed or metabolised by the liver cells. Unlike glucose, amino acids cannot be stored by the body. They are broken down or deaminated in the liver. In the process of deamination the amino $-NH_2$ group is removed. This is then converted to ammonia (NH_3) and then to urea. The urea then enters the bloodstream and is taken to the kidneys to be excreted from the body. The remaining fragment of the amino acid (which we described in Chapter 4 as a carbohydrate-like compound) is then fed into the series of reactions for glucose metabolism, or broken down to release energy. In fact, in situations of starvation where no other forms of energy are

In the liver:
• amino acids are deaminated to form urea and a carbohydrate fragment

available, the liver is capable of breaking down tissue protein and amino acids to keep the blood glucose concentration constant and supply cells with energy.

In a similar way, the liver handles fats from the bloodstream. When not required for energy or building purposes, the products of carbohydrate, protein and fat digestion are converted to fats in the liver and transported to fat depots for storage. When other energy supplies are not available, fats are broken down in the liver and converted to compounds which can be used by the tissues to release energy.

In addition to its most important role as the final dispatch centre for the products of digestion, the liver has many other vital functions. Some of these are shown in Fig 10.14.

Only the most important of these functions are described here. Liver cells produce bile, a fluid which is stored in the **gall bladder** before secretion into the small intestine. Bile contains several excretory products, in addition to bile salts, which are important in the breakdown of fats.

The liver acts as a storage organ for some vitamins and minerals, particularly iron. The liver also serves as a cleansing or filtering organ. It removes worn-out red blood cells from the circulation and destroys them, inactivates hormones, and detoxifies or inactivates a variety of toxic chemicals or drugs which reach the liver in the bloodstream. These inactivated chemicals can then be excreted safely via the kidneys.

- products of carbohydrate, protein and fat digestion can be converted to fat
- when molecules which provide energy are in short supply, fat can be broken down to release energy

Other liver functions:
- production of bile
- storage organ for vitamins and minerals (especially iron)
- cleansing organ:
  - breaking down red blood cells
  - inactivating hormones
  - making toxic chemicals or drugs harmless

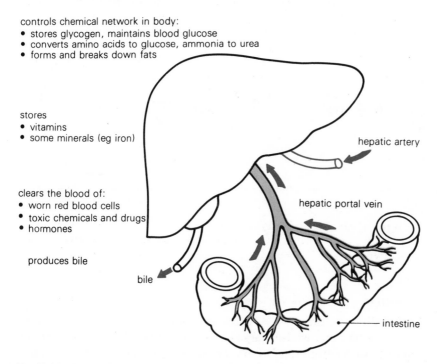

controls chemical network in body:
- stores glycogen, maintains blood glucose
- converts amino acids to glucose, ammonia to urea
- forms and breaks down fats

stores
- vitamins
- some minerals (eg iron)

clears the blood of:
- worn red blood cells
- toxic chemicals and drugs
- hormones

produces bile

bile

hepatic artery

hepatic portal vein

intestine

Fig 10.14 *Some important functions of the liver*

Balancing the fuels

We have seen how the carbohydrate, protein and fat we eat are refined by the digestive system and then fed into the body's chemical network. The small refined molecules are used for immediate energy release; as the building blocks for construction activities within the cells; or, after chemical conversion, as energy storage molecules in the body.

The energy requirements of the human body were discussed in Chapter 4. We saw that in most individuals there is normally an energy balance between the amount of energy required for all the activities of daily living (the total energy requirement) and the amount supplied in the food we eat. An energy imbalance occurs when the energy (food) intake is greater than the total energy required, or where the amount of energy (food) required is greater than the energy intake.

When the energy intake is greater than the energy requirement, fuel molecules are converted into fats, which accumulate in special connective tissue cells—fat or adipose cells. The process of fat accumulation in a fat cell is shown in Fig 10.15. Fat first appears as droplets in the cytoplasm of the fat cell. As fat storage continues, droplets join to form larger globules until, finally, almost the entire cytoplasm is filled by one large fat globule. In the fat person, large areas of connective tissue, particularly under the skin and in the abdominal cavity, become filled with fat cells. These areas are known as adipose tissue. Figure 10.16 shows a section of adipose tissue.

In most individuals the amount of energy required = the amount of energy supplied by food

When energy intake is greater than the energy required, fuel molecules are converted into fats; these are stored in fat cells

In fat people the number and size of fat cells is increased

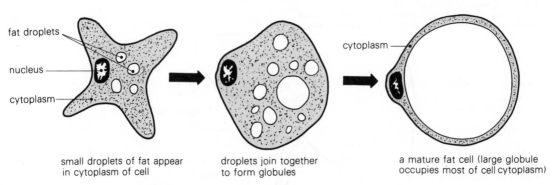

fat droplets

nucleus

cytoplasm

cytoplasm

small droplets of fat appear in cytoplasm of cell

droplets join together to form globules

a mature fat cell (large globule occupies most of cell cytoplasm)

Fig 10.15 *Accumulation of fat in a cell*

Obesity

The condition of excessive fat deposition in the tissues is known as obesity. It is ironic that whilst a large proportion of people in the developing countries suffer from starvation, almost as large a proportion of people in the Western world suffer from obesity.

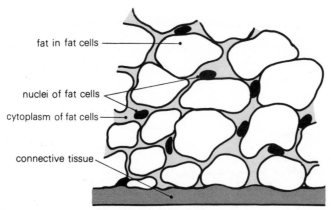

fat in fat cells

nuclei of fat cells

cytoplasm of fat cells

connective tissue

Fig 10.16 *Section of adipose (fat) tissue*

Why is obesity a problem? Above all other reasons, there is now very strong evidence that obesity contributes significantly to a very large proportion of ill-health in our society. People who are overweight are far more likely to suffer from:

- high blood pressure
- disease of the blood vessels (atherosclerosis), which may result in coronary heart disease or strokes (Chapter 6)
- disease of the kidneys or liver
- diseases of the joints—particularly arthritis—as a result of the extra load-bearing stress to which the joints are subjected.

As a result of all these factors, obesity is associated with a reduced life expectancy.

There are other reasons, too, why it is undesirable to be overweight. One of these is 'cosmetic'—fashion today dictates that obesity is unattractive. As a result, overweight can lead to self-consciousness, social isolation, loneliness and depression. Obesity may also interfere with sporting ability: the overweight person may be handicapped in his physical activity—his joints become less mobile, his body less flexible, and his tolerance to exercise greatly reduced. In fact, this restriction of physical activity becomes a vicious circle. Lack of exercise means that the total energy requirement is decreased. If energy (food) intake is not decreased by a corresponding amount, fat stores will increase and obesity will develop. The obesity that results may further limit exercise, so perpetuating the inactivity–obesity cycle (Fig 10.17). Finally, overweight women are far more likely to have fertility problems and complications during pregnancy and childbirth.

Why then is obesity such a common problem in our society? What are the causes of obesity? There is still a lot we do not understand about why some people are fatter than others. It is certainly true that some people become overweight far more easily than others. (Some people seem to

Overweight people are far more likely to suffer from
- high blood pressure
- atherosclerosis
- kidney and liver diseases
- joint disease
and therefore have reduced life expectancy

Obesity–inactivity cycle:
decreased activity
↓
decreased energy requirement
↓
increased fat stores
↓
decreased activity

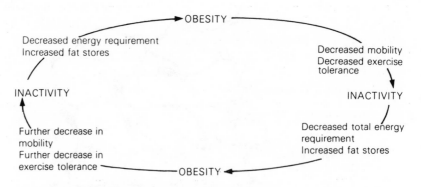

Fig 10.17 *Inactivity–obesity cycle*

be able to eat as much as and whatever they like and not gain weight. Others gain weight as a result of only small changes in their food intake or exercise level.)

Some of these differences are probably explained by differences in the levels of different hormones in the body. As we shall discuss further in Chapter 13, a number of different hormones interact to determine the rate of different chemical reactions in the body. Insulin tends to decrease blood glucose levels and increase the formation of fats; adrenalin has the opposite effect—it increases blood glucose and breaks down fats. The thyroid hormone, secreted by the thyroid gland, affects the rate of many of these chemical reactions. It is quite likely that a different balance of all these hormones in different people may be responsible, at least in part, for differences in build—fat, thin, muscular and so on.

The contraceptive pill is another example of the effect of hormones on weight gain. Most women taking the pill gain weight, sometimes as much as 6 kg in six months. It is for this reason that many women find the pill an unsuitable form of contraceptive device (see Chapter 17).

However, by far the most common cause of obesity is dietary excess—in other words, eating more food than the body needs to meet its energy requirements. (This principle holds even for those people whose hormone balance makes it difficult for them to maintain their body weight within normal limits—enlargement of fat cells and obesity occurs *only* when you consume more energy than your body requires.)

Recent research has shown that there are probably two main types of obesity. When a person becomes overweight during adulthood, fat deposition occurs in the way which we explained earlier—fat droplets accumulate in the fat cells and the fat cells simply enlarge to store the surplus energy. If a person becomes overweight during childhood, the process is rather different. This is because during childhood (and up to the age of 15 to 25 years) fat cells can divide. Obesity during childhood may therefore result in both increased number and increased size of fat cells.

Causes of obesity:
• hormone imbalance
• contraceptive pill
• dietary excess, ie more energy consumed in food than the body requires = energy imbalance

Two main types of obesity:
• develops during adulthood—fat cells enlarge to store surplus
• develops during childhood—fat cells both enlarge and divide (increase in number)

This information also helps to explain why it is more difficult for some people to lose their excess weight than it is for others. Basically, as excess weight is lost, the fat stores are used up and fat cells decrease in size. However, if overweight people have fat cells in increased numbers as well as increased size, it is more difficult for them to reduce their weight. With dieting, they can reduce fat cells to their normal size, but they cannot reduce the number of cells. Because of the larger mass of fat cells, they remain overweight. It is easy, then, to see the dangers of overeating in childhood. Once you have extra fat cells, they remain for life, and it may be much more difficult to lose any excess weight. Table 10.3 summarises these theories about obesity.

As excess weight is lost, fat cells decrease in size but not in number

Table 10.3   *Types of obesity*

Body weight	Fat cells	Effect of dieting
Normal	⊙⊙⊙⊙⊙ Normal size and number	∘∘∘∘∘ Decreased size, weight loss
Type 1 obese	Increased size, normal number	∘ ∘ ∘ ∘ ∘ Cells reduced to normal size, normal weight
Type 2 obese*	Increased size and increased number	Cells reduced to normal size, numbers remain increased, therefore remains overweight

* To lose further weight this person must reduce fat calls *below* normal size — possible, but difficult

Source: Based on A Borushek, *The Complete Diet Manual for Australian Weight Watchers*, Diet Publications for Weight Watchers, 1315 Hay St, West Perth, Western Australia, 1978

In nearly all cases of overweight or obesity, however, regardless of why the extra fat deposits developed, the only way of removing fat stores and reducing weight is by using them up in the body's chemical network. To do this the energy balance between energy intake in food and energy output in physical activity must be altered. In theory, either an increase in physical activity (output) or a decrease in food (intake) would alter this balance. In practice, however, the most effective method of weight reduction is a decrease in food (energy) intake. This is what we call **dieting**. (If dieting is combined with a programme of increased exercise, the weight reduction programme is likely to be even more successful.)

Most effective method of weight reduction is a decrease in energy (food) intake, ie dieting

As Table 10.1 illustrates, however, the foods we eat vary markedly in content. And as we saw in Chapter 4, the energy value of fats, carbohydrates and proteins differs. Fats, the high energy store in both animals

To regulate energy intake, we must understand nutritional and energy values of different foods

and plants, release twice as much energy per mole as proteins and carbohydrates. Sensible weight reduction or dieting therefore involves an understanding of the nutritional value of different food substances. A diet can then be selected that provides for all the body's chemical needs and at the same time helps to reduce the amount of energy taken into the body in food.

Nutritional value of foods

A balanced diet contains appropriate proportions of
• proteins
• fats
• carbohydrates
• minerals
• vitamins
• water

We saw in Chapter 3 that all foods are made up of different combinations of the five basic nutrient types, plus water. These are:
• proteins
• fats
• carbohydrates
• minerals
• vitamins.
All of these groups of chemicals are important for the proper working of the body. A balanced diet contains appropriate amounts of all these food types.

Proteins contain essential amino acids necessary for
• growth and repair of tissues
• formation of
  −enzymes
  −antibodies
  −some hormones

Proteins are an essential part of any diet, because of the body's need for essential amino acids. These are the amino acids, required for protein production in the body, that cannot be formed in the body. Proteins are essential in building and repairing body tissues. Enzymes, antibodies and some hormones are other important proteins. Not all proteins in food are of equal food value. The best-quality proteins are found in eggs, meat, fish, poultry, milk and dairy produce. The next best are in soy beans and nuts. Lower-quality proteins are found in cereals, lentil beans, gelatin, some fruit and vegetables. Larger amounts of the lower-quality proteins are required, but if small amounts of high-quality protein are mixed with lower-quality proteins, the mixture is of a high quality; for example, breakfast cereal (low quality) mixed with milk (high quality).

Fats are the most concentrated energy source available

Fats are the most concentrated energy source available to the body. (Refer to Table 4.1, p 64—the energy value of fats is almost twice that of proteins and carbohydrates.) There are some essential fatty acids which must be supplied in the diet to maintain a healthy body. However, the amount of these fatty acids required is very small and adequately provided in most diets. As we shall soon see, a dietary excess of fats is a far more common cause of problems. Fats are an important ingredient of all milk products, meat, eggs and nuts, as well as being the major ingredient of cooking fats, oils, margarine and butter.

Carbohydrates are the most readily available energy source

Carbohydrates, although not as energy rich as fats, are the most readily available energy source in the body. Many fad diets recommend the reduction or even total elimination of carbohydrates from the diet. As we have already said, however, overweight occurs because total energy intake in food exceeds the energy requirement for body maintenance and physical activity. Since carbohydrates actually have a lower energy value per gram than fats, what is the basis of this discrimination against carbohydrates?

Carbohydrates are available in a variety of·food sources. Bread, cereals, fruit, potatoes, rice, corn, vegetables, honey and sugars are all rich in carbohydrate. However, the energy value of these different foods varies tremendously. This is because the concentration of carbohydrate in these different foods varies.

Most natural or **unrefined carbohydrate** foods are obtained from plants. Their carbohydrate content is diluted with a large volume of indigestible fibre (cellulose) and water. High-fibre carbohydrate foods are of good nutritional value, even to people on weight-reducing diets. We have already explained that fibre or roughage is important in assisting the passage of material through the alimentary canal. In addition, the extra chewing time as well as the filling effect of high-fibre foods can reduce the total food eaten and hence the energy intake. Natural, unrefined carbohydrates provide the greatest volume of food for the least energy intake. (An example may help to illustrate this point. We would normally want to eat only one fresh orange at a time. To make an orange drink, however, we may use two oranges. Twice the amount of energy would be consumed, and yet we would still feel that we had not eaten anything at all.)

Moreover, carbohydrate foods are often wrongly thought to be high kilojoule or energy value foods. The potato is perhaps the best example of this. Potatoes, eaten on their own (for example, boiled) have an energy value of only 2.5 kJ per gram. Baked in fat, their energy value is doubled; fried as chips their energy value triples; and made into potato crisps their energy value per gram is increased more than six times. This change in their energy value is related entirely to the addition of fats to the potatoes—the basic carbohydrate content of the potato is not altered.

Refined or 'artificial' **carbohydrates** are quite a different proposition, however. Refined carbohydrates, such as sugar and white flour, and all the foods we make from them, are very low in fibre and contain carbohydrate (mainly sugar) in a very concentrated form. For example, one sugar cube contains an amount of sugar equivalent to that in two oranges.

The average Australian eats more than one kilogram of sugar each week, yet we buy only a fraction of this as packeted sugar. A very large proportion of the sugar we eat is what we call 'hidden' sugar—sugar already present in foods we eat, which, often, we are unaware that we are eating. As we shall see later, many snack foods such as chocolates, sweets and soft drinks contain very high concentrations of sugar. Breakfast cereals and ice cream are other examples of foods with high concentrations of hidden sugar. The sugar content of some common foods is shown in Table 11.2, Chapter 11. You will realise, then, that by eating large quantities of these types of foods or refined sugars, it is very easy to have an excess energy intake in the diet.

Carbohydrate foods are of two types:
- unrefined (natural)
- refined (processed)

Unrefined carbohydrate foods generally
- are high in fibre
- are high in water
- contain vitamins
- have low energy value per unit volume

Refined carbohydrates
- are low in fibre
- contain carbohydrate (mainly sugar) in very concentrated form
- can increase total energy intake dramatically

Hidden sugars—the sugar present in concealed form in many of the foods we eat, eg snack foods, soft drinks, cakes

Vitamins and minerals are not energy-providing chemicals. They are necessary in small quantities, however, to maintain a healthy body. The role of vitamins and minerals in cell reactions was discussed in Chapter 3 and is summarised in Table 10.4. As Table 10.4 indicates, different foods are rich in different vitamins. However, a balanced and varied diet normally ensures an adequate supply of all vitamins and minerals. Only when the diet is restricted or severely unbalanced will symptoms of vitamin deficiency develop. When vitamin deficiencies do occur, they seldom occur singly. An unbalanced diet (for example, the alcohol-dominated diet of the chronic alcoholic—see Chapter 16) often produces a deficiency of several vitamins.

Dietary imbalances

It is beyond the scope of this book to outline specific diets for weight reduction, growth, pregnancy or any other special requirements. For information about any of these you should consult a nutrition textbook or diet manual. However, recent trends in diet and eating patterns place many of us at risk from particular dietary imbalances. We shall finish this chapter by describing some of these briefly.

'Take-away' foods

One of the major trends in our society is the increased consumption of 'take-away' meals—meals that are prepared and cooked outside our homes, in pizza bars, fried-chicken shops, hamburger and fish and chip shops. In Australia, one meal in four is purchased in prepared form. In the United States this figure is at least one in three. Consumed occasionally, there is probably no harm in any of these foods. However, when they form a regular part of the diet, the diet may become seriously unbalanced. Why is this so?

Whilst most of these foods contain significant amounts of valuable ingredients in the form of protein and carbohydrate, many of them are cooked in fat. As a result, their fat content and energy value are very high. In addition, most of these 'fast' foods have a rather low fibre content. For both these reasons, when take-away foods form a significant proportion of the diet, it is very easy to consume quantities of energy well in excess of the body's requirements. The resulting energy imbalance leads to overweight and obesity. A further problem with take-away foods is that they rarely contain fresh fruit and vegetables. Fruit and vegetables are valuable sources of a variety of vitamins, as well as fibre.

Disadvantages of take-away meals:
- generally high fat (and energy) content
- low fibre content
- low vitamin content

Snack foods

Snack foods are the foods we eat between meals (although they are frequently used to replace a proper meal). They include such foods as potato crisps, chocolates, sweets and fizzy or carbonated soft drinks. These foods are all made from cheap food ingredients—sugars, fats and

Table 10.4 *Role of vitamins in the body*

Vitamin	Role	Food sources	Signs of deficiency
Vitamin A	• helps to keep skin clear and smooth • increases resistance to infection (keeps linings of respiratory and alimentary tracts healthy) • assists night vision	• milk, butter, yellow cheese • margarine • liver • deep yellow, green and red fruit and vegetables	• scaly dry skin • decreased resistance to disease • poor vision in dim light
Vitamin B$_1$ (thiamine)	• stimulates appetite and digestion • necessary for health of nerves • helps body cells obtain energy from food	• all meats, fish and poultry • whole grain cereals • eggs, milk • green vegetables (small amounts in most foods) • yeast	• decreased appetite • weight loss • nervous disorders • fatigue
Vitamin B$_2$ (riboflavin)	• helps in cellular respiration reactions • promotes health of skin, particularly around mouth	• meat and poultry • milk and milk products • eggs • green vegetables • yeast	• inflammation of tongue and lips • skin disorders on face
Vitamin B$_6$ (nicotinic acid)	• helps in cellular respiration reactions	• yeast • liver • lean meat • peas, beans	• skin disorders • inflammation of the intestinal tract mucosa • pellagra
Vitamin B$_{12}$	• important in formation of red blood cells • necessary for health of nerve tissue	• liver, kidney • meat, eggs • milk, cheese	• anaemia—reduced numbers of red blood cells • nervous system disorders
Vitamin C (ascorbic acid)	• important in strength of blood vessel walls • helps resist infection and heal wounds • important in formation of teeth and bones	• citrus fruits • tomatoes, strawberries • potatoes • leaf vegetables (destroyed by boiling)	• sore and bleeding gums • delayed wound healing • scurvy
Vitamin D	• important in formation of strong bones (helps bones use calcium and phosphorus)	• fish and liver oils • milk and milk products (produced in skin when exposed to sunlight)	• soft weak bones • enlarged joints
Vitamin E	• function uncertain	• very widespread in foods	deficiency effects not proved
Vitamin K	• necessary for production of blood clotting factor	• green vegetables • tomatoes	• delayed blood clotting

salt—and contain negligible quantities of protein, no vitamins and no fibre.

We have already explained the dangers of high-fat diets, and there is very little other than fat and salt in a potato crisp. Refined sugar, the sugar which is present in all forms of sweets, is also a very concentrated energy source, and many snack foods contain very large amounts of sugar. (An average can of soft drink contains 12 teaspoons of sugar—the

Snack foods:
• made from sugar, fats and salt
• very little protein
• no vitamins
• no fibre
• very easy to over-eat
• sugar and salt make them habit forming

same amount as more than 20 oranges, without of course the valuable vitamins and fibre which the oranges provide; chocolate contains only sugar and fat.) As with take-away food, it is very easy to overeat when snack foods are a regular part of the diet.

Finally, both sugar and salt—major ingredients of snack foods—are habit-forming substances. Let us now look at the dangers of excessive salt intake.

Excessive salt intake

Normal salt is eaten in the form of sodium chloride (NaCl). It is the sodium that plays an important part in the regulation of body fluids. There is a significant amount of salt in many of the foods we eat—foods of animal origin tend to be high in sodium; foods of vegetable origin are low in sodium. Many processed or prepared foods—canned/packet soups, Marmite/Vegemite, bacon, ham and take-away foods, for example—have very high salt concentrations. In addition, salt is frequently added to many foods during cooking. Sodium is necessary for the proper functioning of all body cells. Frequently, however, our salt intake far exceeds our requirements. This is because, as we said earlier, salt is a habit-forming substance. In other words, we become accustomed to the salty flavour in all the foods we eat and find food unpalatable without it.

Excessive salt intake
↓
fluid retention
↓
may lead to high blood pressure

Why is excessive salt intake a problem, then? You have no doubt experienced many times the thirst which follows a particularly salty meal. This occurs because the body must take in extra water to dilute the salt in the body to normal concentrations. The excess fluid is held in the body until the excess salt can be excreted. It is easy to see, therefore, that if excessive amounts of salt are consumed regularly, excess fluid will be retained in the body most of the time. Fluid retention contributes to hypertension (high blood pressure) with all the associated risks of heart disease and strokes.

High blood fats

We have already discussed some of the dangers of excessive fat consumption. Fats are very energy-rich compounds, and by consuming large quantities of them, it is very easy to have a dietary energy excess. The consumption of large quantities of fats may also lead to other problems for some people. These are the health problems associated with a high level of blood fats.

High blood fat levels contribute to the development of atherosclerosis (disease of the artery walls)

In Chapter 6 we discussed the condition of atherosclerosis, a disease of artery walls which may lead to heart disease or strokes. This condition is caused by a combination of many factors; one of these is high concentrations of fats circulating in the blood. Exactly what causes a rise in the normal concentration of fats in the blood is not understood. As you would expect, increased fat and sugar intake tends to increase blood fats. In some people, blood fats may be high even if they do not overeat. Because high blood fat levels increase the risk of artery disease, many doctors advise patients at risk from heart disease to reduce their fat intake.

You may remember that in Chapter 3 we described two types of fatty acids—the saturated fatty acids and the unsaturated fatty acids. Saturated fatty acids are present largely in animal fats; polyunsaturated fatty acids are present in vegetable oils and margarine. In a number of experiments it has been found that the fats from animals (saturated fats, and another special fat present in some animal tissues, cholesterol) increase blood fat levels more than fats of vegetable origin. As a result, many doctors advise patients at risk from heart disease to substitute polyunsaturated vegetable oils for animal fats in their diet.

Fats from animal sources (saturated fats and cholesterol) tend to increase blood fat levels more than vegetable fats (unsaturated fats)

Patients at risk from heart disease are often advised to substitute vegetable fats for animal fats in their diet

Chapter 11

Teeth and a healthy mouth

The role of the teeth in the digestion of food has already been explained in Chapter 10. They are agents of mechanical digestion—responsible for the breakdown of food particles at the beginning of the alimentary canal. This chapter is devoted to the mouth alone, particularly the teeth and gums. It is about the health of the mouth, some common disorders of the mouth, and how we can prevent them.

Why is a discussion like this necessary? A healthy mouth is important for a number of reasons. Unless our teeth and gums are healthy we are unable to chew properly and so gain full enjoyment from our food. (If you are not convinced of this, ask anyone who has dentures!) Clear speech, also, depends on the correct number of healthy teeth. Finally, healthy gums and teeth contribute significantly to a generally pleasant appearance.

However, despite all these apparent advantages of a healthy mouth, we tolerate far more illness or disease of our teeth and gums than we do of any other part of our bodies. Dental decay (caries) affects 95 per cent of the community (when fluoride is not in the drinking water), and gum disease (periodontal disease) affects at least 50 per cent of the population. Both of these diseases, untreated, may result in loss of tooth structure, and both may be prevented by regular care of the teeth. Dental health and care of the teeth are the subject of this chapter.

Types of teeth

Humans, like all other mammals, have four types of teeth: **incisors, canines, premolars, molars**.

The mature adult has 32 teeth. In each jaw there are 4 incisors, 2 canines, 4 premolars and 6 molars. Figure 11.1 shows the arrangement of these teeth in the upper jaw. When the jaws are closed together, the inner faces of the upper incisors normally fit outside the outer faces of the lower incisors. You can feel this with your finger when your jaws are closed.

Two sets of teeth appear during a person's lifetime:
• milk (deciduous) teeth
• permanent teeth

During a person's life-span, he possesses two sets of teeth. The first teeth are called the **milk teeth** or **deciduous teeth**. They begin to appear at approximately 6 months of age and the set is usually complete by the time a child is about 2½ years old. (The ages at which these teeth appear (or erupt) vary widely.) As Table 11.1 shows, there are only 20 milk teeth in a full set—small children have no premolars, and only 4 molars in each jaw. From approximately 6 years of age the permanent teeth start to appear, and as they do so, the deciduous (milk) teeth are lost. Table 11.1 shows the approximate ages when the permanent teeth erupt. The last permanent teeth to appear are the third molars (wisdom teeth). These may appear at any time between 15 and 30 years of age.

The two central teeth of both jaws are called the central incisors. These are surrounded on both sides by lateral incisors and canines. The canines

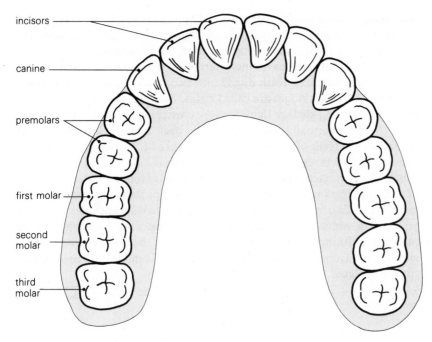

incisors

canine

premolars

first molar

second molar

third molar

Fig 11.1 *Arrangement of teeth in the jaw*

Table 11.1 *Average ages at which teeth appear*

Deciduous teeth	Age (months)	Permanent teeth	Age (years)
Central incisors	6–8	First molars	6
Lateral incisors	8–12	Central incisors	7
First molars	12–14	Lateral incisors	8
Canines	18	First premolars	9–10
Second molars	24–30	Second premolars	10–11
		Canines	9–12
		Second molars	10–13
		Third molars (wisdom teeth)	15–30
Total number of milk teeth = 20		Total number of permanent teeth = 32	

Note: The ages given are averages only; wide variations occur

are often called cuspids or eye teeth. All these teeth have a single root, and a cutting or biting edge for cutting and tearing through food. The canine tooth is somewhat thicker, with a single spearlike point or cusp. These teeth developed in our evolutionary ancestors for ripping or tearing.

Following behind the canines are the cheek teeth. The first and second premolars are often called bicuspids. Behind these are the first and second molars. The third molars are often called wisdom teeth. The cheek

Incisors and canines have a single root and a cutting or biting edge for cutting or tearing through food

Molars and premolars have broad, chewing or grinding surfaces, called their occlusal surfaces. Their function is to chew and crush food

teeth usually have two or more roots. They have broad, chewing, grinding surfaces called their occlusal surfaces. Cheek teeth perform the heavy work of chewing and crushing food for digestion.

While the front teeth have single narrow biting edges, the chewing surfaces of back or cheek teeth divide into two sets of ridges. The pointed projections of these ridges are called **cusps**. Between the cusps in the centre of the chewing surface there are tiny crevices, or **fissures**. When jaws close together normally, the cusps of the back teeth fit into the central fissures of the teeth of the opposite jaw. Figure 11.2 shows the difference between the surfaces of back and front teeth.

Stop for a moment and think about how your teeth go about their task of breaking food into smaller pieces. You will probably realise that your teeth act in two ways: chewing and biting. Chewing includes sideways grinding in which the slanting walls of the opposing cusps slide along each other. Biting, on the other hand, involves the up and down movement of the front teeth, in which firm contact is made between the two cutting surfaces.

> When the jaws close, the cusps of the back teeth fit into the fissures of the teeth of the opposite jaw

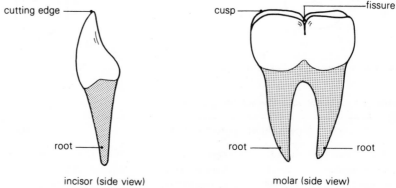

Fig 11.2   *Shapes of front and back teeth (using the incisor and molar as examples)*

Structure of the tooth

> A tooth consists of 3 regions:
> • crown
> • neck
> • roots

Each tooth is composed of three parts: the **crown**, the **neck** and the **root(s)**. These are shown in Fig 11.3. This illustration actually shows a tooth which has been cut lengthwise (a longitudinal section of a tooth). When a tooth is sectioned in this way the tissue layers which make up the tooth can be seen. Refer again to Fig 11.3. Three distinct layers make up all teeth. These are the enamel, the dentine and the pulp.

> The three layers of a tooth:
> • enamel
> • dentine
> • pulp

Enamel

> Enamel—hard, brittle substance containing calcium

The crown of the tooth is covered by a layer of a substance called enamel. This is probably the hardest animal substance known. The tremendous strength of enamel comes from its content of calcium and phosphate. In the enamel these minerals are arranged into crystals, lined

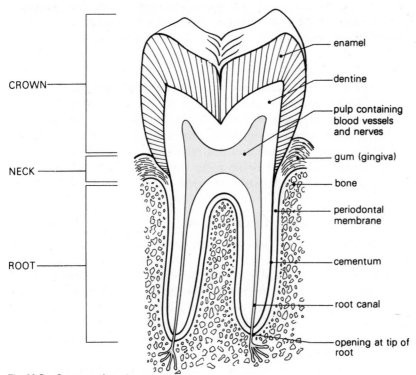

enamel

dentine

pulp containing blood vessels and nerves

gum (gingiva)

bone

periodontal membrane

cementum

root canal

opening at tip of root

CROWN

NECK

ROOT

Fig 11.3 *Cross-section of a tooth*

up perpendicular to the tooth surface. Just as neatly arranged bricks build a strong wall, so the crystal atoms form a strong lattice.

However, in about 4 per cent of sites in the neat crystal lattice, the calcium ion is replaced by another metal, for example sodium, zinc, lead, fluorine or strontium, or the phosphate is replaced by carbonate. The exact composition of enamel varies from person to person, and even from tooth to tooth. Some of these 'intruder' ions are smaller than calcium. Just as a small brick will weaken a wall, so these sites in the lattice may become weak spots in the enamel. The significance of these weak spots in the development of tooth decay will be discussed later in the chapter.

Mature enamel is not considered to be a living tissue. The colour of the enamel on the crown normally ranges from a yellowish colour nearer the root to a greyish white towards the tip.

Dentine

Dentine is more like bone in structure than is enamel. Unlike enamel, it is not brittle, and is elastic and compressible. It is similar to ivory in nature and contains a high proportion of mineral salts. Recent studies using the electron microscope have shown that fine canals of cytoplasm and tiny

Dentine:
• bone-like
• elastic
• compressible
• similar to ivory
• contains small nerves and canals of cytoplasm

nerves penetrate the dentine. Dentine is considered to be alive. It constitutes the inner bulk of the tooth and supports the harder outer enamel surface of the crown.

Pulp

Pulp:
- housed inside the dentine
- contains nerve endings which make the tooth sensitive to heat and cold
- contains blood capillaries which carry oxygen and food for pulp and dentine
- small lymph vessels which carry white blood cells for defence

Inside the dentine is a chamber called the **pulp chamber**. This chamber contains soft connective tissue called pulp. The pulp contains sensory nerve endings and blood capillaries. The nerve endings of the pulp make the tooth sensitive to heat and cold. The capillaries carry food and oxygen which enable the pulp and dentine to live and the tooth to grow. Small lymph vessels in the pulp carry white blood cells, which help to protect the tooth from bacterial invasion.

Teeth are anchored in the jaw

Cementum—thin, hard, bone-like substance surrounding roots of teeth

Root—lower part of tooth, supported in the tooth socket by the periodontal membrane

The portion of the tooth which is anchored in the jaw is called the root. There is no enamel covering the surface of the root. Instead, the root is surrounded by a thin, hard, bone-like substance called the **cementum**. At the bottom of the root, there is an opening in the cementum, through which the nerve endings and capillaries can enter the pulp of the tooth.

The root of the tooth fits into a tooth socket in the bone of the jaw. However, it is not set rigidly into the bony socket. Instead, it is supported by tissue called the **periodontal membrane**. The periodontal membrane acts as a shock absorber, allowing the tooth to move slightly in its socket. It is made up of elastic tissue, and joins the cementum of the tooth to its bony socket in the jaw (see Fig 11.3).

Dental caries

Dental caries (tooth decay) is the most common disease of teeth.

Factors leading to tooth decay

The exact cause of tooth decay or dental caries is not yet known. However, we do know a lot about the types of factors that contribute to its development. Certainly, some people's teeth do seem to be more resistant to decay than others. This may be related to the strength (hardness) of the enamel layer of their teeth (see p 217). More than anything else, however, the development of tooth decay depends on the types of foods eaten, and on how well the teeth are cleaned.

Many experiments in animals have shown that tooth decay does not occur in the absence of sugars. Of all the sugars we eat, solid or sticky sugars are the most important in causing decay. How often these sugars are eaten also contributes to the progress of decay. Each meal or snack we eat allows another attack on the teeth.

Why are these sticky sugars so important? The other important factor in the development of tooth decay is the presence of particular micro-organisms called bacteria. We saw in Chapter 7 that many families of bacteria live in harmony with our bodies, on the skin surface and on the body linings. Bacteria are also present in the mouth. Most bacteria are quite harmless here unless they become involved in the formation of **dental plaque**. Dental plaque is a sticky, nearly invisible film, consisting mainly of bacteria, which accumulates on the surface of teeth. (If the teeth are not cleaned properly you can feel dental plaque with your tongue as a furry film. In contrast, clean (plaque-free) teeth feel shiny.) Dental plaque grows more rapidly when the foods eaten contain sugar. The *longer* these sugary foods remain in the mouth, the *more* plaque will form.

Plaque—a sticky, almost invisible film of bacteria which grows on teeth

The importance of both dental plaque and sugary foods in the development of tooth decay depends on the presence of a particular bacterium which is found in dental plaque. This bacterium is called *Lactobacillus acidophilus* (*lactos* = milk; *bacillus* = germ; *acid* = acid; *phillus* = loving). Research workers have found that lactobacilli multiply rapidly in an environment of refined sugars and starches and produce a waste product that is harmful to teeth.

The important bacterium found in dental plaque is called *Lactobacillus acidophilus*

Let us now examine the sequence of events in the decay of a tooth.

Lactobacilli bacteria play an important part in tooth decay

Stages in development of tooth decay

The tooth decay process seems to begin with the thin film of saliva covering the tooth, called a **pellicle**. Lactobacilli present in the mouth accumulate in the pellicle. The film of bacteria which now covers the tooth is known as plaque. If foods containing sugars stick to the surfaces of the teeth after a meal this plaque grows rapidly. This is because lactobacilli living in the plaque can multiply rapidly by using the sugars in the food particles as a source of energy for their growth and division. As they do this, they produce a waste product called lactic acid. Lactic acid is responsible for the damage to the tooth that follows.

Pellicle—film of saliva covering tooth

Pellicle + bacteria
↓
plaque

In presence of sugars from food:
lactobacilli
↓
acid

As we explained earlier, enamel is the hard covering material of the tooth, which protects the other softer tooth structures from damage. The acid produced by lactobacilli in the plaque attacks the enamel and causes its basic chemical framework to break down. As a result, minerals—particularly calcium and phosphate—are released from the enamel and are able to diffuse into the plaque. This process is known as **demineralisation**.

Acid attacks enamel
↓
loss of calcium and phosphate—demineralisation

As the calcium and phosphate leave the tooth, a brown discoloured area develops and a small cavity appears in the enamel. As the cavity grows larger, plaque bacteria invade deeper into the tooth enamel. The cavity develops only slowly in the hard enamel layer, but once the softer dentine is reached, the demineralising process occurs more rapidly.

Demineralisation
↓
cavity in tooth
(enamel decay)

In the dentine, the decay spreads rapidly, both sideways and downwards in the tooth. If a tooth with dentine decay is not treated, the

Cavity deepens
↓
dentine decay

Spread of infection to pulp
↓
death of pulp

Spread of infection to
surrounding gum and bone
↓
dental abscess

Dental abscess—bacterial infection of the gum and bone beneath a decaying tooth. Gum becomes swollen and red and pus forms

bacteria will soon enter the pulp of the tooth, causing extreme pain and further complications It takes approximately four months for tooth decay to progress to this stage.

When bacteria enter the soft pulp of the tooth, it rapidly becomes inflamed and fills with pus. The damage caused by the invading bacteria and the inflammatory response soon results in the death of the pulp. The inflammation may then spread further through the pulp to the surrounding bone and gum. At this stage this infection is called a **dental abscess**. If not treated, the abscess may spread to the lip or cheek.

These stages in the development of tooth decay are illustrated in Fig 11.4.

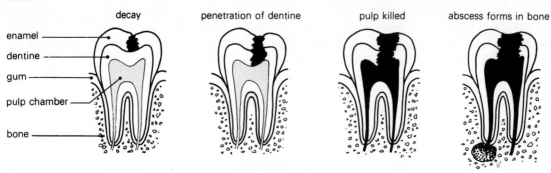

decay   penetration of dentine   pulp killed   abscess forms in bone

enamel
dentine
gum
pulp chamber
bone

Fig 11.4 *Progression of dental caries*

Periodontal disease

Normal, healthy gum is firm, resilient and pink in colour

Gum—gingiva

The gum clings closely to the base of the crown of a tooth

The gingival crevice is a small crevice where the gum meets the tooth

The tooth bulges above the crevice to protect it from collection of food debris

Plaque bacteria that are allowed to remain in the gingival crevice cause slight infection of the gum

The gum or **gingiva** is a layer of soft protective tissue covering the jawbone. It is normally firm, resilient and pink in colour. Between the gum and the bone is a membrane called the **periosteum**. This membrane provides nutrition for the bone from the outside and attaches the soft tissue of the gum to the bone.

The gum meets and surrounds the tooth at the base of the crown (Fig 11.5). Although the gum clings closely to the tooth, it is not completely attached to the tooth at this point. There is a small crevice under the gum edge called the **gingival crevice**. Since the gum clings closely to the tooth, this crevice is normally closed and free from debris. Protection of the crevice is provided by a small bulge at the base of the tooth crown. This curving bulge provides shelter for the crevice somewhat like the eaves of a roof sheltering the walls of a house from rain. It deflects the food debris away from the gingival crevice, which must be kept clean to avoid infection of the gum.

Sometimes plaque bacteria do penetrate into the gingival crevice. Gum tissue in this region stretches and swells, changing from a thin, firm pink structure to a swollen, tender, red area of infection. This is called mild

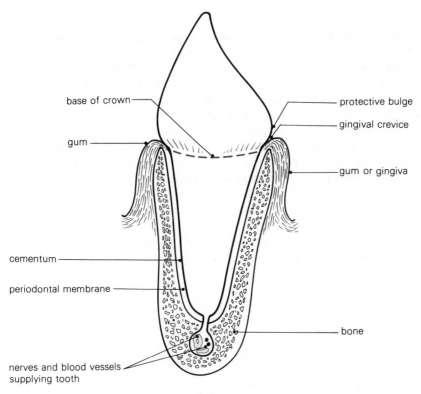

base of crown

protective bulge

gingival crevice

gum

gum or gingiva

cementum

periodontal membrane

bone

nerves and blood vessels supplying tooth

Fig 11.5 *Relationship between the tooth and the gum*

gingivitis. Swollen gums increase the size of the crevice, providing space for more bacteria to settle and grow. Further production of bacterial toxin (poison) in the area causes more swelling. The infected tissues become delicate and tender, and brushing the teeth may cause slight bleeding.

Infected areas of gum may bleed when the teeth are brushed

Sometimes, unremoved deposits of plaque, food debris, and broken-down mouth tissue cells harden on the teeth (by mineralisation with calcium salts) to form **calculus** or **tartar**. Neglected calculus deposits become harder and harder. Calculus often develops on the surface of the tooth, in the gingival crevice, during or following mild gingivitis. These deposits of calculus may further aggravate the gum disease, and a vicious cycle may begin. The surface of the calculus is rough, which encourages more plaque to form. Further calculus develops and spreads down the side of the tooth, inside the gum margin towards the root of the tooth. As this happens, more bacteria (plaque) invade the area, separating the tooth from the gum and creating still larger pockets. More food debris and bacteria enter these pockets, and further infection of the gum tissues results. Breath becomes foul-smelling, and gums swell outward, becoming increasingly reddened and more painful. Teeth may become loose, and gum ulcers may appear in the infected gum region. At this stage, the patient is said to have advanced periodontal disease.

Calculus (tartar)—a combination of plaque and food debris which becomes hardened to form crusty deposits on teeth

Calculus may form in the gingival crevice during mild gingivitis

If gingivitis is allowed to develop, larger pockets form between tooth and gum

This may lead to the development of advanced periodontal disease

If the condition is still not treated, bacteria in periodontal pockets eventually destroy the periodontal membrane and the bony socket which supports the tooth roots. As a result the tooth begins to loosen and the space between root and socket widens. This allows greater tooth mobility and the opportunity for deeper bacterial infection. The final outcome of untreated advanced periodontal disease is loss of the affected tooth. The progression of periodontal disease is illustrated in Fig 11.6.

In the early stages, gum disease is treated by the removal of calculus by the dentist, and by the patient attempting to minimise plaque formation by regular brushing. If the patient cooperates at this stage and maintains a good standard of oral hygiene, the disease can be controlled.

Advanced periodontal disease is treated by periodontal surgery. This is a type of plastic surgery around the teeth. The objective of periodontal surgery is to remove dirt-trapping pockets in the gum margin, and to re-shape the surrounding tissues to help maintain cleanliness around the tooth.

Early periodontal disease is treated by the removal of calculus by the dentist, and by regular brushing

Advanced periodontal disease may require surgery

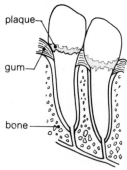
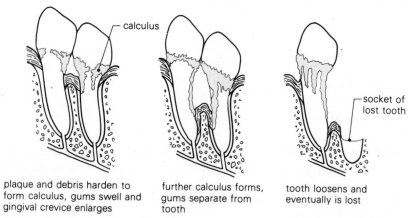

plaque accumulates in the gingival crevice

plaque and debris harden to form calculus, gums swell and gingival crevice enlarges

further calculus forms, gums separate from tooth

tooth loosens and eventually is lost

Fig 11.6 *Progression of periodontal disease*

Prevention of tooth decay

We have now seen how tooth decay develops. In the presence of sugary foods, plaque bacteria grow on teeth and produce an acid which attacks the enamel of the tooth. Knowing these facts, we are in a position to prevent, or at least minimise, tooth decay.

Factors affecting plaque development

A few more points need to be made about the development of plaque on teeth. Bacteria are always present in the mouth, and it is almost impossible to brush plaque completely from the teeth. If you examine the surface of a tooth under a microscope, you will find that it is not smooth—it has many imperfections (such as pits and grooves) which may retain plaque, even when the teeth are brushed. However, the amount of plaque on teeth may vary from person to person, even when diet and cleaning procedures are the same. More plaque builds up around crowded teeth and when the teeth have more imperfections—pits, grooves and rough patches. For this reason, dentists may recommend special treatment to reduce these traps for plaque formation on the teeth.

More plaque builds up
• around crowded teeth
• in rough patches

The mouth does have some natural defences against the development of tooth decay. Enamel itself is probably the greatest barrier to decay. This is particularly so if the enamel has been strengthened with fluoride (see p 226). In addition, saliva is a very important cleaning agent. We have already mentioned the washing action of saliva (and other body fluids) in Chapter 7. With the assistance of the lips and tongue (which are very sensitive to the presence of food particles stuck on or between the teeth), saliva is able to clean most food particles from the mouth within about 15 minutes of a meal. However, sticky sweet foods take much longer to wash away. As you are no doubt aware, the flow of saliva increases dramatically in response to eating. The importance of this flow of saliva is clearly seen in people who suffer from a disease in which saliva is not produced. Their teeth decay very rapidly.

Natural defences against tooth decay:
• enamel
• saliva

Tooth decay can be effectively prevented by a combination of the following three measures:

Tooth decay can be prevented by:
• restricting sugar
• regular cleaning
• use of fluoride

• restricting sugar in the diet

• removing plaque by regular cleaning

• the use of fluoride.

Importance of sugar in the diet

As we have said before, sugary foods are necessary to produce tooth decay. Acids are produced by plaque bacteria within minutes of sugary substances entering the mouth. If the sugar is in a particularly sticky form, the acid attack on the tooth may continue for up to 30 minutes. You will realise, therefore, that the more frequently sugar enters the mouth, and the stickier it is, the more constant the acid attack on the mouth will be. (Constant nibbling of sweet things or sipping of sweet drinks leads to almost continuous acid attack.)

Obviously, then, to prevent tooth decay, sugary foods should be eaten as little as possible, particularly between meals. The important factors are:

• the amount of sugar eaten

• how often it is eaten

Tooth decay is affected by
• amount of sugar eaten
• how often sugar is eaten
• how long sugar remains in mouth

• how long it remains in the mouth (which depends on how sticky the sugar is).

As we discussed in Chapter 10, there is often far more sugar than we realise in the foods we eat. This is the 'hidden' sugar added to many foods—cakes, sweets, jams and soft drinks—during their preparation. The sugar in all of these foods will promote acid production and tooth decay. Table 11.2 lists the sugar content of some common foods and drinks.

Starchy foods do not cause tooth decay

It is perhaps worth mentioning at this stage that starchy foods such as bread, potatoes and chips do not cause tooth decay. Very little sugar is produced from these carbohydrates in the mouth. Only when jam or honey are added to bread does a sandwich become harmful to the teeth!

Table 11.2 *Sugar content of common foods and drinks*

Food/drink	Sugar content (teaspoons)	Food/drink	Sugar content (teaspoons)
Chocolate bar (average size)	7	Average can of soft drink	12
1 toffee mint	3	1 tablespoon of jam or marmalade	3
1 serve of iced chocolate cake	15	1 tablespoon of honey	3
1 doughnut	4	1 serve (sweetened) tinned peaches, apricots	3½
1 gingersnap biscuit	1	5 dried apricots	4
1 serve (1½ cups) plain icecream	5–6	½ cup (sweetened) orange or grapefruit juice	2

Source: Based on J Matthews and A Patterson, *An Investigation into Tooth Decay*, Sorrett, Melbourne, 1975

Cleaning teeth

along cusp

gum → tooth tip

Removing plaque by regular cleaning

There is, at present, no way in which plaque can be prevented from growing on the tooth surfaces. The only effective way of dealing with plaque formation is to remove it regularly, by brushing teeth, before it has grown sufficiently to become harmful.

Whenever possible, the teeth should be cleaned with a toothbrush and toothpaste immediately after each meal. To remove plaque effectively, brushing must be done thoroughly and systematically. One recommended procedure for brushing teeth is as follows. First the cusps and cutting surfaces of the teeth are brushed with sideways vibrating motion. Particular care must be taken with the back teeth. Then a vertical brushing action, in which the brush is moved from gum to tooth tip, is used to remove food from between teeth. Finally the gum margin region is cleaned with a gently vibrating movement of the brush. This will remove food debris and plaque from the area near the gingival crevices. Following cleaning, a rinse and swill helps to remove loosened material.

Often it is impossible for the bristles of the toothbrush to penetrate the small gap between adjacent teeth. Plaque may grow here and tooth decay develop. The plaque can be removed from these areas using dental floss, which is drawn across the tooth surfaces between the teeth.

Plaque between the teeth can be removed by dental floss

The triangular space between teeth where gum and teeth meet is another area often not accessible to the toothbrush. Wood points can be used to clean this region. Usually this treatment is necessary only in cases where gums have receded slightly, since the space is normally filled with gum.

The triangular space where gum and teeth meet can be cleaned with wood points

Although, ideally, the teeth should be cleaned by brushing after every meal, this is not always possible. When it is not, two other procedures will help to clean the teeth of food particles. However, *neither* of these procedures will remove plaque from teeth. Brushing teeth is the only effective means of doing this.

If non-sugary fibrous foods are used to finish a meal, they will help to clean the teeth of food particles. Rinsing the mouth vigorously with water after a meal also helps to remove food particles, but not plaque.

Dental plaque takes about 24 hours to grow to the stage where it is harmful to teeth. Therefore, if these cleaning procedures are adopted after each meal, and the teeth are brushed thoroughly at least once a day, plaque should be restricted to relatively harmless levels. Of course, the success of this programme will depend very largely on how effectively dental plaque is removed from the teeth during brushing. (Plaque-disclosing tablets, which contain a harmless dye that stains plaque, will show you how effective your technique is!)

The dentist's role

Finally, the dentist can play a very valuable role in limiting the development of tooth decay. For this reason regular dental examinations are essential. Early stages of dental decay can be treated with simple fillings. Advanced decay, or periodontal disease, requires complex and expensive treatment.

Early stages of decay are treated with fillings

The dentist can use a number of specialised techniques to prevent tooth decay. One of these involves sealing the fissures or pits between the cusps of molar or premolar teeth. The material used is a hard plastic substance, which prevents plaque from accumulating, and therefore decay developing, in the fissures.

Tooth decay can be reduced by sealing fissures or pits between cusps of molar and premolar teeth

The dentist also has special apparatus for removing calculus. A small circular grinder attached to the drill will remove this hard material. It should not re-form if the patient is careful to remove plaque by regular brushing.

Calculus can be removed by the dentist

Fluoride, an element which is taken into and strengthens enamel, can also be applied to teeth in the form of a gel or solution. It acts to restore some of the minerals lost by demineralisation. Replacing of minerals in teeth is called **remineralisation** (see below).

Fluoride gel can be applied to teeth by the dentist

Strengthening the enamel barrier

So far we have discussed ways in which acid attack on the teeth can be reduced. In addition, there are ways in which we can strengthen the enamel barrier against acid attack.

Fluoride

Fluoride added to the water supply can reduce tooth decay

Fluorine is an element which occurs in very small quantities in most of the world's natural water supplies. It is extremely reactive, combining readily with other elements such as calcium to form very stable compounds. Evidence accumulated over the past 30 years from many countries has shown that when water containing 1 mg per litre (1 ppm) of fluoride ions is consumed by a person during the period of tooth development and maturation, dental decay is considerably reduced. Figures from areas in which fluoride has been used show up to 60 per cent reduction of tooth decay in young people. Such benefits continue into adulthood. On the basis of these findings all dentists now recommend the use of fluoride in the prevention of tooth decay.

Two ways in which fluoride can be given to help strengthen enamel:
• oral doses to babies and children while the teeth are forming
• surface applications to teeth after they have erupted from the gums

There are two ways in which fluoride can be given to help strengthen enamel. The first and most valuable of these is to give doses of fluoride to babies and children while the teeth are still forming. At this stage, swallowed fluoride is absorbed and carried in the bloodstream to the teeth (and also to the bones). The presence of fluoride in the enamel appears to strengthen the enamel, so that minerals do not dissolve out of the enamel as readily when exposed to acids.

Development of the enamel layers of teeth occurs from 4 months after conception in the mother's uterus until 12 years of age

Fluoride taken in this way is of value *only* while the teeth are forming. The formation of enamel begins before a baby is born, during its period of development in the mother's uterus. When the developing baby (foetus) is only 4 months old, the enamel and dentine layers are already beginning to form in the tooth buds in the gums (Fig 11.7). From this stage onwards fluoride may help the developing enamel. The formation of all the permanent (adult) teeth is completed by approximately 12 years of age. (Although some of the permanent teeth may not erupt until several years after this, all are fully formed in the gum by this age.)

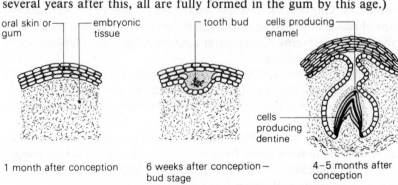

oral skin or gum — embryonic tissue   tooth bud   cells producing enamel

cells producing dentine

1 month after conception   6 weeks after conception — bud stage   4–5 months after conception

Fig 11.7 *Formation of the tooth*

How can this fluoride be obtained? Because of the proven value of fluoride in preventing tooth decay, the water supplies of many towns and cities now have small amounts of fluoride added to them. Only one part per million of fluoride ion is sufficient to provide significant protection against tooth decay. Where fluoride is *not* added to the water, it may be given in the form of fluoride tablets (or drops). These are recommended for both expectant mothers and children up to the age of 12 years.

Fluoride may be obtained
• in town water supplies
or
• as fluoride tablets or drops

The other form of fluoride treatment involves application of fluoride directly to the teeth surfaces. The dentist first cleans the teeth thoroughly, to remove all plaque. Fluoride, as a gel or a paint, is then applied. This technique is less effective, as fluoride enters only the enamel close to the surface. As the enamel wears in normal use, the weaker fluoride-lacking enamel becomes exposed again. However, surface fluoride application is still of value. It improves the strength of enamel, both in children who have had oral fluoride while their teeth are forming, and in adults who have previously received no fluoride treatment. In the same way the use of fluoride toothpastes may help to strengthen enamel, when they are used in conjunction with these other methods.

Surface application of fluoride is
• valuable for both children and adults
• less effective than fluoride given while the teeth are forming (fluoride enters only the surface enamel layers)

When fluoride toothpastes are used in conjunction with these procedures, they also help to prevent tooth decay

There has been a good deal of concern about the possibility that 'unnatural' additions of fluoride to town water supplies might harm other parts of the body. Suggestions that water fluoridation might cause mental retardation, heart disease or cancer have been extensively investigated. American research has shown that fluoridation at the level of 1 ppm in no way relates to any of these conditions. Studies of humans and lower animals using the electron microscope give substantial proof that even doses considerably higher than those used in water fluoridation have no ill-effects on the soft organs of the body. In contrast, the crystalline structure of bone and enamel has been found to be greatly strengthened by fluoride.

Other dietary factors

Remember that earlier in the chapter we likened the enamel barrier to a brick wall—the bricks being composed of calcium–phosphate crystals. Remember, also, that in about 4 per cent of sites in the enamel, the calcium may be replaced by other ions. Some scientists believe that the sites of these ions may become weak spots in the enamel—sites at which demineralisation may occur more rapidly during acid attack.

As we have said, the formation of enamel begins in the mother's uterus and continues until about 12 years of age. During this time, therefore, it is important that the growing child receives all the nutrients necessary to promote the growth of healthy, strong enamel. In particular, the diet must contain adequate amounts of calcium, phosphorus and vitamin D. Tooth development is best, however, when the diet contains a balance of the four major food groups—milk and dairy products, meat and fish, vegetables and fruits, and bread and cereals. Information about the appropriate balance of these different food types in the diet of a growing child can be found in a nutrition textbook.

Treatment of caries

Dentists use several different procedures to treat dental caries.

Fillings

When filling teeth, all decayed material must first be removed by drilling

Fillings are used to restore decayed spaces in teeth. Before placing a permanent filling in a partly decayed tooth, all decayed material must be removed from the infected area of the tooth. This is done using a drill. It is most important that slightly more tooth material is removed than just the decayed region. This ensures that there is no possible chance of further decay in areas that will be buried under the filling material. The tooth cavity must also be shaped in a way that will enable it to hold the filling material.

Silver amalgam is commonly used to fill drilled cavities

Silver amalgam, often called silver or amalgam for short, is the dentist's most serviceable filling material. After the cavity has been prepared, the amalgam mix is made up from two basic materials: a silver alloy powder and liquid mercury. When these are mixed they make a soft, putty-like mass, which is inserted into the prepared tooth cavity. Hardening of the mixture starts to occur immediately. While this is happening, the dentist carves off excess amalgam, to shape the contour of the tooth.

An insulating material is placed beneath the silver amalgam to prevent conduction of heat and cold to the pulp

One disadvantage that silver shares with other metals is that it conducts heat or cold readily. Such conduction through to the pulp may cause sensations of pain. To prevent this, dentists often place protective insulating material below the metal restoration.

Gold fillings are used when a more stable filling material is needed

Sometimes, gold is used to fill cavities in cases where a silver amalgam filling would not hold. Gold fillings are made by pounding small pieces of gold into the drilled cavity. The gold welds itself together and forms a very stable filling material.

Porcelain fillings can be made to match the colour of the teeth

It is natural that people should want fillings in the front of the mouth to be of the same colour as the teeth themselves. Synthetic porcelain fillings are often used for this purpose. A porcelain powder is mixed to give a colour matching that of the other teeth. The soft plastic material is placed in the cavity, left to harden and finally carved to the shape of the tooth.

Gold inlays

Inlays are used to restore teeth when not enough undecayed tooth remains to hold a filling

Many teeth can be saved by filling. However, sometimes a tooth is so neglected that not enough undecayed tooth material remains to hold a filling. Such teeth may be restored by a technique called inlaying. First, the decayed part of the tooth crown is removed. The tooth is then tapered near the edges so that a gold restoration, which replaces the missing parts of the tooth, can lock tightly on to the tooth base. Gold inlay material consists of a combination of gold and other metals, which does not crumble or fracture like silver amalgam. The inlay is made in a laboratory, and must be done with extreme care, so that it fits exactly on to the shape of the prepared tooth. The process of inlaying is shown in Fig 11.8.

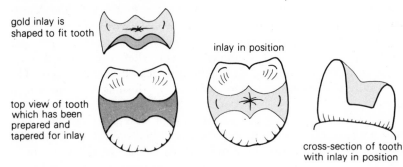

gold inlay is shaped to fit tooth

inlay in position

top view of tooth which has been prepared and tapered for inlay

cross-section of tooth with inlay in position

Fig 11.8 *Repairing a tooth with a gold inlay*

Jackets, caps and crowns

Inlays fit or lie largely within the tooth. Sometimes, when all the decayed portion of a tooth has been removed, a large proportion of the softer dentine becomes exposed. In this case a material is needed to cover the whole outside of the tooth. Such coverings are called jackets, caps or crowns (all different names for the same thing). A full crown replaces almost the entire crown of the tooth. It is like a small barrel, closed at one end. It can be made of metal, or porcelain to match the colour of the other teeth. The crown is slipped over the prepared stump of the tooth, and provides maximum protection to the tooth and its contents. In some instances one or even two walls of the tooth may remain intact. Restoration of these teeth usually involves a three-quarter or half gold crown (Fig 11.9). Crowns are also used to restore teeth that have been broken accidentally; for example, during a game of football or by falling heavily on to the ground.

Jackets, caps or crowns are used to cover large areas of exposed dentine

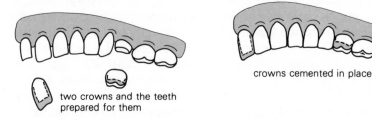

two crowns and the teeth prepared for them

crowns cemented in place

Fig 11.9 *Repairing teeth with crowns*

Root fillings

If not treated, dental decay that penetrates the pulp will result in the formation of a dental abscess. This is followed by death of the pulp. In these

A tooth with infected pulp may be restored by a root filling:
- abscessed tooth is drained
- a root canal is cleared to the abscess beneath the tooth
- the pulp cavity and root canal are sterilised

- a rubber-like cement is injected into the root canal to seal it
- the remainder of the tooth is filled with permanent filling

situations the tooth is often removed. If treated in time, however, only the pulp needs to be removed, not the whole tooth.

Once an abscessed tooth is discovered, the immediate objective is to release the pressure of infection from within the tooth. First the dentist creates a drainage canal to the pulp cavity by using a drill. Pus and blood may immediately gush from the opening, and with the release of pressure within the pulp cavity, there is immediate pain relief. The pulp is then removed from the cavity, and a root canal is cleared to the abscess. The pulp cavity and canals are then sterilised by flushing with medicated solutions.

The final procedure in this restoration process is filling the tooth. There are two stages in this procedure. In the first stage, the root canal is sealed, right up to the tip of the root, with a mixture of soft silver and a rubber-like compound. This cement is often injected into the canal using a syringe. Once the pulp cavity has been filled, the decayed crown can then be restored or filled with normal filling material.

Missing teeth—how to fill the gap

The loss of a tooth may cause
- crooked teeth next to the gap
- the tooth above the gap to become loose

Bridges or partial dentures are used to replace missing teeth

If a tooth has to be extracted because of dental decay, a gap is left in the row of teeth. Normally the teeth from the upper and lower jaws fit closely together as shown in Fig 11.10a. The removal of one tooth, either by extraction or injury, causes sideways pressures on the teeth beside the gap. As a result these teeth may become crooked. The tooth above the gap may also begin to drift out of the gum, owing to lack of pressure from below (Fig 11.10b). For these reasons it is essential that any lost teeth be replaced with artificial teeth.

Teeth may be replaced by either a bridge or a partial denture. Bridges use the teeth on either side of the gap to support one or more artificial teeth. The artificial tooth is attached permanently to the teeth on either side. The bridge cannot be removed by the patient and is no more bulky than the tooth it replaces. A number of different types of bridges can be used. In one method of bridging, a metal backing (usually gold) is cemented to the two support teeth and the replacement tooth pinned to this metal strip. In other cases, a row of joined porcelain teeth may be fitted to two supporting teeth which have been carefully cut to shape (Fig 11.11).

A partial denture consists of a false tooth or teeth attached to a plastic or metal plate, or to a metal framework which clips on to the other teeth. Unlike a bridge, a denture must be removed regularly for cleaning.

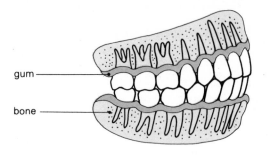

teeth stabilised by pressure
from adjacent teeth and by
contact of upper and lower
teeth

gum

bone

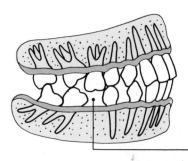

tooth has been lost or
removed from here

Fig 11.10   *Effects of tooth loss*
(a) Normal arrangement of the upper and lower teeth
(b) The results of neglecting to replace a lost tooth

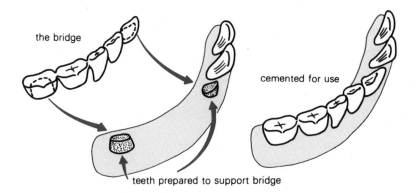

the bridge

cemented for use

teeth prepared to support bridge

Fig 11.11   *The use of shaped teeth to support a bridge consisting of a row of joined artificial teeth*

Chapter 12

The kidney—a living filter and regulator

Chemical reactions are going on all the time in the body. In every cell, compounds are being oxidised to release energy. Others are being used to build up new cell structures, and worn or damaged cell structures are being broken down and replaced. In many of these reactions proteins are involved. You may recall from Chapter 4 that excess dietary proteins (as well as those from worn-out cellular structures) are broken down in the liver. In this process their amino acids are deaminated; that is, the nitrogen (amino group) is separated from the remainder of the molecule (which is a carbohydrate fragment). The carbohydrate fragment can be used again in a variety of cell reactions. The amino group is converted to a waste product, urea.

Ammonia forms during deamination

Ammonia is highly toxic to cells

If we look more closely at this process, we find that the first stage of urea formation is the conversion of the amino group ($-NH_2$) to ammonia (NH_3). This ammonia is highly toxic to body cells, even in very low concentrations. In order to avoid any harmful effects it might cause, ammonia is immediately converted to urea, which is a less poisonous nitrogenous compound. Urea cannot be re-used in any body processes. As it, too, becomes harmful to body cells if it builds up in the liver and bloodstream, a process must be available to remove urea from the body.

Ammonia is converted to urea, which is less toxic to cells

Because urea is a product of chemical reactions in the body and has no useful function in the body (ie it is a waste product), it is termed an excretory product. The excretory organs employed in the body to remove this excretory product are the kidneys. Figure 12.1 shows the arrangement of the kidneys, liver and circulatory system.

The kidneys are excretory organs

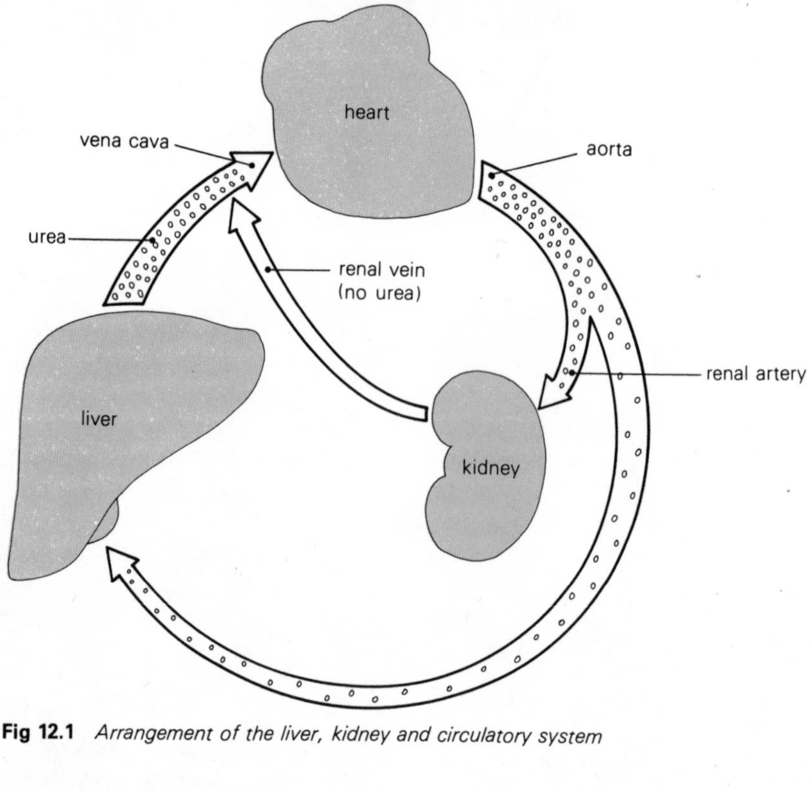

Fig 12.1   *Arrangement of the liver, kidney and circulatory system*

The kidneys are, however, far more than mere excretory organs. As we shall see later, the kidneys can excrete in the urine a variety of other substances, in addition to urea, if these substances are present in excessive quantities in the blood. In this way they regulate the composition of the blood. Any of these waste products must be excreted dissolved in a certain amount of water. Water, in the correct amounts, is essential to the well-being of all the body's cells. The kidney, therefore, has a very vital job in regulating the amount of water lost in urine, and so controlling the body's water content. Later in this chapter we shall see how it fulfils this role. We shall begin, however, by discussing the kidney's role as an excretory organ.

Kidneys also help to regulate
• the composition of the blood
• the amount of water in the body

The problem of urea removal

Consider how you would separate a container full of pebbles of varying sizes into groups of stones of similar size. An easy and efficient method of doing this would be to pass the stones through a number of sieves with varying mesh sizes. In this way we could obtain groups of large, medium and small-sized stones. However, a problem arises if we then want to separate stones of different shapes, all of which are the same small size.

This problem is the one that the kidney faces in separating urea (and other waste products) from other important chemicals in the bloodstream that are of a similar, small molecular size. Basically, in removing waste products from the blood the kidney acts as a filter (or fine sieve). Whereas objects in a sieve are separated using a wire or fabric mesh, the kidney filters blood through a special arrangement of membranes. This arrangement of membranes prevents large molecules and blood cells from leaving the blood. All the smaller molecules—glucose, amino acids, mineral salts and water, in addition to waste products—pass through the

Glucose, mineral salts and amino acids pass through the filtering membrane of the kidney with urea

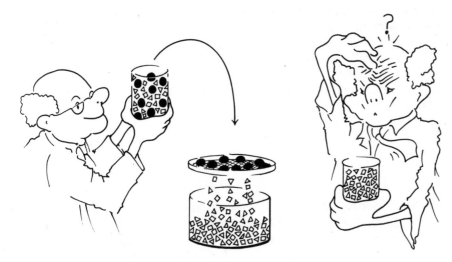

membrane to form the **kidney filtrate**. Many of the molecules in the filtrate are, clearly, very valuable to the body, and a method must be devised to return them from the filtrate to the bloodstream. Obviously, since their size is often similar to that of urea and other waste products, filtration is of no value. How, then, are these essential chemicals re-captured?

The technique the kidney uses to recapture valuable chemicals from the kidney filtrate and return them to the bloodstream is **reabsorption**. Once a filtrate of small chemicals has been obtained, the kidney can selectively reabsorb those molecules that are valuable to the body. Glucose, amino acids, mineral salts and water are recognised, reabsorbed and returned to the bloodstream. Other unwanted chemicals, particularly urea and other waste products, remain in the filtrate and are discharged from the body in urine.

Valuable chemicals filtered out of the bloodstream in the kidney may be recaptured by reabsorption

Visible structures of the urinary system

Urinary system—kidneys, ureters, bladder and urethra

The term urinary system is used to describe the kidneys and their associated structures, the **ureters**, the **bladder** and **urethra**. There are two kidneys, each about 10 centimetres long, in the adult. They lie in the abdomen, on the posterior (back) abdominal wall, one on either side of the vertebral column, just above the waist. Each kidney is supplied with blood by a **renal artery**, which branches off the aorta. Blood leaves the kidney in the **renal vein**, which returns blood to the **vena cava**. The arrangement of the kidneys in the abdominal cavity is shown in Fig 12.2.

Renal artery supplies kidney with oxygenated blood

Blood leaves kidneys in renal vein
↓
vena cava

If a kidney is cut lengthwise (longitudinally), three regions can be distinguished: an outer **cortex**, an inner **medulla** and a **pelvis**. These are shown in Fig 12.3. The cortex or outer zone is normally a darker red-brown colour, whilst the inner medulla is much lighter. (We shall see shortly why this is so.) The pelvis is really the flared end of the ureter. It is a hollow cavity surrounded by connective tissue and embedded in fat.

Urine passes from pelvis of kidney
↓
ureter
↓
bladder
↓
urethra

From the pelvis of the kidney, the ureter (one for each kidney) carries urine to the **bladder**. The bladder acts as a reservoir, which periodically empties urine to the outside through another tube called the **urethra**. The urethra is short in females and much longer in males.

Structure of the filtration unit

We have described the kidney as a special filter which purifies the blood by first filtering it and then selectively reabsorbing from the filtrate those molecules that are valuable to the body. However, each kidney is actually

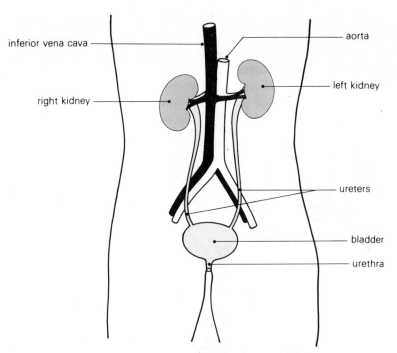

inferior vena cava

aorta

right kidney

left kidney

ureters

bladder

urethra

Fig 12.2   *Position of the urinary system in the body*

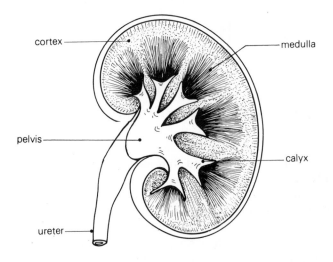

cortex

medulla

pelvis

calyx

ureter

Fig 12.3   *Section through the kidney*

composed of approximately one million microscopic filtration units. Each one of these is capable of producing urine independently of other units. We can therefore understand how the kidney works by studying just one of these tiny units.

Nephron—the kidney's
working filtration unit

Nephron = glomerulus +
kidney tubule

Glomerulus—tuft or knot
of capillaries

The microscopic filtration unit or working unit of the kidney is called the **nephron**. Figure 12.4 shows the structure of a nephron. The nephron is formed from two parts: a long tube, closed at one end, which has specialised segments, and a tuft or knot of capillaries, called a **glomerulus**.

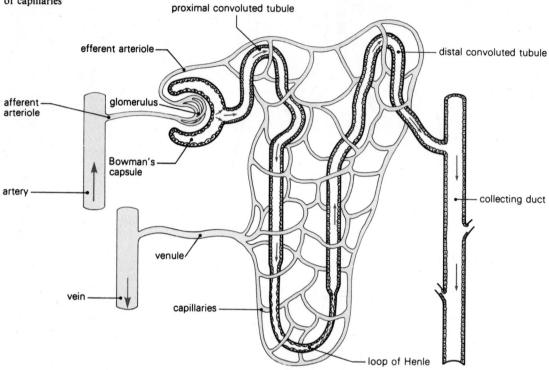

Fig 12.4 *A nephron — the working unit of the kidney*

Bowman's capsule—cup-
shaped expansion of kid-
ney tube which surrounds
the glomerulus

Specialised segments of
kidney tube:
• Bowman's capsule
• proximal convoluted
  tubule
• loop of Henle
• distal convoluted tubule
• collecting duct

Look again at Fig 12.4. The closed end of the tube is expanded to form a cup-like structure called **Bowman's capsule,** which surrounds the capillaries of the glomerulus. The remainder of the tube is specialised to form a number of different segments, each with a different task to perform in the production of urine. The segment closest to the glomerulus is very coiled and twisted. In anatomical terms it is said to be convoluted. Because it is the part of the kidney tubule closest to the glomerulus, it is called the **proximal** (near) **convoluted tubule**. Most of the glomeruli (and the proximal convoluted tubules) lie in the cortex of the kidney. Their presence contributes to the darker colouring of the kidney's outer layer. The convoluted tubule leads into a straight 'U' (or hairpin)-shaped segment called the **loop of Henle**, which dips down into the medulla and then up again. (The single-celled walls of the kidney tubule are even thinner in the loop of Henle than they are in other segments of the tube.) This then leads to another coiled segment, the **distal convoluted tubule**, and finally into the **collecting duct**. The collecting duct receives urine from a number of nephrons and then joins with others to carry urine to the **pelvis** of the kidney. The functions of these different specialised parts of the nephron will be described later.

Blood supply of the nephron

The arrangement of blood vessels around the nephrons in the kidney is different from any other arrangement in the body. Each nephron (working unit) is supplied with its own arteriole (a branch of the renal artery). This arteriole breaks up as it enters the glomerulus to form a network or knot of capillaries. These capillaries then join up again and leave the glomerulus. However, they do *not*, as you might expect, form a vein. Instead they form a second system of capillaries. This system of capillaries closely surrounds all the tubular parts of the nephron. Finally, blood from these tubular capillaries drains into small veins and then to the renal vein.

Blood supply of nephron:
arteriole
↓
capillaries of glomerulus
↓
arteriole
↓
capillary network
around kidney tube
↓
small vein
↓
(renal vein)

How the nephron functions

We have already explained, at the beginning of the chapter, that because of the particular demands of blood purification, the excretory process (or urine production) involves two steps. These are, first, the filtration of blood in the glomerulus, and second, the selective reabsorption of particular molecules from the filtrate in the tubule. These two stages can conveniently be described as separate processes.

Two stages of excretion in the kidney:
• filtration
• selective reabsorption

Filtration in the glomerulus

Earlier in this chapter we explained that filtration occurs in the glomerulus across a system of membranes. Let us now look at this system in a little more detail. Figure 12.5a shows the relationship between the glomerulus and Bowman's capsule, and Fig 12.5b shows an enlargement of the structures that are important in the filtration process. These are:

• The single cell of the capillary wall. Studies with the electron microscope have shown that glomerular capillary cells possess tiny holes or pores in their cytoplasm. These pores allow the passage of plasma but not blood cells out of the capillary.

• The epithelial cell of Bowman's capsule. These cells are also unique. Unlike other epithelial tissues (see Chapter 2), they do not form a continuous sheet. There are small gaps between adjacent cells, which allow the passage of plasma. In addition, the cells of Bowman's capsule do not lie flat against the capillary wall. Instead, they stand up away from the capillary, supported by tiny extensions of cytoplasm called **foot processes**. Between these foot processes there are tiny gaps, through which plasma can pass (Fig 12.5b).

Filtration in kidney occurs through
• pores in capillary cell wall
• basement membrane
• gaps between Bowman's capsule cells (and between foot processes of cells)

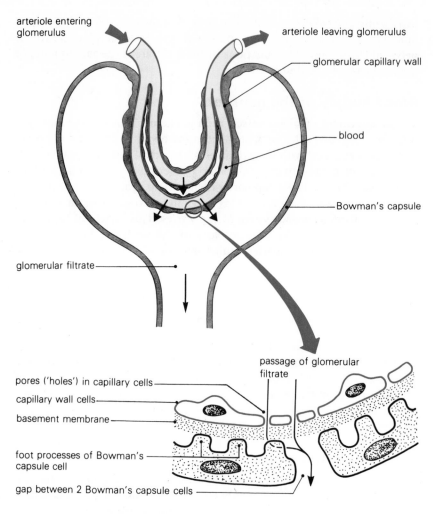

arteriole entering glomerulus

arteriole leaving glomerulus

glomerular capillary wall

blood

Bowman's capsule

glomerular filtrate

passage of glomerular filtrate

pores ('holes') in capillary cells

capillary wall cells

basement membrane

foot processes of Bowman's capsule cell

gap between 2 Bowman's capsule cells

Fig 12.5 *Structures that are important in the filtration process*
(a) Glomerulus and Bowman's capsule
(b) The 'barriers' of the filtration system

Glomerular filtrate contains
- no blood cells
- no plasma proteins
- smaller molecules in same concentrations as blood plasma

- A thin layer of membrane sandwiched between the capillary cell and the Bowman's capsule cell. This membrane is called the **basement membrane.** You can think of it as being like a layer of porous cement supporting both the capillary cells and the Bowman's capsule cells, which lie on either side of it. This membrane is the only continuous barrier to filtration in the kidney. It is believed to be the membrane that prevents large plasma proteins from leaving the blood. Smaller molecules, however, pass through it readily.

Figure 12.6 is a scanning electron micrograph of a glomerulus.

Fluid leaves capillaries in glomerulus as a result of pressure differences between capillary and tubule

The filtration of blood is a fairly straightforward process which occurs as a result of pressure differences between the capillaries of the glomerulus and Bowman's capsule. Blood pressure in the capillaries of the glomerulus is much higher than in normal tissue capillaries. This is because

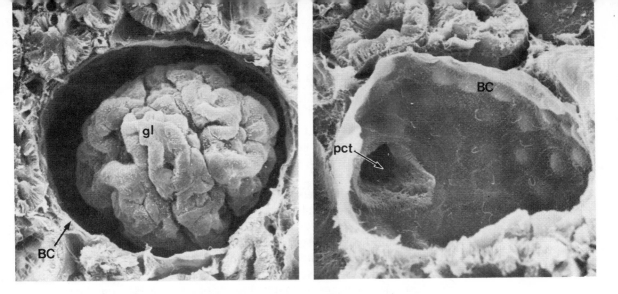

Fig 12.6 *A glomerulus and Bowman's capsule (scanning electron micrographs); on the left, the glomerulus is shown in position; on the right, the glomerulus has been removed to show the cells of Bowman's capsule and the proximal convoluted tubule leading from it. (gl = glomerulus, pct = proximal convoluted tubule, BC = Bowman's capsule)*

the arteriole leading away from the capillary has a much smaller diameter than the arteriole leading to the capillary. The high blood pressure in the capillary therefore forces water and small molecules out of the capillary and into the kidney tubule (Fig 12.7). These small molecules include glucose, amino acids, mineral salts (Na^+, Cl^- etc) and urea.

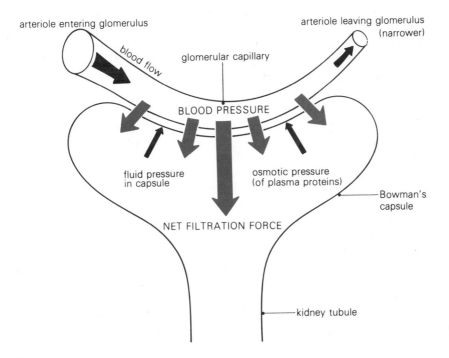

Fig 12.7 *Summary of the pressure forces in glomerular filtration*

Reabsorption in the kidney tubule

The second stage in the formation of urine involves **selective reabsorption** of particular molecules present in the filtrate which was formed in the glomerulus. The basic mechanisms by which these molecules move in and out of cells in the kidney are really no different from those in other parts of the body. It may, therefore, be helpful to refer to p 23 during this discussion.

After the filtrate has passed through the glomerulus, it is collected in the Bowman's capsule and flows into the proximal convoluted tubule. Here all amino acids and glucose, and approximately 80 per cent of salt (sodium chloride), are absorbed into the epithelial cells of the proximal tubule. From these cells the chemicals move across into the adjacent network of capillaries and so re-enter the bloodstream. The transfer of chemicals such as glucose, sodium chloride or amino acids from the kidney tubule back into the bloodstream is known as reabsorption.

Since the movement of each of the chemicals out of the kidney tubule occurs against a concentration gradient (from an area of low concentration to an area of high concentration), it can be assumed that an active transport process is involved here (p 24). Thus the reabsorption of chemicals in the proximal tubule requires energy. This fact is supported by studies of tubular epithelial cells, using an electron microscope. Tubular cells contain large numbers of mitochondria, which could provide the energy needed for an active transport process (Fig 2.12a, p 27).

Once glucose, amino acids and salt have been transferred from the filtrate back into the bloodstream in the capillaries, a flow of water will follow in the same direction. This is because the transport of glucose, amino acids and salt causes the fluid in the capillaries surrounding the kidney tubule to become more concentrated than the fluid in the tubule. As a result, water travels from the kidney tubule into the capillaries by the process of osmosis (p 24).

A similar system works in the loop of Henle. Here, sodium is pumped by active transport out of the kidney tubule into the fluid in the surrounding tissue spaces. This causes a high concentration of sodium ions in the medulla. The collecting duct is also in this area of the medulla, close to the loop of Henle (refer to Fig 12.4). The high concentration of sodium ions therefore draws water out of the collecting duct by osmosis. Once outside the collecting duct, the water moves into the nearest capillaries and re-enters the bloodstream.

Any salt not reabsorbed in the proximal convoluted tubule and the loop of Henle can be removed from the filtrate in the distal convoluted tubule. This is again brought about by active transport. Water follows the salt into the capillaries by osmosis. The fluid that finally collects in the pelvis of the kidney is called urine.

The movements of water, salt, amino acids and glucose between the kidney tubule and the surrounding capillaries are summarised in Fig 12.8.

Glucose, salt and amino acids are reabsorbed from the kidney tubule into the bloodstream

Movement of many chemicals from the kidney tubule is by active transport

Water moves from the kidney tubule into the surrounding capillaries by osmosis

Sodium is pumped by active transport out of the loop of Henle

Remaining salt is reabsorbed in the distal convoluted tubule

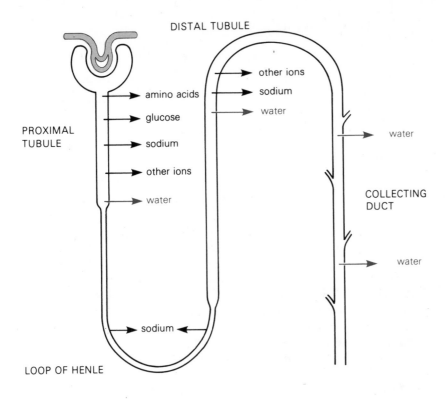

Fig 12.8 *A kidney tubule, showing where substances are reabsorbed*

In total, 125 mL of filtrate passes through the glomeruli of the kidneys per minute. But they are extremely efficient at reabsorbing water, since only 1 mL of this filtrate becomes urine. Most of the glucose, amino acids and salts are also removed from the filtrate. Only if glucose or amino acids are present in excess in the blood will they appear in the urine. A small amount of sodium chloride can usually be detected in normal urine.

It is important at this stage to recall the basic function of the kidney— that is to remove urea and other waste products from the bloodstream. Since none of the urea is actively reabsorbed in the kidney tubule, almost all of it is allowed to flow from the body in the urine. Urine may also contain other toxic substances and drugs which have been filtered out of the blood in the same way. Table 12.1 compares the composition of the final urine with that of blood.

More than 99 per cent of the fluid filtered through the glomeruli of a kidney is reabsorbed

Urea is not actively reabsorbed in the kidney tubule and so leaves the body in the urine

The kidney as a regulator

We have now described how the kidney operates as an excretory organ, constantly clearing the body of urea and other poisonous waste products. Because of the way in which it performs this excretory function, first

Table 12.1 *Concentrations of dissolved substances in blood and urine*

	Concentration in blood (%)	Concentration in urine (%)
Water	90–91	95–96
Urea	0.03	2
Sodium chloride and other salts	0.7	1.5
Proteins	7–9	0
Glucose	0.08	0
Other compounds	0.005	0.2

filtering the blood and then selectively reabsorbing those molecules required by the body, the kidney is very well equipped to regulate the composition of the blood. We shall now examine how it does this.

> The kidney tubule is concerned with water regulation

Approximately 100 mL of water is filtered out of the blood and into the kidney tubule every minute. Normally about 99 mL of this are reabsorbed from the tubule, but this amount can be varied. Varying the amount of water that is reabsorbed in the tubule is therefore a suitable way of controlling the amount of water in the body.

> Antidiuretic hormone (ADH) is released from the hypothalamus

The regulation of water absorption in the kidney tubule is controlled by a chemical called **antidiuretic hormone** (ADH). ADH is produced by cells in a small area of the brain known as the hypothalamus (see Chapter 13). It is carried in the bloodstream to the kidney, where it acts on the kidney tubule. If the proportion of water in the blood falls (ie the osmotic pressure rises), ADH is released from the hypothalamus and travels to the kidney tubule. Here ADH makes the distal convoluted tubule and collecting duct more permeable to water. As a result more water is reabsorbed into the tubule epithelium and from there into the bloodstream. The result of this is that the proportion of water in the blood rises, and a more concentrated urine is produced. This is likely to occur either after the intake of excess salt in a meal or during dehydration. In both cases the salt concentration of the blood increases, causing the proportion of water to decrease. Conversely, if the blood contains too much water, less ADH is produced by the hypothalamus, and less water is reabsorbed in the kidney tubule. In this case a more dilute urine will be produced. This sequence of events is summarised in Fig 12.9.

> ADH causes more water to be reabsorbed in the
> • distal convoluted tubule
> • collecting duct

The kidney also regulates the concentration of sodium (salt) in the blood. This control is brought about by a chemical called **aldosterone**, which is produced in the adrenal glands (see Chapter 13). Aldosterone increases the reabsorption of sodium by kidney tubule cells.

The bladder

Urine flows into the bladder from the kidneys via the ureters. When filled to capacity, the elastic walls of the bladder stretch to provide a maximum volume of about 450 cm^3. Voiding of urine occurs when the muscular rings

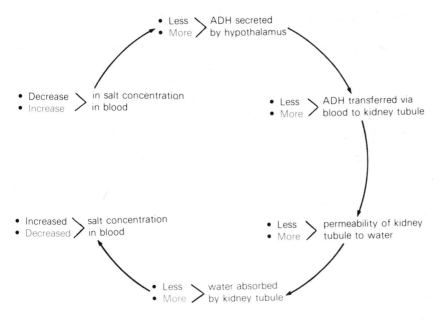

Fig 12.9 *Regulation of water retention in the body*

or sphincters which close the outlet from the bladder to the urethra relax, and urine is allowed to pass out of the bladder. The flow of urine is aided by the contraction of both the bladder and the abdominal muscles. This relaxation of the sphincters is triggered by stretch receptors (nerve endings) in the bladder walls. Two sphincters control the flow from the bladder, but only the external one is under voluntary control. This control is a 'learned' reaction. It is not present in babies and is lost when a person's spinal cord is severed.

Voiding of urine is initiated by stretch receptors in the bladder wall

Relaxation of the external sphincter of the urethra is under voluntary control

Other forms of excretion

As we have explained earlier in this chapter, excretory products are compounds resulting from the body's network of chemical reactions that must be removed from the body. The liver, as well as forming urea from amino acids, breaks down the haemoglobin of old and damaged red blood cells. The haemoglobin is converted to greenish–yellow pigments called bile pigments. These are excreted in the bile into the small intestine. Bile pigments can therefore be regarded as excretory products of the liver.

The liver breaks down haemoglobin and converts it to bile pigments

Bile pigments are excretory products of the liver

In the process of maintaining a constant body temperature, sweat is produced in sweat glands and secreted through ducts onto the skin's surface. The evaporation of sweat on the body surface helps to cool the body. The fluid known as sweat contains sodium chloride and urea, and

Sweat is responsible for the excretion of small quantities of urea and sodium chloride

although sweat is not the major avenue of excretion of these compounds, it is nevertheless worthy of mention.

Carbon dioxide is excreted by the lungs

Finally, the role of the lungs in disposing of carbon dioxide from the body has already been described. Carbon dioxide, a by-product of cellular respiration, which is in no way useful to the body, is also an excretory product. In this case the lungs act as an excretory organ.

Chapter 13

Nerves and hormones— agents of communication

The need for communication systems

Just as the players on a stage need a means of communicating among themselves in order to maintain a harmonious performance, the organs of the body need a method of communicating with each other. For example, if the carbon dioxide concentration in the bloodstream rises during vigorous exercise, the cells of the body will be unable to operate with maximum efficiency. Before this happens the body must somehow *detect* the rise in carbon dioxide and *instruct* those structures responsible for removal of carbon dioxide to act to remove the excess. In Chapter 7 we saw how the body does this—in simple terms, the breathing rate increases; more precisely, the rate of rhythmic contraction and relaxation of the intercostal muscles and diaphragm increases. In some way the vessels carrying the blood have communicated with the intercostal muscles and diaphragm.

Rapid communication is necessary between organs of the body

In many situations this communication between the body's organs must be very rapid. During a 100 metre sprint, carbon dioxide accumulates in the sprinter's blood very quickly. The muscles concerned with breathing must be equally quick in responding to this change, before the body's efficiency is greatly impaired. Such rapid communication between blood vessels and breathing muscles is carried out by the nervous system. The nervous system provides the most rapid means of communication within the body.

Rapid communication is carried out by the nervous system

Not only does the nervous system provide rapid communication between the body's organs, it also provides a constant and vital link with the environment. This can be thought of as the body's survival kit—a car suddenly turning the corner as you cross the road requires split-second action; a tennis ball slammed across the net at you gives you a fraction of a second to react; the hand that you place on a hot plate must be quickly withdrawn before it is burned and damaged. In all of these cases, sense organs in the body receive information, in one of a variety of forms: light, sound, pressure, heat and so on. This information is then relayed as messages to the brain or spinal cord. These, in turn, send further messages to the muscles of the body, instructing them to produce the appropriate response—to jump, run, hit, stop or move a limb. Again, it is the nervous system that provides the link, the means of rapid communication between the sense organs monitoring the outside world and the muscles that must respond to any change.

The nervous system provides a communication link between the body and the environment

Sense organs receive information from the environment

Messages are relayed from the sense organs to the nervous system

Further messages may be sent from the nervous system to muscles, instructing them to contract

As a rapid communication system, the nervous system operates with amazing efficiency. However, one nerve impulse will make a muscle contract for only a fraction of a second. In order to produce a prolonged muscle contraction, nerve impulses must be sent in rapid succession to the muscle for as long as the contraction is required to last. The same is true for glands whose secretory activities are controlled by the nervous system. One short burst of nerve impulses will cause the gland to secrete for only a short time.

One nerve impulse will make a muscle contract for only a fraction of a second

However, another system of communication operates in the body, which is particularly useful when a prolonged response is required. This system involves *chemical messages* in contrast to the *electrical messages* of the nervous system. The chemical messages are called hormones.

Chemical messages do not travel as rapidly in the body as nerve impulses. They are carried in the bloodstream to their target. However, hormones usually produce a more prolonged effect on their target. The secretions of many glands are controlled by hormone messages. The hormones are produced by a number of special glands in the body which together form the **endocrine system.**

Hormone messages
• are relayed more slowly than nerve impulses
• usually have a more prolonged effect than nerve impulses

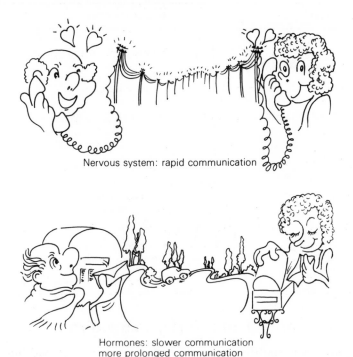

Nervous system: rapid communication

Hormones: slower communication
more prolonged communication

Elements of a communication system

Although the messages are relayed in different ways in the two systems discussed above, the basic elements of communication are the same in both cases. What are they?

In both cases, the communication systems are concerned with monitoring changes in the environment (either inside or outside the body). Any change in the environment that can be detected by some structure in the body is known as a **stimulus.** Mechanical forces, sound, light, heat and chemical substances are all stimuli to different receptors in the body.

Monitoring or detecting a stimulus, alone, however, would be of no value to a person. The importance of both communication systems lies in

Elements of a communication system:
• stimulus
• receptor
• link which relays messages to the
• effector

the fact that they allow the body to respond or react to the change. In other words, the communication system forms the link between the **receptor** or monitor that detects a change and the **effector** (muscle or gland) that responds to that change. As we have seen, in the nervous system the link between receptor and effector is formed by nerve fibres. In the endocrine system the link is formed by chemical messengers—hormones. These elements of communication systems are summarised in Table 13.1.

Table 13.1 *Elements of communication systems*

Nervous system		Endocrine system
	STIMULI	

• Light
• Pressure
• Stretch
• Sound etc
		• Change in concentration
		  of chemical
		• Nerve impulse (from a
		  special receptor)

Nerve endings, nerve cells	RECEPTOR	Cells of endocrine gland
Nerves	LINK	Hormones
Muscles, glands	EFFECTOR	Any body tissues or organs, eg ovary, kidney, breast

• Contraction
• Altered volume of
  secretion
	RESPONSES	• Altered chemical
		  reactions in cells
		• Growth or cell division
		• Contraction of muscles

Arrangement of the nervous system

Nervous system = central and peripheral nervous systems

CNS = brain and spinal cord

CNS functions as
• collector
• analyser
• coordinator

Signals from the environment or within the body are picked up by receptors

Signals are carried from receptors
↓
CNS
↓
muscle/glands (effectors)

All signals are carried to and from CNS by peripheral nerves

In humans, as in most animals, the nervous system is divided into the **central** and **peripheral nervous systems.** The central nervous system (CNS) consists of the brain and spinal cord, and functions as a collector, analyser and coordinator of incoming information. The peripheral nervous system consists of the peripheral nerves.

Signals from the external environment and from within the body are picked up by receptors. Some receptors are special sense organs, such as the eyes and ears which receive light and sound, or specialised areas in arteries which are sensitive to the carbon dioxide concentration in the blood. Other receptors are simple nerve endings, such as those in the skin which respond to heat or pain signals. These signals are passed on to the CNS via the peripheral nerves in the form of nerve impulses. Peripheral nerves also carry nerve impulses from the brain to the muscles and glands of the body. Such organs receiving impulses from the CNS are known as effectors. This is summarised in Fig 13.1. (We shall deal with receptors in detail in Chapter 15.)

RECEPTORS   NERVOUS SYSTEM   EFFECTORS

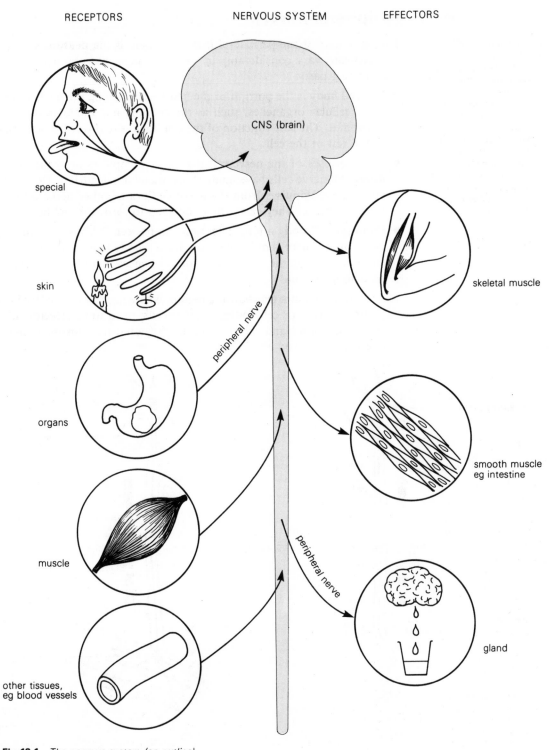

Fig 13.1   *The nervous system (an outline)*

Peripheral nerves

Neuron consists of
- cell body (contains nucleus and organelles and directs activities of rest of cell)
- dendrites (carry nerve impulse towards cell body)
- axon or nerve fibre (conducts impulses away from cell body)
- transmitting region (impulses are passed to dendrites of other cells in this region)

The basic unit of the peripheral nervous system is the **neuron** or nerve cell. Neurons vary considerably in size and shape, but any neuron has four distinct parts:

- The **cell body** is the portion of the neuron containing the nucleus and other cellular organelles, such as the endoplasmic reticulum and its ribosomes. The sole function of the cell body is to direct the activities of the rest of the cell.

- The processes of the nerve cell that receive impulses are called **dendrites**. All nerve cells have many short branching dendrites. Dendrites may receive impulses from the nerve endings of other nerve cells or from receptors. They carry these impulses towards the cell body.

- From the cell body a long extension can be seen. This is the **axon** or **nerve fibre**. There is only one axon per cell body, and it conducts impulses away from the cell body. Axons can be less than 1 mm in length or as long as 1 m.

- The axon ends in a **transmitting region**, where impulses are passed on to the dendrites or cell bodies of other cells, or to some effector such as a muscle or a gland. The transmitting region often consists of many finely divided axon ends.

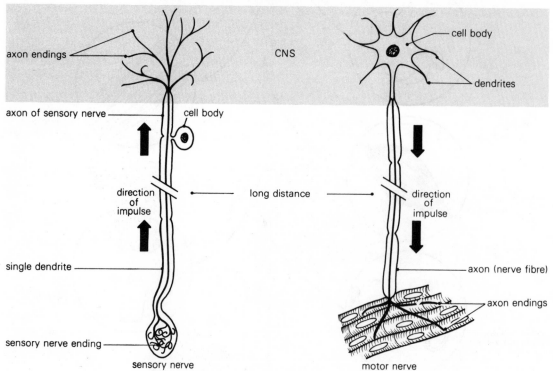

Fig 13.2 *Structure of sensory and motor nerves*

The neurons that conduct nerve impulses from a sensory organ or receptor are known as **sensory neurons**. Those that conduct impulses from the brain to an effector are known as **motor neurons**. Although both of these types of nerves possess the four main regions outlined above, there are differences in the arrangement and size of the regions in the two types of neuron. Outline diagrams of a sensory and a motor nerve are shown in Fig 13.2.

In mammals, many of the neurons are surrounded by a sheath of fatty material known as **myelin**. This sheath is actually composed of a long, flat, thin cell which has wound around the axon many times. You can imagine this sheath cell being like a sheet of paper rolled a large number of times around a pencil (Fig 13.3). This fatty myelin sheath serves as insulation for the axon and enables nerve impulses to travel approximately 200 times as fast as in unmyelinated cells.

Nerves are bundles of nerve fibres, usually myelinated and surrounded by a sheath of white connective tissue. Nerves can be seen as white threads or thin cords in the body, and many can be dissected out with relative ease (Fig 13.4).

Sensory neurons carry impulses from receptors to the brain

Motor neurons carry impulses from the brain to muscles or glands

The myelin sheath increases the speed at which nerve impulses travel

Nerves—bundles of nerve fibres surrounded by a connective tissue sheath

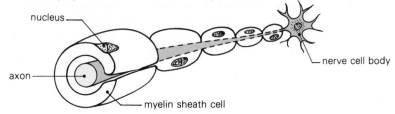

Fig 13.3 *Formation of the myelin sheath*

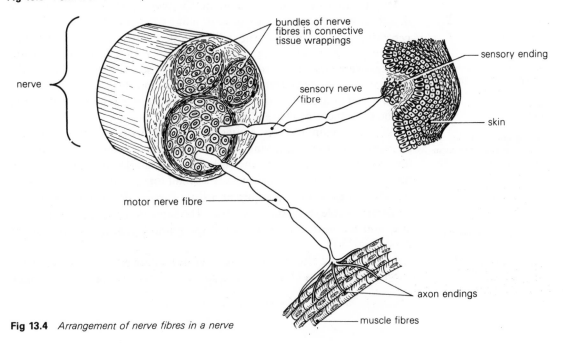

Fig 13.4 *Arrangement of nerve fibres in a nerve*

What is a nerve impulse?

The nerve impulse is
electrical

The message which passes along a nerve fibre is called a nerve impulse. It passes through the dendrites, cell body and axon of a neuron, and may then pass on to another neuron. The impulse is electrical, and we can think of the axon conducting the impulse as acting like a piece of telephone cable.

When an axon is not con-
ducting a nerve impulse,
the outside of the axon has
an overall positive charge
compared with the inside

When an axon is not carrying an electric impulse, there are unequal concentrations of ions on the inside and outside of the axon. A higher concentration of (positive) sodium ions is found on the outside of the axon than on the inside. Higher concentrations of negative ions are found on the inside of the axon than on the outside. The overall result is that there is more positive charge on the outside of the axon than on the inside (Fig 13.5).

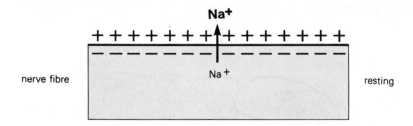

Fig 13.5 *Distribution of sodium ions inside and outside the resting axon membrane*

In our discussion of diffusion in Chapter 2, we pointed out that dissolved substances or gases move to make equal any differences in concentration. The same is true with charge. The only thing stopping positive charge from moving from the outside to the inside of the axon, or negative charge from moving from the inside to the outside of the axon, is the axon membrane. The same situation is found in the dendrites and the cell body, where the surrounding membrane provides the barrier to the movement of charged ions.

The axon membrane
prevents positive charge
from moving from the
outside of the axon to the
inside

When an axon receives a message, this property of its membrane changes, and the membrane suddenly becomes permeable to sodium ions. As a result, sodium ions rush into the interior of the axon. This movement of charged ions releases a small amount of electrical energy which then causes the membrane a little further down the axon to become permeable to sodium ions, too. The same thing happens at the next site, and the next, and so on, until the impulse reaches the end of the axon (Fig 13.6).

When a nerve impulse
reaches an axon, the mem-
brane becomes permeable
to sodium ions
↓
causes sodium ions to
rush into the axon
↓
releases electrical energy

causes next section of
membrane to become
permeable

A split second after sodium ions have been allowed to flow through the axon membrane, ATP is used as a source of energy to pump the sodium ions back to the exterior of the axon membrane. During this process the membrane becomes impermeable again, and the unequal concentrations of sodium are maintained until another impulse comes along. The membrane has returned to its resting state and is ready to relay another message.

ATP is used to pump sodium ions back to the outside of the neuron membrane

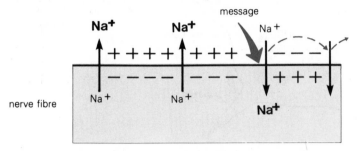

Fig 13.6 *Changes in the distribution of charged ions as an impulse is conducted along a nerve*

Bridging the gap

We have already said that the nervous system provides a means of communication between receptors and effectors in all parts of the body. There must be a process, therefore, which allows signals received by one nerve cell to be relayed to other nerve cells. There are, in fact, special sites on nerve cells where impulses are relayed from one neuron to another.

The unique fact about these points at which impulses travel from one neuron to another is that there is *no* cytoplasmic contact. In fact there is a small gap between the membranes of the two neurons. On the side of the gap from which the impulse is being passed, the axon ends in a small knob-shaped structure. The membranes on both sides of the gap are capable of being made permeable to sodium ions, but the impulse travels *only in one direction.*

There is no contact between cytoplasm of the two neurons at points where impulses are relayed from one neuron to another

Nerve impulses travel in only one direction across the gap

The gap, together with the axon knob and the potentially permeable membranes, is called a **synapse**. The knob is often called a synaptic knob. Synapses occur between axon endings and dendrites or axon endings and cell bodies. Figures 13.7a and 13.7b show examples of both these kinds of synapses; Fig 13.7c shows details of a synapse that are visible only under an electron microscope.

The gap between neurons is called a synapse

How is the nerve impulse carried across the gap of the synapse? When a nerve impulse arrives at a synapse, a **transmitter substance** is released from the membrane of the synaptic knob. In a fraction of a second this

A transmitter substance carries a nerve impulse across a synapse

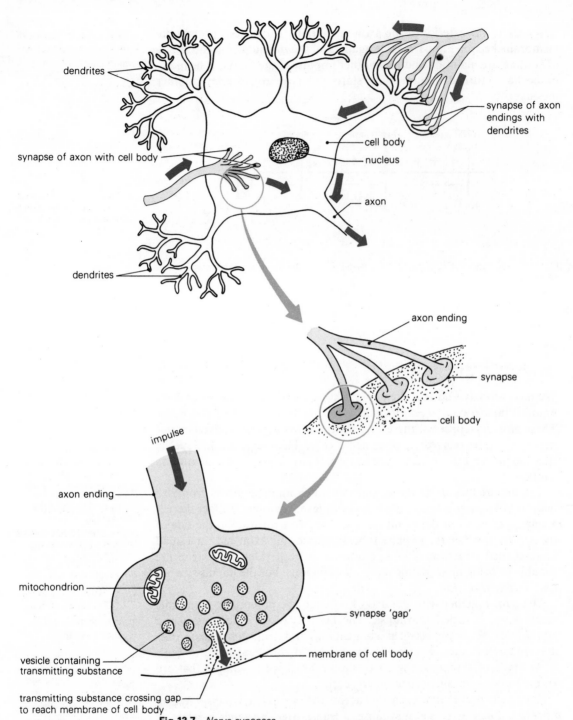

dendrites

synapse of axon endings with dendrites

synapse of axon with cell body

cell body

nucleus

axon

dendrites

axon ending

synapse

cell body

impulse

axon ending

mitochondrion

synapse 'gap'

membrane of cell body

vesicle containing transmitting substance

transmitting substance crossing gap to reach membrane of cell body

Fig 13.7 *Nerve synapses*
(a) Two types of synapse between neurons
(b) Enlargement of synapses between axon endings and cell body
(c) Cross-section of a synapse (as seen with an electron microscope)

substance travels across the gap and causes the membrane on the other side to become permeable to sodium ions. Once sodium ions begin to rush through this membrane, electrical energy is released and the impulse is passed up the dendrite or cell body as described earlier in the chapter.

The transmitter substance causes the membrane on the other side of the synapse to become permeable to sodium ions

The same method of nerve impulse transmission is also seen at the nerve–muscle junction. Here the ending of the axon is splayed out to form a **motor end plate**. Again, a gap exists between the motor end plate and the membrane surrounding the muscle cell. The same transmitter substance relays the impulse from the nerve to the muscle.

It is interesting to note that certain drugs can interfere with the action of this transmitter substance. Curare, the poison used on the tips of arrows by South American Indians, prevents the transmitter from acting on the muscle cell membrane, and therefore causes paralysis. Various drugs that are used to produce relaxation of muscles during operations under general anaesthesia act in the same way.

Some drugs interfere with the action of the transmitter substance

The central nervous system

The central nervous system consists of two parts: the spinal cord and the brain.

The spinal cord

The spinal cord is essentially a receiver of impulses from sensory nerves, a carrier of these impulses to the brain, and a direct link between sensory and motor nerves. For protection, it is enclosed within the bony canal formed by the vertebrae of the backbone (spine).

The spinal cord
• receives impulses from sensory nerves
• carries impulses to the brain
• carries impulses from the brain
• provides a direct link between sensory nerves and motor nerves

A cross-section of the spinal cord reveals two regions: a central region which is grey in colour and is known as the grey matter, and an outer region which is white and is known as the white matter. The grey matter takes the shape of an 'H' in such a cross-section (Fig 13.8).

The central grey matter is made up of cell bodies and non-myelinated nerve fibres. Some of these nerve fibres may be short and confined only to the grey matter. Some may be the ends or beginnings of motor or sensory nerves which lead in and out of the spinal cord. The white matter consists of sections of sensory and motor nerves which are myelinated. It also contains myelinated nerve fibres which run vertically up to or down from the brain. The extensions of the white matter through which sensory and motor nerve fibres enter and leave the spinal cord are called the roots of the spinal cord. Sensory nerves lead into the spinal cord through the **dorsal** (back) **root**, whilst motor nerves leave through the **ventral** (front) **root**. The dorsal and ventral roots join before they leave the spinal canal to form a **spinal nerve**. Spinal nerves are the origins of peripheral nerves.

Grey matter of the spinal cord is made up of non-myelinated nerve fibres

White matter consists of myelinated nerve fibres which run vertically up and down to the brain

Sensory nerves enter the spinal cord through the dorsal root; motor nerves leave through the ventral root

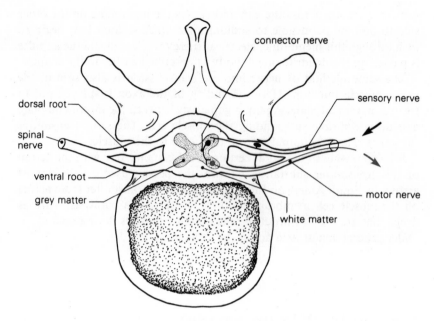

connector nerve

sensory nerve

dorsal root

spinal nerve

ventral root

grey matter

white matter

motor nerve

Fig 13.8 *Section through a vertebra and the spinal cord*

The brain

In the brain:
- grey matter (cell bodies) is on the outside
- white matter is on the inside

The brain is a soft (almost jelly-like) mass of nerve fibres and cell bodies, weighing about 1.3 kg in an adult man. Like the spinal cord, it possesses areas of grey and white matter, but these areas are the reverse of the spinal cord; that is, the grey matter is on the outside, and the white matter is on the inside. The grey area possesses billions of interconnecting cell bodies, the short dendrites of each cell body being connected to the fine axon ends of many other nerve cells. It is this construction that makes the brain the most complex and finely tuned of computers. The white matter is again a mass of myelinated nerve fibres.

Role of the brain:
- receiver
- analyser
- coordinator
- storer
- initiator
of nerve impulses

The brain's role in the nervous system is that of central receiver, analyser, coordinator, storer and initiator of nerve impulses. For example, impulses from sensory endings may be relayed along peripheral nerves and through the spinal cord to the brain.

Here, a rapid analysis of the impulses is carried out. This analysis may involve coordination of impulses reaching the brain from a variety of receptors—eyes, ears, heat or pain receptors in the skin, for example. Following coordinated analysis of all these impulses, further signals may be transmitted from several areas of the brain, through nerves in the spinal cord, to a number of different muscle groups.

Memory involves a permanent chemical change within the brain

An impulse may leave its mark within the brain resulting in some permanent chemical change; this is the origin of memory. This memory may modify the way in which the brain analyses further sensory signals of the same type on a later occasion. As a result, memory may modify the response initiated by brain cells to a particular sensory stimulus or situation.

A simple example may help to demonstrate some of these features of brain function. All small children are naturally curious. They will grasp at and play with any object they see. When a small child sees a shiny, glowing radiator, sensory stimuli pass as nerve impulses from the eyes to the brain. The brain analyses the impulses it receives and responds by relaying signals along many motor neurons which produce coordinated movement—the child reaches for the radiator. However, the radiator is hot. Heat and pain receptors in the skin send more impulses to the brain, which tell the brain that the shiny glowing object is painful to touch. This sensory information is stored in the brain in the form of memory.

The next time the child sees the radiator, the brain analyses the sensory stimulus differently. Despite the attraction of the glowing object, memory of the previous sensory impulses modifies the brain's analysis and response. The child resists his urge to grasp at the radiator, because of the memory of the painful stimulus he received.

Protection of the brain and spinal cord

The brain and spinal cord are composed almost entirely of nerve tissue—nerve cell bodies and their processes. These are very soft, delicate

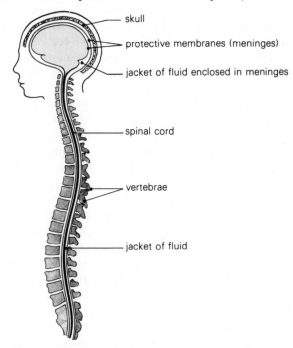

— skull
— protective membranes (meninges)
— jacket of fluid enclosed in meninges
— spinal cord
— vertebrae
— jacket of fluid

Fig 13.9 *Protection of the central nervous system*

structures which are easily damaged. It is obviously essential that this delicate tissue be well protected. The brain and spinal cord are protected by several mechanisms, which are outlined in Fig 13.9 and are listed here:

The brain and spinal cord are protected by
• a bony case
• a jacket of fluid
• three connective tissue wrappings—meninges

- A bony case. The brain is entirely enclosed by the bones of the **skull** (cranial bones) (see Chapter 18). The spinal cord is enclosed along its length in the spinal canal, which is a hollow tube formed by the vertebrae.

- A jacket of fluid. Inside the bony case the brain and spinal cord are surrounded by a jacket of fluid called **cerebrospinal fluid**. This acts as a cushion or shock absorber for the brain and spinal cord in any impact.

- Three connective tissue wrappings called the **meninges**. These membranes surround the brain and spinal cord and help to protect them. The innermost one is attached to the nerve tissue. Cerebrospinal fluid is enclosed between the two inner membranes.

The reflex arc

We have now examined the basic principles of how the nervous system operates—how messages are relayed along nerve fibres in the form of electrical impulses, and how these impulses can be transmitted from one nerve cell across a gap to another nerve cell. We must now see how these principles of communication are organised in the nervous system to allow very precise and efficient communication between all the receptors and the effectors of the body.

The nervous system allows the body to react or respond to changes or stimuli both inside and outside the body. The response to the change may be automatic (or involuntary) or under conscious control (voluntary). As

Reflex responses are automatic; that is, they occur without any activity by the brain

we shall see soon, responses which involve conscious control are organised by the brain. They are often very complex responses. The simplest responses are automatic or involuntary responses. We call these responses reflex responses.

Many reflex responses have a protective function

You can probably think of several responses to change (or stimuli) that are automatic or reflex. Many of these responses have a protective function. For example, we automatically or unconsciously pull our hand away if we touch a hot object, or lift our foot from the ground if we tread on a pin. We are certainly aware of the pain of the pin or heat of the object, but our body has responded almost before we are conscious of the sensation. We shall now see how these simplest responses are organised in the nervous system.

The parts of the nervous system through which impulses have to pass to bring about an involuntary or reflex response are called the reflex arc.

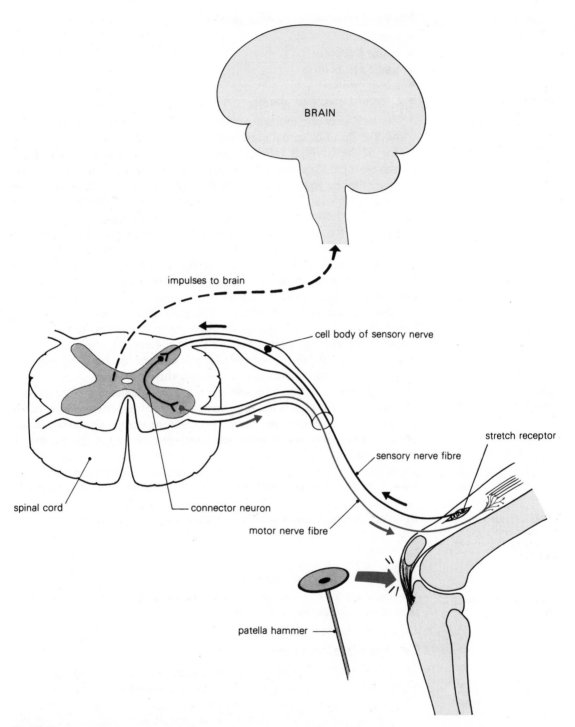

Fig 13.10 *The reflex arc (knee-jerk reflex) — the simplest system of communication*

The basic elements of a reflex arc are:

- receptor
- sensory neuron
- connector neuron
- motor neuron
- effector (muscle or gland).

The link between the sensory and the motor signals always occurs within the brain or spinal cord (central nervous system).

One of the simplest reflex responses, which we can demonstrate on ourselves, is the knee jerk—a tendon is tapped firmly just below the knee cap and the leg jerks forward involuntarily. What is happening in the nervous system in this sequence of events? You will find it helpful to refer to Fig 13.10 as you read the following explanation.

When the tendon is tapped, fibres in the muscle joining the tendon are stretched. This stimulus or change is detected by stretch receptors in the muscle. Nerve impulses are relayed from the receptors along sensory nerves to the spinal cord. The axon of each sensory nerve synapses with a **connector neuron** (often called an interneuron) inside the spinal cord. Another process of the interneuron synapses with a motor neuron. The impulses are therefore relayed through the interneuron to the motor nerve. When the impulses reach the effector (muscle), the muscle contracts and the knee jerks forward. As you can see, no brain activity (or conscious control) is necessary to produce this movement.

The change and the response do not go undetected by the brain, however. Why is this? When the sensory nerve enters the spinal cord, it synapses not only with the interneuron, but also with another sensory neuron. This nerve relays messages from sensory nerves up the spinal cord to the brain. These messages reach the sensory areas of the brain at about the same time as the other messages reach the effector muscle in the leg. By the time the person has realised that his knee has been tapped, his leg is already jerking in response. This stimulus has been detected by the brain, but the response is quite independent of the brain.

More about the brain

We shall now look at how the various parts of the brain make special contributions towards the brain's coordinating role.

The cerebral cortex

If we examine the nervous system of animals at different points along the evolutionary scale, we find that the simpler the animal form, the simpler its nervous system. Simple animals such as flat worms have almost no brain at all. Their nervous system is two single large nerves running the length of the body, with a small swelling of cell bodies at the head end, known as a ganglion.

In the course of evolution the head region of animals has become more specialised, with the development of special sense organs: eyes, ears, smell receptors in the nose, and taste buds in the mouth. The head end of the spinal cord has therefore enlarged—more nerve cell bodies must be housed in this area of the spinal cord than in any other area, and more processes enter and synapse in the cord. In all advanced animals, such as mammals, this front region of the brain has become greatly enlarged and forms the distinct structure which we know as the brain.

The development of the brain is far greater in humans than in any other animal. It is partly this difference which has made them superior to all other animals. The region of the human brain that is particularly enlarged and developed is called the **cerebral cortex**.

During development in the uterus the brain grows from a simple tube of nerve tissue. This swelling, which is in the head region of the nerve tube, can be divided into three regions: **forebrain, midbrain** and **hindbrain**. Figure 13.11 shows that during development the forebrain enlarges more than any other parts of the brain. As it does so, it folds back over the midbrain and swells out on either side of the nerve tube. By this tremendous growth, the forebrain develops into the right and left **cerebral hemispheres**. The midbrain and hindbrain develop to form a number of other specialised brain areas. The fully developed human brain is shown in vertical section in Fig 13.12.

The cerebral cortex is the layer of grey matter on the surface of the cerebral hemispheres. The cortex possesses motor areas and sensory areas. The sensory areas receive impulses from sensory nerve fibres leading into the brain. The motor areas send out nerve impulses to all the voluntary muscles of the body. It has been shown that different regions of these sensory and motor areas receive and send impulses to different areas of the body. Some of these areas are shown in Fig 13.13.

Other areas of the cerebral cortex are responsible for memory, imagination, thought, intelligence, emotions and feelings. These are also shown in Fig 13.13. Further regions known as association areas are responsible for the analysis and coordination of incoming nervous impulses—the sorts of processes involved when the child who has been burnt keeps away from the radiator.

Their large brain makes human beings superior to other animals

The area of the human brain that has become particularly enlarged is the cerebral cortex

The brain begins development as a tube. This tube consists of
- forebrain
- midbrain
- hindbrain

The forebrain folds back over the midbrain and swells to become the cerebral hemispheres

The cerebral cortex is the layer of grey matter on the surface of the cerebral hemispheres

The cerebral cortex contains
- sensory areas
- motor areas
- areas responsible for memory, imagination, thought, intelligence, emotions and feelings
- association areas

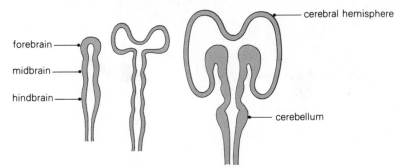

Fig 13.11 *Development of the brain*

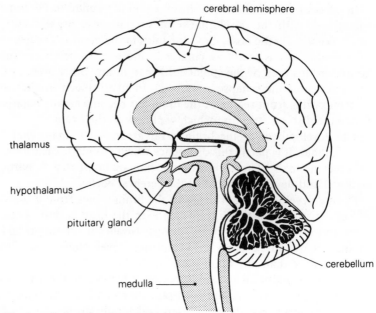

Fig 13.12 *A vertical section through the brain*

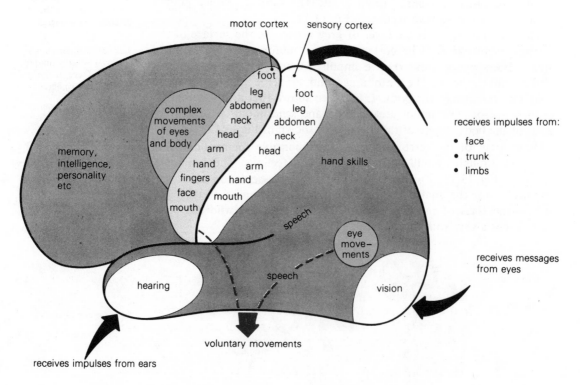

Fig 13.13 *Some functional areas of the cerebral cortex*

Let us consider an example which illustrates how the sensory, motor and association areas of the cortex operate. There is an apple lying on the table in front of you. You look at it and decide whether you are hungry enough to eat it. You finally pick it up and eat it!

First, impulses from the eye, reaching a sensory area of the cortex via sensory nerves, inform you of the apple's presence. Second, impulses are directed to an association area to allow a decision to be made about the apple; the association area then passes impulses to the motor area of the cortex. Finally, the motor area sends impulses down the motor nerves to the muscles of the hands and arms which enable you to pick up the apple.

A tremendous amount is still not known about the functions of the cerebral cortex. A certain amount has been learnt from animals whose cortex has been removed. These animals remain alive, and can eat and sleep and, although blind, walk in a coordinated way. However, such animals lose all their past learning and are incapable of learning new habits. This is perhaps the best clue we have to the function of the cerebral cortex—it is the site of intelligence, thought and emotions, all the higher activities of the brain.

Sensory areas of the cortex receive impulses from receptors

Association areas analyse incoming impulses

Motor areas send impulses to muscles or glands

Other areas of the brain

As was pointed out in the previous section, the midbrain and hindbrain develop into other structures, each of which has a different set of functions. The midbrain and hindbrain structures are generally concerned with more primitive or basic activities than the cerebral hemispheres:

- The **cerebellum** controls balance and posture.

- The **hypothalamus** controls circulation of blood, breathing, digestion, vomiting, body temperature, water content of the body, sleep and adjustments for rage and fear.

- The **thalamus** acts as a relay station through which all sensory information passes before going to the cerebral cortex.

- The **medulla** controls many basic bodily functions such as breathing, heart rate and constriction of blood vessels.

Two important nerves arising from the medulla are the sympathetic nerve (which forms the sympathetic chain) and the vagus nerve. These nerves control the body's involuntary activities, such as secretion of acid in the stomach, peristalsis in the intestine, the dilation of arteries, the rate of breathing and the contraction of the bladder. This part of the nervous system is called the **autonomic nervous system**. The autonomic nervous system controls all bodily activities over which we have no conscious control. This includes the activities of most of the glands and internal organs.

Other areas of the human brain:
- *cerebellum (balance, posture)*
- *hypothalamus (circulation, breathing, body temperature etc)*
- *thalamus (relays impulses to cerebral cortex)*
- *medulla (breathing, heart rate etc)*

The sympathetic and vagus nerves control involuntary activities, eg peristalsis, release of acid from the stomach

Introducing the endocrine system

The endocrine system is a collection of special glands that secrete chemical messengers called hormones. There are basically two types of glands in the body. One group, which includes glands such as the sweat glands of the skin and the salivary glands of the mouth, produces secretions that drain to a particular site (such as the surface of the skin or the mouth cavity) and have an effect near, or where, they are released. Moreover, such glands release their secretions through a small tube called a duct. These glands are known as **exocrine glands** (*exo* = outside).

Exocrine glands:
• release their secretions through a duct
• secretions act near their site of release

In contrast, the other group, known as the **endocrine glands**, manufactures chemicals that pass directly into the bloodstream (*endo* = inside) without passing through a duct. These chemicals circulate all over the body and act at places far from the glands where they are produced. Such circulating chemicals are able to act over a considerable period of time.

Endocrine glands:
• secrete chemicals directly into the bloodstream
• chemicals circulate in the bloodstream and may act far from the glands where they are produced

You will remember from Chapter 6 that there are all sorts of chemicals circulating in the blood plasma, and that many of these act in some way in body cells. What, then are the distinguishing features of the chemical messengers—hormones—of the endocrine system? The properties of hormones can be summarised as follows:

• They are secreted from ductless (endocrine) glands into the bloodstream.

• They are carried in the bloodstream.

• They act at sites distant from the site of their production.

A simple example may help to show how hormones act in the communication system, and how their action differs from that of nerves. (Refer again to Table 13.1, which shows the elements of communication systems.) During pregnancy, a woman's breasts develop, so that by the time of birth all the structures necessary for the production of milk are present. However, almost no milk is actually produced until after the baby is born. Then, within a few days of birth, large volumes of milk begin to be secreted, and this secretion may continue for many months. How does the baby's birth trigger the secretion of milk?

Birth of baby
↓
chemical change in mother's body
↓
endocrine gland below the brain
↓
hormone
↓
gland cells of breast
↓
milk production begins

As a result of a chemical change which takes place in the mother's body when the baby is born, cells of an endocrine gland just below the brain begin to release a hormone. The hormone circulates in the bloodstream and reaches its target—the cells of the breast. Here, the hormone 'instructs' the cells to begin producing milk. The chemical change which takes place at birth is, therefore, the stimulus. The gland cells of the breast are the effectors. The hormone serves as the link between the receptor (endocrine gland) and the effector. (The control of milk secretion is discussed further in Chapter 17 and illustrated in Fig 17.18.)

In the example above, the hormone stimulates the gland cells of the breast to secrete milk. Different hormones can stimulate different types of cells in a variety of ways. For example, hormones may stimulate growth and division of cells, contraction of muscles, secretion from glands and may alter many of the chemical reactions occurring inside cells.

Control of blood sugar concentration

One very important role of the endocrine system is the control of the concentration of glucose in the blood. It is essential that the concentration of glucose in the blood remains between approximately 4.4 and 7.7 mmol/litre (80 and 140 mg/100 mL). If the concentration of glucose falls much below 4.4 mmol/litre (80 mg/100 mL) of blood, the brain is deprived of glucose, which is its sole source of energy. (Remember that, under normal circumstances, the brain cannot use fats or proteins for energy.) Glucose levels above about 7.7 mmol/litre (140 mg/100 mL) also severely disturb body functions.

It has been known since the end of the previous century that the pancreas plays a major part, not only in digestion, but in the control of blood glucose. More recently, small groups of pancreatic cells called the **islets of Langerhans** have been shown to secrete a hormone called **insulin** directly into the circulating blood (Fig 13.14). Experiments have shown that one function of insulin is to assist the absorption of glucose from the bloodstream into cells. Insulin also causes blood glucose to enter the cells of the liver and to be converted there to glycogen. In addition, it accelerates the manufacture of fats.

An important role of the endocrine system is the control of blood sugar

The pancreas produces a hormone called insulin

Insulin
- assists the transport of glucose from the bloodstream into cells
- assists the formation of glycogen in the liver
- assists the manufacture of fats

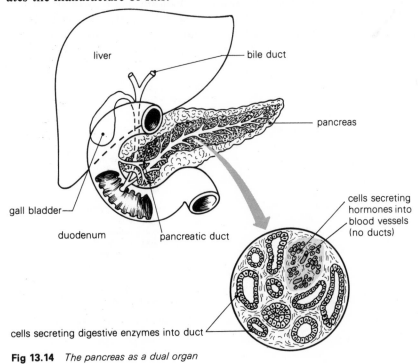

liver — bile duct

pancreas

gall bladder

duodenum   pancreatic duct

cells secreting hormones into blood vessels (no ducts)

cells secreting digestive enzymes into duct

Fig 13.14 *The pancreas as a dual organ*

As you can see, the chemical insulin has all the characteristics of a hormone:

- It is secreted by the cells of an endocrine gland directly into the bloodstream. (Note that the pancreas can also be regarded as an exocrine gland in that other pancreatic cells secrete digestive enzymes through a duct, into the duodenum.)

- It is a chemical.

- It is carried around the body in the blood and acts at numerous sites far from its site of production.

The secretion of insulin by the pancreas is controlled by blood glucose concentration:

- blood glucose increases
  ↓
  insulin increases

- blood glucose decreases
  ↓
  insulin decreases

Glucagon breaks down glycogen to raise blood glucose

Diabetes—a disease resulting from lack of insulin

Prolonged lack of insulin causes death

The secretion of insulin from the pancreas is controlled by the blood glucose concentration. When blood glucose rises after a meal, the pancreas detects this increase. It then increases the rate of insulin secretion. Insulin assists in the transport of glucose into cells for use in respiration, or into liver or muscle cells for storage as glycogen. The concentration of glucose in the blood is thus reduced to the normal level.

If blood glucose falls, for example after exercise, the pancreas again detects this change and reduces the secretion of insulin. In addition, another hormone called **glucagon** is secreted by the pancreas. Its effect is to break down glycogen in the liver to glucose, which then enters the bloodstream. The net effect of reduced insulin and increased glucagon is a rise in blood glucose (Fig 13.15).

Sometimes the islet cells of the pancreas cease to function properly. This can occur early in childhood, but often develops over a number of years during adulthood. It causes a condition called **diabetes**, which results from a lack of insulin circulating in the body. People suffering from diabetes can be treated by regular injections of artificial insulin. Failure to do this results in excessively high glucose concentration in the

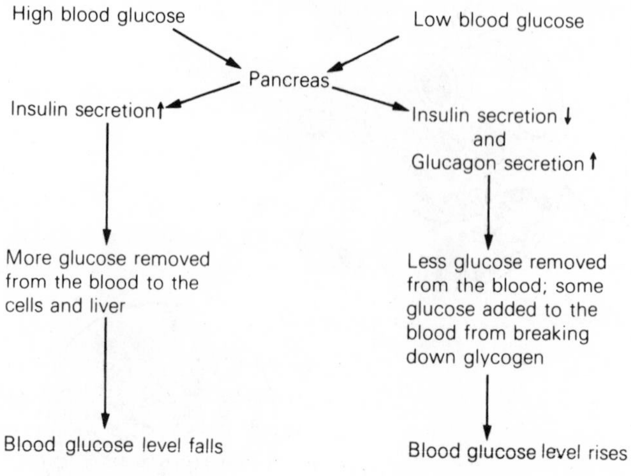

High blood glucose   Low blood glucose

Pancreas

Insulin secretion↑   Insulin secretion↓
                                      and
                                      Glucagon secretion↑

More glucose removed   Less glucose removed
from the blood to the   from the blood; some
cells and liver   glucose added to the
                                      blood from breaking
                                      down glycogen

Blood glucose level falls   Blood glucose level rises

Fig 13.15 *Effect of blood glucose concentration on insulin secretion*

blood after a meal, loss of glucose (and increased amounts of water) in the urine, and eventually coma and death.

Let us examine a little more closely what happens to a person who fails to produce the hormone insulin. As we have already said, glucose is vital for the brain cells. After a meal, the glucose concentration in the blood becomes very high for a short time. However, in the absence of insulin, much of this glucose cannot be transported into body cells. Instead, it is lost through the kidneys (with increased amounts of water) in the urine.

When the glucose concentration in the blood falls, glycogen in the liver is split to form glucose molecules, which then enter the bloodstream to maintain a satisfactory blood glucose level. However, the reserves of glycogen are very limited and cannot maintain blood glucose concentrations for very long.

In the absence of glucose, many of the body cells switch from using glucose to using fats as their source of energy. (Some proteins are broken down, too, to release energy, which causes muscle wasting and weakness.) However, the breakdown of fats is only partly satisfactory. This is because the large-scale breakdown of fats results in the much increased formation of chemicals called ketone bodies. High concentrations of ketone bodies, which develop in severe cases of untreated diabetes, are very harmful to the brain. Unless treated with injections of insulin, a person in this situation would die within a week or two.

When blood glucose falls, fats and proteins are broken down to release energy

Breakdown of large quantities of fats results in the increased formation of ketone bodies

High concentrations of ketone bodies are harmful to the brain

You can see from this description how important it is that the diabetic person obtains a regular supply of insulin. It is equally important, however, that he eat his meals (his supply of glucose) at regular intervals. An example may help to illustrate why this is so.

A diabetic fisherman injects himself with his morning dose of insulin, eats his breakfast, and then sets off in his small boat for a morning's fishing. As he fishes, his morning dose of insulin (which must last until his next injection in the evening) is helping his breakfast glucose to be transported into all the cells of his body. As it does this, the blood glucose concentration gradually falls. Then, unexpectedly, a storm blows up and the boat is washed further away from the shore. The fisherman now faces an alarming situation. Unlike the normal person, his pancreas cannot adjust the secretion of insulin minute by minute, according to his body's altered needs. When he takes his morning dose of insulin, he must predict his requirements for the day. Now, as his boat is swept further from the shore, his blood glucose concentration is falling rapidly (assisted by his morning dose of insulin), and without his lunch he has no supply of glucose to reverse the fall. In this situation, the brain suffers first. Untreated, the fisherman would fall into a coma—known medically as a hypoglycaemic coma. Such is the diabetic's plight. To avoid this eventuality, most diabetics always carry a supply of sugar in some form with them. In addition, they may wear a label identifying them as a diabetic, so that, if found in a coma, they may be given the sugar their body so desperately needs.

Other endocrine glands

Figure 13.16 shows the site of a number of other endocrine glands in the body. Each produces a different hormone which plays an important role within the body as a communicator and a coordinator.

You will notice that both the testes and the ovaries are included in the endocrine system. This is because special cells in both these organs produce sex hormones. In Chapter 17 we shall describe the vital role these hormones play in controlling the production of sex cells.

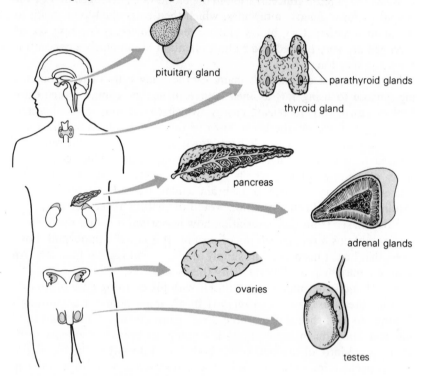

Fig 13.16　*Endocrine glands of the body*

Adrenal glands

Adrenalin is produced by the adrenal gland. Large amounts of adrenalin are produced under conditions of stress

The adrenal glands consist of an outer and an inner part, known as the **adrenal cortex** and **adrenal medulla** respectively. The adrenal medulla manufactures a hormone called **adrenalin.** A certain amount of adrenalin is secreted in the body all the time. However, its effects are most noticeable under conditions of stress or fright. For this reason it is sometimes known as the 'fight or flight' hormone. (Imagine how you would feel after a narrow escape from a motor car accident, or as you approach the starting line in an important race—at times like these you would have a lot of adrenalin circulating in your bloodstream.)

Adrenalin acts to assist you to face a taxing situation. For example, it causes heart and breathing rates to increase, raises the blood pressure and constricts surface blood vessels; it also decreases the activity of the bladder and intestine and causes a rise in blood sugar. Its release is stimulated by nerve impulses reaching the adrenal medulla from the brain.

The activity and secretions of the adrenal cortex (outer part of the adrenal gland) are quite separate from those of the adrenal medulla. Several different hormones are produced in the cortex, including **aldosterone,** which is involved in the regulation of the sodium (salt) concentration in the body (Chapter 12), and **cortisone,** which helps the body to adapt to stress.

Adrenalin
- raises blood pressure
- increases heart and breathing rates
- decreases activity of bladder and intestine
- raises blood sugar concentration

Thyroid gland

Many people complain of a weight problem. Some find they cannot reduce their weight despite controlled dieting; others say that it is impossible for them to put on weight, regardless of what they eat. There must be something basically different about these two types of people—and not necessarily just their eating habits.

The thyroid gland secretes a hormone known as **thyroxine.** This hormone accelerates the rate of respiration of glucose in cells. It also tends to increase heart rate and a person's general level of activity. Herein may lie the key to some weight problems. If the thyroid gland is underactive, it will not produce enough thyroxine, and the person may thus appear lethargic and overweight. This is because when thyroxine is lacking, insufficient glucose is oxidised in cells. As a result, cells do not release energy to maintain their normal level of activity. The excess glucose that is not broken down to carbon dioxide and water is subsequently converted into fat. (This is why people with underactive thyroid glands are usually overweight.)

Conversely, a person whose thyroid gland is overactive will have blood thyroxine levels that are higher than normal. As a result, glucose is consumed rapidly in cellular respiration, and the energy released allows the person to be abundantly active. Fats are also rapidly respired; hence the thinness of this kind of person. Sometimes people who have an enlarged or over-active thyroid gland can be treated by surgical removal of part of the gland. The remaining portion can then secrete the correct amount of the hormone. People with underactive thyroids are treated by regular doses of thyroxine.

Thyroxine is produced by the thyroid gland

Thyroxine increases the rate of glucose and fat respiration in cells

Lack of thyroxine causes lethargy and obesity

Excess thyroxine causes overactivity and inability to gain weight

Parathyroid glands

Normally, there are four small parathyroid glands in humans, lying behind and attached to the thyroid gland. Their role is entirely different from that of the thyroid gland.

The parathyroid glands are concerned with the control of the concentration of calcium in the blood. When the blood calcium concentration falls, the parathyroid glands release **parathyroid hormone** into the bloodstream. This hormone increases the uptake of calcium from the gut and also its reabsorption in the kidneys.

The pituitary—the 'master' hormone gland

The pituitary gland is called the master hormone gland

Pituitary gland
↓
hormone
    ↓ bloodstream
secondary endocrine
    glands
    ↓
hormones
    ↓ bloodstream
body cells

The thyroid gland is actually stimulated to secrete thyroxine by another hormone called the **thyroid stimulating hormone**. This is secreted by a small structure at the base of the brain called the **pituitary gland** (Fig 13.17). You will realise immediately that another reason for a lack of thyroxine may be a malfunctioning pituitary gland.

The pituitary controls the secretions of a number of other endocrine glands, in a similar way to the thyroid gland. Because of this control, it is often called the master hormone gland. Figure 13.17 summarises the secondary endocrine glands which it affects and lists the effects of the hormones produced by these secondary glands. Some of the hormones from the pituitary have a direct effect on body organs or tissues. For example, growth hormone affects body cells directly, causing an increase in tissue growth rate. Other examples of the direct effect of the pituitary gland are also shown in Fig 13.17.

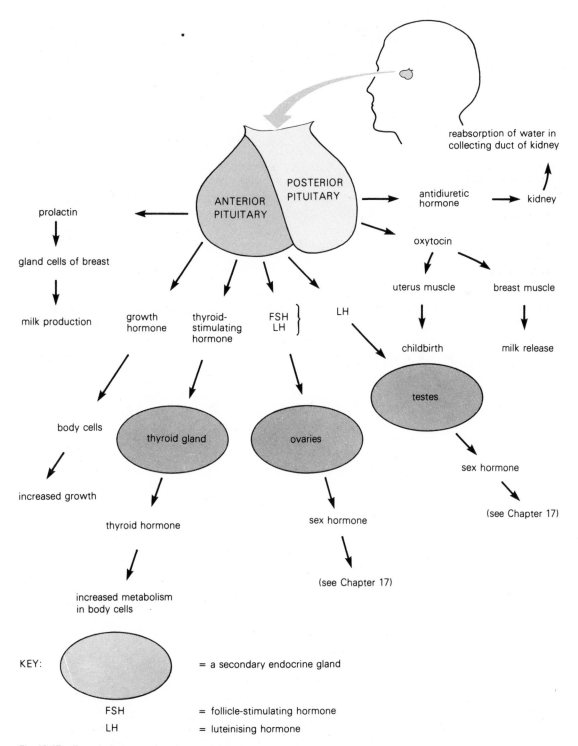

Fig 13.17 *The pituitary gland and the secondary glands under its control*

Chapter 14

Drugs—foreign chemicals in the body's systems

- What is a drug?
- Different types of drugs
- How drugs are taken
- What happens to a drug after administration
- Factors affecting the way drugs act
- Weighing up the risks
- Drug use during pregnancy
- Analgesics
- Mood-altering drugs
- The alternative to drugs

Drugs have a long history of use

People have been taking drugs since the beginning of their history—they experimented with materials they found in the natural world around them and discovered that some of these materials could ease pain or even apparently cure disease. Stone Age people are believed to have cultivated and used opium, and as early as 700 BC the Assyrians were using cannabis.

Many primitive drugs have been refined to produce more powerful medicines

People are still experimenting with drugs today. Many of the primitive drugs have been purified or refined to make them more powerful and effective medicines. New drugs have been made in laboratories by chemists.

Nowadays we know much more about how these drugs work. We know that many of the medicines we use can have dangerous and damaging effects on the body if they are not used very carefully. Because of this, the use of many medicines is very strictly controlled. Most are available only from doctors or, with a doctor's prescription, from a chemist. However, many quite potent drugs can be bought from chemists or supermarkets by anyone who feels a need for them.

The use of most powerful drugs is strictly controlled

But how do we know when we need a drug, and what drug do we choose to take? In the Western world today we take much larger quantities and a far greater variety of medicines than any of our ancestors did. Many more drugs are available to provide relief from both serious and minor illnesses, and in addition, drug taking has become almost a social habit. For some, the habit is a serious and life-threatening one, involving drug dependence, overdose or withdrawal symptoms. But for many more the habit is less conspicuous—pain relievers, sedatives or 'pep' pills are used day by day in the battle to cope with the problems of living.

Drug taking has become almost a social habit

In this chapter we shall examine what drugs are and how they act in our bodies. Then we shall look at particular, important groups of drugs and how they affect the way our bodies work.

What is a drug?

Before we begin to talk about drugs, we must ask the basic question—what is a drug? Some people, when they use the term 'drugs', mean chemicals that affect primarily the mind. Others use the term 'drug' to refer particularly to pain relievers or sedatives. However, many chemicals that affect the body do not fall into either of these categories, and we have chosen a much wider definition of drugs. A drug is any chemical substance that, when taken, alters the way the body works. (This does not include the foods we normally eat.) We can organise all these chemical substances into groups according to how they affect the way the body works or which system or organ they affect.

A drug is a chemical substance that alters the way the body works

Different types of drugs

From our definition you will see that a vast number of very varied chemicals can be classed as drugs. The important drugs, however, are those that we use to prevent or treat diseases. Most of these can be obtained only from a doctor, and are administered by injection or as a short course of tablets to treat a particular disease. In this group are the anti-biotics used to treat bacterial infections and drugs used to regulate blood pressure, control the heart beat, control kidney function, and so on. The doctor supervises the use of these drugs closely.

There are some drugs, however, that are available for us to administer to ourselves. We use them to relieve the discomfort of a variety of minor illnesses: colds, headaches, hayfever, backache and so on; or we use them to alter our mood: to calm us, help us to sleep, or make us more alert. Some of these are available only with a doctor's prescription; others can be purchased from a chemist or even a supermarket. Because we are able to administer these drugs to ourselves, it is essential that we understand the effect they have on our bodies, and are aware of anything that may alter the effect of a particular drug.

In addition, there are some drugs that may not only alter our mood but may also have very harmful side-effects. These drugs cannot be obtained legally from doctors or chemists. They may, however, be obtained from illegal sources. Because of the dangers of such drugs, their effects also will be discussed in this chapter.

All drugs can be grouped according to their use and their effects. Each group has a particular medical name. The most common classes of drugs that we can administer to ourselves are listed here:

'cold' medicines:	decongestants
	expectorants
	cough suppressants
allergy relievers:	anti-histamines
pain relievers:	analgesics
mood-altering drugs:	stimulants
	tranquillisers (relaxants)
	sedatives (depressants)
	narcotics (opiates)
	hallucinogens

Before we are able to discuss the different effects which drugs may produce, we must know the answers to some other questions: how do drugs enter the body; what happens once they are inside the body; and how does a drug find its target?

How drugs are taken

Except for some creams and ointments that we use on body surfaces, all drugs act at target sites inside the body. Therefore, all drugs must some-how cross the surface of the body before they can act. The method used to get drugs inside the body is called the route of administration.

Some drugs are freely available for the treatment of minor illnesses:
• colds
• headaches
• hayfever

Others assist us to alter our mood:
• help us to sleep
• make us more alert
• calm us down

Some mood-altering drugs have very harmful side-effects

All drugs act at target sites inside the body

The method used to get drugs into the body is called the route of administration

The route a doctor chooses to deliver a drug to the inside of the body is very important. This choice depends on a number of things:

- the drug's chemical structure
- how quickly it must act
- for how long it must act.

There are very few drugs that can cross the skin surface to enter the body—the skin is designed to provide protection against foreign chemicals and organisms. There are other body surfaces, however, that are more easily crossed: the epithelium of the stomach and small intestine and the surfaces of the nasal cavity and air sacs (alveoli). All of these surfaces are used as routes of administration for different drugs (Fig 14.1). Some drugs may enter the body through more than one surface.

Oral administration

Any drug that enters the body by absorption from the stomach or intestine must first be swallowed, as a tablet, capsule or liquid. This route of administration is called the oral route (meaning 'by mouth'). Obviously this is a very convenient way for drugs to enter the body. Also it is a relatively safe method, as the drug is absorbed fairly slowly into the body and reaches the target site gradually. In addition, the drug need not be as highly purified or sterilised before it is given, as the gut lining acts as a barrier to most impurities and contaminants which may be present in the medicine.

There are limitations and disadvantages to the oral route, however. Some drugs may be destroyed or made inactive by the acids in the stomach or by the enzymes of the stomach and intestines. The liver, too, may inactivate some drugs in the bloodstream before they reach their target organ. The presence or absence of food in the digestive system may also alter the *rate* at which absorption occurs and the *amount* of drug which is absorbed. Because of this, it is often necessary to give a larger dose of a drug orally than would be necessary by other routes.

Other drugs may irritate the stomach lining and cause nausea and vomiting. Some drugs that must be protected from stomach acid or the stomach lining are given in gelatine capsules or as specially prepared tablets. These capsules do not dissolve to release their content until they reach the alkaline environment of the small intestine.

Inhalation

We have already seen (Chapter 8) that gases such as oxygen enter the body by passing through the cells lining the alveoli and through capillary cell walls to reach the blood. Some drugs can also enter the body this way: anaesthetic drugs such as ether and halothane, nicotine in tobacco smoke, and cannabis. Because they enter the bloodstream very quickly, these drugs tend to reach their target organ very rapidly and produce

---

The route of administration depends on
- structure of the chemical
- how quickly the drug must act
- for how long it must act

The skin is the body's barrier to foreign chemicals and organisms

Chemicals can cross the epithelium of the stomach and small intestine and the surfaces of the nasal cavity and alveoli

Drugs entering the body by absorption from the stomach or intestine must be swallowed as a tablet, capsule or in liquid form

Orally administered drugs enter the body slowly and reach the target site gradually

Drugs may be destroyed or inactivated by enzymes in the stomach and intestine

Drugs that may irritate the lining of the stomach are enclosed in a gelatine capsule

Drugs entering the body through the alveoli enter the bloodstream, and thus the target organ, rapidly

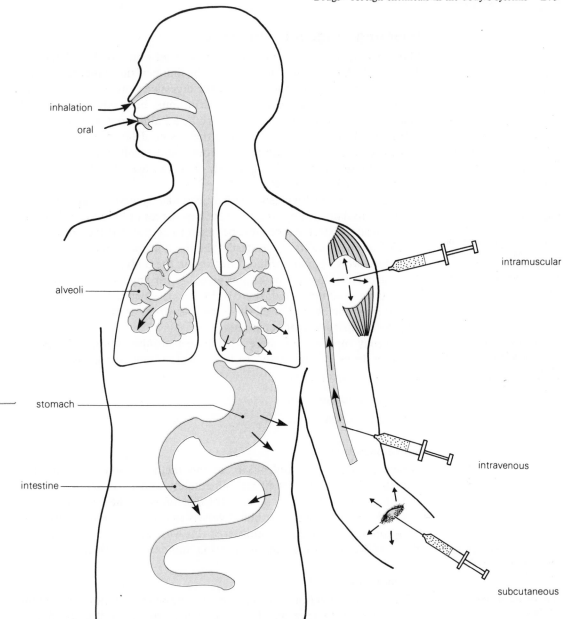

Fig 14.1 *How drugs enter the body—routes of administration*

their effect very soon after administration. If they leave the body by the same route, their effect may wear off almost as rapidly.

Some drugs can also enter the body through other parts of the respiratory passages—the surface of the nasal cavity is used as a route of administration for many 'nose medicines', such as decongestants and anti-histamines. A smaller number of drugs are absorbed through the lining of the bronchi and act on the muscle cells around the bronchi.

Drugs may also be absorbed through
• surfaces of the nasal cavity
• lining of the bronchi

Injecting drugs into the body

Many drugs, however, cannot be administered orally or by inhalation. This may be because they may damage the lining of the alimentary canal, or because the drug is inactivated in the digestive system before it is absorbed, or because the effect of the drug must be produced extremely quickly. All these drugs must therefore be administered by injection.

Some drugs must be given by injection

When a drug is given by injection, there is no delay in its entry to the bloodstream as there is with the oral route, and usually it reaches its target organ more rapidly. This is clearly an advantage when the drug's effect is required immediately.

Drugs given by injection enter the bloodstream and reach the target organ more rapidly than drugs given orally

There are some drawbacks with injections, however. Care must be taken not to damage any structures such as nerves or blood vessels at the injection site. Extreme care must be taken to ensure that the syringe, the needle and the drug itself are sterile; that is, that they contain no microorganisms which could produce infection in the body. It is also essential that the correct dose of the drug is given. If for any reason an overdose of the drug is administered, there is no way in which the drug can be removed from the body. For all these reasons, drugs are generally injected only by qualified doctors or nurses.

Care must be taken to ensure that
• no damage to nerves or blood vessels occurs
• needles are sterile
• the correct dose is given

You may suppose that there is an almost infinite number of sites for injecting drugs into the body. In fact, there are only three basic routes:

Three ways in which drugs can be administered by injection:
• subcutaneous route
• intramuscular route
• intravenous route

• the subcutaneous route

• the intramuscular route

• the intravenous route.

Subcutaneous route

Sub-cutaneous means under-skin. In this method, the drug is injected into the loose connective tissue immediately under the skin. This is a convenient and relatively safe area for injections, as there are few structures such as large nerves or blood vessels to avoid. However, only relatively small doses can be administered this way, and the route cannot be used for drugs that may cause irritation and excessive stinging.

Subcutaneous injection is a safe method of drug administration

Only small doses can be given subcutaneously

Intramuscular route

Intramuscular injections are delivered into muscles. Muscles are good injection sites for two reasons. In the first place, they are well supplied with small blood vessels which can absorb the drug. In the second, they have fewer pain-detecting nerve endings than subcutaneous areas and can therefore be used for injection of drugs that would cause pain if injected under the skin. Although any muscle could, in theory, be used for intramuscular injection, certain sites in the body are much preferred. This is because it is essential to avoid injecting near the path of major nerves, which could be damaged by the needle or by the drug itself. The areas most commonly used for injection, because of their relative safety, are the gluteal muscles of the buttocks and the muscles of the upper arm.

Muscles are suitable sites for injection, since
• they are richly supplied with blood vessels
• they have few pain-detecting endings

Intravenous route

In an intravenous injection, part of the needle penetrates the wall of a vein, just below the skin surface, and the drug is therefore delivered directly into the bloodstream. As you would expect, this route gives the quickest results. Also, because all the drug enters the circulation so quickly, a far higher concentration of the drug reaches the target in the initial stage. In many situations these features make this route the most useful. For the same reasons, however, the intravenous route is by far the most hazardous. Nicotine provides an example of the hazards of intravenous injection (see Chapter 9). When a cigarette is smoked, the nicotine is absorbed into the bloodstream gradually and its effects are, in the short term, relatively mild. However, if the nicotine from one cigarette were injected intravenously, it would be sufficient to kill a person within a short time. Far too much nicotine would enter the bloodstream too quickly by the intravenous route.

The drug reaches its target most rapidly by the intravenous route

Any contamination of drug, syringe or needle that enters the body intravenously will be spread very rapidly throughout the body. Toxic reactions to drugs administered in this way are produced extremely quickly, and there is no direct way in which the drug can then be removed from the circulation. Any drug delivered intravenously must be soluble in water and in blood plasma, and must be prepared in such a way that it does not damage blood cells, plasma proteins or the walls of blood vessels.

Hazards of intravenous administration:
- *contamination from the drug or syringe spreads rapidly throughout the body*
- *the drug cannot be removed from the circulation*
- *higher concentrations of drug reach the target very quickly*

(The intravenous route is also used, sometimes, to ensure constant blood levels of a drug, by slow intravenous drip.)

What happens to a drug after administration

After a drug has been administered, we are not usually aware of its presence in the body until some time later, when it acts on the target site. Furthermore, a drug has its normal effect on the target site only if an appropriate amount of the drug reaches the target. This depends on the dose or amount of the drug that is administered and on what happens to the drug when it enters the body.

A drug will produce the expected effect on its target only if the correct dose is given

The circulatory system is the carrier system for all substances moving around the body—oxygen and carbon dioxide, fuel molecules for the cells, hormones and molecules for excretion are all carried in the blood. In the same way, drugs are carried from the site of administration to their target in the bloodstream.

Figure 14.2 illustrates what happens to a drug after it enters the bloodstream. We can think of the blood as a pool in which the drug molecules dissolve and spread out evenly. Drugs reach this pool by injection or absorption.

The blood is a pool in which drug molecules can dissolve and disperse evenly

The absorbed drug then travels in the bloodstream and reaches its target organ or organs. Inside the target organ, it leaves the blood vessels

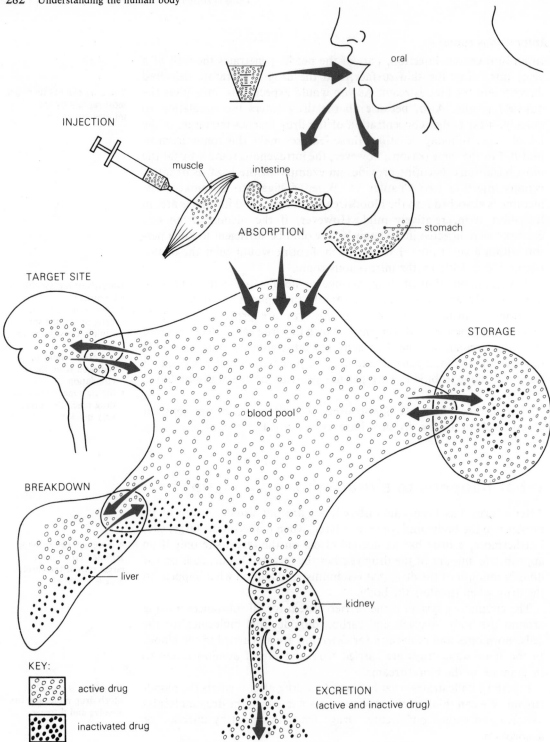

INJECTION

oral

muscle

intestine

stomach

ABSORPTION

TARGET SITE

STORAGE

blood pool

BREAKDOWN

liver

kidney

KEY:

active drug

inactivated drug

EXCRETION
(active and inactive drug)

Fig 14.2 *What happens to a drug after it is absorbed?*

and enters the cells of the target organ. This may be a process of active transport (see Chapter 2) or of simple diffusion. In either case, however, the rate at which it occurs and the concentration of drug which accumulates at the target depends on the concentration of drug in the bloodstream.

The drug begins to have its effect as soon as the concentration in the target organ reaches the critical level. All drugs act by altering in some way the chemical processes which normally go on inside cells. How strongly they act is determined by their concentration.

How long the drug continues to act depends on how long its concentration can be maintained at the target site. This in turn depends on the balance between the amount of new drug entering the bloodstream and the amount leaving the bloodstream. There are three ways in which the drug may leave the bloodstream. First, it may be excreted, unchanged, from the kidneys or in the breath or sweat. Second, it may be broken down by the liver and the products excreted. Third, it may leave the bloodstream to be stored in various storage tissues in the body. As we shall see later, many of the drugs that act on the brain can be stored in fatty tissues. This storage can be a very important consideration in understanding how the drug works and the long-term effects of its use.

The rate at which a drug accumulates at the target organ depends on the concentration of the drug in the bloodstream

Drugs alter chemical processes occurring in cells

How long a drug acts depends on how long its concentration is maintained at the target site

Drugs may leave the bloodstream by being
* *excreted unchanged from the kidneys, breath or sweat*
* *broken down in the liver and then excreted*
* *stored in tissues*

Drugs that act on the brain are often stored in fatty tissues

Factors affecting the way drugs act

As we have said, the way in which a drug acts depends on the concentration at the target site. As Fig 14.2 shows, this concentration is the result of a balance of different factors, all of which determine the drug's concentration in the blood pool. Let us now look at some of these factors more closely.

The first and most obvious way of modifying the amount of drug reaching the target site is to alter the size of the dose administered. Normally, if a larger dose of a drug is administered, the drug's concentration in the blood pool and at the target site rises. This effect can be seen very clearly in the case of alcohol consumption (see Chapter 16). As the amount of alcohol consumed increases, the blood alcohol concentration rises. This causes the concentration of alcohol at the target sites in the brain to increase, so that the alcohol's effects on brain functions are more pronounced. The dose size of certain drugs must be calculated very carefully, since a drug concentration at the target organ which is higher than that required to produce a particular medical effect may produce damaging side-effects, or **toxic reactions**.

Many of the drugs we take are so powerful in their pure form that they must be diluted either in a solution, or with some inactive powder in a tablet, to make a conveniently sized dose that is safe to take. Altering the strength or concentration of drug in the injection, medicine or tablet, then, is another way in which we can alter the effect of a particular drug.

The way in which a drug acts depends on its concentration at the target

A drug's concentration in the blood depends on
* *dose size*
* *blood volume of the receiver*
* *frequency of the drug's administration*

In calculating the correct dose for a particular patient, a doctor takes into consideration that patient's body weight. This is because body weight gives a reasonable guide to blood volume. Blood volume is important, because a drug's concentration in the blood depends not only on the size of the dose, but also on the volume of blood in which the drug is dissolved. Imagine altering the size of the blood pool in Fig 14.2, and see how the drug's concentration in the blood alters. The effect of body weight on drug action is seen very clearly with many drugs. For example, a sleeping tablet that may make a grown man only slightly drowsy may cause a little child to sleep heavily for several hours (Fig 14.3).

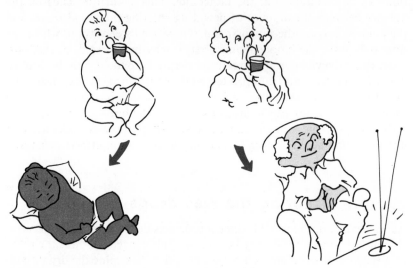

Fig 14.3 *The effect of a certain dose of a drug may be dramatically different in people of different sizes*

We can also change the drug's concentration in the blood by administering the drug more or less frequently over a particular period of time. Again, the effect of frequency is seen clearly in the case of alcohol. Five glasses of beer taken at intervals over 24 hours will produce only a slight increase in blood alcohol concentration. Five glasses of beer consumed in less than one hour, however, increase blood alcohol concentration to levels which affect body function markedly.

Weighing up the risks

Drugs change chemical processes in cells

As we have already noted, all drugs produce their effects by changing in some way the chemical processes which normally go on inside the cells of particular organs or tissues. This change is not usually permanent—it lasts only as long as the drug is present inside the cell.

Anything that interferes with the way a cell normally works, even if only for a short time, has some dangers. This is because when drugs alter chemical processes, they often produce other effects on the body, in addition to the ones required to treat a particular illness. These effects are called **side-effects**. When advising a patient to take a drug, a doctor must weigh the advantages of the drug in treating the illness against the danger of side-effects.

Drugs may have harmful side-effects

Side-effects vary, depending on the size of the drug dose. Generally, as the size of the dose increases, side-effects become more noticeable and possibly dangerous. Large doses that damage organs or tissues are called toxic doses. Side-effects may vary, too, from one person to another, and even from one occasion to another. Most drugs, though, are fairly predictable in their action, and there is a wide safety margin between the dose that can safely be used to treat an illness and the dose that produces toxic side-effects.

Doses of a drug that cause damage to organs or tissues are called toxic doses

Some drugs are considered so safe that they can be obtained without a doctor's prescription. How safe are these drugs? The safety code or poisons schedule for medicines, which determines how readily available medicines are, is based on the concentration or strength of a drug in a particular preparation. A medicine may be regarded as safe because it contains a particular drug only in small quantities. The same drug, in a more concentrated form, might be available only on prescription. For example, until quite recently medicines containing low concentrations of morphine were freely available to the public for the treatment of diarrhoea. But nobody could deny that morphine is a very dangerous drug. In its more concentrated form, it is considered so dangerous that even doctors are restricted in how they can use it. Only because the dose of morphine in the diarrhoea medicine was so small was the medicine considered safe.

The safety rating of a drug depends on
• the drug
• the strengths in which the drug is available

Many drugs are regarded as safe only because they are available in very low doses

Many other medicines that are freely available are only considered safe for this same reason. Cough medicines, anti-histamines and decongestants come into this group. If the size of the dose is increased, their side-effects become toxic and dangerous. Consuming any drugs, therefore, is not without its risks, and because one tablet is an effective dose, two tablets will definitely not be twice as good.

In addition to these risks, which may be associated with the use of any drug, some drugs have particular risks—the risk of **drug dependence**. All the drugs on which people may become dependent belong to a particular group. They are all **psychotropic** drugs. Psychotropic drugs are chemical substances that act on the brain, and affect mood, behaviour, consciousness and powers of perception. For this reason the psychotropic drugs are often called **mood-altering drugs**.

Drug dependence may result from the continued use of some drugs. The drugs that may cause drug dependence are all psychotropic (mood-altering) drugs

When such drugs are taken to alter mood they usually produce a satisfying effect—relieving anxiety and tension, providing a sense of well-being, helping users to feel they cope better with their daily life. It is because of this feeling of satisfaction that drug dependence occurs.

Psychotropic drugs may affect
• mood
• behaviour
• consciousness
• power of perception

Drug dependence is defined as a state of compulsion, where the user feels driven to continue taking the drug regularly to produce these satisfying changes in mood. A number of terms have been used in the past by doctors, lawyers and social workers to describe different forms of drug dependence and people who are dependent on drugs. Many of these are now considered confusing or inaccurate. Most people now recognise two main forms of dependence:

There are two forms of drug dependence:
* *psychological*
* *physical*

* **Psychological dependence**, when the user feels driven to take a drug for emotional reasons—to help him cope, to think or work properly.

Common features of physical dependence:
* *withdrawal symptoms*
* *drug tolerance*

* **Physical dependence**, a state in which continued heavy use of the drug has altered normal biological processes.

Withdrawal symptoms are painful or unpleasant signs that develop when a drug is withheld from a person dependent upon it

When a drug that has caused physical dependence is withheld from the user, he experiences painful or unpleasant **withdrawal symptoms**. This form of dependence is often called **addiction**. Once people have become physically dependent, the same dose of the drug seems to have less effect. The user therefore has to increase the dose to produce the desired effect. This situation is called **drug tolerance**. But because the drug *appears* to have less effect on the tolerant user, it is not less harmful. Increasing the dose of any drug increases the risk of harmful effects, even if the user has become tolerant of it.

Drug tolerance—the same dose of a drug seems to produce less and less effect

Whether a drug has the ability to cause physical dependence seems to depend on its chemical properties. Drugs that can cause physical dependence include alcohol, barbiturates, probably nicotine, and the opiates heroin, morphine, pethidine and methadone. However, some of the most serious drug risks in our society don't come from these drugs. Whilst the withdrawal symptoms of the heroin addict have been given a great deal of publicity and are indeed terrible to witness, psychological dependence on other drugs—such as sedatives, analgesics, tobacco and so on—involves a far greater proportion of the population. As a risk to individuals and society these drugs deserve equal attention, particularly as it is much more difficult to overcome psychological than physical dependence.

Psychological dependence is more difficult to overcome then physical dependence

Drug use during pregnancy

A whole new problem in drug safety was uncovered by a tragedy which occurred in the late 1950s and the early 1960s. This tragedy involved the drug thalidomide, which was prescribed and sold in many countries of the world as a tranquilliser—a sleeping tablet. It was included in many combination pain relievers, for the treatment of pains, coughs, insomnia and other minor illnesses. It was extremely popular, and tests in mice and other laboratory animals, as well as in humans, had shown it to be so 'safe' that in several countries (particularly West Germany) it was available even without a doctor's prescription.

However, by 1961 there had been an alarming increase in the birth of very deformed babies—babies born without legs, arms, or even without both. Almost simultaneously, medical researchers in Europe and in Australia discovered that the mothers of these deformed babies had all taken thalidomide in the early stages of pregnancy. It was the thalidomide that caused the deformities to the developing foetus. Thalidomide was immediately withdrawn from the market throughout the world.

Thalidomide causes abnormalities of growth of the foetus

Since then we have discovered a great deal about the risks of drug-taking during pregnancy. We now know that many of the drugs we take are able to cross from the mother's circulation to the foetal circulation. Their effects may be quite different in the developing foetus. As we shall see in Chapter 17, the most rapid period of the foetus's development occurs during the first three months. This is when all the structures and organs of the foetal body begin to form—after three months these organs then mature and grow. Because of this, drugs have their most damaging and permanent effects during the first three months, by interfering with the formation of new organs, tissues, limbs and so on. This is a particularly serious problem, since at this critical time (as early as three weeks after fertilisation) the mother is very likely to be unaware that she is pregnant. She may be using prescribed or 'over-the-counter' drugs, quite unaware that she is harming a developing foetus.

Many drugs can cross from the maternal to the foetal circulation

Drugs have their most damaging effects during the first 3 months of foetal growth. Drugs may affect the growth of limbs, organs and tissues

The list of drugs that medical research workers now believe may have a damaging effect on the foetus continues to grow. It includes analgesics, anti-histamines, tranquillisers and antibiotics. In addition, excessive alcohol consumption throughout pregnancy may be very dangerous to the developing baby ('foetal alcohol syndrome' will be discussed in Chapter 16), and mothers who smoke have smaller and less healthy babies (see Chapter 9). In general, all doctors now agree that unless there is a very good medical reason for prescribing a particular drug, the use of any drugs during pregnancy, particularly during the first three months, should be avoided.

Drugs that may affect the foetus:
• analgesics
• anti-histamines
• tranquillisers
• antibiotics

Doctors agree that during the first 3 months of pregnancy drug use should be avoided as far as possible

Only one other aspect of drug-taking during pregnancy need be mentioned here—the case of pregnant women who are physically dependent on drugs. Most dependence-producing drugs may enter the body of the foetus from the mother's circulation. The baby then, like its mother, may become physically dependent on the drug that is abused. Not only is the baby of a drug-dependent mother born prematurely, underweight and ill-nourished, but within a few days of birth it may experience all the painful symptoms of drug withdrawal, as its supply of the drug is removed.

Physically drug-dependent mothers may give birth to physically drug-dependent babies

Within the first days after birth, a drug-dependent baby may experience painful withdrawal symptoms

Analgesics

With the exception of alcohol, nicotine (in tobacco smoke) and caffeine (in coffee, tea and cocoa), the most commonly consumed drugs are analgesics. Analgesics are pain relievers (sometimes called pain killers).

They are designed to give short-term relief from minor aches and pains.

Analgesics may be purchased 'over-the-counter', in chemist shops and supermarkets, as tablets or as powders. They are sold by a number of pharmaceutical companies, and under many different brand names. They all contain varying amounts of one drug or a combination of several drugs. Table 14.1 lists some of the analgesic preparations available in Australia and their active ingredients. In terms of their chemical structure and activity, there are three types of pain relievers: salicylates, phenacetin and paracetamol, and codeine.

Three types of pain relievers:
• salicylates
• phenacetin and paracetamol
• codeine

Table 14.1 *Active ingredients of some analgesic preparations*

Type of analgesic	Trade name	Ingredients
Salicylates	Aspro	Aspirin
	Disprin	Aspirin
Paracetamol	Paralgin	Paracetamol
	Panadol	Paracetamol
Combination analgesics	Codral red	Paracetamol + codeine
	Veganin	Aspirin + codeine
	Codis	Aspirin + codeine
	Panadeine	Paracetamol + codeine
	Ascotin	Aspirin + codeine
	My-zone	Aspirin + codeine

Salicylates

The first salicylates to be used as pain relievers were obtained, centuries ago, from the bark of the willow tree (*Salix alba*). Salicylates are now manufactured in laboratories, but their pain-relieving properties still depend on their basic salicylic acid content, like that found in willow bark. Two of the most widely used salicylates are aspirin and salicylamide. Figure 14.4 shows how closely the chemical structure of these resembles that of salicylic acid.

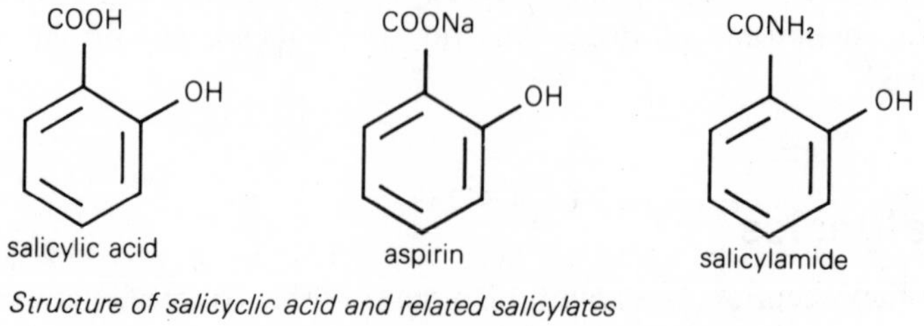

Fig 14.4 *Structure of salicyclic acid and related salicylates*

Salicylates are useful in the treatment of minor illnesses such as toothache and influenza. They are effective because they act in three ways:

- They reduce fever.
- They reduce pain.
- They reduce inflammation.

How they produce these effects is not very well understood. It seems that salicylates reduce fever by affecting the temperature-regulating area of the brain, the hypothalamus. Salicylates can produce a rapid reduction in body temperature in a person whose temperature is abnormally high, but do not alter normal body temperature.

Salicylates produce relief from pain by affecting the areas of the brain that receive pain sensations. Thus salicylates are useful as pain killers for ailments such as strained ligaments, strained muscles or toothache. They may also be used for other conditions such as nervous tension. Basically, salicylates act by making us less aware of the pain sensations. They are useful drugs for this purpose, as they do not cause drowsiness, changes in sensation or other mental disturbances. However, they are only of value in providing relief from low-intensity pain.

Salicylates also act to reduce inflammation. Inflammation contributes considerably to the pain of many conditions. Therefore, some of the pain relief obtained with salicylate treatment may be due to reduced inflammation. It is for this reason, too, that aspirin is frequently prescribed for people suffering from arthritis (inflammation of the joints).

Because salicylates are so readily available and commonly used, they are often regarded as very safe drugs. However, aspirin does have side-effects, which can make its use extremely dangerous, particularly to children. In many patients aspirin is an irritant to the gastric mucosa (the lining of the stomach). It may cause nausea, vomiting and abdominal pain. Aspirin is believed to contribute to the formation of gastric ulcers and haemorrhage in some patients who take large quantities of aspirin for prolonged periods.

If the printed dosage instructions supplied with the drug are followed, side-effects are unlikely to occur. However, if the suggested dosage is exceeded, some alarming effects may occur. The main symptoms of salicylate overdosing (intoxication) are effects on brain function: headache, dizziness, confusion, drowsiness, disturbances of sight and hearing, and rapid breathing. If the poisoning continues, depression, coma and death may result. Because of these side-effects, aspirin should never be combined with any other drugs that affect the central nervous system, for example alcohol.

Phenacetin and paracetamol

Phenacetin and paracetamol are very similar chemicals to salicylates. Like salicylates they reduce temperature when a person is fevered and

---

Salicylates reduce
- fever
- pain
- inflammation

Salicylates affect the temperature-regulating centre of the brain—the hypothalamus

Salicylates affect the areas of the brain that receive pain sensations

Salicylates relieve low-intensity pain. They make us less aware of pain sensations

Salicylates reduce inflammation and may thus reduce pain

Some salicylates produce side-effects:
- aspirin may act as an irritant to the stomach lining
- aspirin may cause gastric ulcers or haemorrhage

Symptoms of salicylate overdosing:
- headache
- dizziness
- confusion
- drowsiness
- disturbances of sight and hearing
- rapid breathing

Aspirin should never be combined with other drugs that affect the central nervous system

Phenacetin and paracetamol
- reduce temperature
- reduce pain

relieve pain. However, they do not reduce inflammation. In the body, phenacetin is easily broken down to paracetamol.

Paracetamol does have some harmful side-effects in higher doses, especially on the liver. But side-effects are more common and more serious in the case of phenacetin. Large quantities of phenacetin may cause anaemia (see Chapter 6), a condition of the red blood cells that reduces the blood's capacity to transport oxygen. Excessive use of these analgesics is also a major cause of kidney disease (see below).

Paracetamol causes few side effects

Phenacetin may cause anaemia

Excessive use of phenacetin or paracetamol may contribute to kidney disease

Mixtures of drugs have been introduced to reduce the dose size of each drug

Combination analgesic preparations

As Table 14.1 indicates, some of the analgesics available are mixtures of analgesic drugs in various combinations. Why are these drugs sold in combination? Mixtures were introduced because they contain smaller doses of each ingredient, which may reduce the toxic side-effects of each drug in the mixture. However, people who take too large or too many doses of such mixtures again lay themselves open to dangerous side-effects.

Caffeine

Caffeine is a mild stimulant

Caffeine in analgesic preparations may cause people to form drug-taking habits

In the past, some common combination analgesic mixtures contained caffeine. Caffeine, the same drug that we find in coffee, tea and cocoa, is *not* an analgesic, but a mild stimulant. It does not increase the effectiveness of the other ingredients of some analgesic mixtures, and it is commonly believed that it may be habit forming—making it more likely that the tablets are taken again and again.

Analgesic use in the community

Analgesics are used in virtually every household in developed countries, and most of the time their use can be justified. However, the consumption of analgesic preparations in Australia has been estimated at 270 tablets or powders per head of population per year—one of the highest consumption rates in the world. A significant proportion of the population abuses analgesics, using them for reasons other than those discussed above. Some people take up to dozens of tablets every day. Why they do this is not always clear. People suffering emotional tension or stress are most likely to abuse analgesics: housewives who reason that they take analgesics to 'stop a headache coming on', industrial workers working in unrewarding and trying conditions, school children who take them for 'kicks'. Analgesics are frequently misused in an attempt to give the user a 'lift' or to help him to cope better with stress—situations in which they are clearly of no value. Whilst analgesics may provide relief from headaches or other minor ailments, it is important to remember that they act only to reduce the sensation of pain. They do not remove the cause of that pain. Continued consumption of analgesic tablets and

A large proportion of the population take far more analgesic tablets than they require medically

Analgesics do not remove the cause of pain

powders may cause any of the symptoms above, in particular anaemia, gastric ulceration and headache, which may themselves lead the person to consume further analgesics.

Analgesic abuse and health

Kidney disease seems to be the most important and most serious disease resulting from overuse of analgesics. The kidney disease that results from abuse of analgesics is quite distinctive—it is called **analgesic nephropathy**. It results in a progressive breakdown of the kidney structures and kidney function, leading eventually to severe kidney failure. At this stage, without dialysis (use of a 'kidney machine') or kidney transplant, death is inevitable.

The most serious disease resulting from analgesic over-use is kidney disease—analgesic nephropathy; death may result from this disease

A report by the Australian Kidney Foundation indicated that from 1971 to 1976, 18 per cent of the patients suffering from kidney failure had analgesic nephropathy. In several surveys, up to 80 per cent of these patients were found to have been using combination analgesics daily or several times each week for several years. How these drugs damage the kidney is not yet known. In fact, which of the drugs causes the damage is unclear. For some time phenacetin was considered the most damaging agent, but it is now thought that the abuse of combinations of drugs is far more damaging than abuse of any one single agent. Efforts have been made in several countries to restrict the sales of combination analgesics.

From 1971–6, 80 per cent of patients who had analgesic nephropathy had been using analgesic mixtures daily or several times each week for several years

Analgesic use in pregnancy

Two Australian surveys have reported that from 7 to 10 per cent of pregnant women use analgesics daily, or on most days. This can have a damaging effect on both the mother and the baby. In the mother it may cause anaemia and increase the risk of haemorrhage before or after the birth. Babies born to mothers who take analgesics regularly have significantly lower birth weights and are more likely to be stillborn or to die shortly after birth.

Effects of analgesics on the pregnant mother and baby:
• the mother risks anaemia and haemorrhage before and after the birth
• babies may have low birth weight
• there is more chance of the baby being stillborn

Mood-altering drugs

The mood-altering drugs are classified according to how they act on the mind. Table 14.2 lists the major groups of drugs, their actions on the mind and some common examples. There are four major groups: sedatives and tranquillisers, opiate narcotics, stimulants, and hallucinogens.

Sedatives and tranquillisers

Sedatives and tranquillisers have a depressing ('switching off') effect on the brain. They may produce a feeling of calmness, relaxation or drowsiness, or, in higher doses, a deep sleep. The term tranquillisers is used for a special type of depressant drug, which is capable of reducing

Mood-altering drugs:
• depressants or sedatives depress the activity of the brain. They produce feelings of
  –calmness
  –relaxation
  –drowsiness
  –deep sleep (high doses)

tranquillisers

sedatives

Table 14.2 *Major groups of mood-altering drugs*

Type of drug	Action	Examples
Mild analgesics	Relieve pain	Aspirin, paracetamol, codeine
Sedatives and tranquillisers (depressants)	Relieve • anxiety • tension • depression Some induce sleep	Benzodiazepines (eg Valium) Barbiturates Alcohol
Opiate narcotics	Relieve intense pain (depress the central nervous system)	Opium, morphine Heroin Pethidine, methadone
Stimulants	Stimulate nervous system → more wakeful → excitement → increased alertness and activity	Caffeine (very mild) Cocaine Amphetamines
Hallucinogens	Alter thoughts, feelings and perceptions	LSD Mescalin, DMT, DET, psilocybin Cannabis (in high doses)

• tranquillisers are a special type of depressant drug which reduce tension and anxiety without causing sleepiness

tension and anxiety without causing sleepiness or interfering with powers of thought. In practical terms, however, it is difficult to distinguish between these drugs; many tranquillisers, taken in higher doses, will cause drowsiness or sleep.

Sedatives and tranquillisers, used to relieve anxiety, tension and depression, are the most frequently prescribed drugs in Australia today. Many of them relieve symptoms of tension and anxiety very effectively, but because of this, they are often regarded as a cure for any problem. Also, used frequently, they may cause psychological dependence.

There is a huge variety of drugs in this group. Some are considered safe enough to be available without any restriction from chemists (for example Seducaps, Relaxatabs and alcohol, which is discussed in Chapter 14). The sedative properties of these preparations are so mild, however, that doctors believe any sedative effect they produce is largely in the mind—the person could probably experience the same effect with a sugar capsule (provided he believed it was a sedative).

Benzodiazepines

Benzodiazepines relieve tension and anxiety

Of the sedative drugs prescribed by doctors to relieve anxiety, the most frequently used are those known as benzodiazepines. (This group of drugs includes the well-known drug Valium or diazepam.) They are regarded by many as being amongst the safest of the prescribed mood-altering drugs. They relieve anxiety and tension effectively, but how they do this is not understood.

Despite their apparent safety, these drugs do have side-effects. These side-effects may be extremely important, because the drugs are so frequently used by apparently well people in their normal day-to-day lives. Overseas studies have shown that these drugs may interfere with powers of perception and judgment, making driving a motor car or using any machines extremely dangerous. In addition, the effect of benzodiazepines is increased when they are taken at the same time as other mood-altering drugs, particularly alcohol.

Benzodiazepines do have side-effects

Benzodiazepines may interfere with powers of perception and judgment; these effects are increased by alcohol

Recent studies have also suggested that diazepam (eg Valium) may temporarily interfere with powers of memory. It would appear, too, that long and excessive use of benzodiazepine drugs may lead to both psychological and physical dependence, and to withdrawal symptoms similar to those seen with other sedatives.

Valium may interfere with powers of memory

Long and excessive use of benzodiazepines may lead to physical and psychological dependence

Barbiturates

In contrast to the benzodiazepines, which are used largely to relieve anxiety, the barbiturates are most commonly used as sleeping pills. Like the benzodiazepines they may also relieve anxiety, but with most some drowsiness always occurs. There are many different barbiturate drugs, *all of which act to depress the brain*. Some, injected intravenously, are used to produce complete unconsciousness or anaesthesia; others, prescribed by doctors and taken orally, are used to help patients to sleep (Amytal, Soneryl, Veronal), to treat high blood pressure and to 'calm' nerves.

Barbiturates depress the brain

Uses of barbiturates:
* *general anaesthesia*
* *sleeping pills*
* *to relieve anxiety and calm nerves (cause some drowsiness)*
* *to treat high blood pressure*

Used wisely under medical supervision, the barbiturates are safe and effective. However, when they are taken in excessive quantities, or self-administered for 'kicks', they are extremely dangerous drugs.

Barbiturates are useful but very dangerous drugs

All barbiturates (like alcohol) depress the central nervous system. This may have a tranquillising effect or may improve spirits (see Chapter 16, p 338), leading the person to use the drug more frequently. Even with small doses, reaction time, perception and powers of concentration are affected (see Chapter 16). These changes make driving a motor car extremely dangerous. In higher doses the depressing activity of barbiturates may interfere with thought processes and cause lack of coordination in walking, speech and other muscular activities. At still higher doses, barbiturates depress the respiratory centre of the brain, so that the breathing rate is slowed. It is this action that causes cessation of breathing and death when an overdose is taken.

Low doses of barbiturates may affect
* *reaction time*
* *perception*
* *powers of concentration*

High doses of barbiturates
* *interfere with thought processes*
* *cause lack of co-ordination in walking and other activities*

Even higher doses of barbiturates cause breathing to slow and finally stop

Barbiturates are commonly used in combination with other drugs, either with alcohol, in a social situation, or with the stimulant drugs. For example, barbiturates are often used with amphetamines. The barbiturates are used to bring on sleep, while the stimulants help the person to wake up again. However, barbiturates and amphetamines do not

Combinations of barbiturates and other drugs often result in unpredictable effects

counteract one another completely. Used with any other drug, the effect of barbiturates may be extremely unpredictable.

'Purple heart' pills are an illegal combination of a barbiturate and a stimulant (amphetamine). They have no medical use and are taken purely to experience the unpredictable changes in mood which they produce.

Barbiturates may cause physical dependence

The great danger of barbiturates is that when taken excessively for any reason, physical dependence on the drug may develop. In the dependent person the drug becomes less effective, so that a larger and larger dose must be taken to produce the desired effect. The person does not become resistant to the toxic effects of the drug, however, so that overdosage and death with barbiturates are common.

Excessive barbiturate use may cause
• staggering gait
• slurred speech
• slow reactions
• emotional instability

Symptoms of addiction to barbiturates resemble, in many ways, those of addiction to alcohol. The barbiturate abuser has a staggering gait and slurred speech. His reactions are slow and he is emotionally unstable—he is easily moved to tears or laughter and may become irritable and aggressive. As with alcohol (see Chapter 16), his brain functions are progressively depressed.

Withdrawal symptoms of a barbiturate-dependent person are among the most severe of any drug. They may cause death

The withdrawal symptoms of the barbiturate-dependent person are among the most severe from any drug. Anxiety, weakness and trembling may lead to a period of temporary madness, very like the alcoholic's delirium tremens (DTs). If the drug is withdrawn very suddenly, convulsions and loss of consciousness are common, sometimes leading to death.

Opiate narcotics

Opiate narcotics are pain killers, related to opium. They depress the central nervous system

The narcotics are a group of painkillers that are related chemically to opium; the group includes opium and its derivatives morphine, codeine and heroin, as well as other drugs, pethidine and methadone, which act in similar ways to the natural opiate drugs. They depress the central nervous system and are used medically to relieve severe pain. They are renowned, above all other drugs, for their ability to produce dependence.

This group of drugs includes
• opium
• morphine ⎫
  codeine ⎬ made from
  heroin   ⎭ opium
• pethidine
• methadone

Opium comes from the unripe seed capsule of a particular type of poppy (Fig 14.5). For thousands of years opium was known as a 'pleasure-giving' drug and the poppy cultivated and its opium extracted.

The narcotics are well known for producing dependence

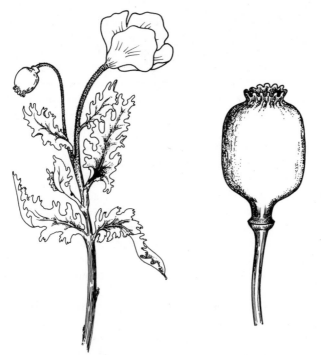

Fig 14.5 *Opium poppy (Papaver somniferum) — plant and seed capsule*

Opium can be eaten or smoked to produce these effects. In past centuries, it was medically a very important drug, but it has now been replaced by the other more powerful opiates.

Morphine is the main active ingredient of opium; it takes almost 15 g of opium to extract 1 g of morphine. It is a very useful drug for the relief of the intense pain which may follow surgery, burns or fractures and is available legally on a doctor's prescription. Like the other opiates, it is available as a white powder, which is taken in tablets or dissolved and used in injections. When used for non-medical purposes it is normally injected into a vein or muscle.

Morphine is an active ingredient of opium

Morphine provides relief from intense pain

Codeine, made from morphine by chemical conversion, is a very widely used medicine. It is only a mild analgesic (pain reliever), but is often sold as a syrup or linctus to suppress coughs.

Codeine is made from morphine

Codeine is a mild pain reliever

Heroin is another drug derived from morphine. It is by far the most powerful and toxic of the opiate drugs. Because of the physical and mental dependence which heroin may cause, it has been banned, even for medical purposes, in many countries of the world. Its importation and manufacture in Australia are forbidden.

Heroin is made from morphine

Heroin is a powerful toxic drug which causes physical and mental dependence

Because of the dependence-producing effects of all these drugs, people have attempted to manufacture drugs which have the same pain-relieving properties but which are not addictive. Pethidine and methadone are two drugs manufactured for this purpose. However, experience has shown that dependence on both these drugs is common.

Pethidine and methadone are effective pain relievers but they also produce dependence

Why is it that these drugs are so likely to be misused, and what makes them such dangerous drugs? The main reason for using all the opiates in medicine is for their tremendous capacity to relieve pain. However, the opiates do more than just relieve pain. In many people they produce a feeling of contentment, well-being and power. General awareness is lowered so much that even feelings of hunger or fear are suppressed. This state of mind, the feeling that nothing needs to be done, because everything is as it should be, is called **euphoria**. For many people it is an extremely pleasant state and leads them to use the drug again.

Let us look more closely at how the opiate drugs work in the body. All opiates act on the brain to depress brain function. They numb pain sensations, reduce anxiety, tensions and fears, and cause drowsiness and lethargy. They lower breathing rate and decrease the movements and secretions of the stomach and intestines. Above all, they may dull intellectual functions and produce a feeling of contentment which removes the normal 'drives' which lead us to involve ourselves in our community.

A user's first experience of morphine or heroin is often quite unpleasant, causing nausea and vomiting. Some people whose first experience is like this may never use the drug again. Others may not use it for days or weeks and then use it intermittently for many months before becoming regular users. For others, though, the first dose may be very satisfying, and the user may then make a conscious decision to use the drug as often as it can be obtained. It is not true, as is sometimes believed, that one becomes an addict after the first dose. However, very many people who thought they knew 'how far they could go' have progressed from occasional doses to true dependence.

As people become dependent on the drug, they become tolerant of it. This means that they need a larger (or sometimes more frequent) dose of the drug to experience its pleasant effects. At this stage, long-term effects of the drug are seen, too. Appetite is reduced, which often results in marked loss of weight. Constipation becomes a continuing problem, and temporary impotence and sterility are common.

At this stage users are physically dependent on the drug; when they cannot obtain their regular supplies, they experience extremely painful and unpleasant withdrawal symptoms. These include violent vomiting, diarrhoea, shivering and twitching, sweating, severe abdominal pain and muscular cramps.

Even more serious than the agony of withdrawal, however, is the problem of psychological dependence on these drugs. After six or seven days without the drug, the physical symptoms of withdrawal begin to subside, and the subjects are left weak, nervous and restless. Their psychological dependence remains, however, and they continue to crave the drug's effects. Why this craving occurs is not understood, but only intensive support and counselling enables them to overcome their desire for the drug and to be 'cured' of their drug dependence.

Continued use of the illegal opiates such as heroin and morphine causes other particular health risks. When these drugs are obtained on

Opiate narcotics both relieve pain and produce a feeling of well-being and power

All opiate drugs suppress brain function

Opiates
- numb pain
- reduce anxiety
- reduce tension
- cause drowsiness and lethargy
- lower blood pressure
- lower breathing rate
- decrease the movements and secretions of the stomach and intestine
- produce a feeling of contentment

First experiences with morphine and heroin may be extremely unpleasant

A morphine- or heroin-dependent person requires gradually larger doses of the drug, as the body becomes tolerant of its effects

Long-term effects:
- reduction of appetite
- loss of weight
- constipation
- sterility

Lack of the drug for the dependent user causes unpleasant withdrawal symptoms:
- vomiting
- diarrhoea
- shivering
- twitching
- sweating
- severe abdominal pains
- muscular cramp

Psychological dependence may cause continued desperate craving for the drug

the illegal market, they are sold as a white (or pink or brown) powder. The quality of this powder—that is, the proportion of heroin or morphine it contains—may vary tremendously. In its long journey from the manufacturer to the smuggler, 'pusher' and drug user, it may be so diluted with other powders that the final mixture contains only 3 to 5 per cent heroin. (Diluting the drug in this way is the easiest way for drug traffickers to increase their profit.) As we saw earlier in the chapter, a drug's effect in the body varies considerably, depending on the strength of the dose administered. Many heroin addicts have died from an overdose of heroin, when the powder they obtained contained more than the usual low percentage of heroin.

These powders carry another danger as well. As we have said, heroin often forms only a very small proportion of the powder which is sold. The remainder may be talcum powder, chalk or glucose. Occasionally, the drug is diluted with much more poisonous powders, for example rat poison or powdered cement. Injection of powders such as these also causes deaths among heroin users.

Another danger of using any illegally obtained drug is the high risk of infection. As we discussed earlier, any drug injected into the body must be sterile, to avoid the risk of infection. Drugs obtained on the illegal market are never sterilised, and serious infections, for example blood poisoning, may result. Using shared and unsterilised syringes and needles for injection can also lead to the formation of abscesses and a serious disease of the liver, serum hepatitis. Hepatitis is one of the commonest causes of death amongst people who take illegal drugs by injection.

Unsterilised drugs and needles may result in
• blood poisoning
• formation of abscesses
• serum hepatitis

Stimulants

This group of drugs includes all the drugs that stimulate the central nervous system, making the user more wakeful.

Stimulants make the person more wakeful

The mildest form of stimulants are the 'stay-awake' pills, for example, No-Doz, which contain the mild stimulant caffeine. The same stimulating effect can be obtained from drinking tea, coffee, cocoa or Cola drinks, all of which, in normal strength, contain a similar amount of caffeine. For the normal healthy person, caffeine is regarded as a relatively harmless drug. However, consumption of large quantities of caffeine can be habit-forming.

This group contains
• caffeine
• amphetamines
• cocaine

Caffeine is the mildest stimulant

The more important and potent stimulants are the amphetamine-like drugs and cocaine. Although the amphetamines and cocaine act in different ways within the target cells of the central nervous system, their effects are very similar. They both stimulate the central nervous system and produce powerful feelings of excitement and well-being. They produce a sense of self-confidence, an increased flow of ideas, talkativeness and bustling activity.

Amphetamines and cocaine are powerful stimulants

Amphetamines and cocaine produce
• feelings of excitement
• sense of well-being
• increased self-confidence
• increased flow of ideas

Amphetamines form a group of drugs which act in a similar way to the body's hormone adrenalin (see Chapter 13). The most common

Amphetamines include
- amphetamine
- dexamphetamine
- methamphetamine ('speed')

Amphetamines are used to
- increase alertness and activity
- reduce appetite

Stimulants do *not*
- assist concentration
- overcome body fatigue

substances in this group are amphetamine, dexamphetamine and methamphetamine—the latter being known as 'speed' when it is injected intravenously. Over the past fifty years they have been used for a variety of purposes. Because of their stimulating, stay-awake properties they were first used by soldiers and air-force pilots during the Second World War. The increase in alertness and activity they cause is accompanied by a reduction in appetite, so they have been prescribed by doctors for patients wishing to lose weight. Students studying for exams, truck drivers travelling long distances and athletes wishing to reduce fatigue and improve their physical performance have also used amphetamines.

However, although the stimulants do help the user to stay awake, they do not help concentration or overcome real body fatigue. For this reason, stimulants are notorious for their damaging effect on students studying for exams. The student may think he has done very well in his exam and that he has in fact offered inspired and original answers. The examiner, on the other hand, sees a talkative, over-confident student who offers disjointed and confused arguments. (One example is recorded of a senior school student who, while suffering the effects of amphetamine, filled an entire examination booklet with his signature, and then left the examination room confident he had performed brilliantly!)

Intravenous injection of cocaine or an amphetamine drug produces immediate powerful effects of wellbeing and excitement. When the effect wears off, anxiety, depression and restlessness follow

Larger and more frequent doses are required by the dependent person

Used for any of these purposes, amphetamines are usually taken as tablets or capsules. The most harmful form of stimulant abuse is the intravenous injection of the drug, either cocaine or methamphetamine ('speed'). These drugs are extremely dangerous because they produce an immediate powerful sensation of well-being and excitement. This is soon replaced by anxiety, depression and restlessness when the effect wears off. This, too, encourages the user to repeat the injection of the drug. Initially, relatively few doses will produce the sensations of excitement and euphoria, but tolerance develops quite rapidly. Larger and more frequent doses are required. In the dependent person 'speed trips' may last several days, with the drug being injected every two or three hours around the clock. At the end of this time the user has become extremely depressed, aggressive, hostile and suspicious—always with the feeling of being watched. However, although disoriented, the user is still quite conscious and coordinated and may become violent and dangerous because of these fears and suspicions.

Cocaine and amphetamine users commonly attempt to overcome their feelings of anxiety and depression by using combination drugs, either stimulant and barbiturate ('purple heart' pills, see earlier), or stimulant and opiate ('speed ball'). In this way users may become dependent on several drugs. Although physical dependence on the stimulant drugs does not seem to occur (people do not suffer withdrawal symptoms when they cannot obtain the drug), the chance of becoming psychologically dependent on these drugs is very high. The severe depression, anxiety and restlessness which follow their use leave the user with a craving for the sense of excitement which another injection will bring.

Stimulant drugs used intravenously may leave the user suspicious, violent and dangerous

Combinations of stimulants–barbiturates/or stimulants–opiates are sometimes used

Stimulant drugs do not produce physical dependence but usually produce psychological dependence

Hallucinogens

Hallucinogen is a term used to describe a group of drugs that can alter our thoughts, feelings and perceptions (that is, how we see things around us). Sometimes our surroundings may seem more pleasant; often, sensations may be unpleasant. With these drugs we experience sensations we would never otherwise experience, except perhaps in dreams. There is a large range of hallucinogenic drugs. The best-known and most powerful of these is LSD. Other hallucinogens are mescalin, psilocybin, DMT and DET. The effects of all these drugs are similar, and we shall discuss only LSD.

Hallucinogens alter our thoughts, feelings and perceptions

Hallucinogenic drugs:
- *mescalin*
- *psilocybin*
- *DMT*
- *DET*
- *LSD*
- *cannabis (in high doses)*

LSD

LSD is an abbreviation of the chemical name of the drug lysergic acid diethylamide. It is one of the most powerful drugs available—only one millionth of a gram per kilogram body weight, when swallowed, will cause a 'psychedelic trip'. On the illegal market the drug may be obtained as a small white pill, or offered in the form of impregnated sugar cubes or biscuits.

LSD is an extremely powerful drug

LSD alters the way we appreciate the sensory stimuli around us and removes our control over what we experience—this is a 'trip'

LSD affects the central nervous system and begins to take effect shortly after being swallowed. As with all the hallucinogen drugs, its effect is completely unpredictable. Some people find a 'trip' an extremely pleasant experience; for others it is a nightmare. The effect may vary from time to time, too—a pleasant 'trip' may be followed by a very frightening one. Basically, LSD alters the way we appreciate all the sensory stimuli we receive and removes our control over what we experience. The changes in perception are so severe that the user may 'see sounds' or 'hear colours'. Food may taste and feel different, and clothes may change their texture. Most important, the user loses all control over these experiences, loses his awareness of his real environment, and may even lose the ability to control his body's movements.

LSD affects emotions

LSD affects emotions too, again in an unpredictable way. It may cause laughter or tears, relaxation and happiness or fear and panic. Very commonly, after four or five hours of a 'trip', the fears of loneliness and loss of self control become so intense that a panic reaction develops. Many people have become so distressed at this stage that they have attempted suicide to escape from it. Others are psychologically damaged by their experiences for months or years. (To prevent dangerous reactions of this kind, LSD users often arrange for a friend, not using the drug, to supervise them during a 'trip'.)

The full course of the 'trip' lasts about 12 hours, after which time the user is again aware of his surroundings and in control of his body. Although dependence on hallucinogens is not a problem, LSD and the other hallucinogens should never be regarded as safe drugs. Their great danger is that, under their influence, people lose their sense of reality and may attempt dangerous actions—they may panic and become suicidal, or even attempt impossible feats, such as 'floating' from the top of a high building. They may be dangerous in the long term, too; the horrifying experiences of a 'trip' may cause permanent mental damage, and it is not uncommon for users to experience 'flash-backs'. LSD sensations may reoccur months later while driving a car or when under stress.

LSD causes loss of sense of reality

Flash-backs of LSD sensations may occur after many months, under conditions of stress

Cannabis (marijuana)

Marijuana is a product of the plant *Cannabis sativa*

The drugs that have caused more controversy than any others are the products of the plant *Cannabis sativa*, sometimes known as Indian hemp (Fig 14.6). Drugs produced from this plant have been known and used since ancient times. The Chinese, as early as 1000 BC, described the plant as 'a remedy which soothes pain, subdues insomnia and restlessness'. The cannabis plant can be grown in almost any part of the world, although it thrives best in hot, dry climates. The drugs produced from the plant are known by many different names in different parts of the world.

The drugs produced from cannabis plants are known as
• marijuana
• hashish

In the English-speaking world, three terms are commonly used:

• Marijuana, which consists of the leaves, flowers and stems of the male and female plants *Cannabis sativa*.

Fig 14.6 *Indian hemp (Cannabis sativa)*

- Hashish, a liquid resin obtained from the flowering tops of the female plant. This is the most powerful form of cannabis. (The male plant contains very little of this resin.)

- Tetrahydrocannabinol (THC), which was identified in cannabis resin in 1965. THC can now be produced by chemical reactions in the laboratory, and it is commonly believed to be the main active ingredient in cannabis.

THC is thought to be the active chemical in cannabis

Marijuana is usually smoked, in hand-rolled cigarettes. Hashish (being a liquid resin) is mixed with tobacco or smoked 'neat' in pipes. It can also be eaten, in various forms of cakes, biscuits and so on. When it is smoked, the effect is experienced almost immediately, so the user is able to keep the effects under his control. When eaten, however, the drug takes longer to produce its effects—the user has less control over the effect and is more likely to take an overdose (see p 278).

Marijuana can be smoked or eaten

Overdosing is more likely to occur if marijuana is eaten

One of the biggest problems in determining the effects of the different forms of cannabis is that the strength of the products varies tremendously. The amount of active ingredients varies with the location in which the plants grow, the time of harvest, and the parts of the plant used. (Like other drugs, cannabis products sold on the illegal market are often diluted with other, inactive ingredients.) The production of THC in

The effects of cannabis are difficult to assess, since the concentration of active ingredients varies from plant to plant

THC has been used in experiments to investigate the effects of cannabis

Physical effects of cannabis:
- increased heart rate
- dryness of mouth and throat
- redness of eyes
- enlargement of pupils

Psychological effects of cannabis:
- feeling of well-being
- lessening of inhibitions
- alterations in the sense of time
- loss of short-term memory
- increased desire to laugh
- production of fear, panic, anxiety and hallucinations

The effects of cannabis last from 2 to 4 hours

There is no hangover after cannabis use

Psychological dependence may develop

Cannabis smoke contains carcinogenic agents

Cannabis reduces powers of perception, thought and concentration

Driving skills are greatly impaired if alcohol and cannabis are used together

the laboratory has greatly aided research into the effects of cannabis on the body. It is now possible to administer measured doses of THC to volunteers and observe its effects. However, it is far from proved that this chemical is the *only* active ingredient of marijuana and hashish.

What, then, are the effects of cannabis? These can be divided into physical and psychological effects. When smoked, cannabis causes a variety of physical effects within 10 to 20 minutes, including:

- increased heart rate

- dryness of mouth and throat

- redness of eyes

- enlargement of pupils, and pain when exposed to bright lights.

The psychological effects are far less predictable. They vary with the dose of the drug, the route and rate of administration, the type of preparation and so on. Like alcohol, they appear to depend, too, on the user's personality, his previous experience, expectations of the drug and so on. There are several commonly reported effects, however:

- A feeling of well-being—inner calm, or euphoria.

- Lessening of inhibitions, so that ideas and thoughts seem to flow freely.

- Alterations in the sense of time.

- Loss of short-term memory, so that the user may forget what he is saying before reaching the end of a sentence.

- An exaggerated desire to laugh or giggle.

- Occasionally, less pleasant experiences are produced: fear, panic, anxiety and hallucinations have been reported. However, unlike LSD and alcohol, these sensations are only shortlived. They tend to occur when much higher doses of cannabis are used.

The effects of cannabis normally last from 2 to 4 hours and may be followed by a deep sleep. Unlike alcohol, there is no hangover, other than some lethargy and sleepiness with continued use. Much research is yet to be done into the effects of the long-term use of cannabis. It is uncertain whether cannabis causes brain damage. Psychological dependence has been demonstrated, and some studies have also described cases of physical dependence on cannabis. Cannabis smoke has been reported to contain carcinogenic substances in concentrations about half of those present in tobacco smoke. Cannabis smokers could therefore be expected to have an increased chance of developing lung and other cancers. As yet no statistics to establish or refute this hypothesis are available.

Many reports have shown that while cannabis is being smoked normal powers of perception, thought and concentration are reduced. This may have dangerous consequences for anyone driving a car while intoxicated with cannabis. Driving skill is impaired even more if alcohol and cannabis are used together (see Chapter 16).

Most research suggests that cannabis is a relatively mild drug, when compared with alcohol and the other mood-altering drugs. It is normally used, like alcohol, to reduce tension and produce a sense of relaxation which makes social interaction easier.

However, possession and smoking of marijuana are illegal in Australia and most Western countries. This is the subject of considerable controversy. Many people claim that its use leads the way to use of the more dangerous drugs. There is little evidence to support this view. Perhaps the strongest argument against legalising its use is our almost complete lack of knowledge of its long-term effects. We now know of the serious dangers associated with the use of tobacco and alcohol, which were once considered harmless. Until the long-term effects of cannabis have been thoroughly researched—the effects on the foetus, its relationship to respiratory disease, its long-term storage in the body, its interaction with other drugs and so on—caution is undoubtedly the best policy.

Possession and smoking of marijuana are illegal in Australia and most Western countries

Little is known about marijuana's long-term effects

The problem of multiple drug use

We have now examined each of the major groups of mood-altering drugs and seen how they act in the body, where their effects can be useful, and the dangers of their abuse. One problem now remains to be considered. This is the question of multiple drug use (and abuse). In other words, the problem of using more than one of these mood-altering drugs at the one time. Table 14.3 describes the effects of the combined use of alcohol with some other common drugs.

Table 14.3 *Interaction of alcohol with some other common drugs*

Alcohol		Drug		Effect
Alcohol	+	Other depressants, eg barbiturates	→	Dramatically increased depressant effect
Alcohol	+	Anti-histamines (normally little or no sedative effect)	→	Marked drowsiness
Alcohol	+	Valium	→	Dramatic and rapid increase in sedative effect (drowsiness etc)
Alcohol	+	Cannabis	→	Decreased coordination, increased reaction time, impaired judgment
Alcohol	+	Aspirin	→	Increased risk of damage to gastric mucosa

From your understanding of how each different type of drug works in the body, it should now be clear that taking more than one drug at any time is a dangerous practice. The effect of any of these drugs can obviously be compounded. For example, if two depressants, alcohol and a

When two drugs are taken at once their effects may be exaggerated and unpredictable

barbiturate, are used together, a very exaggerated depressing effect may be produced. Clearly, this could be disastrous for anyone driving a car or operating machinery. Perhaps even more dangerous, though, than this effect is the unpredictability of response to any drug when it is combined with other drugs in the body. We still have a lot to learn about how different drugs interact in the body, and how the presence of one drug may interfere with the way another drug operates.

Multiple drug abuse may lead to multiple drug dependence

Finally, there is the problem of multiple drug abuse. We have seen how dependence may result from abuse of any of the mood-altering drugs and have described the damaging effects of this dependence on the user. Frequently, however, a person abuses not just one, but several, drugs—in fact he will abuse whichever drug he can obtain. As we have said, the interactions of these drugs in the body are complex and unpredictable. In addition, this practice frequently leads to multiple drug dependence—dependence on a number of drugs.

The alternative to drugs

Drug taking has been a social habit in almost every human civilisation. In different societies particular drugs have been permitted or socially accepted: opium in ancient China, marijuana in the Middle East and South East Asia, tobacco among North American Indians and, later, Europeans.

The types of drugs used may depend on
• social pressures
• living conditions
• reasons for using drugs

In this chapter, we have examined some of the mood-altering drugs that are taken today. Which drugs are taken depends on social pressures: living conditions, a person's reasons for using drugs, and what is available. Some drugs are more accepted than others—nicotine and alcohol have all the pressures of social custom and powerful advertising behind them. Others are taken out of boredom or curiosity.

Drugs may be used when emotional needs are not met

For most people, drugs are not a problem. They limit drug use to manageable and fairly harmless levels. For the remainder, drug taking is uncontrolled and represents a danger to their mental and/or physical well-being. We have seen why this is so. For these people, drug taking fills an emotional need which they find they cannot meet from their own resources. All people have emotional needs, amongst other things for security, friendship and love, independence, self-respect and a sense of achievement. When any one of these needs cannot be met, drugs may be sought as an alternative.

Drug abuse in any form is rarely a problem for mature, well-adjusted people. It is most often a problem for the insecure or those who are under considerable stress. It often occurs among people deprived of an emotional need or people who are unable to accept themselves as they really are. By using drugs, a person may be trying to become the 'someone' he would like to be.

An alternative to mood-altering drugs involves understanding our needs and learning to understand who we really are. If we can accept ourselves as we really are, our need for the security of being part of a group is reduced. We no longer need to conform to the habits of that group, in drug taking or any other activity. If we can involve ourselves in recreational activities that develop our self-esteem and give us a sense of achievement, we will not turn to drugs for 'kicks' or out of curiosity or boredom.

Sometimes our unfilled needs or the stresses of life may be too great for us to cope with on our own. However, mood-altering drugs cannot solve these problems. Some drugs may provide valuable temporary relief from depression, anxiety or tension, but they must be taken under medical supervision. Solutions to problems can be found only by confronting the problems honestly and examining the possibilities realistically. In achieving this understanding of ourselves and our needs, we may have to rely heavily on the support of our friends and family. And no one should hesitate to seek additional help from school or community counsellors—that's what they are there for.

Taking drugs cannot solve problems. To solve problems we must understand ourselves and our needs and seek help when necessary

Chapter 15

The sense organs—a link with the outside world

In Chapter 13 we saw that the body is similar to a group of actors performing a play. Coordination occurs at two levels—actors must coordinate their activities with one another, to present the correct sequence of speeches and actions which make an understandable and enjoyable play; and actors must also be receptive to the audience's mood and modify their performance (even if only a little) in order to communicate more effectively with the audience.

In the same way, communication occurs between organs and tissues within the body, and between the body and the external environment. Communication within the body ensures a constant internal environment, so necessary for the body's efficient working. It also ensures minimum wastage of vital body fuels, which are often available in only limited quantities. Communication between the body and the external environment provides an essential awareness of sources of harm—heat, objects that may damage the body, and predators, for example. In addition, knowing where to find vital commodities such as food and shelter depends on communication with the environment. In short, this contact with the exterior is the basis of survival in the wider world. We have already seen that, within the body, messages are transmitted via the endocrine and nervous systems. How does the body receive information about the external environment?

Contact between humans and the external environment is necessary for survival

Receptor cells

All animals, except the very simplest, possess specialised sensitive cells which respond to different stimuli such as light and heat. Such sensitive cells are often referred to as receptor cells. The following table and Fig 15.1 classify four main types of receptor cells according to the stimuli to which they respond.

Specialised sensitive cells are known as receptor cells

Types of receptor cells:
- *photoreceptors*
- *chemoreceptors*
- *thermoreceptors*
- *mechanoreceptors*

Table 15.1   *A classification of receptor cells*

Receptor cell	Stimuli
Photoreceptors	Light
Chemoreceptors	Chemicals
Thermoreceptors	Heat, cold
Mechanoreceptors	Mechanical stress, eg pressure, tension (stretch)

A receptor cell may be a sensory neuron whose dendrites are sensitive to a stimulus

Receptor cells can be of two types. The most common is a sensory neuron in which the endings, or dendrites, are especially structured to receive a stimulus. Such endings are present in the skin and are sensitive to touch, pain, heat, cold and pressures. The endings of these receptor cells are often branched and may develop small knobs or bulbs (Fig 15.2). Others, such as stretch receptors, are found in the tissues of the joints, ligaments and muscles of the limbs. Gaseous molecules are detected in the nasal passages by similar dendrite endings.

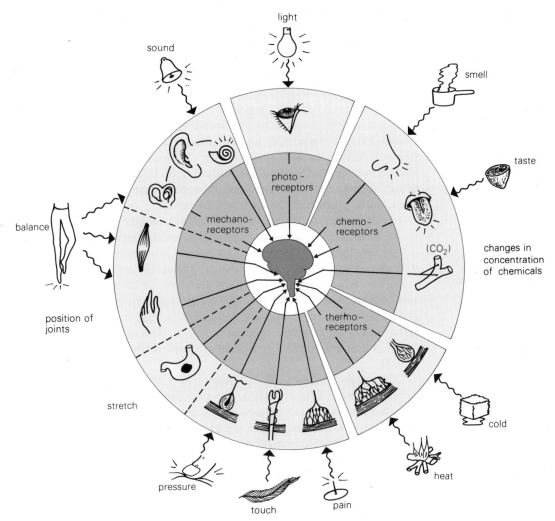

Fig 15.1 *Types of receptor cells and the stimuli to which they respond*

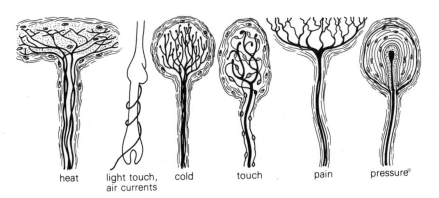

Fig 15.2 *Receptor nerve endings, responsible for six different sensations*

A receptor cell may be an epithelial cell with a particular structure that enables it to receive a stimulus

Nerve impulses are passed from a receptor cell
↓
spinal cord
↓
brain

Receptor cells may be grouped together in sense organs

When the endings or dendrites of a receptor cell (sensory neuron) are stimulated, nerve impulses are produced in the endings and pass along the sensory neuron to the spinal cord. From here, the impulses travel to the brain, where they produce a particular sensation or feeling.

The second kind of receptor cell is an epithelial cell especially structured to receive a certain stimulus. Examples of this kind of receptor cell are found in the eye and tongue. When light falls on the light-sensitive receptor cells in the eye, a nerve impulse is produced. This impulse is passed directly to a sensory neuron, which then relays the message to the brain. When the impulse finally reaches the visual area of the brain, the person sees or experiences the sensation of light. A similar chain of events is produced when dissolved chemicals stimulate taste receptors in the mouth, producing the sensation of taste.

The two types of receptor cell are shown in simple outline in Fig 15.3.

We have already seen that different particular types of receptor cells are present in large numbers in organs such as the eye, skin, tongue, nose and ear. These organs are known as the sense organs. The types of stimuli to which these sense organs are sensitive correspond to the five basic human senses: sight, hearing, touch, smell and taste. Thus the eye contains receptor cells that are sensitive to a large range of colours and intensities of light, giving the sense of sight. The tongue contains receptor cells that are sensitive to a wide range of chemicals, giving the sense of taste.

One of the purposes of this chapter is to examine the human sense organs in detail. This will enable you to understand how the human body detects changes in its environment, a feature that is necessary for its survival. You will also realise that when the senses are carefully investigated, it has to be admitted that far more than five senses exist in humans. We have already seen, for example, that the skin is sensitive to heat, cold and pressure, as well as touch. In addition, there are such things as the vital sense of balance, and the sense that enables us to place our legs and arms in certain positions and to be aware of their exact positions without having to watch them.

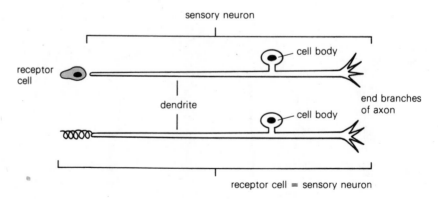

Fig 15.3 *Two types of receptor cells*

The eye

The eyes can be regarded as our 'window to the world'. (The importance of sight can be readily appreciated if you attempt an apparently simple task while blindfolded.)

Structure and function

The important features of the eye are identical to those of a camera: an *aperture* or opening through which light can enter, a *lens* for focusing the rays of light, and a *sensitive surface* on which an image can fall.

The eyes are composed entirely of soft tissues, so it is essential that they have supporting structures to protect them from mechanical or chemical damage. Several protective structures surround the eyes. The eyeballs are well padded by fatty tissue and protected by the bony **orbits** (sockets) of the skull. At the front, each eye can be completely covered by two eyelids. The movement of the eyelids (blinking) occurs reflexly in response to dangers, as well as routinely to help bathe the surfaces of the eyes with tears. Tears are produced by **tear glands** which open on to the surface of the eyes, under the upper eyelids. Tears contain a solution of sodium bicarbonate and sodium chloride and help to keep the outer surfaces of the eyes moist. The flow of tears, assisted by blinking, helps to wash away dust particles and other stray material. In addition, tears contain an enzyme which helps to protect the eyes against bacterial infection (see Chapter 7). After bathing the eyes, excess fluid from the tear glands drains into the nasal cavity, through **lacrimal ducts**, situated at the inside corners of the eyes. The arrangement of the tear glands and lacrimal ducts is shown in Fig 15.4.

The eyeball is protected by
- the bony orbits of the skull
- pads of fatty tissue
- the eyelids
- tears, which wash the surfaces of the eyes (tears also contain an antibacterial enzyme)

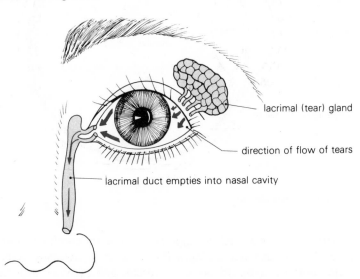

lacrimal (tear) gland

direction of flow of tears

lacrimal duct empties into nasal cavity

Fig 15.4 *Position of the tear gland and lacrimal duct*

In the eye:
- the conjunctiva protects the front of the eyeball
- the sclera provides support within the eyeball
- the cornea helps to bend light rays as they enter the eye
- the choroid provides the eye with food and oxygen
- the retina contains light-sensitive cells
- the aqueous humour helps to bend light rays
- the lens focuses light rays onto the retina
- the suspensory ligaments support the lens
- the ciliary muscles alter the shape of the lens
- the vitreous humour fills the hollow in the centre of the eyeball
- the iris regulates the amount of light entering the eye

Figure 15.5 shows the structure of the eye itself. A transparent, thin layer of epithelial cells lines the inside of the eyelids and passes across the front of the eyeball. This layer is called the **conjunctiva**. Its main function is to protect the outer surface of the eye. Beneath the conjunctiva a tough, non-elastic coat of white connective tissue called the **sclera** surrounds, and provides support for, the eyeball. This coat is opaque (does not allow light to pass through), but becomes transparent at the front to form the **cornea**. The cornea is partly responsible for bending light rays as they enter the eye.

Inside the sclera, except in the region of the cornea at the front of the eye, are two further layers: the **choroid** and the **retina**. The choroid is rich in blood vessels which carry food and oxygen to the eye. The choroid is also heavily pigmented with black melanin, which prevents distortion of the image due to reflection of light inside the eye.

Inside the choroid is the retina. This is a light-sensitive surface which contains the light receptor cells. Sensory neurons, which synapse (see Chapter 13) with these cells, pass across the front of the retina and join together to form the **optic nerve**. This nerve relays nerve impulses from the eye to the brain.

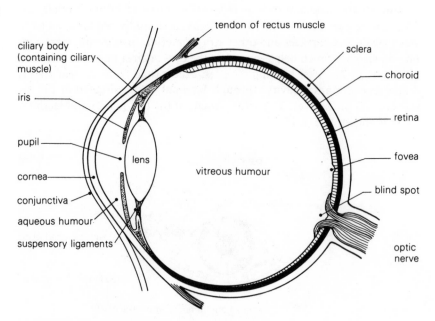

Fig 15.5 *Section through the eye*

After light has passed through the transparent conjunctiva and cornea it reaches an area containing a fluid known as **aqueous humour**. This fluid contains carbohydrate and protein, and together with the cornea begins the refraction (or bending) of light towards a point of focus.

From the aqueous humour light passes through the **lens**. The lens is made up of transparent epithelial cells. When removed from the eye, the lens takes on a spherical shape. However, in the eye the lens is supported under tension by fibres called **suspensory ligaments**, which radiate from its edge. These attach it to part of the choroid which has become expanded and is known as the **ciliary body**.

Within the ciliary body the suspensory ligaments are attached directly to muscle fibres known as the **ciliary muscles**. The shape of the lens can be altered by the contraction or relaxation of the ciliary muscles.

The lens, like the cornea and aqueous humour, refracts (bends) light, thus contributing to the focusing of light rays on the retina. However, the lens's ability to refract light is not as great as that of the cornea. The importance of the lens lies in the fact that, being elastic, its focal length can be changed rapidly by the pull of the ciliary muscles on the suspensory ligaments. This makes it possible to adjust the eye's focus from near to far objects, within a fraction of a second.

The importance of the lens lies in the fact that it can rapidly change its focal length

A further section of the eye contributes to the refraction of light to a point of focus. This is the **vitreous humour**. The vitreous humour is a clear, jelly-like substance which fills the hollow in the centre of the eye. It has a chemical composition similar to that of the fluid aqueous humour.

The lens's external surface is partly covered by an opaque disc of tissue. This disc is known as the **iris**. The iris is the pigmented part of the eye which can be seen through the cornea. Depending on the pigment content of the iris, eyes are said to be blue, brown or some other colour. The opening in the centre of the iris is the **pupil**. The size of this opening is controlled by the contraction and relaxation of muscle fibres within the iris. This in turn controls the amount of light entering the eye.

Let us return to our analogy of the eye and the camera. A detailed comparison is set out in the following table.

Table 15.2 *Comparison of the eye and the camera*

Eye	Camera
Sclera	Camera case
Choroid	Black paint
Retina	Light-sensitive film
Iris	Iris diaphragm
Most refraction of light occurs at the air–cornea boundary. A small amount occurs at the aqueous humour–lens boundary	Refraction of light occurs only at the lens
Focusing objects is automatic and is carried out by altering the shape, and thus the focal length, of the lens	Focusing different objects is achieved by moving a lens of fixed focal length towards and away from the film
The intensity of light entering the eye is automatically controlled by movements of the iris	The intensity of light entering the camera is adjusted manually, by adjusting the diaphragm covering the lens

Focusing

Most refraction in the eye occurs at the air–cornea boundary

The eye is an optical system in which light rays are focused on the retina. It is at the air–cornea boundary that most of the refraction occurs. Here the amount of refraction is the same, regardless of whether the object is near or distant.

Refraction also occurs at the aqueous humour–lens boundary

Further refraction occurs at the aqueous humour–lens boundary. The amount of refraction here depends on the curvature of the lens. Figure 15.6 shows the refraction of light through a curved surface.

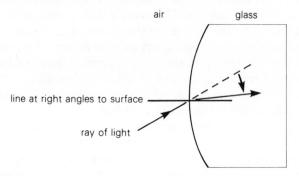

Fig 15.6 *Refraction of light. In passing from air into glass (from an optically less dense to an optically more dense medium) a ray of light is bent towards the line at right angles to the surface*

In order to understand how the lens bends light rays entering the eye, refer to Fig 15.7. Note the following points:

Objects close to the eye are focused with a more curved lens

- Light rays from near objects penetrate the lens at sharper angles than light rays from far objects.
- In order to focus light rays from near objects onto the retina, the rays must be refracted more sharply than rays from far objects.
- Sharper refraction of rays from near objects is brought about by a lens with more curved surfaces.

Distant objects are focused with a flatter lens

- Almost parallel rays from far objects are brought to focus by a lens with flatter surfaces.

The shape of the lens is altered by changes in tension in the suspensory ligaments

How is the shape of the lens changed in the eye? The lens is normally held under tension by the suspensory ligaments which are attached to the ciliary body. Changes in the tension of the suspensory ligaments therefore cause changes in the shape of the lens. The tension can be changed by the contraction or relaxation of the ciliary muscles within the ciliary body. These muscles are arranged in such a way that their contraction reduces the tension of the ligaments and allows the lens to bulge. This enables light rays from objects near the eye to be focused on the retina. Relaxation of the muscles increases the tension of the ligaments, which draws the lens into a flatter shape. This allows light rays from distant objects to be focused on the retina. The changes in the shape of the lens, which make it possible to focus light from near or distant objects on the retina, are called **accommodation**. This is illustrated in Fig 15.8.

Contraction/relaxation of the ciliary muscles decreases/increases the tension in the suspensory ligaments

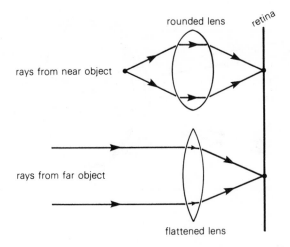

Fig 15.7   *Changes in the lens of the eye for near and distant vision*

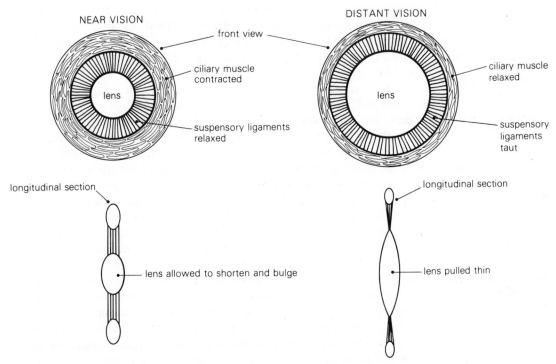

Fig 15.8   *Lens accommodation*

After light rays have passed through the cornea, aqueous humour, lens and vitreous humour, they reach the light-sensitive layer of tissue called the retina. Here the converging rays form an upside-down, back-to-front image. The image is much smaller than the object. Such image formation is shown in Fig 15.9.

Light rays form an upside-down, back-to-front image on the retina

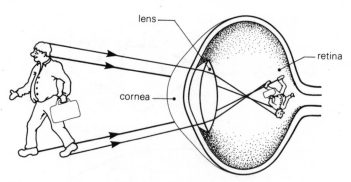

Fig 15.9 *Forming an image of a complex object*

The retina

The retina consists of a layer of cells which are sensitive to light. There are two such types of receptor cells, called **rods** and **cones**. Rods are highly sensitive to all wavelengths (colours) of light. However, they do not transmit any information to the brain about colour. They merely tell the brain how much light is falling on different areas of the retina. Rods alone cannot give sharp images with clear boundaries. About 95 per cent of light-sensitive cells in the retina are rods.

Cones are less sensitive to light (they require more light to stimulate them) and are responsible for colour vision. There are three types of cone cells, each type being most sensitive to a particular colour, or wavelength, of light. One kind of cone is most sensitive to blue light, whilst the other two have maximum sensitivity to green and red light.

The cones are most numerous in the centre of the retina, whereas the rods tend to be concentrated around the edge (periphery). Since the rods are more sensitive to light, one can actually see a dim object more clearly by gazing slightly to one side of the object. This allows the light to fall on the area of the retina that has the higher concentration of rods.

In the region where the nerve fibres which are connected with the rods and cones leave the eye to join the optic nerve, there are no light-sensitive cells. This is known as the **blind spot**. If some of the light rays from the image hit this area, no message is relayed to the brain. However, we do not have to view life with a persistent blank space in our field of vision. This is due partly to the fact that our eyes are continually scanning the field of view. It also happens that the blind spot never coincides with the part of the image we are concentrating on.

In the centre of the retina is a small depression called the **fovea**. The fovea is the area of the retina that produces most acute vision, and the eyes are automatically moved so that the important image in the field of view falls on this area. Several factors are responsible for this acuteness of vision:

Light-sensitive cells in the retina:
- rods are responsible for black and white vision of shapes
- cones are responsible for colour vision

Rods are more sensitive to light

The blind spot contains no light-sensitive cells

The fovea is the region of the retina that provides most acute vision

- There are only cones in the fovea.
- There is the greatest concentration of sensory cells in the fovea.
- There are fewer blood vessels and neurons covering the sensory cells in the fovea region.

Eye defects

In order for an object to appear clear to the observer, the light rays from the object must converge or meet on the retina. If light rays meet in front of or behind the retina (supposing that the retina was not in the way), a blurred image is formed.

Two common defects of the eye are shortsightedness (nearsightedness) and longsightedness (farsightedness). People suffering from short-sightedness can focus near objects accurately, but cannot focus distant objects. Light rays from distant objects converge in front of the retina. This occurs because light rays are refracted (bent) too much by the lens. There are a number of reasons why this may occur, but it often develops at school age when the eyes are used for a great deal of near vision. In other cases, shortsightedness is caused by the eyeballs being too long; that is, the distance from the lens to the retina is too great. Glasses with concave lenses, which diverge the light rays before they enter the eye, are used to correct this condition (Fig 15.10b).

Shortsightedness (distant objects cannot be focused):
- light rays from distant objects converge in front of the retina
- concave lenses are used to correct the condition

In longsightedness, distant objects can be seen clearly but near objects cannot be focused. This is because the rays from near objects cannot be bent sufficiently and converge behind the retina. Longsightedness is often found in infants, where the lens reaches adult size long before the rest of the eyeball has grown. It may also be due to a lens system that is too weak to refract light rays sufficiently. This problem arises when the ciliary muscles lose some of their ability to contract. As a result, the tension in the suspensory ligaments is never adequately reduced, and the surface of the lens never becomes sufficiently curved to focus rays from a near object onto the retina.

Longsightedness (near objects cannot be focused):
- light rays from near objects converge behind the lens
- convex lenses are used to correct the condition

Longsightedness is often found, also, in elderly people. This is because, with increasing age, the lens tends to become less flexible and elastic. As a result, the lens can be stretched by the suspensory ligaments, but when they relax, the lens may not return to its curved shape. The lens, which remains flat, is not able to focus close objects.

Longsightedness is corrected by a lens that causes light rays to converge partly before they reach the lens. This is done using spectacles with convex lenses (Fig 15.10c).

Figure 15.11 illustrates the difference between shortsightedness and longsightedness.

A further defect of the eyes is astigmatism. This is caused by the deformation of the cornea. As a result, light rays from a point source form either a vertically or horizontally elongated image of the point source on the retina.

Astigmatism:
- caused by a deformed cornea
- produces lengthened or widened image

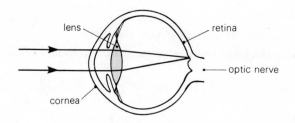

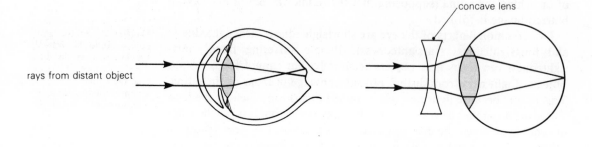

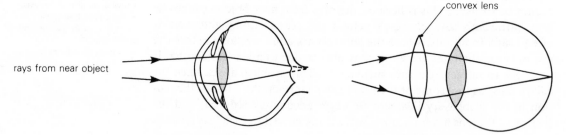

Fig 15.10　*Eye defects and the lenses used to correct them*
(a) Normal vision
(b) Shortsightedness
(c) Longsightedness

The ear

Sound is transmitted as
pressure waves in the air

Sound is transmitted as pressure waves in air or some other medium through which it may pass, such as water. The ear is the sense organ that detects these pressure waves in the air. It relays nerve impulses to the brain, where they are interpreted as sound. The pitch of sound is determined by the frequency of the pressure waves. The ear is capable of detecting sound corresponding to frequencies ranging from 20 to 20 000 waves per second.

Fig 15.11 *Defects in focusing*
(a) Longsightedness — close objects appear blurred while distant objects are seen clearly
(b) Shortsightedness — distant objects appear blurred while close objects are seen clearly

The ear is divided into three sections: the outer ear, middle ear and inner ear. Figure 15.12 shows how these are arranged.

Outer ear

The outer ear consists of the **pinna**, which is attached to a tube (the **auditory canal**), which leads to the **ear-drum**. The pinna is an extension of skin and cartilage and helps to direct the sound into the tube or auditory canal. Sound waves directed down the auditory canal strike the ear-drum and cause it to vibrate with the same frequency as the pressure waves in the air.

Outer ear:
• pinna
• auditory canal
• ear-drum

Middle ear

The middle ear is an air-filled cavity inside the bones of the skull. Inside this cavity three small bones (**ossicles**) connect the ear-drum with the membrane covering the opening between the middle and inner ears. This opening is called the **oval window**. The bones are arranged so that the vibrations in the ear-drum are magnified and passed to the oval window and so to the inner ear. The **malleus** (hammer) is the largest of the three ossicles. It is attached to the ear-drum at one end and meets the **incus** (anvil) at the other. The incus, in turn, joins with the **stapes** (stirrup), whose inner end fits into the oval window. This arrangement of the ossicles causes the membrane lying across the oval window to vibrate with the same frequency as the ear-drum.

Middle ear:
• ossicles:
  −malleus
  −incus
  −stapes

The ossicles
• magnify the vibrations of the ear-drum
• cause the oval window to vibrate with the same frequency as the ear-drum

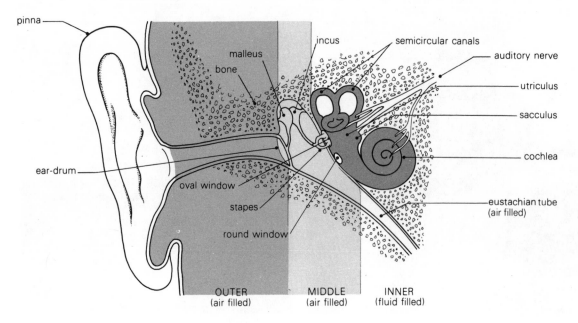

Fig 15.12 *Section of the ear*

The eustachian tube ensures that air pressure in the middle ear = external air pressure

A thin tube joins the cavity of the middle ear with the pharynx, at the back of the mouth. This is called the **eustachian tube**. The tube opens each time swallowing occurs and allows air to enter and leave the middle ear. The eustachian tube therefore ensures that air pressures remain equal on both sides of the ear-drum (that is, that the middle ear pressure = atmospheric pressure). (This prevents rupture of the ear-drum as a result of sudden changes in atmospheric pressure, such as may occur in aeroplanes.)

Inner ear

Membranous labyrinth—complex arrangement of tubes and sacs, fitted into the skull

Membranous labyrinth contains fluid called endolymph

Bony spaces in skull housing membranous labyrinth—the bony labyrinth

Perilymph—fluid between bone of skull and membranous labyrinth

The inner ear consists of a series of membranous tubes and sacs, arranged in different planes. These tubes and sacs contain a fluid known as **endolymph** (*endo* = inside). Because of the complex arrangement of the tubes and sacs, they are sometimes referred to as the **membranous labyrinth** (*labyrinthos* = a maze). Figure 15.13a shows the shape of the membranous labyrinth.

The membranous labyrinth is loosely fitted into a series of spaces and cavities in the bone of the skull. These bony spaces are often called the **bony labyrinth** and are shown in Fig 15.13b. Between the membranous tubes and sacs of the membranous labyrinth and the bony case of the bony labyrinth is a fluid called **perilymph** (*peri* = around).

The structures of the inner ear have two functions. One of these functions involves the sense of hearing, whilst the other is concerned with the sense of balance.

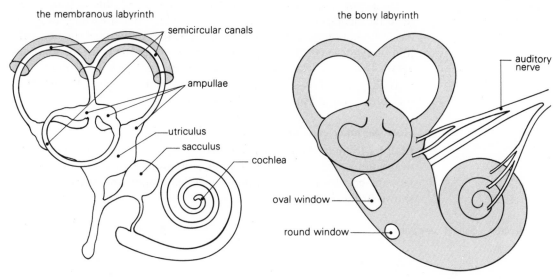

Fig 15.13   *Labyrinths of the inner ear*
(a)   The membranous labyrinth
(b)   The bony labyrinth

The structure that senses sound is the **cochlea**. If you were able to make a plaster cast of the inside of this bony cavity, it would resemble the coiled shell of a snail. The cochlea can be seen in Fig 15.12. Inside the cochlea are a number of membranes which are important in translating the vibrations from the oval window into nerve impulses. These membranes are part of the membranous labyrinth.

The cochlea is divided into three chambers, which are shown in Fig 15.14. The central chamber is bounded by two membranes: the **basilar membrane** and the **vestibular membrane**. Within this chamber are housed the cells which are sensitive to vibrations produced in the inner ear by the oval window. These are called **hair cells**. Also enclosed in the central chamber is the fluid known as endolymph. The two chambers on either side of this central chamber contain perilymph.

The cochlea is similar to a coiled shell of a snail

The cochlea contains three chambers:
- the central chamber containing endolymph and hair cells
- the side chambers containing perilymph

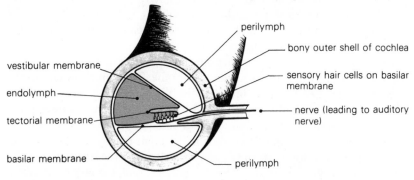

Fig 15.14   *Cross-section of the cochlea*

Hair cells are sensitive to vibrations in the inner ear

The auditory nerve relays nerve impulses from the inner ear to the brain

The sensory mechanism consists of a thick membrane known as the **tectorial membrane** and the layer of hair cells which are attached to the basilar membrane. At their bases on the basilar membrane the hair cells join or synapse (see Chapter 13) with nerve fibres to form the **auditory nerve**. This nerve relays impulses from the ear to the brain. At their other ends they have hair-like structures which extend towards the tectorial membrane but are not attached to the membrane.

How the inner ear operates

In order to understand how the inner ear translates the vibrations of the oval window into nerve impulses, it is important that you understand how the cochlea is arranged in an uncoiled longitudinal section. This is shown in Fig 15.15.

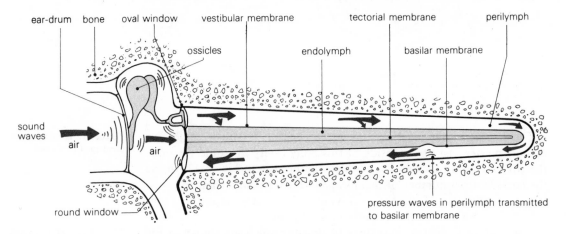

Fig 15.15 *Longitudinal section of an uncoiled, shortened cochlea*

The oval window produces pressure waves in the perilymph

The pressure waves cause different sections of the basilar membrane to vibrate

As the oval window vibrates, it sends a series of pressure waves through the perilymph of the cochlea. These pressure waves cause the basilar membrane to vibrate. Different sections of the basilar membrane vibrate with pressure waves of different frequency. For example, low frequencies cause the basilar membrane to vibrate most strongly near the apex of the cochlea, whereas high frequencies cause it to vibrate most strongly near the base of the cochlea.

When hair cells attached to the basilar membrane vibrate and contact the tectorial membrane, nerve impulses are relayed to the brain

The vibration of the basilar membrane causes the hair-like endings of the hair cells to contact the tectorial membrane. This somehow causes the hair cells to trigger off nerve impulses in the attached neurons. Such impulses travel to the auditory nerve and then to the brain, producing the sensation of sound. Thus, sounds of different pitch are distinguished, owing to the stimulation of hair cells in different regions of the cochlea.

Louder sounds cause larger vibrations in the basilar membrane

The intensity or loudness of sound is translated by the size of the vibrations in the basilar membrane. The louder the sound, the larger the vibrations of the ear-drum and, therefore, of the ossicles, the oval window, the cochlear fluid and finally the basilar membrane. The larger vibrations of the basilar membrane result in more impulses being transmitted through the neurons to the auditory nerve. As a result, more impulses reach the brain per second, and the sound is interpreted as being louder.

The balance organs

The organs responsible for the maintenance of balance are also contained in the inner ear. These are the semicircular canals, utriculus and sacculus.

Semicircular canals, utriculus and sacculus, are responsible for balance

The semicircular canals

The semicircular canals are located in a part of the bony labyrinth (see Fig 15.13) consisting of three bony tubes, arranged in three planes at right angles to each other. Inside these spaces in the bone there are similarly shaped membrane-bound tubes which are part of the membranous labyrinth. These tubes (canals) contain fluid, endolymph (which is continuous with the endolymph of the cochlea). At the end of each canal is a swelling called an **ampulla** (see Fig 15.13). Each ampulla contains a gelatinous plate or **cupula**, in which are embedded the endings of **sensory hair cells**. The hair cells are stimulated by the movement of fluid within the canals.

Semicircular canals consist of three tubes which are part of the membranous labyrinth and contain endolymph

Ampullae are swellings at the ends of the semicircular canals. An ampulla contains a cupula (gelatinous plate) in which sensory hair cells are embedded

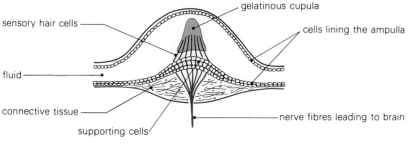

Fig **15.16** Section through an ampulla
(a) With the head at rest
(b) During movement of the head

The semicircular canals are stimulated when the head is rotated in the vertical or horizontal planes (Fig 15.16). For example, when the head is suddenly turned to the left in a horizontal plane, the fluid in the horizontal canal displays inertia and lags behind the movement of the canal. As the fluid in the canal pushes the cupula in the reverse direction, some of the hair cells of the cupula are pulled (Fig 15.16b), generating nerve impulses which are transmitted from these to the auditory nerve and so to the brain. Such signals reaching the brain from the semicircular canals are coordinated in the brain and result in nerve impulses being relayed to the muscles to assist the body in maintaining balance.

Inertia of the endolymph causes movement of the cupula and stretching of the hair cells

Utriculus and sacculus

The utriculus and sacculus are sacs in the membranous labyrinth

Two other swellings in the membranous labyrinth of the inner ear are the utriculus and sacculus. These contain small particles of calcium carbonate called **otoliths**, which are embedded in a membrane attached to sensitive areas of the labyrinth lining by the otoliths hairs. These hairs are extensions of sensory cells located in the labyrinth lining (Fig 15.17a). The density of the otoliths is greater than that of the surrounding fluid, so when the head is tilted, the otoliths push or pull on the sensory hairs (Fig 15.17b). The nerve impulses triggered off in these hairs are relayed to the auditory nerve and then to the brain. From the brain, impulses may again be relayed to body muscles, to help to control

These contain otoliths which are attached to the labyrinth by the hairs of sensory cells

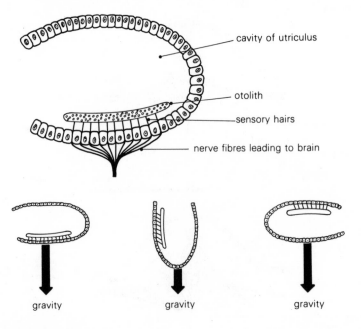

cavity of utriculus

otolith

sensory hairs

nerve fibres leading to brain

gravity   gravity   gravity

Fig 15.17 *The utriculus*
(a) Cross-section
(b) Positions of an otolith within the utriculus or sacculus depend on the position of the head. The otolith either pulls or presses down on the sensory hair cells

balance. Because of their different arrangements in the membranous labyrinth, sensory cells of the utriculus and sacculus can detect tilting movements of the head (or whole body). In contrast, the semicircular canals respond to rotation of the head. It is important to remember that the eyes and ears also receive information from the surroundings which helps to control balance.

Nerve impulses from the hair cells in the ampullae and the utriculus/sacculus are relayed to the brain

Taste and smell

The receptor cells for taste and smell are chemoreceptors. They are stimulated when contact is made with particular chemical substances. The taste receptors depend upon substances being dissolved. Smell receptors are sensitive to gaseous substances, or substances in the vapour phase.

Taste receptors

The taste receptors are small oval structures situated mainly on the tongue, but also on the palate and pharynx. Each receptor, or taste bud, contains about 20 long receptor cells which are part of the epithelium. These cells have hair-like tips which project through a pore above the tongue surface. It is these hair-like tips that are the sensitive surfaces of the cells. Chemical stimulation of the tips of the cells triggers the production of nerve impulses in the sensory neurons which are wrapped around the receptor cells (Fig 15.18). These impulses are relayed to the brain along cranial nerves.

Taste receptors consist of groups of sensory epithelial cells

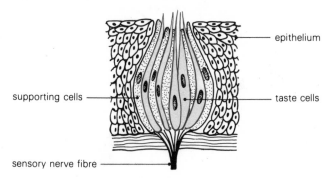

Fig 15.18 *Section of a taste bud*

It is generally thought that there are four primary taste sensations: sweet, sour, salt and bitter. These correspond to four types of taste receptor cells. Certain areas of the tongue seem to be most sensitive to these four taste categories (Fig 15.19). However, individuals differ in the precise areas in which they experience the primary taste sensations, as well as in general sensitivity to taste. For example, some people may be

There are taste receptor cells that are sensitive to
• sweet
• sour
• salt
• bitter
substances

completely insensitive to certain chemicals. A well-known example of this is phenylthiocarbamide (PTC), which can be tasted by only 80 per cent of the population.

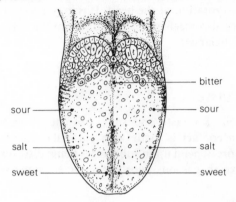

Fig 15.19   *Areas of the tongue responsible for the four taste sensations*

Smell receptors

Smell receptors are nerve cells

The receptors for smell lie in a small patch of **olfactory membrane** in the nasal cavity (Fig 15.20). They are situated above the stream of air that passes in and out during normal breathing, but are reached by eddy currents and diffusion. Whereas taste receptor cells are attached to neurons, smell receptors are themselves nerve cells.

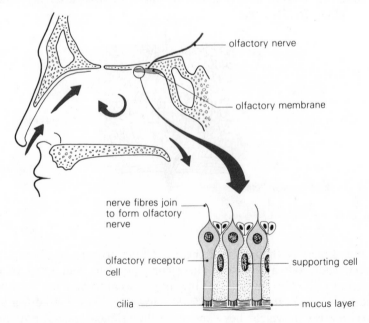

Fig 15.20   *Position of the smell receptors*

The olfactory membrane contains 10 to 20 million small receptor cells. Each of these is actually a nerve cell, with its own axon and dendrite. The dendrite extends to the epithelial surface and its hair-like endings project beyond the surrounding cells. For a substance to stimulate these endings, it must be volatile enough to enter the nose in the airstream and sufficiently soluble to dissolve in the mucus layer covering the cells of the olfactory membrane. Stimulation results in nerve impulses being transmitted to the brain via the **olfactory nerve**.

The sense of smell is far more sensitive than the sense of taste, since we are able to detect more than 3000 different odours. A search has been made for so-called primary odours. In one proposed system there are seven primary odours: camphoraceous, ethereal, floral, musky, pepperminty, pungent and putrid. Furthermore, it has been suggested that the odour of a substance depends upon the shape of the molecule. For example, it has been claimed that all spherical molecules have a camphoraceous smell.

For a substance to stimulate the smell receptors, it must be
- *volatile*
- *able to dissolve in the mucus layer covering the receptor cells*

3000 different odours can be detected by the human smell receptors

Deep receptors

Even with the eyes closed, it is possible to describe fairly precisely the position in which any part of the body has been placed, or to place a finger on an ear. The sensory receptors which make this possible are called **proprioceptors**. They are located in tendons, ligaments and joints.

In addition to these proprioceptors, there are two special types of proprioceptors found in tendons and muscles. These are stretch receptors; in other words, they trigger nerve impulses when the muscle or tendon surrounding them is stretched. As we shall see in Chapter 18, stretch receptors have a vital role in both the maintenance of posture and body tone and the coordination of contraction of different groups of muscles Stimulation of these proprioceptors probably usually stays below the level of our conscious awareness.

(There are also some free nerve endings in muscles and tendons, which produce sensations of pain or deep pressure.)

Proprioceptors are located in muscles, tendons, ligaments and joints

They provide information about the position and movement of the limbs

Skin receptors

We have already described the variety of skin receptors which allow us to distinguish the texture, temperature, shape and size of all the objects we touch. However, our ability to make these observations does not result only from the activity of individual receptors. The information we receive about the environment depends on the summation (addition) of impulses reaching the brain from many receptors in the skin of a particular region.

The number of skin receptors in a particular area of skin varies in different parts of the body. A very simple experiment helps us to determine which areas of the skin are best supplied with receptors. This experiment uses the **two-point discrimination test**. In this test the subject is blind-folded and then touched lightly with two pins, on different regions of his skin surface. He is asked to determine whether one or two pins are used to produce the sensation. On the back, the subject can usually dis-criminate two pin-pricks only when they are at least 10 to 15 mm apart. The skin of the finger-tips, however, is far more richly supplied with receptors. In these areas, pin-pricks as little as 1 mm apart may be dis-tinguished individually.

If you refer again to Fig 13.13 you will see that these variations in the distribution of receptors are reflected also in the sensory areas of the brain. The fingers and thumbs, which are so richly supplied with recep-tors, are represented by a correspondingly large area of the sensory cor-tex. The back is represented by only a small area of the sensory cortex.

The protection of the body from injury is possibly the most obvious function of skin receptors. However, skin receptors are vital in a number of other ways. People who, as a result of injury or disease, lack skin receptor function in the hands experience a variety of difficulties. With-out skin receptors they are unable to judge pressure, making it difficult to grip a hammer and almost impossible to play a musical instrument. They are also unable to judge the weight, shape or texture of objects. They cannot select the required coin from a pocket simply by feel, but have to look. Where skin receptors (or their nerves) are damaged in the legs, posture and walking may also be impaired.

Chapter 16

Alcohol—stimulant or depressant?

A mug of beer with icy droplets on a frosted glass surface; a small tumbler of rich, red port; a delicate crystal glass filled with smooth brown sherry—a variety of drinks for every social occasion. But despite their differences of character and taste, all these drinks have an important ingredient in common. They all contain the chemical commonly known as alcohol. In scientific terms this chemical is called **ethyl alcohol** or **ethanol**.

Alcoholic drinks have been known throughout recorded history. The oldest alcoholic drinks on record are beers and wines. In the Middle Ages the Arabs developed the science of distillation and were thus able to produce highly alcoholic drinks such as whisky and gin. The alchemists proclaimed these concentrated alcoholic solutions to contain the long-sought elixir of life. Thus alcohol came to be used therapeutically as well as socially. However, it was some time before the exact nature of the intoxicating component of these drinks was discovered. Since then we have gained an insight into the reasons why yeast cells produce alcohol, as well as the effects of alcohol consumption on the body's normal functioning.

Alcohol—a by-product of energy release

In Chapter 4 we saw how glucose is oxidised in body cells to release energy. While oxygen is used in this process of cellular respiration, carbon dioxide and water are given off as waste products. In rapidly contracting muscle tissue, oxygen cannot be supplied rapidly enough for this cellular respiration to provide the muscle cells with their total energy requirement. Another process then comes into action. Glucose is converted into lactic acid, a process which releases a smaller amount of energy but does not require oxygen. This process is sometimes known as **lactic fermentation**. Lactic fermentation occurs in situations where oxygen is not available; that is, in anaerobic situations. The chemical equation for lactic fermentation can be summarised as follows:

Lactic fermentation provides energy for muscle in the absence of oxygen

$$\text{Glucose} \rightarrow \text{lactic acid} + \text{energy}$$

In symbols:

$$C_6H_{12}O_6 \rightarrow 2\,C_3H_6O_3 + E$$

Alcohol is produced in yeast cells by a process very similar to lactic fermentation. Yeasts are single-celled plants belonging to a group called fungi (Fig 16.1). Just as muscle cells in animals require energy to enable them to contract, yeast cells require energy for growth and division. And just as muscle cells have to rely on lactic fermentation when oxygen is in short supply, so yeast cells have to rely on a similar process for obtaining energy in situations where there is little oxygen. This process is called **alcoholic fermentation**.

Alcoholic fermentation provides energy for yeast cells

In this process yeast cells break down glucose to release energy. Ethyl alcohol (a liquid chemical) and carbon dioxide (a gas) are produced as

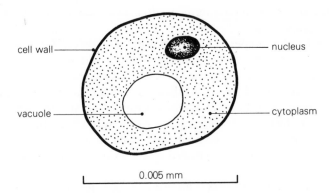

Fig 16.1 *A yeast cell. (Note the absence of chlorophyll; hence the cell's inability to manufacture its own sugar)*

waste products of the reaction. The equation for alcoholic fermentation can be summarised as follows:

$$\text{Glucose} \rightarrow \text{ethyl alcohol} + \text{carbon dioxide} + \text{energy}$$

In symbols:

$$C_6H_{12}O_6 \rightarrow 2\ C_2H_5OH + 2\ CO_2 + E$$

Equation for alcoholic fermentation

As is shown in the equation, ethyl alcohol consists of carbon, hydrogen and oxygen atoms. These atoms are linked together in a three-dimensional arrangement which can be represented thus:

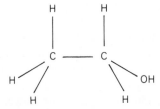

Fermentation and wine making

The process of alcoholic fermentation is used widely to produce a number of types of alcoholic drinks. The simplest procedure involving fermentation is wine making. The most widely consumed wines are made from grapes.

Wine is made from grapes

When the wine maker judges the grapes to be exactly ripe for picking, they are taken to the winery for crushing and fermenting. In the process of becoming wine the juice of the grapes undergoes fermentation. Ripe grapes have yeast in the form of a bloom or fuzz on the outside of their skins. While the juice is inside the unbroken skin of the grape it is protected from these yeasts. But once the skin is broken the yeasts are able to enter the juice and begin breaking down the glucose to ethyl alcohol and

Yeast fuzz is responsible for alcoholic fermentation in wine making carbon dioxide. Alcoholic fermentation thus occurs in the juices of the crushed grape cells.

When to pick grapes is a very important decision. Grapes contain a number of acids (mainly tartaric, acetic, malic and lactic acids), and during the course of ripening some of these acids are converted to glucose. If the grapes are picked too early, they will contain too much acid and not enough sugar, and the wine will be sour and lack alcohol, which is produced from the sugar. If the grapes are picked too late, they will contain too much sugar and not enough acid. Such wines will lack the quality which results from the presence of a certain proportion of the different acids.

The time at which grapes are picked is important, since grapes must contain the correct balance of acid and sugar

The fermentation process is allowed to occur for six days. To produce white wines, the skins of the grapes are removed before fermentation, so that the juice retains a pale yellow-green colour. In red wine production, the skins are left in the juice during fermentation, for it is from the skins that the wine obtains its colour. Also, the skins provide the wine with tannin, which helps to preserve it from bacterial contamination.

Skins are removed in fermenting white wines

After fermentation the wine is run into wooden casks, where it is allowed to stand for some time to acquire its distinctive flavour and character. After about eighteen months red wines are transferred to bottles, and it is desirable for them to stand for a number of years to attain full maturity. White wines may be transferred to bottles after seven to eight months. Once in the bottle, it may take only a few months for them to mature to a satisfactory drinkable flavour.

Longer bottling time is used for red wines

Beer making

Beers are normally produced by a single fermentation process but their production is more complicated than that of wines. The brewing of beer differs from wine making in two important ways: the raw materials from which the fermentable sugars are obtained are different and the alcohol content of the final product is significantly lower.

Malted barley is the principal raw material in beer production

The main raw material in the brewing of beer is malted barley, ie barley that has been allowed to partially germinate. The barley is soaked in water and then germinated under strictly controlled conditions of temperature and moisture content. During germination, enzymes (**amylases**) are produced that will be used, during brewing, to convert the starch in the grain to maltose. When this process has gone far enough it is stopped by drying the grain in a kiln. The barley is now said to have been malted and can be stored until required.

One of the main purposes of the malting process is to produce enzymes which convert starch to maltose later in brewing

The malted barley is crushed and mixed with water at a specific temperature. The mixture, called a **mash,** is allowed to stand for a certain period of time at a controlled temperature. During this period the enzymes produced during malting convert the starch in the grain to soluble maltose. Unlike starch, maltose can be fermented by yeast.

The sugar solution that forms is called **wort**. This is then drained off, liquid cane sugar or liquid glucose is added and the mixture boiled for one to one and a half hours. At this stage a hop extract is normally added to provide *some* of the typical flavour of beer. After boiling, the wort is cooled to a temperature suitable for fermentation (10°C). Until the yeast is added and fermentation begins, the liquid remains non-alcoholic.

Wet yeast is then added to start the fermentation, which results in the formation of ethyl alcohol and the release of carbon dioxide gas. The carbon dioxide is collected from the fermenter and compressed before being added to the beer just before final filtration (see later). Fermentation proceeds for about 100 to 120 hours, after which the beer is chilled to about 0°C. The bulk of the yeast which settles out is removed from the fermenter. The beer is then further chilled to about −1°C and passed to storage vessels. During this period a concentrate of the bitter flavoured components derived from hops is added to provide the characteristic bitter, hoppy flavour of beer.

> The starch in malted barley is converted to a fermentable sugar, maltose

> Fermentation is carried out by yeast

During storage, which may last from seven days to two or three months, material which could impair the appearance, flavour and shelf-life of the finished beer is allowed to precipitate and settle.

At the end of storage the beer is injected with carbon dioxide gas previously collected from the fermenters and filtered to provide a crystal-clear product. This beer is then packaged into bottles, cans or casks (in the case of draught beer).

> Hops provide the basic flavour of beer

Beer is pasteurised to prevent the growth of any remaining yeast cells or other micro-organisms that may be present in the beer after packaging. If the beer has been bottled or canned, it is pasteurised in the package. Draught beer is pasteurised before packaging.

Figure 16.2 summarises the wine-making and beer-brewing processes.

> Beer is pasteurised to ensure biological stability

Fortified wines and distillates

An alcoholic drink that is produced by a single fermentation process is known as a **ferment**. In any fermenting suspension, yeast is capable of producing alcohol until the alcohol reaches a concentration of 15 per cent by volume. At this concentration the alcohol which is a waste product of fermentation becomes toxic to yeast, kills its parent yeast cells and thus stops fermentation. Thus the maximum alcohol concentration in any ferment is 15 per cent.

> Ferments are produced by simple fermentation

In order to increase the alcohol content in wine, ethyl alcohol can be added. This process is known as fortification, and the resulting wines are known as fortified wines. When alcohol is added to a part-fermented wine, it immediately stops fermentation by killing the active yeasts. However, the alcohol has an additional effect of protecting the wine from many bacteria. Thus fortified wine may be left in a decanter or in

> Fortified wines are made by adding ethyl alcohol to a ferment

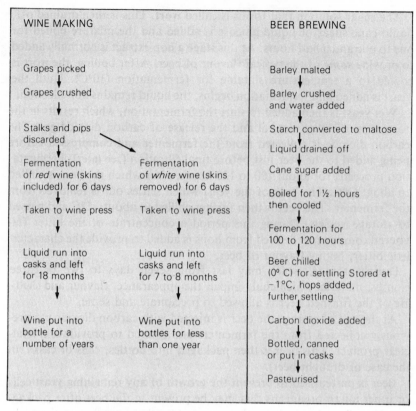

Fig 16.2   *Summary of wine-making and beer-brewing processes*

an open bottle, without going sour or turning to vinegar. Port, sherry and sweet dessert wines (such as muscat) are all examples of fortified wines.

Boiling point of ethyl alcohol is lower than that of water

Because ethyl alcohol has a lower boiling point than water, a fermented mixture can be heated to a temperature of 90°C, resulting in a vapour of ethyl alcohol being given off while the water and other solids are left behind. The vapour can then be condensed to re-form a liquid. The apparatus used in this procedure is shown in Fig 16.3. During this process a small amount of water may be carried across with the alcohol vapour, and thus on first distillation the alcohol content of the liquid product may be only about 40 per cent by volume. In order to create more and more concentrated solutions, the liquid product can be distilled further. In the end it is possible to reach ethyl alcohol concentrations of 85 per cent by volume. A drink prepared by the process of distillation is called a **distillate**. The method of producing a distillate is summarised in Fig 16.4.

A concentrated alcohol solution is prepared by distillation

A distillate is prepared by the distillation of a ferment

Depending on the raw material used to produce the original ferment, distillates of different tastes can be produced. For example, a grape ferment is used to make brandy, potatoes are used for vodka, and barley is

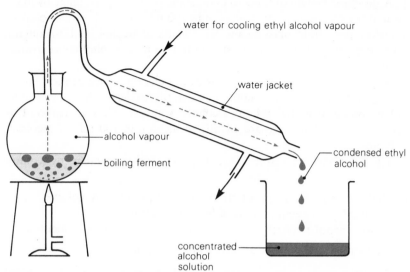

Fig 16.3 *Apparatus for distilling a fermented solution*

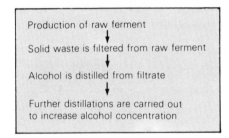

Fig 16.4 *Summary of the preparation of a distillate*

used for whisky and gin. In some cases the characteristic flavour of the distillate gained from the raw materials is supplemented by adding the juice of another fruit. For example, juniper berries are used in gin production.

Strength of drinks

Early in the history of wine-making people used to designate alcohol concentration by *proof* units. A solution described as 100 per cent proof in strength (written 100%) was an alcoholic solution which contained enough alcohol to allow gunpowder to burn slowly when saturated with the solution. Today these units are known as British proof strength units. The Americans have also developed a proof scale to measure alcohol concentration. One hundred per cent proof on the British scale is equivalent to approximately 88 per cent proof on the American scale.

British proof strength is one method of indicating alcohol concentration

American proof scale can also be used to indicate alcohol concentration

A far easier system of units to understand is that of percentage by mass, or number of grams of pure alcohol in 100 mL of the alcoholic solution. Fourteen per cent by mass means that 100 mL of alcohol solution contains 14 g of alcohol. This is the most common unit of alcohol concentration used today.

Another common method of indicating alcohol concentration is percentage by volume. As the name suggests, this indicates the volume of alcohol contained in 100 mL of alcoholic solution. Thus 14 per cent by volume means that there are 14 mL of alcohol in 100 mL of alcoholic solution.

The relationship between British proof and percentage by volume units is:

100 per cent British proof strength = 57 per cent by volume

A simpler connection is given by the equation:

British proof strength = $\frac{1}{4}$ × percentage by volume of alcohol

A number of strengths of different kinds of drinks are listed below:

Name of drink	Type of drink	Average % by mass	Average % by volume	Average British proof strength
Beer, ale	Ferment	4.25	5.35	9.36
Dinner wines: hock claret riesling moselle	Ferments	8.0	10.08	17.63
Fortified wines: sherry vermouth port muscat	Fortified	14.00	17.63	30.86
Sparkling wines	Ferments	10.00	12.60	22.04
Rum Brandy Gin Whisky	Distillates	33.47	42.15	73.77

Distillates clearly contain more alcohol than fortified wines, which contain more alcohol than simple ferments. A a result, we tend to drink smaller quantities of the more concentrated drinks. Figure 16.5 shows the volumes of the typical glasses used for the different types of drinks. Each of these glasses contains the same quantity of alcohol—8 grams.

Alcohol in the body's chemical network

Alcohol is rapidly absorbed from the stomach and small intestine. It can be detected in the blood within five minutes of being swallowed. From the digestive tract it passes into the bloodstream. It is carried first to the

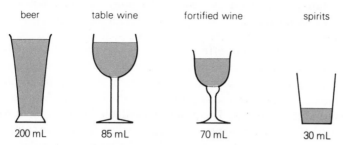

beer	table wine	fortified wine	spirits
200 mL	85 mL	70 mL	30 mL

Fig 16.5 *Volumes of the typical glasses used for different types of drinks (each glass contains approximately 8 grams of ethyl alcohol)*

liver, where the liver cells change it to another chemical called acetaldehyde. This is far more toxic than ethyl alcohol and must be rapidly converted by the liver cells into a chemical which is closely related to acetic acid:

Liver cells change ethyl alcohol to acetaldehyde and finally to acetic acid

$$\text{Ethyl alcohol} \rightarrow \text{acetaldehyde} \rightarrow \text{'acetic acid'}$$

Once in the form of 'acetic acid' it can then continue its path around the body, to be absorbed by the different body cells. Once in the body cells the 'acetic acid' can be fed into the chain of reactions which make up the process of cellular respiration. In these reactions, the 'acetic acid' is finally broken down to carbon dioxide and water, and energy is released in the form of ATP. In this way alcohol acts as an energy source for body cells.

Ethyl alcohol is an energy source

People who frequently consume large quantities of alcoholic drinks are, therefore, supplying their bodies with large quantities of energy or fuel in the form of ethyl alcohol. Because the supply of energy is greater than the body's demands for it, fats which are normally broken down to release energy accumulate in the fat storage areas of the body.

Excess alcohol may also increase the fatty acid concentration of the blood. This is mainly due to the increased absorption of fats through the gut wall caused by alcohol present in the gut. The higher concentrations of fat in the blood and the reduced use of fat for energy cause large amounts of fat to be laid down in the abdomen and other fat storage areas. This causes the 'pot-belly' which is common amongst heavy drinkers. Increased fat concentrations in the blood may also speed up the process of atherosclerosis (see Chapter 6).

The fatty acid concentration of the blood increases as a result of increased absorption of fatty acids in the gut

The liver is an organ that is particularly affected by alcohol. Not only does it accumulate fat because of the high concentrations of blood fat caused by the alcohol, but it is able to manufacture its own fatty acids from the 'acetic acid' chemical. This conversion is carried out by means of special enzymes.

The liver is able to manufacture fatty acids from alcohol

Extra fat accumulated in the liver tends to swamp the inner cytoplasm of the liver cells. As a result, liver cells produce fewer structural proteins and enzymes. Gradually such changes interfere more and more with the function of normal liver tissue. Instead of the liver carrying out its role as

Extra fat in the liver tends to swamp the cytoplasm of the liver cells, which in turn reduces the production of liver enzymes

an important centre of fat, protein and carbohydrate metabolism, large parts of it become merely a fat storehouse. Such a condition is known as fatty liver.

Excessive alcohol intake reduces blood glucose concentration

Another possible serious effect of an excessive intake of alcohol is the lowering of the concentration of glucose in the blood. This may happen when a person drinks alcohol at the expense of eating a balanced diet. Such a lack of glucose also causes glycogen, which acts as the body's glucose reserve, to disappear. The presence of alcohol also slows down the breakdown of amino acids into urea and a carbohydrate-like compound. This process is a valuable source of blood glucose, particularly when blood glucose levels become very low. Because this process is reduced, it is more difficult to raise blood glucose from its low level.

Low glucose concentrations in the blood may affect the brain

Very low blood glucose concentrations due to alcohol may have a harmful effect on the brain. Brain cells cannot use fat in cellular respiration. They must use glucose as the only fuel providing energy for growth, repair and other cellular processes such as active transport. Low glucose levels in the bloodstream supplying the brain may cause permanent cell damage and may interfere with the normal working of the brain.

Immediate effects of alcohol

The immediate effects of excessive alcohol intake are seen more in the central nervous system than in any other system in the body. Here, there is a great deal of evidence to show that alcohol depresses brain function rather than stimulates it. To the onlooker, the alcohol may appear to stimulate the drinker—abounding confidence, witty speech and jovial laughter can suddenly transform an ordinarily dull person. However, this apparent stimulation is seen because alcohol depresses, inhibits or 'switches off' the function of certain parts of the brain.

Alcohol is a depressant of the brain

Alcohol reduces the effect of the brain's control centres. As a result, people's emotions become less inhibited

The parts of the brain most affected by alcohol are those responsible for controlling our emotions and our behaviour amongst other people. Alcohol tends to stop these control areas from working. As a result, behaviour that is normally held in check is suddenly allowed a free rein.

Thus, a person whose blood alcohol concentration is raised may use abusive language that is quite uncharacteristic of him; he may become aggressive and even violent in situations that would not normally provoke him—his feelings of anger are now uncontrolled. Equally, a shy person, under the influence of alcohol, may lose his inhibitions and find conversation and social interaction much easier. Others, whose cheery manner normally covers an inner mood of depression, may become morose and despondent after a few drinks (Fig 16.6). All these effects are the result of the depressant action of alcohol on the control areas of the brain.

Very high blood alcohol concentrations depress parts of the brain that control speech, vision and balance

As the blood alcohol concentration reaches still higher levels, further areas of the brain are depressed or inhibited. Speech becomes slurred and then incoherent. Vision is affected in several ways:

     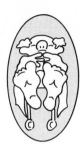

dry and decent   cheerful, judgment   erratic behaviour,   slurred speech,   oblivious,'falls
and behaviour   quarrelling   staggering,   in the gutter'
may be affected   double vision,
loss of memory

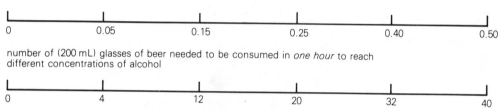

blood alcohol concentration (grams per 100 mL)

| 0 | 0.05 | 0.15 | 0.25 | 0.40 | 0.50 |

number of (200 mL) glasses of beer needed to be consumed in *one hour* to reach different concentrations of alcohol

| 0 | 4 | 12 | 20 | 32 | 40 |

Fig 16.6 *Changes in behaviour with increasing blood alcohol concentrations*

- It may become blurred.
- Gaze may become unsteady and a person may not be able to fix his vision on one particular point (often called nystagmus).
- The field of vision may be reduced. Normally our eyes can scan a field of more than 180° in front of us. Alcohol produces so-called telescopic or tunnel vision, in which our field of vision is greatly reduced, making us feel as if we are looking through a long tunnel.

High blood alcohol may also cause loss of balance, fumbling and staggering. Ultimately, if consumption of alcohol continues, the brain is depressed to the point where loss of consciousness occurs. By preventing further alcohol intake, this unconsciousness saves the person from death caused by acute alcohol poisoning.

Finally, immediate effects of alcohol are seen in changes in blood pressure and pulse rate. In moderate doses alcohol causes dilation of the small blood vessels in the skin. This allows more blood to reach the skin surface and gives the person a warm, flushed appearance. The larger volume available for accommodation of the blood after this widening of the blood vessels may cause a simultaneous small drop in blood pressure. However, often there is an increase in the heart rate at the same time, which causes an increase in blood pressure. Rises in blood pressure are often found in people who have drunk excessively over a long time.

Alcohol causes
- a dilation of small blood vessels
- increase in heart rate

Prolonged heavy alcohol consumption may result in an increase in blood pressure

Long-term excessive consumption of alcohol

The immediate effects of alcohol are those experienced by *anyone* who drinks in excess, on any occasion. As we shall soon see, these effects are enormously important, because they involve the drinker's behaviour, self-control and mood, as well as his ability to perform skilled tasks, such as driving a motor car. For some people, though, alcohol consumption introduces a whole range of other problems. These people are the heavy drinkers, who drink excessive quantities of alcohol over long periods of time. Long-term or chronic alcohol excess may lead to a variety of problems, which are summarised in Fig 16.7.

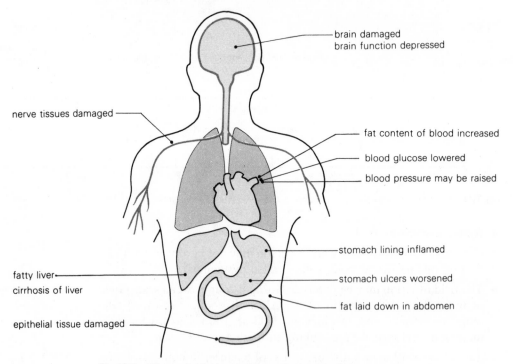

Fig 16.7 *Effects of drinking alcohol over a long period*

Physical effects

Consumed in excess, alcohol has been reported to have damaging effects on almost every organ and tissue. Some of these are direct effects of alcohol on the cells; others are probably indirect effects, the result of deficiencies of particular vitamins and foodstuffs. (Vitamin and other deficiencies are common in 'problem drinkers' and alcoholics, because such a large proportion of their diet is made up of alcohol.) The effects on the various body systems described below are the most common and important of the effects of alcohol on the body.

On the liver

We have already described how an alcohol excess may lead to the development of a fatty liver. At this stage, the liver's function is not severely disturbed and the condition can be reversed if alcohol is withheld. With further alcohol consumption, however, further damage may occur to the liver. Prolonged high concentration of alcohol in the blood may kill liver cells, which are then replaced by fibrous tissue. This is merely a coarse 'filling' of connective tissue. It is in no way able to produce the enzymes normally manufactured by liver cells, which are essential to body metabolism. If such replacement of liver cells by fibrous tissue continues, a condition called **cirrhosis of the liver** results.

Excessive alcohol intake often causes damage to the liver, which may result in cirrhosis of the liver

On the cardiovascular system

As we have already explained, excessive consumption of alcohol may cause an increase in the blood pressure, or hypertension (see Chapter 6). Also, as was explained earlier, consumption of large quantities of alcohol increases the concentration of fatty acids in the bloodstream. We saw in Chapter 6 that both these factors—high blood fat concentrations and hypertension—can lead to the development of atherosclerosis, a serious disease of the blood vessels. Excessive alcohol consumption therefore increases the risk of coronary heart disease or strokes. In addition, a consistently high intake of alcohol may cause damage to the heart muscle. This causes the heart's pumping efficiency to decrease and may finally lead to heart failure.

Excessive alcohol intake may cause hypertension, atherosclerosis, coronary heart disease and strokes

On the digestive system and nutrition

Other effects of alcohol are seen in the alimentary canal. Excessive alcohol consumption may damage epithelial tissues lining the inside of the stomach and small intestine. This may result in a reduced ability to absorb food materials and often leads to malnutrition. In addition, the stomach lining may become inflamed and stomach ulcers may become worse.

The direct damage to the epithelium of the small intestine may also interfere with the absorption of some of the vitamins which are important to the human body. The vitamins most affected are those belonging to the B group. Vitamin B deficiency leads to a number of disabilities: damage to peripheral nerves, decrease in the efficiency of sense organs, heart failure, muscular weakness and damage to the cerebellum resulting in loss of balance and a general sense of confusion. Many of these symptoms are frequently seen in chronic alcoholics.

Vitamin deficiencies in people who drink excessively can also be caused by two other factors. First, a large proportion of the diet of alcoholics is made up of alcohol, so that their diet is likely to be deficient in protein and vitamins. Second, in the metabolism of ethyl alcohol to carbon dioxide and water, a number of vitamins are necessary. The constant use of B vitamins in this role may result in any of the disabilities caused by vitamin B deficiency in the body.

Damage to the epithelium of the small intestine may
- *reduce the absorption of food materials*
- *cause inflammation and worsening of stomach ulcers*

Vitamin deficiencies in alcoholic people may be caused by
- *lack of vitamins in the diet*
- *use of B vitamins in metabolising alcohol*
- *damage to the intestinal epithelium preventing absorption of vitamins*

On the nervous system

Excessive alcohol intake over long periods causes physical damage to brain and nerve tissue

Excessive alcohol intake over long periods of time may affect the nervous system permanently, by causing physical damage to brain and nerve tissue. This may result in loss of feeling and muscle power and often causes lack of balance. Brain damage also causes loss of memory, of powers of concentration, and of the ability to think and reason. (Some of these effects on the nervous system may be the result of direct damage to the nerve cells by alcohol. Others are indirect effects—the result of deficiency of particular vitamins—as explained above.)

On the developing baby—foetal alcohol syndrome

Many doctors advise women not to drink alcohol at all during pregnancy

Among the most damaging effects of alcohol on the body are the effects of alcohol on the unborn baby (foetus). These effects have been recognised only in the past ten years, but they are now considered so dangerous that doctors advise women not to drink alcohol *at all* during pregnancy, and particularly not during the first three months.

The dangers to the baby are associated with the fact that alcohol in the mother's blood can cross to the baby's bloodstream via the placenta. Consistently high blood alcohol concentrations may interfere with cell division and differentiation in the embryo and lead to the development of the foetal alcohol syndrome. Babies suffering from the foetal alcohol syndrome are born with a number of defects: abnormalities of the face, brain damage and mental retardation, heart damage or deformities of the limbs. In addition, if the mother consumes quantities of alcohol that consistently lower her blood glucose concentration, the growing foetus will be deprived of its glucose requirements and fail to grow. Babies of mothers who drink heavily are frequently born prematurely, are of low birth weight, and fail to thrive after birth.

Alcohol in the blood of the foetus interferes with cell division and differentiation

Foetal alcohol syndrome:
• deformities of face
• brain damage
• mental retardation
• heart damage
• deformities of limbs
• premature births
• low birth weight

Finally, the effects of alcohol dependence can occur even before birth. Cases have been recorded in which babies born to alcoholic mothers suffer considerably shortly after birth as a result of the so-called withdrawal syndrome (see Chapter 14).

Social consequences of heavy drinking

The great majority of people who drink do so in moderation, in social situations. There are some people, however, who cannot control their drinking. Although they may have begun as moderate social drinkers, alcohol becomes a means of escaping from boredom, anxiety or feelings of inadequacy. Over a long period of time this excessive or heavy drinking may become uncontrolled. The drinker repeatedly drinks excessively, despite seeing the damage it causes to health, employment, personal relationships, family and so on. What is the change taking place in people that allows them to continue drinking, despite the damage which they see it causing to themselves? Uncontrolled drinkers have become physically dependent on alcohol.

People who become dependent on alcohol cannot control their drinking

We discussed drug dependence on a variety of mood-altering drugs in Chapter 14. Dependence on alcohol is far more common, in our society, than dependence on any of the other mood-altering drugs. The dependence is both physical and psychological. In other words, people who are dependent on alcohol suffer withdrawal symptoms when their supplies of alcohol are withheld. After overcoming this physical dependence, they continue to crave for alcohol because of their psychological dependence on the drug.

Dependence on alcohol may be both physical and psychological

It is widely believed that the alcoholic's withdrawal symptoms are even more severe than those of people dependent on narcotics or barbiturates. The withdrawal symptoms may begin within a few hours after the last drink. The person feels sick, becomes weak and anxious, and perspires freely. Later, cramps and vomiting may occur, and the person may begin to suffer from hallucinations. Heart rhythm may be upset and delirium may set in. People suffering from these symptoms require watchful and careful medical care. Having weathered the discomfort of withdrawal symptoms and physical dependence, psychological dependence remains. At this stage, counselling and group therapy is essential to help the person to resist the craving for alcohol.

Lack of alcohol causes withdrawal symptoms in physically dependent people:
• sickness
• anxiety
• weakness
• hallucinations
• heart failure
• delirium

People who are dependent on alcohol are commonly referred to as alcoholics. We may think of alcoholics as being homeless, destitute people, but in fact less than 3 per cent of alcoholics are in this category. There are alcoholics in every level of society, in most age groups and of both sexes. One estimate suggests that of all people who drink, one in twenty may become a problem drinker or an alcoholic. There are at least 300 000 people dependent on alcohol in Australia.

We have already described the health problems which arise from excessive drinking. Drinking may affect every area of the alcoholic's life, however, as well as the lives of his or her family and many others in the community. We shall see shortly how important alcohol is as a cause of injury and death in road accidents. Many crimes, too, are committed after the offender has been drinking excessively. Alcohol interferes with normal behaviour—the alcoholic may become unreliable or irresponsible—making it difficult for a person to 'hold down' a job. More than anything else, though, the alcoholic's family is seriously affected. Financial hardship caused by unemployment and/or excessive spending on alcohol, loss of friends, breakdown of marriages, and even violence and ill-treatment of children are the price some people have to pay for alcoholism.

Significance of blood alcohol concentration

As we have said, alcohol is absorbed very rapidly from the digestive tract into the bloodstream. It circulates in the blood until it is converted in the liver cells to its inactive products, acetaldehyde and the 'acetic acid'

Blood alcohol concentration (BAC) is a measure of alcohol consumed

chemical, and, finally, to carbon dioxide, water and energy. The concentration of alcohol in the blood is therefore a good measure of the amount of alcohol that has recently been consumed and the degree to which the body, and in particular the brain, is likely to be affected.

Surveys of large numbers of people have enabled standards of blood alcohol concentration (BAC) to be established. On the basis of these, acceptable units of blood alcohol concentration have been determined, above which it is considered unsafe to drive a car. The legal limit of BAC throughout most of Australia is 0.08 per cent (0.08 g in 100 mL of blood), although in many people driving skills may be impaired well below this blood alcohol concentration. A BAC of 0.05 per cent, which is the legal limit in the State of Victoria, can be reached by drinking four 200 mL glasses of beer within one hour.

The legal BAC limit is 0.08%, except in Victoria, where it is 0.05%

As we have noted, the body is able to use up alcohol, converting it to carbon dioxide, water and energy. The maximum rate at which the body is able to do this causes the BAC to drop by 0.02 per cent per hour. In most people, a more realistic figure for this is a drop of 0.015 per cent per hour. This is equivalent to one and a half 200 mL drinks per hour. This means that a person's BAC will continue to rise if he consumes more than one and a half 200 mL drinks per hour. As a rule, the BAC of a person who has consumed four 200 mL glasses of beer in one hour may remain above 0.05 per cent for thirty to sixty minutes without further drinking.

In most people alcohol is used at the rate of about one and a half 200 mL glasses of beer per hour

A person's BAC may remain above 0.05% for 30 to 60 minutes after drinking four 200 mL glasses of beer in one hour

Blood alcohol concentrations can be measured in two ways: directly or indirectly. In the direct method a sample of the patient's blood is analysed by chemical tests in the laboratory. This technique is often used in hospitals, to determine the BAC of road accident victims on arrival at the hospital.

BAC is measured directly by chemical tests in the laboratory

The indirect method of measurement is that used by the police force, and involves an instrument known as a breathalyser. In the lungs, alcohol circulating in the bloodstream diffuses out of the capillaries into the alveoli and then vaporises to form gaseous alcohol. The amount of alcohol vapour in the exhaled air is directly related to the concentration of alcohol in the blood circulating through the lungs. The breathalyser measures the amount of alcohol vapour in exhaled air. The machine is calibrated to convert this figure into a value for the concentration of alcohol in the blood.

BAC is measured indirectly by a breathalyser

Alcohol and driving

BAC is the most important factor contributing to road crashes

There is a great deal of evidence to show that *excessive use of alcohol is the most important single factor contributing to serious road crashes*. With regard to fatal crashes, Australian data gathered in 1975 show that about one half of drivers killed, about one quarter of pedestrians killed, about one quarter of motorcyclists killed and about one fifth of passengers killed had a BAC of 0.05 per cent or greater. This means that approximately one in three of the persons killed in road crashes in Australia in 1975 had a BAC above 0.05 per cent. (Figure 16.8 is a graph showing the number of car drivers of different ages killed on the roads in 1975, who had a BAC of more than 0.05 per cent.) Further research has shown that a driver with a BAC of 0.08 per cent is two to three times more likely to be involved in a crash than a sober driver, and with a BAC of 0.15 per cent, twenty to fifty times more likely to be involved in a crash.

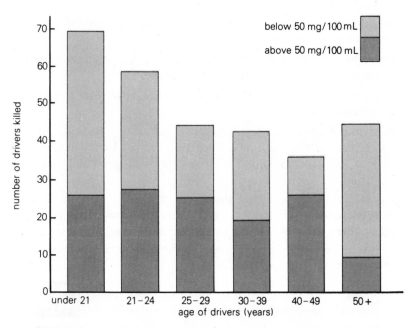

Fig 16.8 *Survey of blood alcohol concentrations of drivers killed in road crashes (Melbourne, 1975). The numbers of drivers killed in each age group, and the numbers with blood alcohol concentrations above 0.05 per cent, are shown*

What is the reason for this dramatic effect of alcohol? When people are learning to drive, they have to think about every action before carrying it out. For example, the process of changing gears involves a great deal of thought and anticipation before the learner actually makes the gear change; questions such as 'When do I depress the clutch pedal?', 'At what engine speed should I do this?', and 'Where should I direct the gear stick?' all have to be considered and answered before the actions are carried out. Even braking may take a split second of conscious thought before the foot is placed on the brake pedal and the pedal depressed.

Learner drivers have to think while operating controls

In contrast, experienced drivers carry out all these actions without consciously thinking about what they are doing—their responses to the situations they face on the roads are reflex actions. As the alcohol concentration in the driver's blood increases, the nerves that control these reflex actions are affected more and more. As a result, the driver's reflexes become slower and they reach a stage when they are not fast enough

Experienced drivers rely heavily on reflex actions

High blood alcohol concentrations slow a driver's reflexes

to cope with the technical demands of driving a car in today's traffic conditions.

Not only does alcohol affect the driver's reflexes, but it also affects a number of other abilities:

- Judgment is affected, so that a person's ability to judge distance, speed or angle becomes distorted.

- Coordination of hands, arms, legs, head and eyes is often impaired, so that the driver becomes clumsy and incompetent in operating the car's controls and guiding it on a safe path.

- Alertness or watchfulness is dulled, and the driver may fail to notice objects outside the car.

- Vision becomes blurred and unsteady. Often tunnel vision occurs (that is, the field of vision is reduced—see earlier).

- Reaction time increases—the driver takes longer to react to anything unexpected.

- Behaviour becomes careless, impulsive and erratic. Because the caution centres of the brain have been switched off by the alcohol, behaviour tends to run wild. The driver may well speed and take risks (Fig 16.9).

It is important to note that the effect of alcohol on each of these abilities is exponential. That is, when the concentration of alcohol in the blood doubles, the effect on the driver's abilities may more than triple.

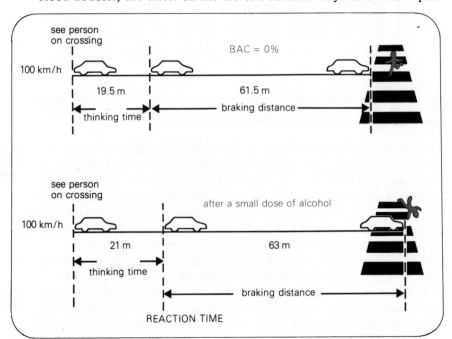

Fig 16.9 *Alcohol and driving*

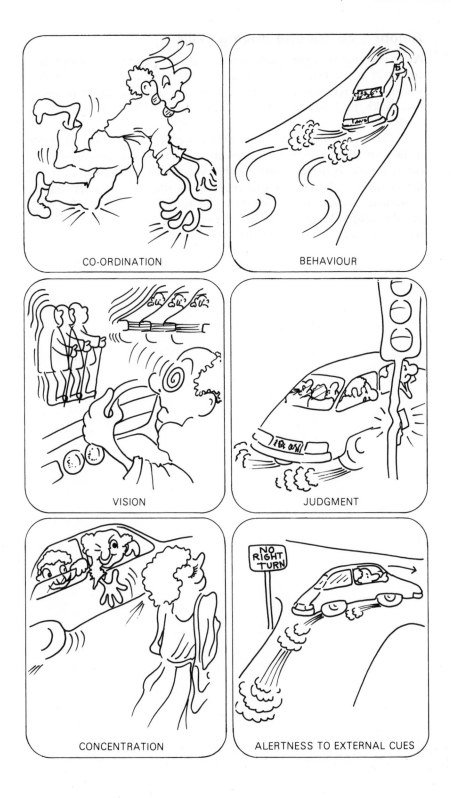

CO-ORDINATION

BEHAVIOUR

VISION

JUDGMENT

CONCENTRATION

ALERTNESS TO EXTERNAL CUES

Alcohol, coffee and driving skills

After consuming large quantities of alcohol, people commonly drink coffee in an attempt to sober up before driving. Experiments have shown, however, that caffeine, the stimulant drug ingredient of coffee, may make the drinking driver even *more* dangerous on the road. Why is this?

Caffeine makes a driver less drowsy, but makes him unaware of his loss of skill. In this condition he is an extremely dangerous person on the road

The effect of caffeine is to make the driver feel less drowsy. However, it does nothing to improve judgment, coordinaton, alertness, vision or reaction time. A driver may *feel* sober and normal after a cup of coffee, but in fact his abilities are still impaired by the alcohol he has recently consumed. Because the driver now fails to recognise his condition, his guard is dropped and he becomes an even more dangerous driver than he would have been without the drink of coffee.

Chapter 17

Reproduction—perpetuation of life

The need for specialised structures

As with all mammals, the method of producing young in humans occurs by sexual reproduction. This involves the joining or fusion of two sex cells or **gametes** in a process known as **fertilisation**. The male gamete is known as a **sperm** and the female gamete as an egg or **ovum**. Each gamete contains a certain amount of DNA from the respective parent. You will recall from Chapter 5 that a normal human body cell possesses 46, or 23 pairs, of chromosomes, so that when fusion occurs, the resulting **zygote** (the first cell of the young individual) must posses the correct 46, or 23 pairs, of chromosomes.

You will also recall from Chapter 5 that each pair of chromosomes controls a different set of body characteristics. After fertilisation, each characteristic of the zygote is controlled by one pair of chromosomes. One chromosome of each pair has come from the father, and one from the mother. Later, all the body cells of the new young individual have the same chromosome make-up as the original zygote cell.

When normal body cells divide, the two daughter cells contain the same number of chromosomes as the parent cell. That is, daughter cells will contain 46 chromosomes. Because sex cells, such as a sperm and an ovum, need to have only 23 chromosomes, the body requires a particular area where cells can divide in a special way to produce half the normal chromosome number. These areas are the **primary sex organs**.

Once the sex cells have been produced by the male and female, there must be a method for ensuring that sperm can travel safely from the male to the female, where fusion of the two gametes occurs. Furthermore, the zygote produced in the female's body must be nurtured carefully to the stage at which it has developed sufficiently (in terms of size and complete differentiation of organ tissues) to be released from its mother and take up a more independent life in the outside world. Once again the physical make-up of both male and female must meet these requirements. Structures concerned with these functions are known as the **secondary sex organs**.

Primary sex organs

Male

The primary sex organs in the male are the **testes** or **testicles** (Fig 17.1a and 17.1b), which produce the male sex cells called sperm. The two testes develop in the abdominal cavity of the foetus (Chapter 5). About two months before birth they descend through an opening in the pelvis into the **scrotum**, a sac of skin which hangs loosely between the legs (Fig 17.2). The testes are egg-shaped bodies and can differ in size from man to man. Since the scrotum is outside the body, its temperature is slightly

Sexual reproduction involves joining two sex cells called gametes

Male gametes—sperm Female gametes—ovum

A human zygote has 23 pairs of chromosomes

In each chromosome pair, one chromosome comes from the father and one from the mother

Gametes must contain half the number of chromosomes present in a body cell

The primary sex organs are special regions in the body where cells with half the normal chromosome number are produced

Secondary sex organs
• ensure safe travel of sperm from male to female
• provide the environment for the zygote to develop

The primary sex organs of the male are the testes

The testes are held in a sac called the scrotum

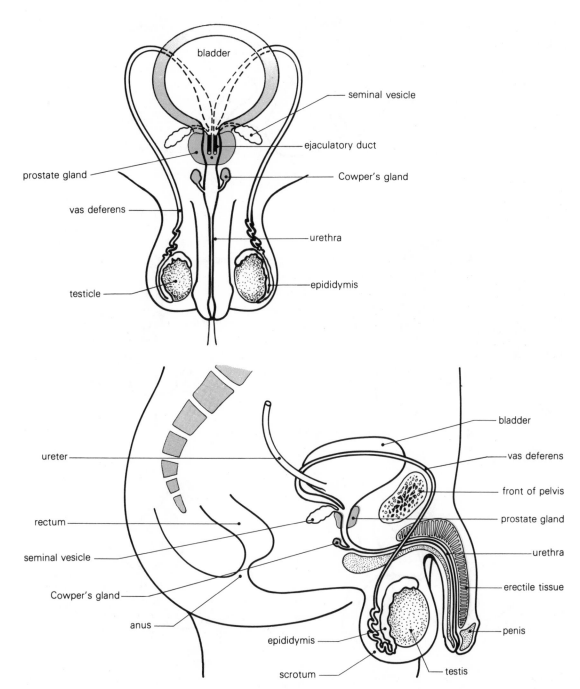

Fig 17.1 *Male reproductive system*
(a) Frontal view
(b) Side view

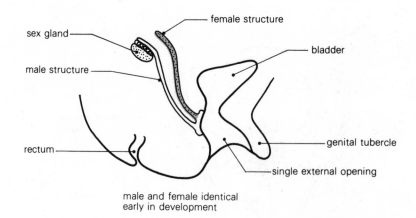

sex gland

male structure

rectum

female structure

bladder

genital tubercle

single external opening

male and female identical
early in development

MALE

female remnants

sex gland (testis)

vas deferens
(male structure)

female remnants

scrotal swelling begins to form

direction of
movement
of testis

penis

groove about
to form
urethra

FEMALE

uterine tube

sex gland
(ovary)

uterus
(female structure)

male remnants

clitoris

at 2–3 months of pregnancy

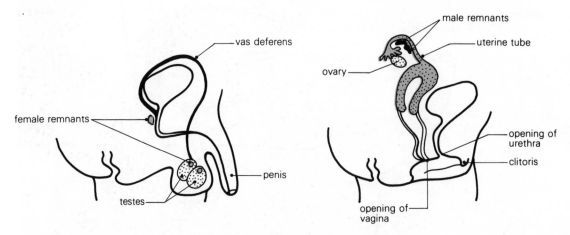

vas deferens

female remnants

testes

penis

male remnants

uterine tube

ovary

opening of
urethra

clitoris

opening of
vagina

at 3–4 months of pregnancy

Fig 17.2   *Development of the reproductive organs*

lower than the rest of the body. This lower temperature is necessary for the production of sperm. The testes are supported by muscle tissue which can contract and relax. In cold weather this tissue contracts, drawing the testes nearer to the warm body. In hot weather the muscles relax, thereby lowering the testes and maintaining the lower testicular temperature.

The temperature of the testes is lower than that of the rest of the body

The testes consist of a mass of sperm-producing tubes. These are called the **seminiferous tubules,** and it is here that the sperm are produced (Figs 17.3 and 17.4a). The process of sperm production is called **spermatogenesis.** In this process 'parent' sperm cells (Fig 17.4c) divide by the method known as **meiosis.** Meiosis is a special form of cell division which, in humans, takes place only in the testes and ovaries. When the parent sperm cells divide in meiosis, they give rise to cells with half the

Sperm are produced in the seminiferous tubules

Sperm are produced by meiosis and contain 23 chromosomes

Fig 17.3 *Section through a seminiferous tubule (scanning electron micrograph). (sfc = sperm-forming cells, sp = sperm)*

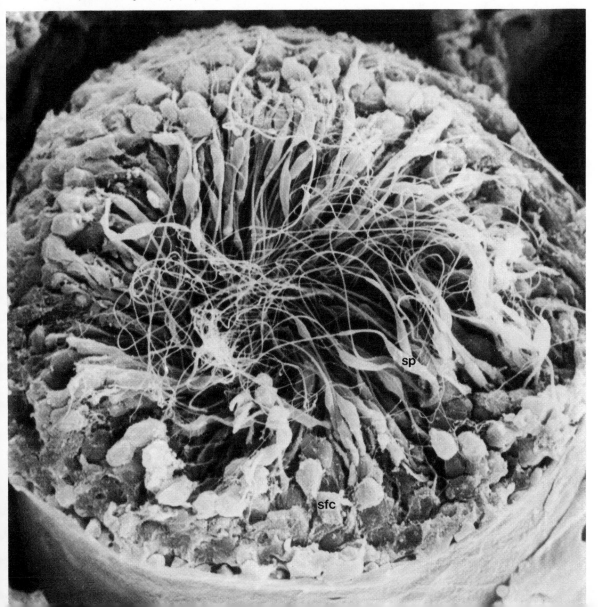

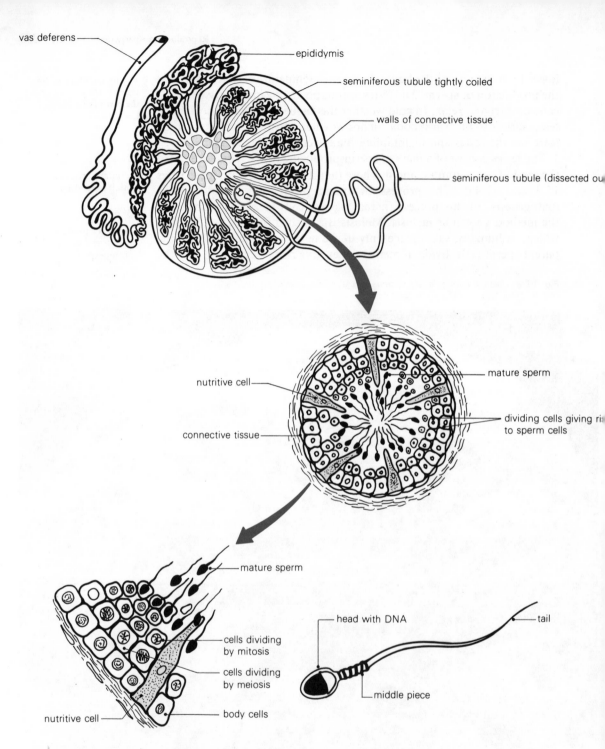

vas deferens

epididymis

seminiferous tubule tightly coiled

walls of connective tissue

seminiferous tubule (dissected ou

nutritive cell

connective tissue

mature sperm

dividing cells giving ri
to sperm cells

mature sperm

cells dividing
by mitosis

cells dividing
by meiosis

body cells

nutritive cell

head with DNA

tail

middle piece

Fig 17.4 *The testis*
(a) Longitudinal section
(b) Cross-section of a seminiferous tubule
(c) Dividing cells in the seminiferous tubule
(d) A mature human sperm

amount of DNA found in normal body cells. These daughter cells, which contain 23 single chromosomes, divide again by **mitosis** and develop into sperm (Figs 17.4b and 17.4c). Each sperm consists of a nucleus surrounded by a little cytoplasm which extends to form a long tail (Fig 17.4d). Although sperm in the seminiferous tubules appear to be mature, they are not yet motile.

A sexually mature male can produce sperm continuously. This is possible because the parent or sperm-producing cells in the testes can continue to divide mitotically throughout a man's life. New parent cells are thus produced continuously to replace those developing into sperm.

Between the seminiferous tubules are cells called **interstitial cells**. These produce the hormone **testosterone**, which is responsible for the development of sperm and the development of the secondary sex organs and characteristics of the male (see p 364).

Between the seminiferous tubules are interstitial cells, which produce testosterone. Testosterone is responsible for the male's secondary sex organs and characteristics

Female

The primary sex organs of the female are the **ovaries** (Figs 17.5a and 17.5b). The ovaries develop in the abdominal cavity as a pair, and in fact develop from the same group of cells as do the testes in the male (refer to Fig 17.2). In this respect there is great similarity between the male and female foetus. However, as development proceeds, the ovaries remain inside the abdominal cavity, whilst the testes descend into the scrotum.

The female primary sex organs are the ovaries

The ovaries are pinkish-grey bodies, each roughly the size, shape and weight of an almond. They consist of connective tissue, blood vessels and potential eggs. At birth the two ovaries of the female infant contain nearly 500 000 cells which are capable of developing into mature ova. In the female, in contrast to the male, this number of potential eggs does not increase after birth; that is to say, no further mitotic divisions of parent egg cells occur. Of these 500 000 cells, only about 400 will actually become mature ova.

The ovaries contain potential egg cells

Between the ages of 10 and 17 years some of the potential eggs begin to grow. The cells around them divide rapidly and increasing numbers of blood vessels develop close to them. The layers of dividing cells which surround the growing ovum develop to enclose a small volume of fluid. This fluid partly encloses the ovum, which also becomes supported by a layer of nutrition-providing cells. The whole sac-like structure which encloses the ovum is called an **ovarian (Graafian) follicle** (Fig 17.6a).

A developing ovum is surrounded by a layer of dividing cells which enclose some fluid. This whole structure is an ovarian follicle

If we were able to look at the ovary of an adult woman, we would see follicles at different stages of development (Fig 17.6b). Some of the follicles would be just beginning to grow, and some would be approaching the time to burst open and release a fully mature ovum. Usually only one follicle becomes fully mature each month and releases an ovum. This process is called **ovulation**. Once this happens, the remaining follicles and their ova begin to disappear. A new set of follicles then begins to grow, which will release another mature ovum a month later.

Ovulation—release of an ovum from a mature follicle

One follicle becomes fully mature each month and releases an ovum

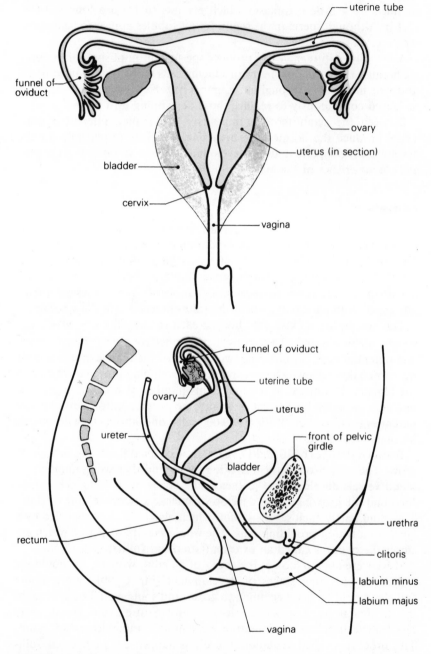

Fig 17.5 *Female reproductive system*
(a) Frontal view
(b) Side view

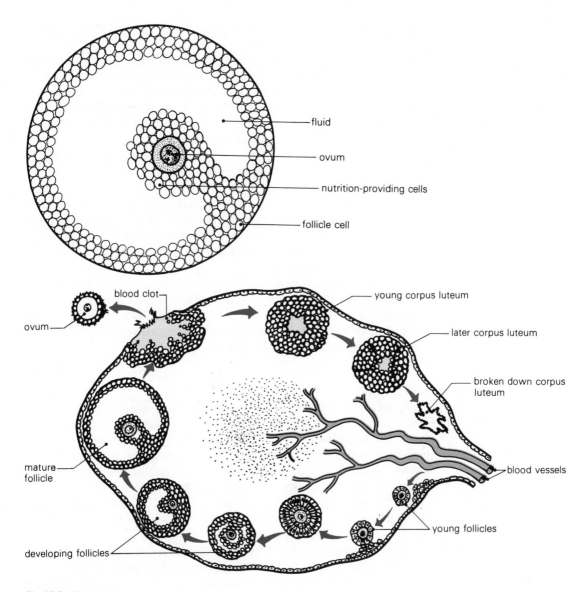

Fig 17.6   *The ovary*
(a) A Graafian follicle
(b) Section through an ovary, showing Graafian follicles at different stages of development

Secondary sex organs and the transport of sex cells

Male

From the seminiferous tubules, sperm pass into the **epididymis**. This is a coiled tube attached to the upper part of each testis (see Fig 17.4a). Here sperm remain for as long as six weeks while the final stages of development occur. When fully mature sperm leave the epididymis, they are able to propel themselves through fluid by means of the whip-like action of their tails.

From the end of the epididymis the sperm continue into another tube known as the **vas deferens**. The vas deferens leads up into the body cavity to the top of the **prostate gland**. This gland is firm, partly muscular and partly gland-like, about the size of a walnut. It is situated immediately below the bladder. The prostate gland produces the greater proportion of the sperm-carrying fluid called **seminal fluid**.

Inside the prostate gland each vas deferens is joined by a duct from the **seminal vesicle**. These glands secrete a fluid which activates, provides nutrition for, and helps to transport sperm.

Where the duct from the seminal vesicle joins the vas deferens, it forms the **ejaculatory duct**. This duct passes through the prostate gland and both ejaculatory ducts open into the single **urethra**. You will recall from Chapter 12 that the urethra carries urine from the bladder, through the penis, to the outside.

On each side of the urethra, just below the prostate gland, are two pea-sized bodies, the **Cowper's glands**. During sexual excitement these glands produce a few drops of fluid which lubricate the male's urethra for the passage of sperm. The final mixture of sperm and seminal fluid which passes into the urethra is called **semen**.

Female

When an ovum bursts from an ovarian follicle in one of the ovaries, it is transferred to one of the two **uterine tubes**. (The uterine tubes are often called the **fallopian tubes**.) These are tubes measuring about 10 cm in length, extending from the region of the ovaries to the upper part of the **uterus**. An ovum is usually transferred to the uterine tube nearest to its 'parent' ovary. It is drawn into the uterine tube by the wafting action of cilia. Cilia are hairy projections on the surfaces of cells at the entrance of the uterine tube (Fig 17.7). Remember that an ovum, unlike a sperm, has no method of self-locomotion.

The ovum's continued movement up the uterine tube is brought about by peristaltic activity within the uterine tube. The beating of cilia inside the tube also assists movement. Once the ovum has completed the journey down the uterine tube, it enters the upper portion of the uterus.

Transfer of sex cells from male to female

Both sexes are equipped with a secondary sex organ to enable the transfer of sperm from the man to the woman. In the case of the male this organ is the **penis**, while in the female it is the **vagina**.

The shaft of the penis contains the urethra and a number of layers of erectile tissue. At the end of the penis is an area which is extremely sensitive to touch, called the **glans penis**. This is covered by a loose flap of

---

Sperm pass from seminiferous tubules
↓
epididymis
↓
vas deferens
↓   ⤏ seminal vesicle
ejaculatory duct
↓   ⤏ prostate gland
urethra
↓   ⤏ Cowper's gland

Seminal fluid 'activates', provides nutrition for and helps to transport sperm

Ova travel from the ovary into the uterine tubes (fallopian tubes)

The ovum is moved up the uterine tube by peristalsis and by the beating of cilia

The penis transfers sperm into the vagina

The penis contains erectile tissue

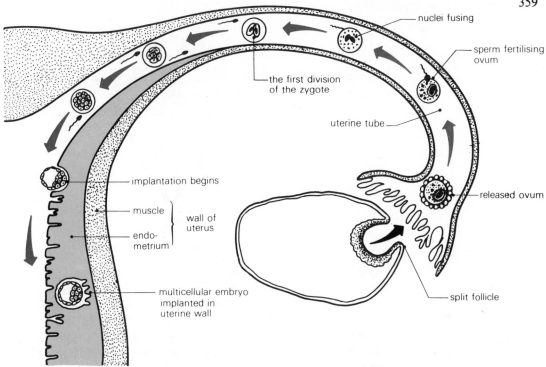

Fig 17.7 *A zygote develops as it passes to the uterus*

unattached skin called the **foreskin** (Fig 17.8). In the operation of circumcision, the foreskin is surgically removed.

During sexual excitement changes in blood flow through the small arteries and veins of the penis cause the spaces within the erectile tissue to become filled with blood under pressure. The blood thus trapped causes the penis to enlarge and stiffen. The penis can then be placed into the vagina of the female.

The vagina is a muscular tube into which the penis can fit during sexual intercourse. It leads from the base of the uterus to an opening between the legs (Figs 17.5a and 17.9). The opening of the vagina is partially closed by a flap of tissue called the **hymen**. This is often broken

The opening of the vagina is covered by the hymen

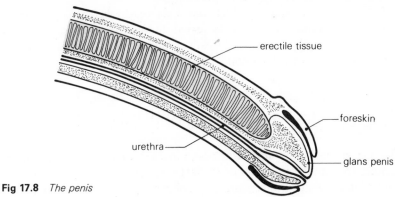

Fig 17.8 *The penis*

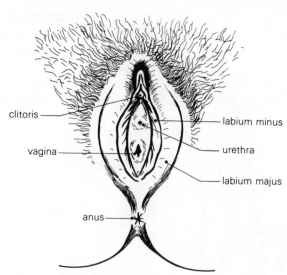

clitoris

vagina

labium minus

urethra

labium majus

anus

Fig 17.9 *External genitalia of the female*

when sexual intercourse first takes place. It may also be broken by the insertion of a vaginal tampon during a menstrual period (p 361).

Around the vaginal opening are two lips or folds of tissues known as the **labia**. These labia enclose an area called the **vestibule** into which the urethra also runs. At the upper end of the vestibule, covered by small lips, is a small round elongated organ known as the **clitoris**. Like the penis, this has a shaft and a gláns; the shaft contains erectile tissue, and the glans is highly sensitive, owing to the presence of a large number of nerve endings. Refer back to Figs 17.2a and 17.2b, which show the close relationship between the male penis and the female clitoris, from the point of view of their development.

The clitoris contains erectile tissue like the penis

Once the penis is inside the vagina, further stimulation causes **ejaculation**. In this stage of sperm transfer, muscular contractions around the urethra in the erect penis cause accumulated sperm-containing semen to be forced out of the penis and into the vagina. It is at this point that the peak of male sexual enjoyment is experienced: this is known as **orgasm**. After orgasm, blood is allowed to flow from the spaces in the erectile tissue, and the penis returns to its normal size.

Muscular contractions force semen and sperm from the penis. This is known as ejaculation

This act of intimacy in which the male places his penis inside the vagina of the female is known as sexual intercourse. During this act, a woman may equally experience great sexual enjoyment. The peak of the female's experience is also known as orgasm.

The uterus—a place for growth and development

The uterus–a place for growth and development– is a muscular organ located in the pelvic cavity

The uterus is a hollow muscular organ located within the pelvic cavity, between the bladder in front and the large intestine at the back. It is pear-shaped and has thick muscular walls, which enclose a triangular cavity. This cavity is normally narrow and slit-like until pregnancy occurs.

For descriptive purposes the uterus is divided into an upper part or body and a lower part or **cervix**. (The word *cervix* means neck and refers to the neck of the uterus in this case.) The cavity of the uterus is narrowest in the region of the cervix and widest in the middle. At the top of the uterus the cavity is continuous with the two uterine tubes.

The uterine wall is made of three layers. The outer one is a thin covering membrane. The middle layer makes up the bulk of the uterine wall and consists of layers of smooth muscle. During pregnancy the outer membrane layer and muscular middle layer allow the uterus to stretch to house the growing foetus.

The uterine wall has three layers:
- an outer covering membrane
- a middle smooth muscle layer
- an inner layer rich in glands and blood vessels—the endometrium

The inner layer is known as the **endometrium**. This is a layer of epithelial and connective tissue which lines the uterine cavity and is rich in glands and blood vessels. Each month the endometrium becomes gradually thicker. This occurs as the uterus prepares to receive a fertilised ovum, which would attach and embed itself in the uterine wall. If fertilisation does not occur during the monthly cycle, much of the endometrium breaks down, releasing blood, fluids, mucous material and fragments of uterine lining. This is known as **menstruation**.

Control mechanisms in gamete production

The production of sex cells in both male and female occurs under the control of the endocrine system. You will recall (from Chapter 13) that this system is responsible for producing chemical messengers called hormones. Hormones are transported throughout the body in the bloodstream and produce their effects some distances from their sites of production.

The endocrine system controls sex cell production

In the male the anterior pituitary gland at the base of the brain secretes a hormone called the **luteinising hormone** (LH). This hormone travels in the bloodstream to the testes, where it causes the interstitial cells to produce another hormone, testosterone. Testosterone is responsible for the proper maturation of sperm produced in the seminiferous tubules. Very little testosterone is secreted before puberty, which occurs between the ages of 10 and 15 years (see the next section). Once its secretion begins, it is produced continuously throughout the man's life. This enables a man to produce sperm continuously from this time.

Male:
anterior pituitary
↓
luteinising hormone
↓
interstitial cells
↓
testosterone

The female system is far more complex and operates on a monthly cycle. In this cycle one ovum is released from one of the two ovaries approximately every 28 days, although this time differs for different women.

Female:
one ovum is released every 28 days:

anterior pituitary
↓
follicle-stimulating hormone
↓
development of ovarian follicle
↓
follicle secretes oestrogen
↓
causes anterior pituitary to secrete luteinising hormone
↓
causes release of ovum from ovary

The cycle begins when the anterior pituitary secretes a hormone called the **follicle-stimulating hormone**, or **FSH**. This hormone has two effects: it causes a number of ovarian follicles to develop in the ovary, and it stimulates the follicles to secrete another hormone called **oestrogen**. The effect of oestrogen is to stimulate the repair and thickening of the endometrium after the previous menstrual period.

Oestrogen has another important effect. As its concentration builds up in the blood, it finally reaches a level at which it acts on the anterior pituitary, causing this endocrine gland to release another hormone called luteinising hormone (LH). This hormone circulates in the bloodstream and is carried to the ovary, where it causes the most mature follicle to burst and release an ovum. This event occurs about 14 days after the beginning of the previous menstrual period. This sequence of events is summarised in Fig 17.10.

An empty follicle forms a corpus luteum

Once the ovum has burst from the follicle, the now empty follicle collapses and the luteinising hormone causes further changes in its structure. At the same time, its colour changes from white to yellow. The follicle has now changed into a **corpus luteum** (Latin for 'yellow body').

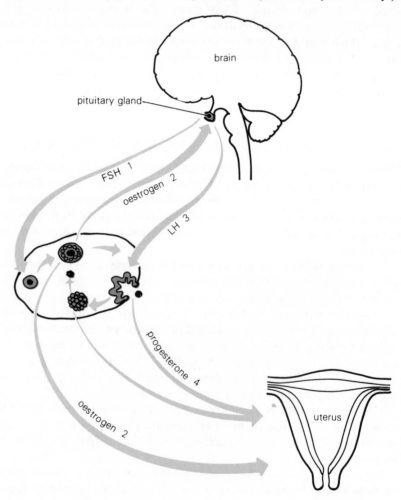

Fig 17.10 *Hormones in the female sex cycle*

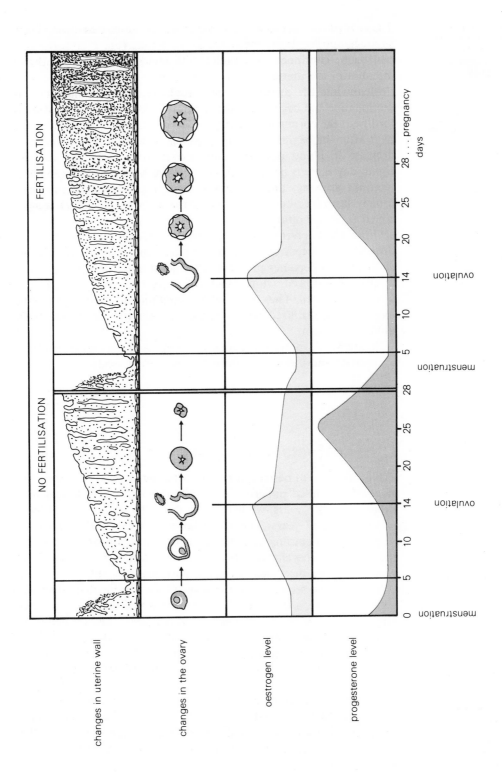

Fig 17.11 *Hormonal and uterine changes during the female reproductive cycle*

Cells of the corpus luteum produce oestrogen and progesterone. Both oestrogen and progesterone repair and build up the endometrium

The cells of the corpus luteum continue to produce oestrogen. They also produce another hormone called **progesterone** (Fig 17.10), which, with oestrogen, continues to stimulate the buildup (growth) of the endometrium of the uterus.

Meanwhile the ovum has been caught in the finger-like ends of the uterine tube and begins its journey towards the uterus. If the ovum is not fertilised, the corpus luteum begins to waste away. This occurs about 22 days after the beginning of the previous menstrual period and causes a decrease in blood oestrogen and progesterone levels. By the twenty-eighth day there is not enough of these two hormones to keep the endometrium growing, and it breaks down. The resulting menstrual flow usually lasts for about five days, at the end of which FSH is again secreted from the pituitary.

If the released ovum is not fertilised, the corpus luteum wastes away
↓
oestrogen and progesterone levels fall
↓
endometrium breaks down

If ovum is fertilised
↓
the corpus luteum continues to produce oestrogen and progesterone
↓
the endometrium continues to build up

If the ovum is fertilised, the corpus luteum continues to grow and produce higher concentrations of progesterone in the blood. In this case the endometrium becomes progressively thicker and more spongy, ready to receive the fertilised ovum, which will implant itself in the surface layers of the uterus wall. The corpus luteum continues to produce progesterone long after the fertilised ovum is implanted, and the uterine wall thus continues to thicken.

Figure 17.11 shows the changing hormone levels and their effects on the ovaries and uterus in different phases of the cycle.

Other effects of testosterone and oestrogen

Puberty is due to a marked increase in testosterone and oestrogen

The production of oestrogen and testosterone increases dramatically at a stage of life called **puberty**. In females this may occur at any time between 11 and 16 years, while in males it usually occurs slightly later, between 13 and 17 years. The rise in hormone levels at this time of life is responsible for causing the development of the **secondary sex characteristics**. Important psychological changes also take place in both sexes at this time. These are discussed in the last part of this chapter.

At puberty, the secondary sex characteristics develop

Psychological changes also take place

What are the secondary sex characteristics? In the male they include: growth of hair on the face, abdomen, groin and under the armpits; enlargement of the penis; enlargement of the larynx and deepening of the voice; and the growth of muscle and bone to give the typical masculine body shape. In the female, oestrogen promotes the development of the breasts, the growth of hair under the armpits and in the groin, and changes in the shape of the hip bones (pelvis).

Growth of secondary sex organs occurs at puberty

In both males and females the first gametes are produced

At puberty, increased production of oestrogen and testosterone causes the growth of the secondary sex organs (Fig 17.12). In addition, in the female the monthly menstrual periods begin, while in the male the first emission of semen may occur. In both males and females, the first gametes are produced.

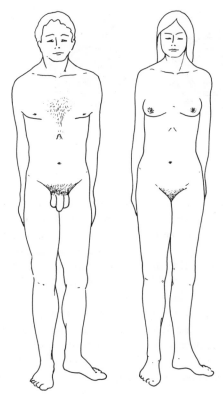

Male
- Hair grows on face, chest, in groin and armpits
- Larynx enlarges and voice deepens
- Muscles and bones grow, shape of body changes
- Secondary sex organs:
  Penis, scrotum, prostate etc enlarge
- Sperm formation begins
- Psychological changes:
  Feelings and sexual drives associated with adulthood begin to develop

Female
- Hair grows in groin and armpits
- Pelvis becomes broader, fat deposited on hips and thighs to give typical feminine contours
- Breasts develop
- Secondary sex organs:
  Uterine tubes, uterus and vagina enlarge
  Uterine and vaginal lining thicken
- Ovulation and menstruation begin
- Psychological changes:
  Feelings and sexual drives associated with adulthood begin to develop

Fig 17.12 *Changes at puberty*

Fertilisation and early development

When ejaculation occurs during sexual intercourse, between 200 and 500 million sperm are deposited in the vagina. The acidity of the vagina is not favourable for the survival of sperm, and many die there. The remaining cells move towards the cervix and only about 10 000 may enter the canal of the cervix. Further death of sperm in the cervix means that only a few thousand enter the uterus. A few hundred may be all that finally complete the journey to the far ends of the uterine tubes.

> Only a small proportion of ejaculated sperm reaches the ends of the uterine tubes

Fertilisation will usually take place in the ends of the uterine tubes nearest to the ovaries. It is thought that by the time the ovum has reached the section of a uterine tube nearest the uterus, it has lost the ability to become fertilised. The ovum is thought to be capable of fertilisation up to 48 hours after its release from the ovary. Sperm deposited in the vagina have a maximum life expectancy of about 72 hours.

> Fertilisation takes place in the ends of the uterine tubes

Fertilisation, once thought to be a simple matter of a sperm joining with an egg, is in fact a complex series of events. When one sperm head penetrates the jelly coat and double membrane of the egg, further sperm are prevented from fertilising the same ovum. This is caused by the immediate thickening of the outer membrane (Fig 17.13).

> Only one sperm is allowed to fertilise an ovum

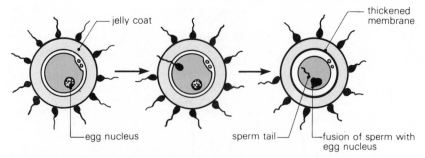

Fig 17.13   *The events of fertilisation*

After fertilisation, the 23 chromosomes of the sperm join with the 23 chromosomes of the ovum to produce a total of 46. Two of these chromosomes are known as the **sex chromosomes**. These determine whether the young individual is male or female. The ovum always contains one X chromosome. A sperm can contain either an X or a Y chromosome. If an X sperm joins with the X ovum, the child will be female (XX). If a Y sperm joins with the X ovum, the child will be male (XY).

The ovum always contains one X chromosome

A sperm can contain either an X or a Y chromosome

Male   = XY
Female = XX

Once fertilised, the ovum embarks on the 3 to 4 day journey through the remainder of the uterine tube to the uterus. Thirty-six hours after fertilisation the single zygote cell has become two cells. Two days later these cells have each divided twice more to give a microscopic ball of 8 cells. In this condition the egg completes its passage through the uterine tube and enters the uterus.

Four days after fertilisation the egg is a cluster of 32 or 64 cells, which then begin to divide more rapidly. This stage corresponds to about day 19 or 20 of the menstrual cycle. This cluster of cells remains unattached for two days.

The uterine wall at this stage is under the influence of the hormone progesterone and is becoming spongy and supplied with numerous small blood vessels. By the twelfth day after fertilisation the ball of cells has further increased in size and is now called an embryo. At this stage the embryo becomes completely buried in the endometrium. This is called **implantation**. (Refer again to Fig 17.7.)

Implantation—the embryo becomes embedded in the endometrium

Growth of the foetus

As the embryo grows, it becomes surrounded by a thin transparent membrane, the **amniotic sac**, containing fluid known as **amniotic fluid**. The embryo becomes suspended within the liquid by its body stalk, which attaches the embryo to the uterine wall.

The embryo becomes surrounded by an amniotic sac containing amniotic fluid

By the sixth week the body stalk has become longer and thicker and is called an **umbilical cord**. This cord contains the major veins and arteries that link the embryo and the mother.

The umbilical cord contains the major blood vessels linking the embryo and mother

A **placenta** has also begun to develop at the end of the umbilical cord. This is a disc of tissue with finger-like projections which clings close to the uterine wall. It is through the placenta that exchange of food, oxygen and wastes takes place between the embryo's blood and the mother's blood. The embryo absorbs glucose, amino acids, mineral salts, vitamins and oxygen into its bloodstream from the mother's blood. Carbon dioxide and urea are in turn absorbed by the mother's blood and removed through her excretory systems. Figure 17.14 shows the relationship between the embryo's blood supply and that of the mother.

Exchange of food, oxygen and wastes takes place through the placenta

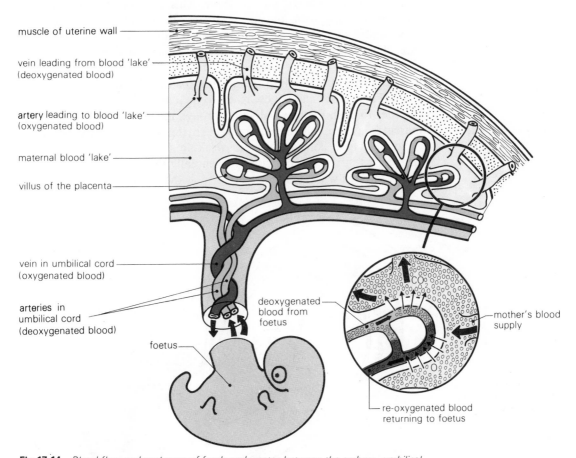

muscle of uterine wall

vein leading from blood 'lake' (deoxygenated blood)

artery leading to blood 'lake' (oxygenated blood)

maternal blood 'lake'

villus of the placenta

vein in umbilical cord (oxygenated blood)

arteries in umbilical cord (deoxygenated blood)

foetus

deoxygenated blood from foetus

mother's blood supply

re-oxygenated blood returning to foetus

Fig 17.14 *Blood flow and exchange of foods and wastes between the embryo, umbilical cord, placenta and mother*

By eight weeks the embryo is called a foetus. The first twelve weeks of foetal development are a particularly critical time. By twelve weeks after conception all the organ systems of the foetal body have formed: the heart pumps blood through the blood vessels; the alimentary canal, excretory system and lungs can all be seen. The limbs, too, are formed, and although the mother cannot feel foetal movements at this stage, the foetus is already quite active. The foetus is recognisably human, and for the remainder of its time in the uterus most of the changes consist of

The embryo becomes a foetus

refinements, or maturing, and growth of all these systems and organs. Obviously, any damaging influence on the foetus can be particularly dangerous during the first twelve weeks. It may cause basic malformations of organs or limbs which cannot be repaired later in foetal life. The case of the drug thalidomide is a tragic example of just such damage occurring during the period of formation of the limbs (see Chapter 14).

At 5 months the foetus is 25 cm long, and the amniotic sac now contains a considerable volume of fluid. This prevents the foetus from damage resulting from outside pressures. It also allows the foetus to move about and helps to maintain the foetus at a constant temperature. The placenta is now large and is similar in size to the foetus (Fig 17.16a).

By the end of a 9-month period, the foetus has usually turned head down (Fig 17.16b) and is now ready to be released to the outside world. In order to push the new baby out through the cervix of the uterus, the muscular layers of the uterus contract rhythmically in what is known as 'labour'. These contractions are weak in the beginning but become stronger as birth becomes closer. Eventually the contractions force the foetus through what is often referred to as the 'birth canal' (Fig 17.15).

The uterus contracts rhythmically in order to expel the foetus

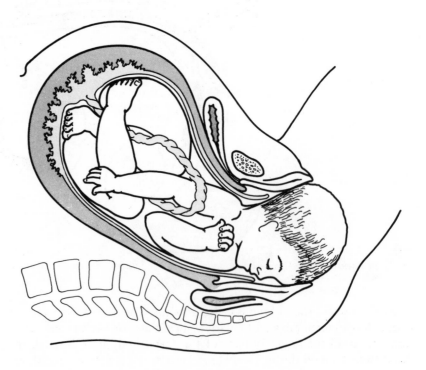

Fig 17.15   *The beginning of birth. Muscular contractions force the foetus through the birth canal*

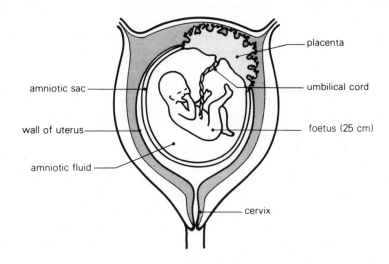

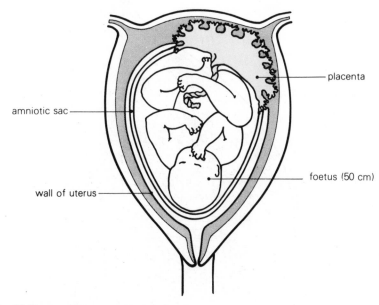

Fig 17.16 *Development of the foetus*
(a) At five months
(b) Shortly before birth

Lactation

The breast contains
• alveoli
• ducts
• nipple (and some fat)

Each alveolus is surrounded by a band of muscle, which forces the milk from the alveoli and into the ducts

Mother's milk contains more
• lactose
• vitamins
• mineral salts
than cow's milk

After birth, the hormone prolactin causes the alveoli to produce milk

Oxytocin causes the muscle bands around the alveoli to contract, forcing the milk into the ducts and out the nipple

The female breast is made up of fifteen sections each containing a large number of **alveoli** (often called glands). These are where milk is produced and are like small sacs. A system of small tubes or **ducts** carries milk from the alveoli to a large central duct which has its opening in the **nipple** (Fig 17.17). Each alveolus is surrounded by a small band of muscle, which can contract and force the milk down the ducts and out of the nipple. The milk produced by the mother is different from cow's milk in that it contains less protein but more milk sugar (lactose), vitamins and mineral salts.

The breasts begin to develop at puberty but often remain relatively small and do not secrete milk. It is not until pregnancy that the breasts develop so that they are capable of producing milk. Early in pregnancy there is a considerable growth of the ducts and alveoli, and the breasts increase in size. After birth, a hormone called **prolactin** is secreted from the pituitary and stimulates the production of milk by the alveoli. However, this hormone does not cause the milk to be released into the ducts, and it is thus unavailable to the baby at this stage.

Another hormone called **oxytocin** causes the muscle bands around the alveoli to contract, thus forcing the milk into the ducts and towards the nipple. The release of this hormone in the mother is stimulated by the baby. As the infant sucks the nipple, nerve impulses are sent to the brain,

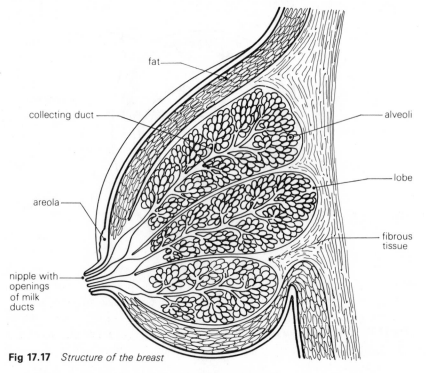

fat

collecting duct

areola

nipple with openings of milk ducts

alveoli

lobe

fibrous tissue

Fig 17.17 *Structure of the breast*

which results in oxytocin being released from the pituitary. This hormone circulates in the bloodstream and soon reaches the breast, where it causes the muscle bands around the alveoli to contract, squeezing milk out of the milk glands and into the ducts of the breast. The milk in the ducts is then available when the baby sucks (Fig 17.18).

Sucking on the nipple by the baby stimulates the release of oxytocin

In some cases the baby may cause oxytocin to be released from the pituitary merely by its crying. The noise of the baby's cries stimulates the mother's brain, again causing oxytocin to be released and milk to be forced out of the alveoli and through the nipple.

The baby's cries may also cause the release of oxytocin

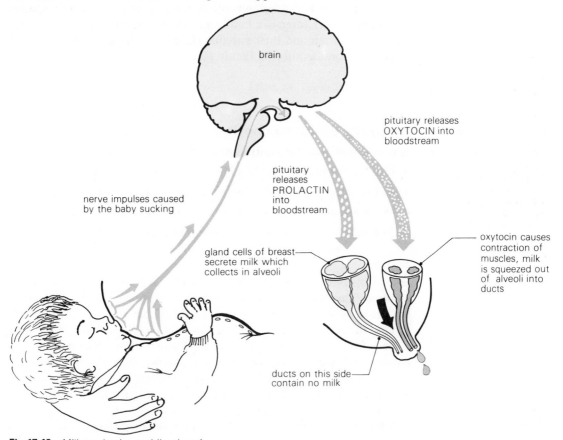

brain

pituitary releases OXYTOCIN into bloodstream

pituitary releases PROLACTIN into bloodstream

nerve impulses caused by the baby sucking

gland cells of breast secrete milk which collects in alveoli

oxytocin causes contraction of muscles, milk is squeezed out of alveoli into ducts

ducts on this side contain no milk

Fig 17.18 *Milk production and 'let-down'*

Birth control

In order to survive, people need sufficient supplies of food, water, shelter and space. In an over-populated country these requirements cannot be met, and hunger, disease and inadequate housing then become daily burdens for the majority of the population. Such a predicament can be seen in many developing countries, where hunger and disease are commonplace.

The solution to such problems lies largely in the control of the birth rate. Birth control can be brought about by **contraception**, which is the prevention of fertilisation or of the development of the zygote by a variety of temporary means. Birth control may also involve the termination of pregnancy.

Techniques of contraception may be used not only to control population growth as a whole, but also to plan individual families. It is important that children are born only into situations where they will receive adequate loving care and attention from their parents during their vital years of growth and development. Because of this, the timing, spacing and number of children in a family may be important to the well-being of both the children and their parents. (Economic factors may also be an important consideration in family planning.)

Methods of contraception

It is useful to think of contraceptive devices in four ways:

● as a barrier preventing the union of sperm and ovum
● as a device preventing the implantation and development of the zygote
● as a substance preventing the production of sperm or ova
● as a schedule of sexual intercourse that prevents fertilisation.

Barriers

One of the most commonly used contraceptive devices in Australia is the **condom**. This is a sheath made of strong, thin rubber which is worn over the penis. At the open end there is a thin rubber ring which fits firmly around the penis, while at the closed end is a small pouch which provides a space for the collection of the semen. There is always a chance that the condom will slip off during sexual intercourse, thus allowing sperm to enter the vagina. In order to increase the safety of the device, sperm-killing creams may be applied around the rim (the open end) of the condom.

A barrier that can be used by a woman is the **diaphragm**. This is a thin rubber dome-shaped cup with a thin metal ring around its margin. The diaphragm is designed to fit over the cervix, and the woman places it in position before intercourse. However, it is difficult to ensure that there are no gaps around the edge of the diaphragm. To prevent sperm from swimming around the edge of the diaphragm, it is necessary to place some sperm-killing cream or jelly around the margin of the diaphragm before insertion.

Neither of the barrier methods is extremely safe, and the failure rate of both exceeds 10 per cent (that is to say, 10 out of every 100 women who rely on these methods become pregnant).

Figure 17.19a illustrates contraceptive barriers.

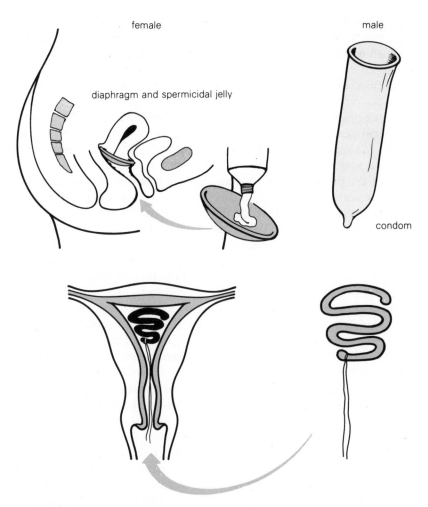

Fig 17.19 *Contraceptive devices*
(a) Contraceptive barriers
(b) One type of intrauterine device (IUD)

Prevention of implantation

If fertilisation is allowed to occur, the implantation of the zygote in the endometrium of the uterine wall can be prevented by a device known as an **intrauterine device** or an **IUD** (Fig 17.19b). This is a small plastic and/or metal device, which is placed inside the uterus. The device is inserted by a doctor and may be allowed to remain in the uterus for a number of years. One type of IUD, known as the Lippes loop, is shown in Fig 17.19b.

Implantation is prevented by an intrauterine device

Prevention of gamete production

The most widely used method of contraception in Australia over the past decade has been the **'pill'**. This method prevents ovulation in the female.

You will recall that ovulation in the female occurs in a cycle of about 28 days and is controlled by a number of hormones. One thing that was not stressed earlier in the chapter is that as the concentration of oestrogen produced by follicles in the ovary rises, this inhibits the production of FSH from the pituitary. That is, at a certain concentration, oestrogen stops the pituitary producing FSH. Thus no development of new follicles can take place, and no development of new ova can occur. Later in the cycle, progesterone has the same effect on the pituitary.

Oestrogen and progesterone inhibit FSH production in the pituitary

The contraceptive pill contains progesterone and oestrogen in different proportions. It works on the principle that oestrogen and progesterone prevent the production of FSH and thus prevent the formation of new ova. Because the concentrations of oestrogen and progesterone are kept at high levels, it is said that the pill produces a false pregnancy.

The 'pill' contains oestrogen and progesterone, which prevent the release of FSH by the pituitary and stop the formation of an ovarian follicle

Pills are usually taken for the full 28 days each month. However, not all the pills contain oestrogen–progesterone; some contain just sugar. Counting the first day of the menstrual period as day 1, the first hormone pill is taken on day 4. By day 5, menstruation will have stopped, since the oestrogen–progesterone of the pill causes the endometrium to repair and begin building up again. Hormone pills are then taken for 21 days, which brings us to day 24. Hormone pills are then stopped and replaced by sugar pills for 7 days. Four days after the last hormone pill there will be little oestrogen–progesterone remaining in the bloodstream, and menstruation begins again. This continues for 2 days after the first hormone pill of the next series has been taken (that is, for 5 days). However, it should be remembered that different women have different sensitivities to the pill, and the length of the menstrual period may be longer or shorter than 5 days. The schedule is summarised in Fig 17.20.

The pill is effective only if taken every day. Even a single forgotten pill may allow pregnancy. However, it is the most reliable method of contraception and is said to have a failure rate of only about 0.3 per cent.

The pill may have a number of undesirable side-effects

Despite its safety, the pill is not used by some women because of the fairly drastic side-effects it can have: headaches, irritability, change of personality and soreness in the breasts are some of these. However, a new 'pill' for men is now under review. This prevents the correct development of sperm in the testes and is at present being tested on men in America and Australia.

A schedule of sexual intercourse to avoid fertilisation

The system of contraception called the **rhythm method** involves abstaining from sexual intercourse during days when an ovum is being produced by the female.

This method relies on three facts. First, ovulation occurs only once in the menstrual cycle, and the egg can survive in the uterine tube for about 72 hours. Second, the ovum is produced about 13 to 15 days after the beginning of the previous menstrual period. Third, sperm can survive for only about 72 hours in the woman.

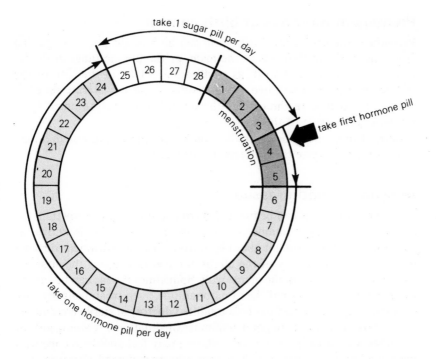

Fig 17.20 *Monthly schedule for taking the 'pill'. (FSH production is prevented, so no new ova are produced)*

Thus, if a couple deliberately avoid sexual intercourse at the time of supposed ovulation, and for three days on either side of these dates, fertilisation should not occur. These days are known as the 'unsafe' period. However, different women menstruate in cycles of different length, and sometimes the cycles can vary considerably in length. Under these circumstances it is extremely difficult to work out which days are 'unsafe' in any one cycle. The statistics show that this method has a 25 per cent failure rate.

Some clue as to when ovulation occurs is given by a woman's temperature. Usually the temperature is slightly lower during the first 13 days of the cycle. At the time of ovulation the temperature drops slightly. This is then followed by a sharp rise of about 0.7°C. By taking the temperature daily during a menstrual cycle, it may be possible to work out when ovulation occurs. This can be checked with similar measurements during following months.

Another clue as to when ovulation occurs may be gained by observing changes in the quality of the mucous secretions from the cervix throughout the menstrual cycle. From both these observations and temperature measurements it may be possible to predict the days of the cycle when ovulation *could* occur. Sexual intercourse would then be avoided for three days before and three days after these days.

Rhythm method—sexual intercourse is avoided for the three days on either side of the day of ovulation

Body temperature can indicate the time of ovulation

Permanent methods of birth control

Permanent prevention of fertilisation can be brought about by cutting and tying both vas deferens in the male, or the uterine tubes in the female. This method is known as **sterilisation**. Thus, in the case of the female, sperm are prevented from passing along the uterine tubes to fertilise the ovum. In the case of the male, sperm are prevented from reaching the outside of the body.

Sterilisation involves cutting and tying the vas deferens or uterine tubes

Both of these methods of sterilisation are permanent, although it may be possible to reverse their effects in some cases.

Abortion—another issue

Abortion is the removal of the fertilised ovum, embryo or immature foetus from the uterus, preventing further growth

An embryo or foetus can be prevented from continuing its growth in the mother's uterus by a number of artificial methods. This is known as abortion. It can be brought about by introducing an instrument through the cervix into the cavity of the uterus and gently scraping the attached amniotic sac away from the uterus wall. Sometimes the sac can be sucked from the uterus by a small suction apparatus. Such treatments are safe provided they are carried out by a qualified doctor, in sterile conditions.

An abortion may be sought in a number of situations. A young girl, or a mother who already has several children, may feel unable to cope with the baby she has conceived. A doctor may recommend abortion of a foetus which is found to have some serious and permanent defect.

The whole issue of abortion is very complex. One point of view is that abortions should not be available to 'careless' young couples. For a woman whose health may be threatened by another child, or whose child will have some permanent deformity, an abortion may be justified. Some people would argue against this, maintaining that even a one-day-old embryo is potential life and that we have no right to destroy life. Others hold the opinion that a foetus does not represent potential life until it reaches 12 weeks of age. This controversy is still debated strongly and may never be resolved completely.

Sexual diseases

Venereal diseases—diseases passed from one person to another by contact with infected sex organs

Some diseases can be passed from one person to another during sexual intercourse. These diseases are called **venereal diseases**. They are caused by organisms that are spread from one person to another by direct contact with the sex organs. In other words, venereal diseases can only be spread from person A to person B, if person B has handled or come into contact with the sex organs of person A with any part of his or her body.

Medical records show that the occurrence of venereal disease has increased dramatically in recent years. Some people have expressed the opinion that this has been due to increased promiscuity in the community. However, others propose that the increased incidence of venereal disease may also be related to the change in the type of contraceptive devices used in recent years. People who use condoms give themselves some protection against venereal disease, as direct sexual contact is reduced. With the increased use of the pill, and the resulting decreased use of the condom, direct sexual contact has increased, and this is a possible factor in the increasing incidence of venereal disease.

Gonorrhoea is a common form of venereal disease. It is caused by a member of a group of very small organisms called bacteria. The name of the bacterium which causes this particular disease is *Neisseria gonorrhoeae*. This bacterium passes from an infected person to a healthy person only when they have sexual intercourse. Within 2 to 5 days the bacteria have multiplied many thousands of times.

Gonorrhoea is caused by the bacterium *Neisseria gonorrhoeae*

In the male, gonorrhoea shows itself by causing inflammation and swelling in the urethra. Pus may also appear from the opening of the urethra. The infection may spread to the bladder and prostate gland, or even as far as the epididymis. This condition can become painful and may cause difficulty in passing urine. In its most severe form it can eventually completely block the epididymis, thus causing sterility.

In the male, gonorrhoea causes
• inflammation and swelling in the urethra
• infected bladder, prostate gland and epididymis
It may block the epididymis, causing sterility

In the female, the symptoms are slow to show themselves, since they occur internally. Inflammation begins in the cervix and continues up into the uterus and finally into the uterine tube. Severe gonorrhoea may cause the uterine tube to be blocked, thus preventing fertilisation from occurring. Signs of gonorrhoea may merely amount to a mucous discharge from the vagina, or an abscess developing in the vaginal opening.

In the female, gonorrhoea causes inflammation of the cervix, uterus and uterine tubes. It may block the uterine tubes, causing sterility

Once the disease has been detected, treatment can be given. The type of drug used is an antibiotic such as penicillin, which is given by injection. Provided the disease is detected early, it can be cured without leaving scars or complications.

Gonorrhoea can be treated with antibiotics

A far more serious venereal disease than gonorrhoea is **syphilis**. Syphilis is caused by another bacterium called *Treponema pallidum*, which is spiral in shape. The disease usually shows itself by the appearance of an ulcer on the sex organs or on some other organ such as the tongue. In the female the ulcer may be internal and therefore go unnoticed. These ulcers or sores are usually painless. After about two weeks the ulcers will heal and disappear by themselves.

Syphilis is caused by the bacterium *Treponema pallidum*

Stages of syphilis:
• ulcer on sex organs
• rash on any part of the body
• dormant stage when no symptoms show
• vital damage to heart, brain, eyes

If the disease is not treated at this first stage, the bacteria then invade all the organs of the body. The second stage of infection now begins, often showing itself as a rash. This rash may appear anywhere on the body. If the rash is scraped and these scrapings examined under a microscope, the small spiral bacteria can be seen. This stage usually clears up after two months.

If the disease is still not treated, the third stage of infection may begin. In this stage, the body's defence cells (white blood cells) kill the bacteria, so that relatively few remain in the body. None infect the surface of the body during this stage. Because the bacteria are still in the body, but do not produce any symptoms, the disease is said to be dormant. This stage may last for up to 40 years.

378 Understanding the human body

After this long period of time the person enters the fourth stage. By this time the bacteria are causing permanent damage to vital organs such as the heart, brain or eyes. Whereas syphilis in the first three stages can be cured with antibiotics, the fourth stage may be incurable.

Syphilis can be treated with antibiotics

Menopause — the completion of a role

A woman's life can be divided into distinct phases. Sometimes the change from one phase to the next is clear-cut, but sometimes these changes occur gradually and are hardly noticeable.

Around the age of 10 to 12 years a girl reaches puberty. At this stage of her life she changes from a girl to an adolescent. Her secondary sexual characteristics develop and menstruation begins. Further development into womanhood brings with it the ability to bear children, and a great number of other responsibilities.

The first set of changes in a woman's life occurs at puberty

Menopause is the gradual change from sexual maturity to the stage when the reproductive function ceases

Later in life, a woman goes through another set of changes, during which her child-bearing ability ceases. This is a gradual process and may take anything from a few months to a number of years. Such a gradual change from sexual maturity to a stage when the reproductive function ceases is called menopause. It usually occurs as the woman approaches middle-age.

At menopause:
• mature ova are no longer produced
• concentration of sex hormones falls
• menstrual periods cease

At menopause, the ovaries gradually cease to produce mature and fertilisable ova, and the supply of hormones produced by the ovaries, especially oestrogen, begins to lessen. The ceasing of the monthly menstrual periods is the most obvious sign that the activity of the ovaries is slowing down. In some women this change in hormonal balance causes very little disturbance. In others there may be some discomfort while the adjustments are still occurring. Here the decrease in ovarian hormones may cause hot flushing sensations in the face, headaches, giddiness, aches and pains and disturbances of mood.

Some discomforts may occur at menopause:
• hot flushes
• headaches
• aches and pains

The changes at menopause are many and varied, and it is impossible to predict with confidence exactly what changes any particular woman will experience. Thus, some may complain to their doctor of tiredness and headache, vague aches and pains. Others will be startled by a sudden hot flush, which they have never previously experienced, and which they cannot explain. Others may feel moody, irritable and depressed. Often these symptoms show themselves before or even after the monthly menstrual periods have become irregular or have stopped.

After menopause, the female sex organs decrease in size

After menopause, the female sex organs (the ovaries, uterus and external organs) begin to decrease in size. The breasts also decrease in size, and fat tends to accumulate both on the shoulders and around the waist-line. Changes occur in the activity of the thyroid and other endocrine (hormone) glands. Decreasing activity of the thyroid gland may be responsible for an increase in tiredness after menopause.

Tiredness may be due to the decreasing activity of the thyroid gland

Occasionally bleeding may occur after the periods have finished, as a result of disturbances of the growth of the uterine lining. When this is severe, or when other conditions of the uterus occur, the doctor may decide to remove the uterus, an operation called a hysterectomy.

Hysterectomy—removal of uterus

One of the main reasons for emotional upset during menopause is that it represents to some women the end of their 'useful' phase, since they can no longer bear children. However, to many women, the time following menopause is seen as an opportunity to channel their energies into activities outside the home and family. At this time many women make their greatest contribution either in their profession or in a range of community activities.

In many ways the changes experienced during menopause are easier to adapt to than the changes experienced during the transition from girlhood to womanhood. If approached in a positive light, this stage of life can be one of a woman's most satisfying, as she develops herself in new spheres of activity and interest.

Sexual feelings in personal relationships

The previous pages of this chapter have dealt with what can be described as the mechanics of sexuality—reproduction and contraception. Sexuality has, however, another most important aspect, because in all these discussions we must remember that we are concerned with people, their emotions and their feelings. Each of us must, therefore, develop a personal understanding of how our own sexuality fits into our pattern of social behaviour and personal relationships.

How we develop such an understanding is beyond the scope of this book, but perhaps a few points can be made. Sociability begins from the day we are born. As tiny babies we respond to only one person—our mother—who provides us with the warmth, comfort, nourishment and love we desire. Before long, we become aware of other people who love and care for us—our father, siblings, grandparents and so on; we learn to respond to their attentions with smiles, laughter and language. As we grow, so our world and the range of our friendships grows, so that, by the time we go to school, we are learning to form friendships of our own, amongst our peers. This stage is one of the biggest steps in our social development, as we learn what sharing and caring involves. And so, as we grow, we develop both physically, emotionally and socially, learning to cope better with ourselves and to balance our own desires with the needs and desires of our friends.

During our early teens we suddenly become aware of ourselves as sexually capable beings. This time of sexual awakening is called puberty. As mentioned earlier, it is during this time that boys and girls begin to produce their respective male and female hormones. Increasing testosterone and oestrogen cause the development of the secondary sex characteristics. In the female, menstrual periods begin, and in both, gamete production begins. It is now that we become capable of producing another human being through a sexual relationship.

This new sexual awareness may greatly influence our established patterns of sociability. We become more conscious of our own masculinity or femininity and may seek out friendships with people of the opposite sex. In these new friendships there may be, in addition to the emotional drives on which all friendships are based, new physical sexual drives.

However, it is most important to realise that these physical drives are not experienced in the same way in all people. In some, the physical sexual drive may be quite close to the surface, so that a relationship based on physical attraction may develop, whilst that person's emotional involvement remains quite casual. Others may feel their physical drives awaken strongly only as a deeply meaningful personal relationship develops.

One message, at least, which comes out very clearly from this discussion, is that as we begin to develop these personal relationships, we must try very sincerely to understand our own drives and feelings, as well as those of our partner. This understanding enables us to be sensitive to the feelings, pressures and desires which our partner is experiencing and to cope with our own reactions. In this way, we are able to prevent ourselves from acting in any way which could hurt, either temporarily or permanently, the girl or boy with whom we have formed even a casual relationship.

Chapter 18

Bones and muscles—a framework for movement

- Organising the frame-work
- Details of the skeleton
- Structure of bones and cartilage
- Where bones meet
- Special joints
- How muscles move joints
- Mechanism of muscle contraction
- Balance and the control of movement

We have now talked about a number of body systems: a transport or circulatory system, a gas exchange or respiratory system, a food processing or digestive system, communication or nervous and endocrine systems, and so on. All of these systems are composed of organs and tissues which are soft in texture. They may have a definite shape of their own, but they could not keep their shape without support and protection. The bony **skeleton** is the framework which supports and protects all the organs of the body. Without a skeleton our bodies could be moulded like soft clay and would be as floppy as a big bean bag.

The skeleton provides stability with flexibility

with bones

without bones

Many familiar objects have firm frameworks—cars, houses, chairs, kites and even scarecrows are built around a firm framework which provides support and stability. The skeleton is a very special framework, though, because as well as providing support and protection, it makes movement possible.

Many small animals have an exoskeleton

Not all animals have skeletons. Some of the simple animals like slugs and earthworms can manage without a skeleton because they are small and slow moving. (There are some much bigger animals without skeletons, like the octopus or giant squid. They can manage without a skeleton because they are supported by the water they live in. On land they would be quite helpless.) Some of the smaller animals such as insects and spiders have a firm covering on the outside of their body for protection and mobility. This is called an **exoskeleton**. The crab is the largest animal with an exoskeleton. Such a skeleton does have a number of disadvantages. Not only is it very heavy compared with the animal's weight, but there is no room for growth or expansion to take place. To accommodate growth, the outer covering must be shed, leaving the animal very vulnerable to attack.

All larger land-living animals have an endoskeleton

However, all the larger land-living animals need a lot of firm support for their large, mobile bodies. They all have an internal or **endoskeleton** made of bone and cartilage supporting tissue. The basic arrangement of the framework which supports them is the same. You may remember from Chapter 1 that humans are members of a large group (or subphylum) of animals called the vertebrates. Vertebrates are animals that have a vertebral column or backbone which forms the central supporting rod for their bodies. This backbone is made of very strong supporting, or connective, tissue. In some fishes, the connective tissue of the backbone is cartilage, whilst in humans, it is bone and cartilage. In addition to the vertebral column, many of the vertebrates have limbs, which make a great variety of movements possible.

Vertebrates have a backbone, which is a central supporting rod for the body

In humans, the backbone consists of bone and cartilage

Humans are capable of an incredible range of movements, far more complex and varied, probably, than almost any other form of life—the cricketer, the violinist, the watchmaker, the tightrope walker, the athlete and the rock climber all train their bodies to perform a huge variety of very complex movements. The movements of which we are capable make up part of the unique nature of human life.

Limbs make a large variety of movements possible

These movements are made possible by the arrangement of the many bones in our skeleton. Our framework or skeleton is composed, not of a small number of rods or girders, but of more than 200 bones. The bones meet one another at joints. Some movement is possible at nearly all of these joints. The total range of movement is therefore enormous.

If we were to construct a human framework from mechanical parts (a robot), it would be made from many rods (bones) joined together with hinges, ball bearings and sockets (joints). We would need a complex system of engines, pulleys and levers to move each of these joints and drive the robot. In our bodies, the joints are powered by muscles which are attached to bones across the joints. We shall see later how the muscles move the body framework.

Organising the framework

The skeleton of all vertebrates can be considered to be made up of two main sections:

- the **axial skeleton,** which supports the structures on the main axis of the body

- the **appendicular skeleton,** which supports the limbs and attaches them to the body.

The skeleton of vertebrates consists of
- axial skeleton
- appendicular skeleton

Figure 18.1 shows these two parts of the skeleton in schematic form.

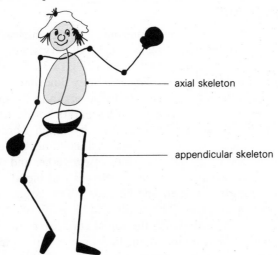

axial skeleton

appendicular skeleton

Fig 18.1 *The framework of the body*

The axial skeleton consists of the skull, the vertebral column, and the ribs and sternum. The skull is made up of a brain case (cranium) which protects the brain, and the face bones and jaw. The vertebral column (often called the backbone or spine) is the central rod supporting the whole body. It also provides protection for the soft organs inside the body.

Axial skeleton:
- skull
- vertebral column
- ribs
- sternum

Appendicular skeleton:
- bones of limbs
- girdles

The trunk consists of three parts:
- thorax
- abdomen
- pelvis

The appendicular skeleton is made up of the bones of the limbs (arms and legs) and the girdles (shoulder and pelvic girdles). The girdles are the frameworks for attaching the limbs to the rest of the body.

While we are talking about the arrangement of the skeleton, we should also mention the **trunk**. This is made up of three parts: the thorax, abdomen and pelvis. Each of these sections of the trunk has a body wall (made of muscle and bone) and a cavity, which is filled with soft organs (called viscera). In the thorax the wall is formed by the vertebrae, the ribs, sternum (breastbone) and muscles (see Chapter 8). The abdominal wall is almost entirely muscular, except for the vertebral column at the back. The walls of the pelvic cavity are formed by the bones of the pelvic girdle, the vertebrae and muscles. The thoracic and abdominal cavities are separated by the muscular diaphragm. There is no actual separation of the abdominal and pelvic cavities—the pelvic cavity is said to begin at the level of the top of the pelvic girdle.

Details of the skeleton

Figure 18.2 shows the bones of the human skeleton and their names. You will find it helpful to refer to this diagram throughout this section.

The skull

The skull consists of:
- cranial bones
- facial bones

The cranium surrounds and protects the brain

In the foetus the cranium consists of separate bones

The bones of the cranium fuse as a person. approaches adulthood

Facial bones
- give face its shape
- house and protect the eyes
and form
- nasal passages
- air sinuses
- hard palate
- upper and lower jaws

All facial bones are fused to the cranium except the mandible

The skull is not a single bone but 22 bones which are arranged to perform some extremely vital tasks. They fall very simply into two groups: the cranial bones and the facial bones (Fig 18.3). The cranial bones form the **cranium** or brain case. This is a bony box which entirely surrounds and protects the most delicate and vital organ in the body, the brain. In the foetus the cranium consists of 8 separate bones. At birth these bones are not joined but are held together by tough fibrous tissue. The places where the bones meet are regarded as immoveable joints. As growth to adulthood continues, the bones fuse together and the cranium becomes a solid box enclosing the brain. Nerves and blood vessels enter and leave the cranium through special holes. The largest of these holes is the **foramen magnum**. This is situated in the floor of the brain case, and is the hole through which the spinal cord leaves the brain.

Below the cranium are the facial bones which make up the face. In all, there are 14 of these bones, and they give the face its characteristic shape. They form the sockets (orbits) which house and protect the eyes (see Chapter 15); they form the nasal passages and air sinuses, the hard palate, and the upper and lower jaws which house the teeth. With the exception of the lower jaw, the **mandible**, the bones of the face are firmly joined to the cranium. They do not move.

The mandible or lower jaw is the only bone in the skull that can move. It is a bone shaped like a horse-shoe which is hinged to the base of the cranium (Fig 18.4). Movements of the mandible open and close the mouth, as in chewing and speaking.

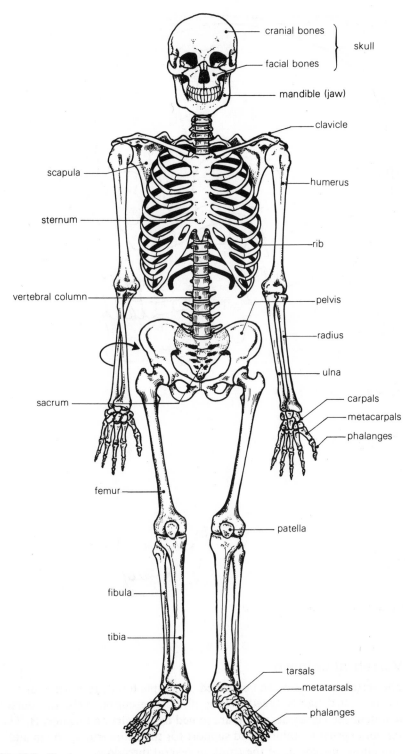

cranial bones
facial bones
} skull

mandible (jaw)

clavicle

scapula

humerus

sternum

rib

vertebral column

pelvis

radius

ulna

sacrum

carpals

metacarpals

phalanges

femur

patella

fibula

tibia

tarsals

metatarsals

phalanges

Fig 18.2 *The human skeleton*

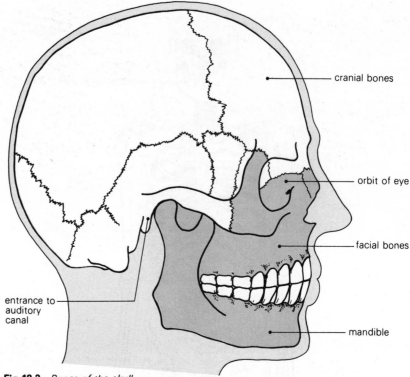

cranial bones

orbit of eye

facial bones

entrance to
auditory
canal

mandible

Fig 18.3   *Bones of the skull*

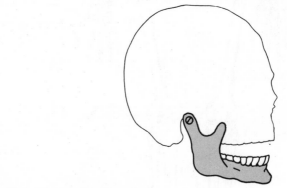

Fig 18.4   *The mandible (lower jaw)*

Vertebral column

The vertebrae
- provide stability and support for the trunk
- allow the movement of the trunk in several directions

The vertebral column can be likened, in simple terms, to a string of cotton reels tied tightly together (Fig 18.5). The cotton reels, of course, represent the vertebrae, which are joined by muscles and ligaments. The vertebrae provide stability and support for the entire trunk, and in addition allow movement of the trunk in several directions.

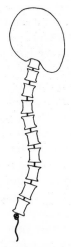

Fig 18.5 *String of cotton reels, representing the vertebral column*

There are 34 vertebrae (singular vertebra) which make up the back-bone or vertebral column. As we shall see soon, their structure varies slightly in different places along the vertebral column. They all have some common basic features, however. These are shown in Fig 18.6. Each vertebra has a hole in its centre. Together all these holes form a bony tube called the **spinal canal**. The spinal canal protects the delicate spinal cord along its length. Each vertebra also has several bony points or projections. Some of these interlock with projections on adjacent verte-brae and help to make the vertebral column stronger. Others are areas where muscles attach to the backbone.

Each vertebra has a hole in its centre. All the holes of the vertebrae form the spinal canal

The spinal canal houses the spinal cord

Projections of vertebrae
• interlock with each other
• provide muscle attachments

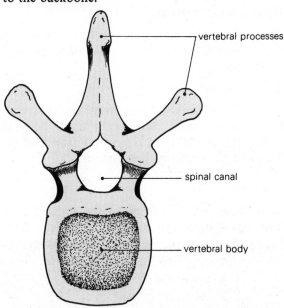

vertebral processes

spinal canal

vertebral body

Fig 18.6 *Structure of a typical vertebra, showing common basic features*

If you look at a skeleton (or a living person) from the side, you will see that the vertebral column is not entirely straight. It has several distinct and important curves. Standing, walking and running in the upright position are activities which we tend to take for granted, but it requires constant unconscious balance control to do these things. The curves of the backbone are very important in helping to balance the weight of the head, the organs of the trunk, and the limbs.

We have already said that the appearance, or structure, of the vertebrae varies along the backbone. This is because at different levels of the backbone the vertebrae have different tasks to perform. Figure 18.7 shows the arrangement of the different vertebrae. These are: 7 neck vertebrae, 12 thoracic vertebrae, 5 lumbar vertebrae, 5 sacral vertebrae (fused together and known as the **sacrum**), and 4 tail vertebrae (fused together and known as the **coccyx**).

Neck vertebrae have short projections allowing great flexibility

Thoracic vertebrae have projections for the attachment of ribs

Lumbar vertebrae have large projections which interlock to provide maximum stability

Sacral vertebrae are fused to form the sacrum

Tail vertebrae are fused to form the coccyx

The neck vertebrae have only short projections. Because of this, this region is the most flexible part of the backbone, allowing quite free movements of the head and neck. The thoracic vertebrae are less mobile and have special projections for attachment of the ribs to the backbone. The lumbar vertebrae are the largest in the backbone. Their projections are large, and they interlock, to provide maximum stability and only a limited amount of movement. The next five vertebrae are fused together to form one bone called the sacrum. The sacrum is almost immoveable and is wedged between the bones of the pelvic (hip) girdle. In humans, the last vertebrae, the tail vertebrae, are very small and have no function. They are fused to form one small bone called the coccyx. The coccyx is attached to the tip of the sacrum.

Ribs and sternum

The structure and movements of the ribs and sternum (breastbone) were discussed in detail in Chapter 8, so they will not be dealt with here.

The girdles

Girdles are bony frameworks which attach the limbs to the trunk

As we have already said, the girdles are the bony frameworks which attach the limbs to the trunk. In the human body, the shoulder and pelvic girdles are very different in structure from each other. This is because of the different functions they perform.

The pelvic girdle

The pelvic girdle
• transmits the thrust of the legs to the vertebral column
• supports the weight of the body on the legs

The pelvis is strong and rigid. It consists of two wide, flattened pelvic bones

To make the whole body move, the thrust of the legs against the ground must be transmitted to the vertebral column. This is achieved via the pelvic girdle. In addition, when a person is standing, the pelvic girdle must support the weight of the body on the legs. The pelvic girdle therefore needs to be very strong and fairly rigid. The pelvic girdle can be likened, then, in very simple terms, to a car's axle. The structure of the pelvic girdle is shown in Fig 18.8. It consists of two pelvic bones which are wide

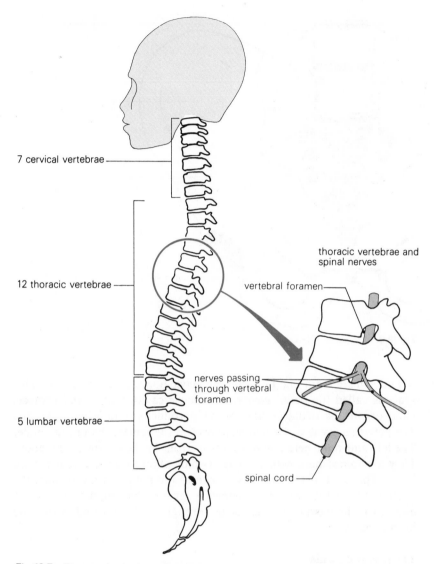

7 cervical vertebrae

thoracic vertebrae and
spinal nerves

vertebral foramen

12 thoracic vertebrae

nerves passing
through vertebral
foramen

5 lumbar vertebrae

spinal cord

Fig 18.7 *The vertebral column (lateral view)*

and flattened. (During development, each pelvic bone actually forms from three separate bones which fuse together early in childhood.) Many very large muscles, which run to the trunk or to the legs, are attached to the broad surfaces of these bones.

Many muscles are attached to the broad pelvic bones

At the back, the pelvic bones are very firmly attached to the base of the backbone—the sacrum. The joint between the pelvis and the sacrum is an immoveable joint, so that forces from the legs can be transferred directly to the body. On the outer and lower surface of each pelvic bone is a socket into which the head of the thigh bone (femur) fits.

The pelvic bones are attached to the sacrum

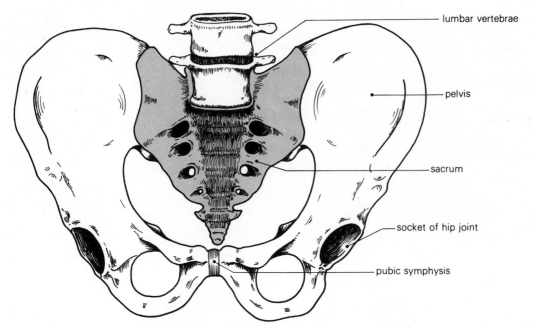

lumbar vertebrae

pelvis

sacrum

socket of hip joint

pubic symphysis

Fig 18.8 *Structure of the pelvic girdle*

The pelvic cavity houses and protects organs of the reproductive and urinary systems

You will see from Fig 18.8 that the pelvic bones enclose a space. This space is called the pelvic cavity. The pelvic cavity houses and protects many organs, particularly those of the reproductive and urinary systems. The pelvic cavity is wider and shallower in the female than in the male. The left and right pelvic bones meet in front in the centre of the body. They are joined here with cartilage (which allows some movement; see later). This area of the pelvis is known as the **pubis**. In the female, the angle between the two pubic bones is greater than in the male. This allows for the passage of the foetus through the birth canal during the birth process.

The pectoral girdle

The shoulder girdle allows maximum movement of the arms

The pectoral girdle (shoulder girdle) is quite different in structure from the pelvic girdle. People do not normally rely on their arms for locomotion and propulsion of the body. Instead, the shoulder girdle is designed to provide maximum mobility for the arms. In this sense the shoulder girdle can be likened to a coat hanger which keeps the arms hung out at the sides of the uppermost part of the trunk (Fig 18.9). In this position movements at the shoulder are totally unrestricted.

The pectoral girdle consists of two bones on each side (Fig 18.10):

The shoulder girdle consists of
- **2 clavicles**
- **2 scapulae**

- the **clavicle** (or collar bone) in front, which is attached to the sternum in the centre

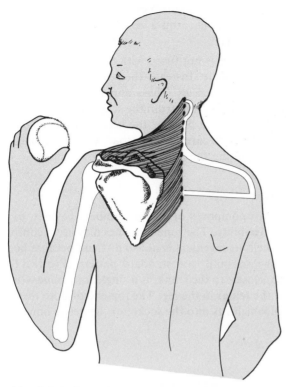

Fig 18.9 *The shoulder girdle is like a coat-hanger, suspending the arms away from the trunk*

Fig 18.10 *Bony structures of the pectoral girdle*

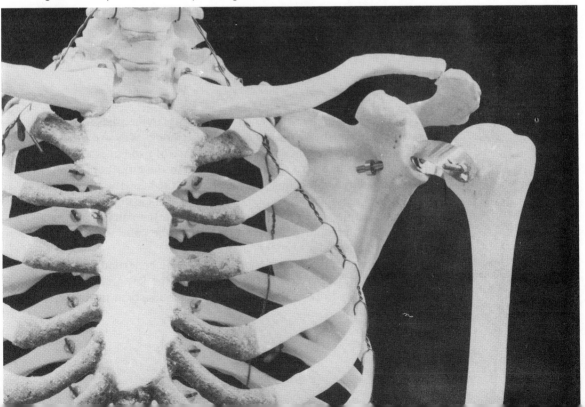

- the **scapula** (plural scapulae) or shoulder blade, which lies on the ribs, behind. The scapula forms a very mobile joint with the top of the arm bone (humerus).

The pectoral girdle is not fused with the bones of the vertebral column, as is the pelvic girdle. Instead, the scapulae are hung on the trunk by large, very strong muscles. These muscles run from the scapulae to the neck vertebrae above, and from the scapulae to the ribs below. (You can feel the muscles at the back of the neck holding up the shoulder blades and arms, when you carry a heavy load in your hands.) The collar bones act as rods, limiting the movement of the scapulae.

The limbs

The limbs are composed of a large number of bones, to provide support as well as flexibility. Their many names may seem confusing, but understanding their arrangement is not so difficult because both the upper and lower limbs are built to a standard pattern (Fig 18.11). At the top of each limb, closest to the trunk, is a single long bone—the **humerus** in the arm, and the **femur** in the leg. The top end of both these bones is shaped like a ball which fits into the socket of the pelvic bones and the shoulder blade.

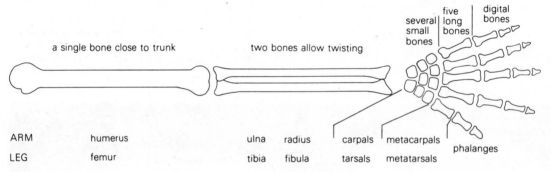

| ARM | humerus | ulna | radius | carpals | metacarpals | phalanges |
| LEG | femur | tibia | fibula | tarsals | metatarsals | |

Fig 18.11 *Bones of the limbs are arranged according to a standard pattern*

From the elbow to the wrist, and from the knee to the ankle, each limb has two bones which are hinged to the upper bone. Why are there two bones in this section of the limbs? The presence of two bones allows the muscles to twist and turn the hand or foot. In the arm, both of these bones, the **radius** and the **ulna**, are hinged with the humerus at the elbow joint. By using muscles which pull on just one of these bones, it is possible to turn the hand over (see Fig 18.12). When the palm of the hand faces up, the ulna and radius are straight. As the palm is turned face down, the radius glides over the ulna.

The two bones of the lower leg are the **tibia** (shin bone) and **fibula** (calf bone). However, because only the tibia forms the knee joint with the femur, the ability to twist the lower leg is much less than the ability to twist the forearm.

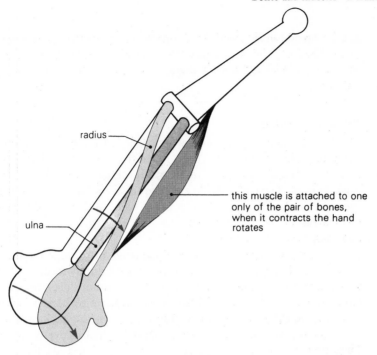

Fig 18.12 _Parallel bones in the forearm allow the hand to turn (rotate)_

The knee and the elbow are similar in structure, too. The bones of each joint are arranged so that they operate like hinges (see Fig 18.13). They can move smoothly and easily, but only in one plane. The knee joint has one other special feature—a small bone called the **patella** or knee cap. The patella provides some protection for the knee joint and also acts as a pivot, making the pull of the muscles across the front of the knee joint more efficient.

In the wrist and hand, and the ankle and foot, the basic arrangement of bones remains the same, too. The wrist has 8 small **carpal bones**, the

Hinge joints are found at the knee and the elbow. The bones at these joints can move only in one plane

The patella
• provides protection for the knee joint
• acts as a pivot

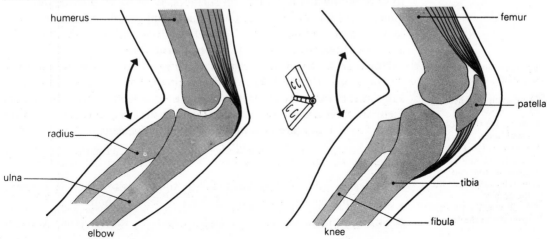

Fig 18.13 _Knee and elbow joints move like hinges_

Wrist:
- 8 carpals
- 5 meta-
  carpals
- 5 digits
  (3 bones)
  (1st digit has 2 bones)

Ankle:
- 7 tarsals
- 5 meta-
  tarsals
- 5 digits
  (3 bones)

The arrangement of the bones and muscles of the wrist and hand allows a large range of movement and manipulations

The fingers are moved by
- muscles in the forearm
- small muscles in the fingers

The foot
- supports the body weight
- acts as a lever to push the body forward when walking

The many small bones in the foot allow flexibility

The bones of the foot are arranged in three arches

These arches are held up by
- the wedge shape of the small bones
- ligaments tying bones together
- tendons from calf muscles helping to lift the arches
- small muscles attached to bones in the foot

ankle 7 **tarsal bones**. There are 5 long bones in the hand, the **metacarpals**, and in the foot, the **metatarsals**. Both hand and foot end in 5 digits, each of which has 3 small bones, **phalanges**, except for the first digit which has only two.

The wrist and hand

The arrangement of the bones and muscles of the wrist and hand make the hand man's most useful tool. More than any other part of the skeleton, the hand allows man a range of movement greater than that of any other animal. The eight small carpal bones allow twisting and rotation of the wrist on the forearm. Muscles in the palm of the hand attached to the metacarpal bones make possible the pincer grip of thumb and fingers, and cupping of the hand.

There are two types of muscles which bend and straighten the joints of the fingers. The more powerful of these are actually located in the forearm and move the fingers by means of long tendons. (Tendons are strong bands of connective tissue which attach muscle to bone.) You can see some of the extensor tendons of the fingers on the back of your hand. Can you feel the muscles in your forearm which move these tendons? The other muscles of the fingers are very small and are located on the fingers themselves. They make it possible to move individual joints on individual fingers.

The foot

The foot is designed for two important functions:

- to support the body's weight
- to act as a lever to push the body forward in walking (see Fig 18.14).

If the foot were made from a single strong bone, it could support the body's weight and propel the body. However, it would have no flexibility to cope with walking on uneven surfaces. In order to provide this flexibility, the foot is a structure containing many small bones. The pull of muscles and tendons on the front of the foot and toes (the 'take-off' area) also greatly increases the force of propulsion.

However, having a foot made of many small bones does present some design problems. Just like a bridge built of stones, the foot can only support the body's weight if it is built in the shape of an arch. In the foot there are three arches: two which run along the foot, and one across the foot. These arches are held up by a number of means:

- The bones of the foot are wedge shaped and so make the arches more stable.
- Underneath the arches, ligaments tie the bones together. (Ligaments are strong bands of connective tissue which join bone to bone.)
- Strong tendons from calf muscles attach to the underneath of the

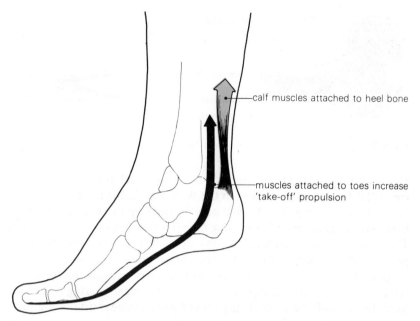

calf muscles attached to heel bone

muscles attached to toes increase 'take-off' propulsion

Fig 18.14   *The foot acts as a lever, and as a 'jointed' lever*

arches and help to lift them up. If these muscles become paralysed, the foot collapses.

- Small muscles, whose ends are attached to small bones within the foot.

Structure of bones and cartilage

From studying a skeleton we may gain the impression that bones are solid, brittle and rather dead sort of structures. In fact, in the living body, bones have none of these characteristics. We shall now look briefly at what bones are made of, and at some of the features of bone which make it the ideal substance for the body's framework.

Figure 18.15 shows a section through the length of the femur (thigh bone). The structures we can see in this bone are typical of all the limb bones in the body.

When we look at them in section, we can see that bones are not solid. They have an outer layer of dense or compact bone, which surrounds a central cavity called the **marrow cavity**. Just as tubular steel can be used to build the legs of a chair, so tubular bone is used in bones. Experiments show that nearly all the stresses on bone are on the outer part. For this reason tubular bone is almost as strong as solid bone, and it has the great advantage of being very much lighter.

A closer look at a section through any bone also shows us that bone exists in two forms: the compact bone which forms the solid outer layer of

Bones have
- outer compact bone
- a central marrow cavity

Nearly all stresses on bones are on the outer part

Two forms of bone:
- compact dense bone
- less dense woven bone

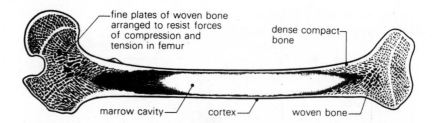

fine plates of woven bone arranged to resist forces of compression and tension in femur

dense compact bone

marrow cavity

cortex

woven bone

Fig 18.15   *Section through the length of the femur*

all the bones, and the less dense 'woven' bone which is found in the centre of flat bones, such as those in the skull, and in the heads of the long bones, close to the joints. Woven bone is made up of very thin plates of bone which are arranged in varying directions within the compact bone. These plates form remarkably strong struts which resist forces of compression and tension on the bone. You can see these thin plates of woven bone in Fig 18.15; some are arranged to resist tension forces in the femur, others to resist compression caused by weight-bearing on the hip joint. In the skull these very fine plates of woven bone resist the compression forces of hits or bumps on the head.

In addition to a variable amount of woven bone, the marrow cavity of bones is filled by a substance called **bone marrow**. Bone marrow is of two types: **red marrow** and **yellow marrow**. Red marrow has been discussed before, in Chapter 6. It is where red blood cells are produced. In the young child, red marrow is found in the marrow cavities of almost all the bones. In the adult, red marrow is found only in the cavities of the bones of the skull, vertebral column, rib cage and girdles. In the limb bones it is replaced by yellow marrow. Yellow marrow is made up of connective tissue cells and, in particular, fat cells, which give it its distinctive colour.

To find out more about the structure of bone we must examine it under a microscope. Bone is a special type of connective tissue. Like all connective tissues, bone is made up of cells, which are surrounded by a non-living substance called the matrix. Bone cells produce or secrete a number of complex chemicals which make up the bone matrix. The most important of these chemicals are:

- A cement-like substance, made of large carbohydrate molecules.

- Collagen, which is arranged as fibres. These fibres become embedded in the cement matrix and are a very important feature of bone. Without these slightly elastic fibres, bones would be brittle, like pieces of limestone or chalk.

- If the bone matrix were composed only of the cement substance and collagen fibres, it would be extremely flexible. It is the deposition of calcium in the bone matrix which makes bones *hard*. (Bones which have had their calcium entirely removed by chemical means can even be tied in knots.) Minerals, mainly calcium, with phosphate and carbonate, make up 65 per cent of bone matrix, by weight.

Woven bone is found
- in the heads of long bones
- in the centre of flat bones
- close to joints

The marrow cavity is filled by
- red marrow (where red blood cells are produced)

or
- yellow marrow

In the adult, red marrow is found in cavities of
- skull bones
- vertebral column
- rib cage
- girdles

Limb bones of the adult contain yellow marrow

Bone is made up of cells, which are surrounded by a non-living matrix

Bone matrix consists of
- a cement-like carbohydrate
- collagen fibres
- calcium (and other minerals)

Bone is therefore a complex chemical substance—soft but tough elastic fibres are blended with hard but brittle calcium material to make a very efficient and light framework material.

One other important feature of bones remains to be mentioned. Bones are living tissues. This means that they can grow and repair themselves if they are broken or fractured. A detailed description of how bone growth, remodelling and repair occurs is beyond the scope of this book. However, it should be understood that, even in the adult, many cells are constantly laying down new bone tissue. Furthermore, the minerals in bone are in a constant state of flux. It is for this reason that deficiencies of calcium or other important factors in the diet may affect the health of bones at any stage of life. Bones are also able to respond to stresses and needs. Thus, if bones are not used for a length of time, they may waste and weaken.

Bones are living tissues which grow and repair themselves

Bones respond to stresses and needs

What is cartilage?

Cartilage is another type of connective tissue. It is found in parts of the body where some support is needed, but where bone would be too hard and not sufficiently elastic. The ears, the tip of the nose, and the larynx (Adam's apple) are all supported by cartilage. We could think of cartilage as a biological equivalent of plastic or nylon, while bone is more like steel.

Cartilage is a connective tissue which provides strength and elasticity

Like bone, cartilage is composed of cells (cartilage cells) which produce an intercellular matrix. The matrix of cartilage is a gel, made of carbohydrates and proteins similar to those found in bone cement. Under normal circumstances, however, cartilage does not contain calcium. The cartilage matrix also contains collagen fibres.

The matrix of cartilage is a gel made up of carbohydrates, proteins and collagen fibres

Different types of cartilage are found in different areas in the body. One type of cartilage acts in the same way as nylon bearings in a machine. This is a smooth, shiny cartilage called hyaline cartilage. Just as nylon bearings are used in machines to provide almost frictionless surfaces, so hyaline cartilage provides almost frictionless surfaces on the ends of bones or the bearing surfaces of joints. Some cartilage is more elastic, because of the presence of elastic fibres. Such cartilage is found in the ear and the epiglottis. In other situations, where strength is important, cartilage contains more tough collagen fibres in its matrix. This type of cartilage is found in tendons and ligaments.

Cartilage may be
- *elastic (as in the ear)*
- *strong but flexible (as in ligaments and tendons)*
- *shiny (hyaline)*

Hyaline cartilage is smooth and shiny and provides a frictionless surface

Where bones meet

The site where two or more bones come together is called a **joint** (whether or not there is movement between the bones). How much movement can occur at any joint depends on how the joint is constructed.

Joint—site where two or more bones come together

Freely moveable joints

Synovial joints—freely
moveable joints

Synovial joints are found
in
• limbs
• jaw
• rib–vertebrae joints

The most familiar joints in the body are the **synovial joints**. Nearly all the
joints in the limbs, the joints of the jaw and the joints between the ribs
and the vertebrae are synovial joints. Synovial joints are designed to permit maximum movement. (Sometimes synovial joints permit free movement only in certain directions. These joints will be described in the next
section.)

All the important features of synovial joints are illustrated in Fig
18.16 (a section through the hip joint) and are described below.

Synovial joints contain
• ligaments
• joint capsule
• synovial membrane and
fluid
• hyaline cartilage
covering bone ends

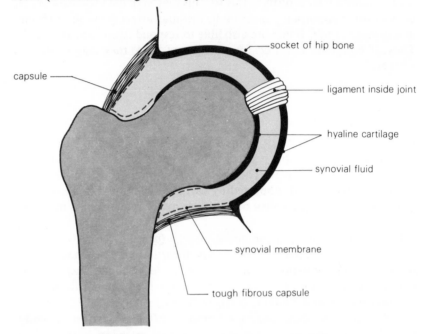

Fig 18.16 *Section through the hip joint – a synovial joint*

Ligaments

The ends of the bones are held together on the outside by tough bands of
tissue called ligaments. Ligaments act rather like very strong rubber
bands. They hold the bone ends together at the joint, preventing disloca-
tion, but stretch slightly to allow the bones to move. (Sometimes ligaments are also found inside the joint capsule.)

Joint capsule

The joint capsule is a tough fibrous layer which entirely surrounds the
bone ends and helps to hold them together. Inside the joint capsule,
synovial joints have a sealed space called the **joint cavity**.

Synovial membrane and synovial fluid

Lining the inner surface of the joint capsule is a layer of cells which is extremely important for the synovial joint. This is the synovial membrane, which secretes a small amount of lubricating fluid, called synovial fluid, into the joint cavity.

Hyaline cartilage

The ends of the bones in synovial joints are covered with a layer of hyaline (shiny) cartilage. Together with the synovial fluid which constantly 'greases' all the surfaces of the joint, this allows smooth and friction-free movement.

Less moveable joints

Cartilage joints

In cartilage joints (Fig 18.17a), the bone ends are separated only by a disc or plate of tough fibrous cartilage. Only a small amount of movement is possible. Cartilage joints are present between the vertebrae in the backbone, and join the two pubic bones in the pelvis.

Fibrous joints

Fibrous joints (Fig 18.17b) are joints where the bone ends are held together by very strong, short bands of fibrous tissue. The bones of the skull are united by fibrous joints which allow no movement at all.

Less moveable joints:
- cartilage joints—bone ends separated by a disc of tough fibrous cartilage (between vertebrae and joining pubic bones)
- fibrous joints—bone ends held together by strong fibrous tissue

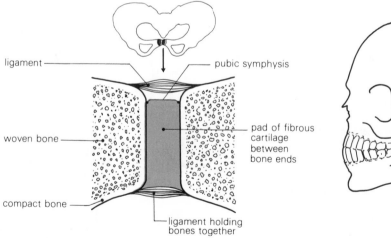

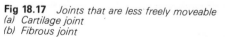

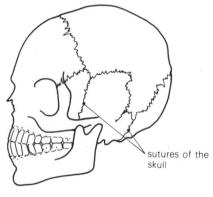

Fig 18.17 *Joints that are less freely moveable*
(a) Cartilage joint
(b) Fibrous joint

Special joints

There are some special joints in the body for particular locations.

Special types of synovial joints

Special types of synovial joints:
• ball and socket joint (shoulder and hip)
• hinge joint (knee, ankle and elbow)

The type of movement that can occur in synovial joints often depends on the shapes of the bones that make up the joints. Different types of joints are found in different locations in the body. At both the shoulder and the hip there are **ball and socket joints**, which allow the limb to swing and turn (rotate) in all directions. (Because the hip joint must bear the entire weight of the body, the socket here is much deeper than that in the shoulder.) The ankle, elbow and knee joints are described as **hinge joints**, because, like hinges, they move only in one plane (that is, swing up and down).

Special cartilage joints

Discs of cartilage attached to the vertebral bodies
• allow one vertebra to tilt or rotate on the next one
• act as cushions which absorb shock

As has been mentioned, the vertebrae are linked by special cartilage joints. Between the body of each vertebra is a pad of fibrous cartilage known as a **disc**. The discs are attached to the vertebral bodies (see Fig 18.18) and allow one vertebra to tilt or rotate a little on the next one. They also act as cushions, absorbing shock along the vertebral column. Occasionally a disc may lose its cushioning properties and then bulge into the spinal canal, putting pressure on the spinal cord and on spinal nerves. This causes the condition known as a 'slipped disc'.

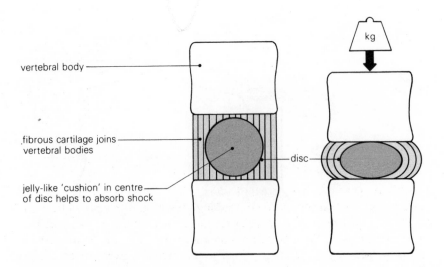

vertebral body

fibrous cartilage joins vertebral bodies

jelly-like 'cushion' in centre of disc helps to absorb shock

kg

disc

Fig 18.18   *Intervertebral disc – special cartilage*

How muscles move joints

So far we have been looking at the framework (skeleton) and the moving parts (joints) of the body. The joints are moved by muscles arranged around them. Muscles are capable of producing movement at joints because muscle cells, if stimulated by a nerve impulse, can contract. When muscle cells contract, the muscle as a whole becomes shorter and thicker. The muscle can then pull on the bone to produce movement. (We shall see in the next section how the special structure of muscle cells enables them to contract.)

The muscles which we can feel in our arms and legs are made up of large bundles of long muscle cells. (Muscle cells are often called fibres. If you tease a piece of muscle tissue apart and examine it carefully under a microscope, you can see these long, thin fibres.) Muscle cells are bound together with strong fibrous tissue, and their ends are attached to bones, across joints. Sometimes muscle fibres are attached directly to bones. In other places muscles are joined to bone by bands of fibrous tissue called tendons. (Note: tendons join muscle to bone; ligaments join bone to bone at joints.) Tendons may sometimes be very long. In joints such as those in the fingers, a bulky mass of muscle would interfere with the movement of the fingers. The strong muscles of the fingers are therefore located in the forearm and connected with the bone, across joints, by long tendons (see Fig 18.19).

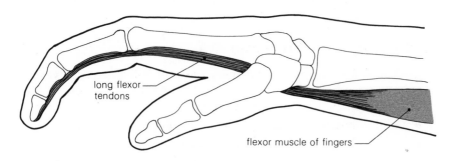

long flexor tendons

flexor muscle of fingers

Fig 18.19 *Long flexor tendons of the fingers*

Muscles can only contract and relax. They cannot lengthen of their own accord. When they stop contracting they have to be pulled back to their original length. For this reason most muscles are in pairs, called antagonistic pairs. Each muscle has an antagonist or a muscle that acts in the opposite way to itself. In hinge joints, where movement occurs in only one plane, the pairs of muscles are easy to identify. Figure 18.20 shows a pair of antagonistic muscles at the elbow joint. The biceps muscle which bends or flexes the joint is called a **flexor**. The triceps muscle

The biceps and triceps muscles form an antagonistic pair:
- when the biceps contracts the triceps relaxes
- when the triceps contracts the biceps relaxes

which straightens or extends the joint is called an **extensor**. As the biceps muscle contracts and shortens, the triceps muscle must relax and lengthen to allow movement at the joint. In this case the triceps muscle is the antagonist of the biceps muscle, and vice versa. As we shall see later, even when we are resting, muscles work in pairs around joints to hold the body in position.

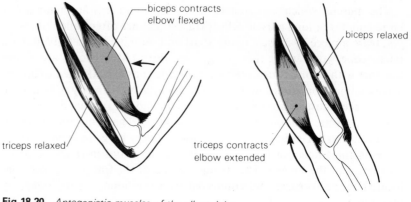

biceps contracts
elbow flexed

biceps relaxed

triceps relaxed

triceps contracts
elbow extended

Fig 18.20   *Antagonistic muscles of the elbow joint*

Mechanism of muscle contraction

In Chapter 2 we discussed some special types of cells and tissues. One of these tissues was muscle tissue, composed of cells that are capable of contraction. Muscle tissue is of three types:

Muscle types:
- cardiac muscle
- smooth or involuntary muscle
- skeletal or voluntary muscle

- Cardiac muscle (Chapter 6). This is the muscle of the heart.

- Smooth or involuntary muscle, over whose activity we have no conscious control. This is found in many of the internal organs—the alimentary canal, uterus, bladder, blood vessels, for example.

- Skeletal muscle, which comprises the muscles that move the bones of the skeleton. Skeletal muscle is sometimes also called voluntary muscle, because the activity of every skeletal muscle cell in the body is controlled by signals sent along nerve fibres from the brain and spinal cord to the muscles. We shall now look at how this is done.

One nerve may control a number of muscle fibres

Each muscle in the body is controlled by one or more large nerves. Nerves are bundles of thousands of individual nerve cell processes (axons and dendrites). A single nerve cell controls the activity of a number of

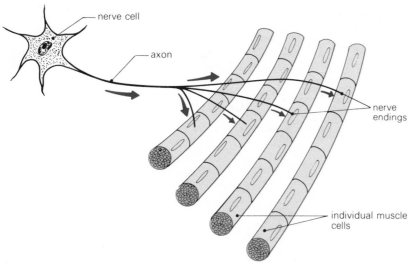

Fig 18.21 *Activity of a muscle is controlled by many nerve cells. One nerve cell controls the activity of several muscle cells (fibres)*

muscle fibres. The activity of a large muscle such as the biceps or triceps muscle is controlled by a nerve consisting of thousands of individual nerve cells (Fig 18.21). When signals (called nerve impulses) are sent from the brain or spinal cord, down a nerve cell, all the muscle fibres supplied by the nerve cell contract at the same time. If only a fine delicate muscle movement is required, signals may be sent along the axons of only very few nerve cells. If a very strong contraction is required, repeated signals will be relayed along many of the nerve cells supplying all the muscle fibres in the muscle. In this way the strength of muscle contraction can be varied or graded (Fig 18.22).

The activity of a large muscle is controlled by one or more nerves, each containing the fibres of thousands of nerve cells

How does the nerve signal cause contraction in the muscle, and how does the muscle fibre become shorter?

In Chapter 13 we saw how nerve impulses could be relayed across the gap between two adjacent nerve cells. In a similar way, messages are relayed across the gap between the end of the motor nerve and the muscle fibre. When a signal reaches the end of the motor nerve, a transmitter substance released from the nerve ending passes to the muscle fibre and causes it to contract.

A transmitter substance released from the end of a motor nerve causes the muscle to contract

How muscle fibres become shorter has been the subject of tremendous debate over the years. It is now thought that the shortening of muscle fibres is best explained by a process known as the 'sliding filament hypothesis' (Fig 18.23). Each muscle cell is believed to be formed of hundreds of long protein threads called **myofibrils**. When the muscle cell is contracted, myofibrils actually become shorter. This is because the protein molecules inside the myofibril are able to slide over (overlap) each other, causing the myofibril to shorten.

A muscle cell is formed of hundreds of myofibrils (long protein threads). During the contraction of a muscle cell, the myofibrils become shorter

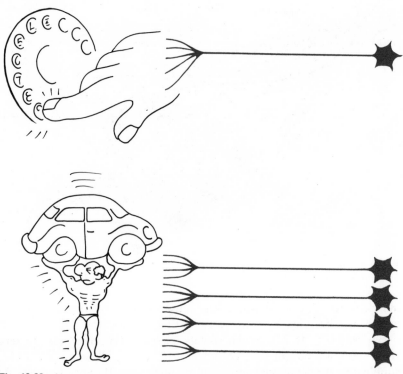

Fig 18.22 *How nerves control muscle contraction. The smallest contraction is the response of one nerve fibre and the muscle cells it supplies. Strong contractions are the response of many nerve fibres and all the muscle cells they supply*

Energy for muscle contraction

You may remember (Chapter 4) that muscle contraction requires energy—energy which is supplied in the body as chemical energy. When muscle cells shorten they use ATP molecules. Before the muscle cell can contract again, these ATP molecules must be replaced. You may also remember from Chapter 4 that certain fuel molecules in the body can be broken down in the presence of oxygen to produce energy in the form of ATP. This process is called aerobic respiration. The most useful fuel is glucose. Glucose can be stored in the liver or muscle as glycogen, which can easily be broken down to glucose when more fuel for the muscle is required (that is, when blood glucose has been reduced). Fats can also be 'burnt' to produce energy. Muscle cells can produce their own ATP, provided they are supplied with blood vessels which deliver glucose and oxygen to the contracting cells and remove the waste products of energy production (carbon dioxide and heat). Muscle cells are also able to produce ATP through anaerobic respiration (Chapter 4). During periods of vigorous exercise when the muscles cannot be supplied with all the oxygen they need, some of the glucose can be broken down without oxygen

Muscle contraction requires chemical energy (ATP)

ATP may be produced by aerobic or anaerobic respiration in muscle cells

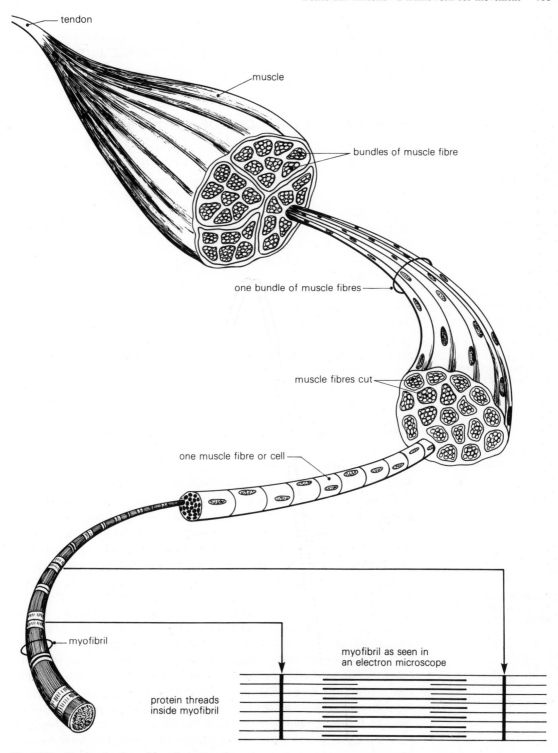

tendon

muscle

bundles of muscle fibre

one bundle of muscle fibres

muscle fibres cut

one muscle fibre or cell

myofibril

myofibril as seen in
an electron microscope

protein threads
inside myofibril

Fig 18.23   *The mechanism of muscle contraction*

to produce some ATP molecules. The waste product of this process is lactic acid (Chapter 4). When it accumulates in muscle cells, this lactic acid makes you feel stiff and sore.

Balance and the control of movement

We have seen that the contraction of every muscle of the skeleton is triggered by impulses sent to the muscle from the brain or spinal cord. We have also seen that even the simplest sort of muscle action, such as the reflex that makes us pull our hand away from a hot object, involves cooperation of pairs of muscles. When the biceps muscle contracts to lift the hand away from an object, the triceps muscle must relax, to allow it to move the joint. Then, when the elbow joint is bent, the triceps must contract again, like a braking system, to stop the hand from hitting the face in an uncontrolled way.

To control muscle movements in this way, the central nervous system must have continual accurate knowledge of what is happening in the muscles. It receives this information from sensory nerve endings located in muscles, tendons, joints and ligaments. These special nerve endings are called proprioceptors (Chapter 15, p 327). They tell the brain the position of the joints, and how much each muscle in the body is being stretched or contracted. Even when we are resting, these stretch receptors prevent any muscle from becoming too stretched and maintain a balance of tone in all muscles.

The brain is the body's computer, which analyses all the information it receives and makes whatever adjustments are necessary. It receives information not only from the muscles and joints but from other areas as well. In Chapter 15 we discussed the balance organs of the inner ear. These organs tell the brain the position of the body in space. Information is sent from these organs to a special area of the brain known as the cerebellum. From there, any signals to correct the balance are relayed, along complex nerve paths, to the appropriate muscle groups. The eyes may also provide the brain with information about the position of different parts of the body.

When we make any conscious or voluntary movement, the nervous coordination necessary is even more complicated. Nerve impulses are triggered from the cerebral cortex and then relayed through the cerebellum and spinal cord to the muscles involved. Some muscles contract; others are prevented from contracting, and relax or stretch. For example, if we make a decision to lift a book from a table, nerve impulses are sent from the cerebral cortex to the arm, causing the biceps to contract and the triceps to relax. Then, as the movement is completed, signals tell these muscles to 'apply the brakes' and control the movement. Walking, running, jumping, in fact all our normal movements, involve a complicated and coordinated sequence of contraction and relaxation of many muscle groups.

Even the simplest movements involve cooperation of muscle pairs

The brain must be continually informed about the positions and activities of muscles

Proprioceptors tell the brain about the positions of joints, and how much each muscle is stretched

The brain receives information from
• muscles
• joints
• balance organs
• eyes

During voluntary movement, nerve impulses pass from the cerebral cortex
↓
cerebellum
↓
spinal cord
↓
muscles of limbs

Chapter 19

Ageing—as old as you feel?

- What is ageing?
- Changes at the cellular level
- Effects of age on body systems
- Loneliness in the elderly
- Accommodation of old people
- Nursing the elderly and terminally ill

What is ageing?

Biologically speaking you are no longer the same person you were when you started to read this sentence. During the past few minutes you have lost about one irreplaceable nerve cell, and thousands of other cells in your body have ceased to function. In short, you have changed. In fact you have aged.

People are in a constant state of change

For a long time people have wondered about old age and the reasons for the changes that alter our bodies in the course of our lives. The prize of eternal youth still hovers beyond our grasp. So far attempts to prevent ageing have failed. For example, even though skin can be treated surgically to make it look less wrinkled, it still retains the texture and type characteristic of people of that particular age. Certainly, if a person's internal tissues are examined closely, the structure of many of them reflects that person's age.

Changes at the cellular level

Why do these changes occur? What are the processes which operate in the body to make us change, or age, probably from the moment we are born? Most research into the processes or mechanisms of ageing has been focused on cells. Cells are the basic units of life. We would expect, therefore, that as the body ages, cells must age also. As a result of this research into the mechanisms of ageing in cells, a number of theories have been developed which attempt to explain why and how ageing occurs. None of these has been verified, but probably all identify factors that contribute to the ageing process. We shall outline the most important suggestions here.

Cells are constantly dividing to
- *build new tissues (growth)*
- *replace dead or damaged cells (repair)*

You may remember that in Chapter 5 we explained that there is a continual turnover of cells in the body. In all parts of the body cell division is occurring, either to build new tissues (growth) or to replace cells that are damaged or dead. It is this process of continual cell division that many people feel is at the centre of the ageing process.

Continual cell division may be at the centre of the ageing process

Cell division and the ageing process

Some time before a cell divides, it must double its content of DNA. Then, when the cell divides, each daughter cell receives an identical set of chromosomes (DNA). The way in which this DNA doubling and division occurs was described in Chapter 5. The successful division of one cell to produce two identical daughter cells relies on the successful doubling and splitting of the DNA. Any mistake made in DNA copying is transferred to a daughter cell, resulting in a cell being produced that is different from the parent cell. During this process, mistakes may develop in the DNA molecules in any of several ways. Two of these are shown in Fig 19.1.

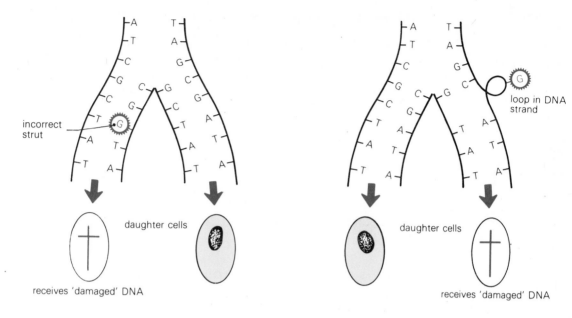

Fig 19.1 *Examples of mistakes that could be made during the copying of DNA*
(a) Incorrect strut (base) pairing
(b) A loop in the parent DNA strand resulting in a missing strut (base) in the new DNA molecule

First, when the new DNA molecule forms on the struts (bases) of the parent molecule, a strut may pair incorrectly. For example, in Fig 19.1a a guanine (G) strut has incorrectly paired with thymine. As a result, the DNA of one of the daughter cells contains a mistake. This mistake in the DNA code may cause a mistake in the formation of a protein. This happens because the mistake area of the DNA codes for the wrong amino acid when the polypeptide chain is forming. If the polypeptide with its incorrect amino acid is one that forms part of the cell's structure, the effect on the cell may be slight. However, if the amino acid is an important one in the active site of an enzyme (Chapter 4), the cell's whole function may be impaired.

Second, when the daughter DNA molecule forms, one or more struts may be missing from the molecule. This may happen because a loop remains in the parent DNA molecule while the new DNA molecule is forming (see Fig 19.1b). Such a mistake may have drastic effects on the cell. For example, leaving out one strut could result in a new sequence of amino acids being coded for by that part of the DNA strand. (Remember that the code for each amino acid is formed by a triplet of three bases, or struts.) In an example such as this a whole enzyme may be changed and replaced by a totally inactive protein structure.

A third way in which mistakes may be produced in daughter cells is by the DNA chains sticking together during the doubling process. This may

Mistakes may occur during doubling of DNA and cell division because
• struts (bases) pair incorrectly during copying
• bases are omitted from daughter molecules
• DNA chains stick together during doubling. This results in unequal division of DNA between two daughter cells

Mistakes made during the doubling of DNA may affect
• cell structure
• cellular enzymes

Unequal division of DNA may cause one daughter cell to lack its full share of DNA. This may result in imperfect cells

result in one daughter cell inheriting more than its share of DNA, whilst the other one may lack large portions of its genetic material. In such cases abnormalities may result in both cells.

DNA mistakes occurring in any of these ways may have far-reaching effects on the individual as a whole. For example, a stomach mucous cell that could not produce mucus would cease to be of any use in the stomach. A muscle cell that lacked an enzyme necessary for energy release would be unable to contract and would become a burden within the muscle.

Ageing may be due to increasing numbers of imperfect cells within the body

Most cells with serious DNA mistakes die rapidly or are destroyed by white blood cells. However, some cells may escape this purification process and continue to divide to produce more and more imperfect cells. Many people think that the gradual accumulation of imperfect cells is a most important factor in the ageing process.

Proteins and the ageing process

Ageing may be due to extra bonds forming between polypeptide chains (cross-linking)

Other scientists hold the view that ageing is mainly the result of slight changes in the chemical structure of some of the body proteins. Many proteins (such as hair protein) normally contain chemical bonds, called cross-links, between different chains of amino acids. These cross-links usually occur between amino acids containing sulphur (S). However, extra abnormal cross-links may also form. There is evidence to show that the number of extra abnormal cross-links increases as a person becomes older.

The number of extra cross-links increases with age

Cross-linking may affect the character of body tissues

The formation of extra cross-links may affect the body in two ways. First, the cross-linking may cause body tissues to change their character. For example, skin epithelium may lose its elasticity while bone connective tissue may become brittle and lose its strength.

Cross-links may affect the active site of an enzyme. Such cross-linking may cause enzymes to become less efficient or completely inactive

Second, cross-links may form in the active site of enzymes (Chapter 4). As a result of these cross-links, the active site of an enzyme may become partly blocked or be forced to change shape. This may prevent the substrate from entering the active site at all. This in turn may drastically reduce the enzyme's efficiency or make it inactive. If such an enzyme is vital to a cell, the cell may become very inefficient or perhaps die. It is thought by some that an increase in the number of cells containing defective enzymes may be one of the important causes of ageing.

The immune system and the ageing process

Ageing may be due to changes in the immune system

Another set of theories attempts to explain the ageing process in terms of changes in the activity of the immune system. It has been suggested that, as age increases, the immune system may produce antibodies directed against normal or 'self' cells (see Chapter 7). This could be the basis of the changes that occur in many tissues as they age.

Effects of age on body systems

So far we have looked only at the events which occur at the cellular level during ageing. How do these changes affect the function and appearance of the tissues, organs and systems of the body (Fig 19.2)?

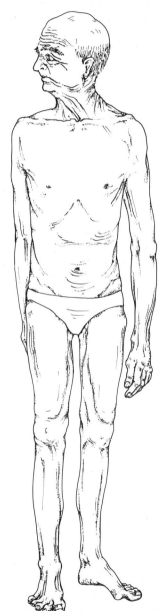

nervous system:
- brain function declines
- nerve conduction speed reduced
- vision less acute
- balance may be unreliable
- sense of touch reduced
- hearing less acute

respiratory system:
- decreased breathing efficiency
- decreased gas exchange

heart and circulation:
- decreased heart output
- decreased blood flow to tissues

digestive system:
- digestion is less efficient

kidneys:
- decreased blood flow leads to less efficient filtration of the blood

changes in
- skin
- hair
- muscles – wasting
- bones and joints:
  posture
  brittle bones
  joint wear

Fig 19.2 *Some effects of ageing on tissues, organs and systems*

Outward appearance

The outer appearance of a person can be a good gauge of age except in cases in which the skin has been treated by plastic surgery. Skin generally becomes wrinkled, less elastic and dry, and small patches of brown pigment may appear. The small blood vessels and capillaries of the skin become increasingly fragile, so that bruises appear far more readily than in younger people. Hair tends to lose its pigment and become grey or white. Baldness may occur in men, but occurs less frequently in women. The rate at which the sweat glands are able to secrete fluid also decreases.

Effects of age:

Skin:
• wrinkled
• less elastic
• dry
• patches of pigment

Bruising occurs more readily; hair loses pigment; sweating may be reduced

Muscles

A common sign of old age is a decrease in muscular strength, endurance and agility. Wasting of muscle tissue is often apparent in elderly people. What used to be large firm biceps or quadriceps muscles become smaller, weaker structures. Hands tend to become thinner and bonier. Microscopic examination would show a decrease in the number of muscle fibres, because as muscle cells die they are not replaced.

Muscles become smaller and weaker

Bones and joints

Changes in posture are another common sign of advancing age. The posture of an older person tends to be stooped, with head and neck allowed to fall forward. The upper limbs often remain slightly flexed (bent) when the arms hang beside the body. This is due to muscle shrinkage, to a decrease in elasticity of ligaments and to shrinkage of tendons.

As bones become older, they tend to lose calcium. As a result they become lighter (Fig 19.3) and far more brittle. This, together with a decrease in elasticity and flexibility, makes elderly people more prone to fractures. Changes to the bones and ligaments of the vertebral column may cause a decrease in height.

Bones and joints:
• changes in posture due to:
  −muscle shrinkage
  −tendon shrinkage
  −decreased elasticity of ligaments
• bones lose calcium and become brittle
• joints wear, leading to arthritis

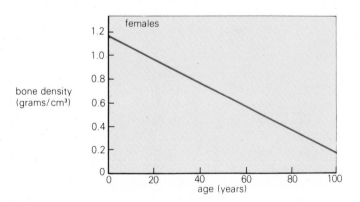

Fig 19.3 *Relationship between bone density and age in females*

Finally, signs of wear frequently develop in joints as age increases, leading to the development of a condition known as arthritis. The term arthritis means 'inflammation of the joint'. Inflammation may result from a number of different causes. When it occurs in old age, however, it is frequently the result of wear and tear on the joint. The shiny articular cartilages may become thin and worn, and small areas of bone in the joint may weaken and crumble (see Chapter 18). As a result, the patient suffers severe pain, and movements of the joint are severely restricted.

Nervous system

There is an overall decline in the function of the nervous system as age increases. Research has shown that there is a loss in the total number of brain cells and their fibres during ageing. This loss of brain cells may occur only in particular areas. Brain weights have been found to decrease by about 20 to 25 per cent from maturity to age 90 or over. This causes a gradual failing of memory capacity, particularly of short-term memory.

General decline in function of nervous system; in particular:
- failing memory (particularly short-term)
- decreased speed of nerve conduction
  - increased reaction time
  - decreased coordination
  - balance impaired

The speed of nerve conduction has also been shown to decrease in people of advancing age. Because of this, reaction times increase and co-ordination of muscle activities is impaired. Balance and coordination, and the ability to adjust quickly to changes in the environment, are often reduced in the elderly.

Special senses

The sense of touch starts to become less accurate after the age of 50. This is true for all parts of the body, but the feet lose their sensitivity to touch and vibration faster than the hands. As well, pain thresholds tend to rise; that is, it takes more pain before the person is able to feel any pain sensation. This loss of pain sensation may have serious consequences for old people. For example, they may ignore some aspect of ill-health in which pain is an important signal. Also, because of the reduced power of their senses, they are more prone to injuries such as burns, or blisters and sores on the feet.

Sense of touch becomes less accurate

Pain thresholds rise

Vision may also be restricted. In particular, the ability to adapt to night vision, and to distinguish two points close together, decreases with advancing age. There is also a gradual loss of the senses of smell and taste. Sensitivity to sound may also decrease. Finally, the balance organs may be affected. This is a factor in the many injuries caused by falls among old people.

Vision becomes less acute. Adaptation to night vision becomes slow

Loss of smell and taste may occur

Balance may become unreliable

Since all the sense organs rely on the nervous system to relay their messages to the brain, the decreased efficiency of the sense organs may be the result of a less efficient nervous system. Less frequent conduction of nerve impulses along nerve fibres would reduce the efficiency with which messages from the different sense organs are relayed to the brain. However, part of the effect is probably due to changes in the sense organs themselves.

The decreased efficiency of the sense organs may be due to
- a less efficient nervous system
- less efficient sense organs

Heart and circulatory system

Mass and strength of heart muscle decreases

The heart's effectiveness as a pump is greatly reduced in later years. A reduction in the mass and strength of the heart muscle means that less blood is pumped with each beat, and cardiac output is reduced (see Chapter 6). As a result, blood flow to the tissues is reduced.

Blood flow to tissues decreases because
• cardiac output decreases
• resistance to flow in blood vessels increases as a result of
  −decreased elasticity of walls
  −atherosclerosis

Increased resistance to flow
  ↓
high blood pressure
  ↓
further strain on the heart

Reduced blood supplies to the tissues are also caused by increased resistance to blood flow in arteries and arterioles. How does this occur? With ageing, arteries and arterioles lose their elasticity. Very frequently, too, fatty deposits develop on the inside of the vessel walls. This hardening of the arteries and accumulation of fat is what we know as atherosclerosis (see Chapter 6). Blood flow is impaired in vessels affected by atherosclerosis.

As we explained in Chapter 6, atherosclerosis also causes an increase in blood pressure (Fig 19.4). At 25, the average blood pressure during systole (heart contraction) is 120 mm Hg, while at 65 the average is 160 mm Hg. Average readings for blood pressure during diastole are 75 for a person of 25, and 90 for a person of 65. The increased blood pressure places further strain on the heart, which must work harder to pump blood to the tissues.

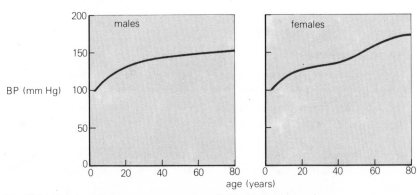

Fig 19.4 *Relationship between average systolic blood pressure and age*

Respiratory system

The amount of air that the lungs can take in and push out decreases as a result of
• weakening of muscles
• reduced mobility of joints
• reduced elasticity of alveoli

Another change which is seen in all people as they grow older is reduced breathing efficiency. In other words, the volume of air which the lungs can take in during inspiration and push out during expiration decreases. This is the result of a number of factors:

● Weakening of the muscle of the diaphragm and intercostal muscles means that they are unable to contract as forcibly.

● Reduced mobility of the joints of the vertebrae and rib cage may impair breathing movements.

- Several changes may affect the alveoli. There is a reduction in the number of alveoli and in their elasticity. (Advanced emphysema is often seen in elderly people—see Chapter 9.) Alveolar walls (the barrier through which gases must be exchanged between the air space and the blood) frequently become thicker.

What do these changes mean to a person's health? First, the changes in the thoracic cage and its muscles reduce the ability of the thoracic cavity to expand and so decrease the volume of air that can be taken into the lungs. The total lung capacity of an average man is normally approximately 5½ litres, and the amount of air that is exchanged in normal quiet breathing is 0.5 litres. Both of these volumes are very much reduced in elderly people. During expiration, the thoracic cavity and lungs decrease in volume, largely as a result of elastic recoil of the lungs. If the lungs' elasticity is reduced, the amount of air that can be forced out of the lungs will also decrease. Figure 19.5 shows how the maximum volume of air that can be forced from the lungs in one breath (the forced expiratory volume) decreases with age, in both males and females. In attempting to maintain an adequate volume of air entering and leaving the lungs, the elderly person may have to expend a great deal of extra energy and effort. Such effort is often seen as a struggle for breath.

Elderly people may have to struggle for breath, to maintain adequate volumes of air exchange

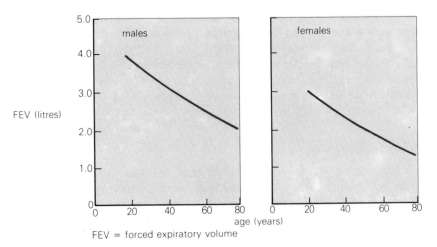

FEV = forced expiratory volume

Fig 19.5 *Relationship between forced expiratory volume and age*

Second, the decreased number of alveoli will result in a decreased surface area of lungs available for gas exchange. Gas exchange is also impaired by thickening of the alveolar walls. Both of these factors reduce the supply of oxygen to the blood and removal of carbon dioxide from the blood. As you can imagine, this imbalance of gases impairs the performance of body cells, particularly during periods of exercise, when demands for gas exchange are high (see Chapter 8).

Gas exchange in the lungs is reduced by:
- *decreased numbers of alveoli, resulting in a decreased surface area*
- *thickening of alveolar walls*

The reduced efficiency of the respiratory system may have further effects on the heart. In order to ensure that as much oxygen as possible is picked up from the less efficient lungs, an increased blood flow to the alveoli becomes necessary. To do this the heart must pump more rapidly. This in turn puts extra strain on the heart. As well, blood pressure may rise, which exposes the person to all the risks of high blood pressure (Chapter 6).

Decreased breathing efficiency puts extra strain on the heart

Digestive system

The most important changes in the digestive system, with ageing, are probably ones that affect the muscles of the alimentary canal. In Chapter 10 we saw that the muscles of the alimentary canal have three important functions:

Muscle layers of the alimentary canal become weaker, causing

• decreased mechanical digestion

• decreased mixing of food with enzymes (reduced digestive efficiency)

• slowing of passage of food

- They aid in breaking down food particles—mechanical digestion.
- They aid the mixing of food with digestive juices, and so help chemical digestion to occur efficiently.
- They are responsible for moving food along the alimentary canal.

In old age, the smooth muscle of the alimentary canal becomes weaker, and all the above functions are impaired. The size of food particles is not reduced as effectively in the stomach. Digestive enzymes can therefore not work as efficiently, and large quantities of valuable food particles leave the body undigested. This reduced efficiency of the digestive system often causes weight loss in elderly people. Reduced strength of the muscles may also slow the passage of food through the alimentary canal, so that constipation becomes a problem. Finally, poor dental structure may also interfere with the mechanical digestion of food (Chapters 10 and 11).

Reduced digestive efficiency may cause weight loss

The kidneys

The changes in the function of the kidneys, with age, are due to the decreased blood flow to them (see 'Heart and circulatory system'). The lowered blood flow through the kidneys results in a reduction in the rate of filtration of blood. (The rate of filtration in the kidneys in persons over 80 is about 50 per cent of that in people of 25.) This may cause an increase in the concentration of urea in the blood. Excessively high levels of urea in the blood may affect the operation of other body cells.

Decreased blood flow to tissues
↓
decreased filtration of blood in kidneys

Endocrine system

The activity of many endocrine glands shows a considerable decrease with advancing age. This is particularly so for the pituitary and thyroid glands. The reduced secretion of the thyroid hormone (thyroxine) causes a slowing down of many of the chemical reactions (metabolism) of the body. Lethargy, continual tiredness and general lack of energy may be seen as a result of this.

Reduction in the activity of the thyroid gland may cause lethargy and lack of energy

With a less active pituitary gland, fewer reproductive hormones may be secreted.

Concentration of reproductive hormones decreases

Temperature control

It is well known that ageing people show an increasing tendency to chilling. You may have seen an elderly person wearing a thick coat even on a warm day. This is primarily due to the body's inability to maintain a constant core temperature when the environmental temperature changes.

Elderly people are less able to keep a constant body temperature

One of the causes of this lack of regulation may be a slowing down in the basic rate of body metabolism, which is caused by a deficiency of thyroxine. The reduced efficiency of the nervous system may also be involved. In a similar way, old people are less able to adapt to extremely hot weather.

All these changes to tissues, organs and systems may seem a little 'clinical'. Perhaps an example may help to show how important they may be to the life of an elderly person.

An elderly woman lives alone. She is really quite fit in mind and body, but her body is undergoing many of the changes of ageing. In the dim light of early morning, she fails to see a fold in a mat on the floor. Her leg muscles are not as strong as they were, and as she walks (with a slight shuffle) her foot fails to clear the small hump in the mat and she trips. With advancing age, muscles become weaker and nervous coordination decreases. Having lost her balance she is unable to save herself and she falls to the ground. Her bones, too, have become brittle through calcium loss, and as a result of only a minor fall she fractures her femur (thigh bone). She must then enter hospital for treatment of the fracture and for nursing care. The fracture will heal, but how well and how quickly it heals will depend on the efficiency of blood flow to the damaged tissues. While she remains immobilised in hospital, the risks of complications arising in many other ageing body systems are increased considerably.

Loneliness in the elderly

One of the harshest consequences of old age is loneliness. This may arise because a partner and close friends have died, and other friends and family live in different areas. But even in circumstances in which family and friends are nearby and available, loneliness may still be feature of the life-style of elderly people.

Perhaps the most common single reason for loneliness in old age is deafness. It is easy for us to speak to those who respond quickly and obviously follow our comments and reasoning, even if they do not agreee with what we say. Difficulties arise, however, when we make a statement or ask a question and receive no response at all. It is very easy to abandon the attempt to communicate and find somebody more able to listen.

If we are persevering enough to put our question or statement a second time, and still fail to produce a reply, we may easily become irritated or even mildly hostile. Our natural reaction may be to give up in our attempts at communication (Fig 19.6).

These situations and reactions frequently develop in relationships with elderly people who suffer from deafness. And it is these reactions of frustration or irritation that alienate elderly people in a group, often leaving them cut off and lonely. Only tremendous patience and understanding on our part can help to overcome these problems and provide the companionship old people need.

Loneliness may be caused by:
• deafness
• slowness in comprehension

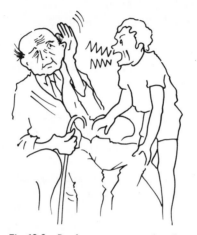 

Fig 19.6 *Deafness may cause loneliness*

The situation can be made even more difficult if elderly people are also slow to comprehend what we say. It may be necessary to put our questions to them two or three times before they can understand what we are asking them. This may occur even though they can hear what we are saying. To help them overcome their difficulties, we may need to embark on slow step-by-step explanations of the points of our argument—an exercise which again requires tremendous understanding and patience.

Tolerance as a listener may help problems of communication with the elderly

Because of these difficulties in comprehension, some elderly people may tend to talk a great deal. Talking, after all, is easier than listening, which requires concentration and unselfishness. But think how boring we find people who want to talk only about themselves and appear uninterested in *our* activities. Again, our natural reaction may be to seek other, more interested, company, leaving the elderly to further isolation and loneliness.

Other factors which contribute to loneliness:
• failure of short-term memory
• intolerance and lack of tact

There are other factors which also contribute to loneliness. Failure of short-term memory is a common condition in old age, and it may be an exasperating one to cope with. Intolerance or lack of tact may also encourage us to avoid an elderly member of the family (Fig. 19.7). No one likes being told how much better life was 'in those days', or how the 'modern generation has gone downhill'. Any of these situations may produce feelings of impatience, irritation or resentment—to which our reaction may be 'why bother?'.

In summary, there are numerous reasons why loneliness is so much part of the life of many old people. It is important, however, that elderly people continue to have contact and friendship with others, particularly at a stage when their lives are becoming less active and more confined. An understanding of the reasons for these difficulties in communication can help us to overcome them. In this way, the gap between young and old which these problems tend to produce may be lessened.

Fig 19.7 *Lack of tact may cause loneliness*

Accommodation for old people

As people approach the stage at which it is no longer possible to live independently, a number of decisions have to be made. These decisions not only affect the elderly people themselves, but are also very much the concern of the families or guardians who have responsibility for them. Broadly speaking, there are four questions to be asked:

Choosing accommodation for elderly members of the family is complex

Four options are available

- Is a move from the family home to a small dwelling advisable? Such a move may bring with it substantial emotional upset, during which period the person has to adapt to a new routine in a new home.

- Should accommodation be found in the home of younger members of the family?

- Is it appropriate for the person to remain in his or her own home and receive some form of day-to-day assistance?

- Is a geriatric hospital necessary for the treatment of illnesses resulting from old age?

An elderly person living in the home of young relatives may become burdensome to the family

In finding answers to these questions a number of issues must be considered. If an elderly person who requires considerable care remains in the home of a younger member of the family, demands made particularly on the daughter or daughter-in-law may become too great. These demands may result in neglect of the other members of the family. If a geriatric home is chosen instead, physical care and attention would be provided, but loneliness and depression might occur as a result of the separation from family and familiar surroundings. The elderly person might feel that the family has a responsibility and duty to look after him or her. Is this feeling unreasonable?

Accommodation which provides for some kind of independence is important for elderly people

Someone who is still capable of being independent may best be accommodated in a small flat or house, which would present fewer physical demands. For the elderly person, the independence enjoyed in such a situation is often the last thread of self-identity. It is most important that such independence is maintained for as long as possible. Even a situation which may prove to be mildly demanding may be preferable to one in which the person feels over-supported, at a time of life when he or she still has the ability to cope.

A satisfactory solution may be one in which a person lives independently in a small flat but receives assistance from a visiting helper

Finding answers to the kinds of questions which have been posed above is obviously extremely difficult and may involve hours of discussion by the family. Very often a compromise may be reached, in which the elderly person moves to a small flat or dwelling and receives assistance during the day from a visiting helper. This helper may be a home nurse if any type of regular medical attention is needed. In this situation, independence is maintained, family burdens are lessened, and sound medical assistance can be provided.

A private hospital or rest home provides constant, concentrated care

For a family who decide that an elderly member should be given closer and more constant attention than even they could offer, a private hospital or rest home may be the answer. In these units, meals are cooked, laundry is attended to, and medical attention is always available. Most important, a caring, watchful staff is always at hand ready to provide companionship, care and guidance. Figures 19.8 and 19.9 show examples of different types of accommodation for elderly people. For those who have an illness or disability which requires special treatment, special geriatric services or units have been developed. These may be attached to a general hospital, or may exist in their own right as geriatric hospitals. Such services should include beds for treating the acutely ill and beds for concentrated rehabilitation (helping people to return to their normal state of health after illness). After concentrated treatment has been completed in the special unit, the elderly people may then be moved to smaller hospitals or nursing homes. If complete health is recovered, they may then return to private accommodation to enjoy a life that is largely independent.

Special geriatric services or units provide expert medical treatment for elderly people with illnesses or disabilities

Fig 19.8 *Examples of accommodation for the elderly.*
(a) Self-contained flats
(b) Bed-sitting rooms

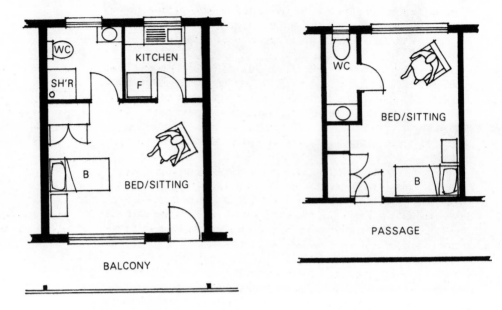

Fig 19.9 *Some floor plans of accommodation for the elderly*
(a) Self-contained flat
(b) Bed-sitting room

Nursing the elderly and terminally ill

One of the most difficult aspects of nursing is caring for the terminally ill (those whose illness will result in death). This task requires great resources of humanity and compassion from nursing staff. Not only is this kind of nursing demanding, but to some it may seem depressing. However, people who are involved with caring for the elderly or terminally ill often show a peace and acceptance of life rarely demonstrated in other professions. The personal rewards in caring for a person during the final days of his or her life may be considerable and long-lasting.

People who are involved in nursing the terminally ill often show exceptional qualities of peace and acceptance

The following extracts are taken from an article by Miss Shirley Jennings. Miss Jennings has worked for many years at the Peter MacCallum Hospital for cancer treatment in Melbourne, and in her writing she illustrates some of the qualities of courage, patience, understanding and cheer which are so much a part of many who care for terminally ill patients.

Many people have commented on the atmosphere at Peter MacCallum Clinic and said that everyone on the staff seems to care and to be happy in their work.

Reassurance and support are vital for patients with terminal illness

If you feel welcome, reassured and supported when you come to the hospital, some of your anxiety will be reduced. If you can then be advised and supported during each step of your treatment, you will cope better. This approach stems from a belief that the patient is an individual and the most important person, and from the desire of the staff to care for each patient as a real person.

People are afraid or anxious to widely varying degrees—in some it is very apparent, others conceal it. One of our main tasks, both within the hospital and from the home, is to assist the patient to adjust to this new experience in his life.

Some people have an ability to take things in their stride, others are thrown by the slightest break in their routine or life. Building a relationship of trust and confidence at the first encounter is of the utmost importance, and for us, this is where everyone in the hospital has a part. There is also a responsibility to build a similar relationship with the family and to help them also to accept progress of disease and to give the necessary support and reassurance to the patient.

A relationship of trust and confidence must be built between patient, nursing staff and family

For me, nursing the patient with cancer is challenging, because it not only requires a wide variety of practical skills but a special care in the emotional and spiritual support of the patient. In my opinion, there are many worse things than cancer. The havoc wrought in people's lives by hatred, greed, resentment and bitterness is recognised in the field of psychosomatic medicine. It is known that worry, anxiety and tension lie behind many other physical conditions.

Emotional and spiritual support are important for patients

Time can be spent on evasion, false cheerfulness and sometimes downright dishonesty, which could often be spent in more simple care and appreciation. Where there exists an open and honest relationship within a family, it is evident that the members of this family together come to terms with the new situation of illness and usually are better able to cope.

Honesty is essential in all relationships with patients

My own approach to this branch of nursing has been influenced tremendously by a patient I nursed many years ago who had advanced cancer, but faced it so courageously that I felt I had learned far more from him than I had given in nursing care.

Throughout this book we have been looking at how our bodies work. We have seen how they may change as we grow older and also in response to such things as disease, drugs and alcohol.

Understanding the human body can help us to understand our own and other people's behaviour: how we react to one another and to different situations. It helps us to make informed decisions about our own health and lifestyle. Knowing the effect of alcohol on the nervous system, for example, we are less likely to drive after drinking or to let friends who have been drinking drive. Knowing the health risks associated with smoking helps us to decide whether we shall take up the habit.

Similarly, knowing what changes take place in the body as a person grows old may help us to treat an elderly relative with more consideration and love. Knowing the discomforts that may accompany menopause may equip us better to provide the support and sensitivity which someone we know may need.

Index

The italic page numbers refer to illustrations.